Case, Shirley Jackson. The evolution of early
   Christianity. Chic. Univ.of Chicago (S) 1914.
   385p. $2.25 net.

   With an understanding of the psychological processes in the
rise and development of all religions and the historical situation in which the Christian lived, the author "seeks to
analyze and interpret the environmental forces which stimulated, nourished, or directed the growth of the new religion,"
giving special attention to the Hellenistic environment, a field
which has had little investigation. A scholarly contribution for
the student.

THE EVOLUTION OF EARLY
CHRISTIANITY

THE UNIVERSITY OF CHICAGO PRESS
CHICAGO, ILLINOIS

Agents

THE CAMBRIDGE UNIVERSITY PRESS
LONDON AND EDINBURGH

THE MARUZEN-KABUSHIKI-KAISHA
TOKYO, OSAKA, KYOTO

KARL W. HIERSEMANN
LEIPZIG

THE BAKER & TAYLOR COMPANY
NEW YORK

THE EVOLUTION OF EARLY CHRISTIANITY

A GENETIC STUDY OF FIRST-CENTURY
CHRISTIANITY IN RELATION TO ITS
RELIGIOUS ENVIRONMENT

By

SHIRLEY JACKSON CASE

*of the Department of New Testament and Early Christian Literature
in the University of Chicago*

THE UNIVERSITY OF CHICAGO PRESS
CHICAGO, ILLINOIS

Composed and Printed By
The University of Chicago Press
Chicago, Illinois, U.S.A.

PREFACE

This book does not aim to furnish a detailed account of the territorial, doctrinal, ecclesiastical, and literary developments of early Christianity. It seeks rather to analyze and interpret the environmental forces which stimulated, nourished, or directed the growth of the new religion. Consequently interest centers mainly in the lives of actual persons whose activities were related to a specific setting within which they worked out their various problems.

This study, accordingly, deals primarily with the origins of the Christian movement and only secondarily with the writings which the movement produced, sporadically and sometimes quite incidentally, in the process of expansion. Later generations have become so accustomed to think of the New Testament as the source of their religion that they with difficulty appreciate the situation of the early Christians during that spontaneous and formative period when the champions of the new faith were performing their work without the aid of any distinctively Christian Scriptures. When the New Testament books were ultimately assembled they preserved records of Christian activity and thinking from different localities and various periods, and so these writings constitute an important source of information for the study of Christian origins; but they render this service truly only when they are interpreted as the product of the movement of whose history they are a valuable though fragmentary record. Hence the student of Christian origins must first orient himself in the life of the times, if he would understand the genesis of the new religion as well as the literature it produced.

The possibility of obtaining this orientation has greatly increased in recent years. Much help may now be derived from the historical study of religions as a whole, which supplies certain broad principles capable of general application. These results emphasize the necessity of taking account of psychological processes in the rise and development of all religions, and they make clear the importance of social and cultural forces for the determination of religious phenomena. But more immediate help comes from observing the actual historical situation in which the early Christians lived. Within the last half-century various scholars have devoted themselves to the study of later Judaism, with the result that the historian can now know, for the most part, the actual religious situation which conditioned the lives of the first disciples on Jewish soil.

But only in its veriest beginnings was Christianity confined to a strictly Jewish setting. Even before the earliest extant New Testament book was written the advocates of the new movement were using the Greek speech of the gentile world; perhaps by the middle of the first century Christians outside of Palestine were more numerous than those residing in the Holy Land; and certainly the membership of many gentile churches was constituted largely of persons whose youthful religious training had been received in some heathen faith. From an early date the cultural, social, and religious environment of Christians had been distinctly Hellenistic, consequently some students of Christian origins have recently insisted upon the necessity of greater familiarity with the Hellenistic setting of the new religion.

As yet this particular field has received all too little attention. Indeed, it is not uncommon even today to find its rights to consideration either denied, or ignored, or greatly minimized. The difficulties of the subject are many, for the sources of information are not readily available. They are vast in extent and are scattered through thousands of pages of Greek and Latin authors, inscriptions, and papyri—not to mention Semitic documents. While some excellent pioneer work has already been done, there are no books treating the Hellenistic environment of the early Christians in the same comprehensive way that Schürer and numerous other writers expound the Jewish setting.

It is in this less-worked field that the present volume aims to render its chief service. The book is necessarily introductory in character, mainly emphasizing a point of view and a method of procedure. It will have fulfilled its intended mission if it has demonstrated the importance of this line of study, if it has made clear the general course to be pursued in such inquiry, and if it has helped in any degree to a better understanding of the vital character of primitive Christianity.

SHIRLEY JACKSON CASE

UNIVERSITY OF CHICAGO
August 12, 1914

TABLE OF CONTENTS

CHAPTER   PAGE

  I. THE DEVELOPMENTAL NATURE OF CHRISTIANITY .   1

  II. THE IMPORTANCE OF ENVIRONMENT FOR CHRISTIAN ORIGINS 26

  III. THE MEDITERRANEAN WORLD IN NEW TESTAMENT TIMES 48

  IV. THE EARLY CHRISTIANS' JEWISH CONNECTIONS . 78

  V. THE BREACH BETWEEN CHRISTIANS AND JEWS . . 123

  VI. THE EARLY CHRISTIANS' CONTACT WITH GENTILE RELIGIONS 166

  VII. THE RELIGIOUS SIGNIFICANCE OF EMPEROR-WORSHIP 195

  VIII. THE RELIGIOUS SIGNIFICANCE OF PHILOSOPHICAL SPECULATION 239

  IX. HELLENISTIC RELIGIONS OF REDEMPTION . . . 284

  X. THE TRIUMPH OF CHRISTIANITY 331

CHAPTER I

THE DEVELOPMENTAL NATURE OF CHRISTIANITY

The Christian religion has undergone numerous changes in the course of its history. Not only has its form in one period differed from that of a subsequent age, but different groups of people within the same period have become exponents of varying types of faith. As a consequence of these variations, modern Christianity in its totality is a widely diversified phenomenon. The Greek and the Roman churches have many distinctive features; Protestantism is sharply differentiated from Catholicism; Protestant denominations differ more or less widely from one another, and divergent tendencies may often be observed among members of the same communion.

These variations, which have persisted in spite of many attempts to establish or maintain uniformity, seem to imply that Christianity is primarily an affair of life, with varying characteristics according to the individuals and the circumstances which have determined its historical manifestation. As each new generation reacts upon its peculiar world of reality, appropriating data from the past and attaining new experiences in the present, its religious activities show new and varying characteristics. While Christians may preserve a keen sense of historical continuity and may acknowledge large obligations to the past, in the last analysis their religion is identical with the spiritual attainments of different individuals, or groups

of individuals, whose experience, conduct, and thinking
have been very effectively influenced by immediate surroundings.   Since Christianity is thus fundamentally an
expression of spiritual life evolved under specific conditions in successive periods of history, its form naturally
varies with the changing circumstances of life.

But change, instead of being made a primary item
in Christianity's nature, is usually thought to be quite
incidental, or even detrimental, to its true character.
Its fundamental constitution is commonly seen in some
static quantity of experience, doctrine, conduct, or
ritual which is assumed to have been established in the
days of Jesus and the apostles, and to be reproduced
in all other circles where this faith is maintained in its
purity.   The fact of variation is disposed of by setting
aside as spurious all phases not in agreement with some
particular type which its devotees call "genuine."   Or,
if more generously inclined, one may find the essentials
of Christianity in a modicum so small and so broadly
defined that it can be thought to exist in several different communities where variations in other respects may
be very pronounced.   Beneath all differences there is
a static quantity called "essence," while all divergent
phenomena are merely excrescences.

This situation suggests a crucial problem.   Is Christianity ultimately vital and developmental in nature,
or is it static and quantitative?   This question is fundamental to any study of the new religion's origin, and
especially to the problem of its relation to other faiths
in the world in which it arose.   Hence the necessity of
ascertaining at the outset the view of Christianity's
nature according to which our interpretation of the early

evolution of the new religion is to proceed. If we think of it as vitally developmental, a genuine growth, the circumstances surrounding the lives of its earliest advocates must form an important consideration in the interpretation of its history. If, on the other hand, it is treated as a static quantity whose essential character and content are fixed at the start, the question of relationship to other faiths is not fundamentally important. This question may have a secondary interest because of its bearing upon external matters, but it has essentially nothing to do with an understanding of Christianity's real genius.

To which of these two main positions is the preference to be given? The static character of Christianity has been maintained from an early date in both Catholic and Protestant circles. Orthodox Romanists have always defined their religion in terms of a God-given quantum of revelation, original in content, complete at the outset, and historically unconditioned except that its completeness and perfection were displayed more fully in the expanding life of the historic church. Changes may be admitted in the course of history, even changes necessitated by contemporary conditions, but Christianity is not in any real sense a product of evolutionary forces. This assertion applies even to its relation to Judaism. While Christianity is assumed to preserve everything of permanent worth in the latter, the relation of the two is not one of organic evolution. Christianity is really a new and fuller revelation, a fresh divine insert into history, for which Judaism has merely prepared the way. In the course of subsequent history popular pagan religion may have affected somewhat the church's rites and ceremonies, and Greek philosophy may have had some influence upon the development of doctrine, but it is a gross error, according to the Catholic view, to think of these outside forces as introducing anything in the least alien to the original substance of the Christian revelation. Historical growth is but the further unfolding of the heavenly robe brought to earth by Jesus, passed on by him to the apostles, and intrusted by them to the divinely established and officered church. The garment never needs to be altered or repaired, but only to be further unfolded.[1]

The older Protestant estimate of Christianity's nature rested upon the same basic principle. The new religion as revealed by Jesus and perpetuated by the apostles was a purely divine deposit, essentially complete from the first. The fundamental divergence between Protestantism and Catholicism lay in their different theories about the preservation of the deposit. According to the latter the infallible church was its perpetual guardian and interpreter, consequently the whole ecclesiastical development within orthodox Romanism was the continuation of genuinely original Christianity. The Protestant Reformers, on the other hand, took the Scriptures rather than the church as their ultimate authority, and so found original Christianity in the Canon. It could be recovered only by a return to the age of the apostles, its divine character being assured by an infallible Scripture. Thus Storrs

[1] Cf. articles "Christianity," "Development of Doctrine," and "Revelation" in the *Catholic Encyclopedia* (New York, 1907 ff.) and the article "Église" in *Dictionnaire de théologie catholique* (Tome IV, Paris, 1911).

in his lectures on *The Divine Origin of Christianity*[1] says of the New Testament books that they hold Christianity as nothing else does. While it has been "variously tinted and refracted" by human representations of it, still these primitive writings continue to reveal its spiritual substance and vital force. They are our inheritance from God, and this faith "is the one system of religion on earth for which the eternal creative spirit, from whom the spirit of man is derived, is directly responsible, and to which his veracity is pledged" (p. 6).

This did not mean that ecclesiastical organization and doctrinal elaboration were thought by Protestants to form no part of Christianity. On the contrary, many features which emerge in post-apostolic times were regarded as legitimate because believed to be scriptural. Thus Anglicans could retain the notion that the church is a supernatural organization, divinely equipped to administer the rites of salvation. Though inculcating only that which is "agreeable to the doctrine of the Old and New Testaments and which the Catholic Fathers and ancient bishops have collected from that very doctrine,"[2] still according to a canon of 1604 the Church of England differs from the Catholics only "in those particular points wherein they were fallen both from themselves in their ancient integrity and from the apostolic churches which were their first founders." According to this conception Christianity is still, as in Catholicism, a purely supernatural contribution to

[1] Boston, 1884.

[2] Cited from the Convocation of 1571, by A. C. A. Hall in the article "Protestantism" in the *New Schaff-Herzog Encyclopedia*, Vol. IX (New York, 1911).

human history, its integrity being carefully preserved within divinely determined limits.

Other sections of Protestantism attached less significance to the perpetuation of the divinely authorized ecclesiastical organization and placed chief stress upon individual religious life. Yet Christianity was a significant historical quantum, more especially on its doctrinal side. While Scripture was the ultimate norm for faith, much genuine Christianity was to be recognized in the doctrinal development of post-apostolic times. This position has been stated more recently by Orr. He believes "the labor spent by myriads of minds on the fashioning of dogma has not, as so many in our day seem to think, been utterly fatuous, and the mere forging of fetters for the human spirit."[1] This work of doctrinal elaboration has not been a merely human affair, but has been pursued in agreement with the divine character and intention of Christianity. The general tendency of this type of interpretation is to define Christianity's essential content in terms of a divinely directed type of metaphysical speculation guaranteed in the first instance by the teaching of Jesus and the apostles. The exposition of sound doctrine never goes beyond this original revelation, nor are the intellectual attainments of a later age ever able to import anything essentially new into its content. If a contribution is new it must in the nature of the case be untrue. The function of interpretation is only to expound in greater detail the perfect original.

These various opinions of both Catholics and Protestants are in fundamental agreement on the question of

[1] *The Progress of Dogma* (New York, 1901), p. v.

Christianity's nature. It is a quantity of divine instruction, supernaturally given and designed to cover all the essentials of true religion. Whether it is more perfectly preserved in an ecclesiastical organization, in a canon of Scripture, in a system of metaphysical speculation, or in some combination of these is only a subsidiary question. In any case it has a truly other-worldly origin and maintains its unique originality in every legitimate stage of its career. Human experience and historical circumstances contribute nothing to its making; they merely provide channels for its spread, in so far as they do not obscure or retard its progress.

The nineteenth century witnessed a general expansion of man's mental horizon and with it came a keener sense of real connection between earlier and later periods of history. Scholars became more vitally conscious of progression in the course of human experience, so that the notion of development entered by degrees into the realm of historical study. Religion was naturally tardy in accepting and applying to itself the conception of evolution, yet some scholars, Catholic as well as Protestant, recognized that the older method of interpretation did not do full justice to the developmental side of Christianity. The changes through which it had passed were felt to be more extensive and thoroughgoing than were possible on the traditional view. Cardinal Newman, from the side of Catholicism, recognized the pressure of this demand and sought to meet it in his *Essay on the Development of Christian Doctrine*.[1] He is more generous than most of his Catholic predecessors in finding extensive changes in the history of doctrine, a fact which, he says,

[1] London, 1845, 1894⁹.

"embarrasses us when we consult history for the true idea of Christianity." While it is a supernaturally revealed religion, its historical manifestation is humanly conditioned and so is subject to "the general method by which the course of things is carried forward."

Have we here a new conception of Christianity's nature according to which it becomes a product of religious life rather than a divine insert into history? Such might, at first sight, seem to be the case, but Newman very quickly assures his readers that this is not his thought. No matter how extensively Christianity may appear humanly conditioned, "the powers which it wields and the words which proceed out of its mouth attest its miraculous nativity." Furthermore, no phases of development are legitimate which do not ultimately fall within the pale of ecclesiastical sanction, and these "natural" and "true" developments were all contemplated by Christianity's author, "who in designing the work designed its legitimate results." Security against error and perversion is obtained by the maintenance of the original type which has remained from first to last unalterable.

Thus it is apparent that Newman does not really believe it is Christianity's nature to evolve, at least not in the sense of genuine, organic evolution. Changes in its history do not inhere primarily in its character as a religion, but are due to the medium through which it is compelled to work. Variation is necessary only because it is the inevitable attendant of "any philosophy or polity which takes possession of the intellect and heart"; it is in the nature of the human mind that "time is necessary for the full comprehension and perfection of great ideas and that the highest and most wonderful truths, though communicated to the world once for all by inspired teachers, could not be comprehended all at once by the recipients . . . . but have required only the longer time and deeper thought for their full elucidation." Thus it is not essential Christianity which evolves but only its historical elucidation, and the two things are in reality treated as separate entities. After all, Newman signally fails to find any vital place for the conception of growth as fundamental to Christianity's nature.

Among Protestants the problem of development was approached from a different angle. Newman had been compelled to face this question in order to legitimize the history of the church in which change and variation no longer could be denied. If the authority of the ecclesiastical organization was to be maintained, the notion of development must be admitted into Christianity far enough to cover the changes which time had wrought in the outward history of the church. Protestants, on the other hand, except those Anglicans who swung far toward Rome in their reaction against liberalism—a movement of which Newman was a leader before his outright adoption of Catholicism—easily dismissed all ecclesiastical developments as mere perversions of true Christianity. Its history was not a vital growth, but a process of degeneration and decay. The problem of so defining Christianity as to give the notion of development any important place in the definition did not become a real issue for Protestant scholars until they felt it desirable to bring religion into more vital relations with the historic life of the human spirit and to recognize that the New Testament, which had constituted the Protestant norm for faith, was itself the product of growth.

A tendency to ally religion more closely with humanity, and so to make it less a thing from without, early appeared in English deism and German rationalism. But these movements were more negative than positive in their results. They denied to Christianity much that had traditionally been regarded as essential to its nature, without formulating a new definition of its character with a view to displaying the real genius of its historical development. But German idealism, especially as expounded by Hegel, made an effort to supply this needed definition. For him the universe is at heart spiritual, or perhaps better, intellectual, being grounded in the divine Idea, the absolute Reason, whose essential nature consists in living development. Ideally the world is the very product of this development of the logical thought of the absolute spirit. Since thought and being are thus a unit, philosophical dialectic reproduces, at least in kind, the evolutionary process of the absolute, and every historic product of the human spirit —custom, law, art, science, philosophy, religion—is a more or less perfect expression of the absolute. Progress is the result of conflict and discord in the general trend of all things which are synthetically evolving nearer and nearer to the divine Idea, itself the ultimate and absolute truth. Similarly in the realm of religion every new stage in the development of the human spirit marks a new revelation of divine truth.

What, then, is the Hegelian understanding of Christianity's nature? Seemingly the notion of development, not only in externals but also in essentials, has been made central. Closer inspection, however, shows that even this mode of interpretation does not find Christianity to have been so thoroughly developmental, a process of vital historical growth, as might at first sight be imagined. To begin with, Hegel had little interest in the historical life of Christianity as a whole. His primary concern was with doctrine only. Nor did he view this in its entirety; much less was he interested in its actual historical growth. In closing his lectures on the philosophy of religion[1] he affirms that his aim has been "to reconcile reason and religion, to show how we know this latter to be in all its manifold forms necessary, and to rediscover in revealed religion the truth and the idea." In other words, he is concerned with supposed abstract elements of universality in Christianity rather than with its concrete phenomena, and he discovers the universal through a process of philosophical reflection acting upon the content of religious ideas. The vital situations out of which these ideas come are not made the norm for estimating their character. That is determined by relating them to the imaginary absolute. Accordingly, Hegel can say of the religious situation in his own day that "philosophy which is theology is solely concerned with showing the rationality of religion," and so "forms a sanctuary apart and those who serve in it constitute an isolated order of priests who must not mix with the world and whose work is to protect the possessions of truth." This is not the attitude of one who thinks Christianity

---

[1] *Vorlesungen über die Philosophie der Religion* (Berlin, 1832, 1840[2]), English tr., *Lectures on the Philosophy of Religion* (London, 1895).

a genuine product of vital historical forces. It is, on the contrary, ultimately an esoteric philosophy constructed according to a pre-arranged divine pattern called the Absolute.

Thus interpreted Christianity is ultimately undevelopmental. The human attainment of truth is, indeed, an evolutionary process, but the real content and substance of that truth are determined from without. The growth of Christianity, as a historical phenomenon, is recognized, but it is not a purely spontaneous growth, since it must conform to a model called the Absolute which fixes the goal before the process of development begins. Thus Christianity is essentially the reproduction of a set of ideas divinely determined beforehand. Man's struggle to attain them may be long and laborious, but they are in no true sense a product of his struggle. He is able to grasp them because of the fortunate circumstance that he is made in their image; he is never to be regarded as their creator. Newman, we found, restricted the notion of development to the historical elucidation of Christianity, leaving its essential content quite untouched by conditions of historical growth. Hegel applied the principle of development more rigorously to the method by which man attains the essential in religion, but he still defined that essence as an independent entity, the Absolute, whose real content was not in the least determined by the developmental forces of history.

Hegel's neglect of historical phenomena was recognized even by his followers, and they early attempted an application of his philosophical principles to the specific data of Christianity, especially in reference to the origins of dogma. F. C. Baur,[1] and the members of the Tübingen school in general, found early Christianity to be a development out of specific, conflicting historical forces. The Jewish particularism of the Palestinian community on the one hand, and Pauline universalism on the other were finally synthesized through an evolutionary process into early Catholicism, and the books of the New Testament were thought to represent different points of view emerging in the course of the controversy. Although Baur's procedure thus approximated to a truly scientific historical method—a fact not always appreciated by critics of the Tübingen school—he confined attention so exclusively to the intellectual side of human activity, neglecting its emotional and volitional phases, that his conception of Christianity's content was not sufficiently comprehensive. He did maintain in a more realistic way than Hegel had done that human ideas and historical events are closely interwoven. Hence early Christianity, on its doctrinal side, was more vitally developmental, but its ultimate essence was still defined in terms of the Hegelian doctrine of the Absolute, and, therefore, necessarily remained undevelopmental in the last analysis.

In more recent years the Hegelian interpretation of Christianity has been considerably modified, especially in the direction of recognizing more fully its concrete, historical character. Accordingly, the Absolute becomes less a predetermined quantum and more a product of historical growth. Troeltsch, for example, maintains that the Christian religion is to be placed

[1] See in this connection his *Das Christentum und die christliche Kirche der drei ersten Jahrhunderte* (Tübingen, 1853, 1860[2]).

side by side with other faiths, and is to be studied by the same general scientific method of investigation. Since they must be treated as normal evolutionary developments in the life of humanity, so it must be viewed as a strictly historical evolution. If it is to take precedence over other religions its supremacy can be maintained solely on the ground of actual merit historically demonstrated. It appears, however, that Christianity as a matter of fact is the best religion, and so has a just claim to the title "absolute." As yet its complete finality may not be fully established, but its development is surely moving toward this end. Enough of its distinctive characteristics have already emerged to furnish adequate ground for faith in its ultimate absoluteness. So Troeltsch can speak of an "essential" Christianity in whose history the fundamental "ideal" is being realized through progress toward the "absolute goal."[1]

Idealistic philosophy, even in this form, does not supply a vitally developmental conception of Christianity's nature. While a process of evolution is recognized, it is supposed to issue in an Absolute no longer subject to the laws of growth. Thus the more essential phases of Christianity have already become static, and when the process of development has reached a further stage it will result in fixing a comparatively complete quantitative entity which will transcend the historic evolution by which it is said to have been

[1] See his *Die Absolutheit des Christentums und die Religionsgeschichte* (Tübingen, 1902, 1912²); also articles "Dogmatik" and "Glaube und Geschichte" in *Die Religion in Geschichte und Gegenwart*, II (Tübingen, 1910); and "The Dogmatics of the *religionsgeschichtliche Schule*," *American Journal of Theology*, XVII (1913), 1–21.

produced. Even if this outcome were possible, how could a result be called "absolute" unless an external criterion were applied for determining the ultimate? So long as history is being made—and it is vain to theorize about a time when history will cease to be in the making —it is quite impossible to be certain that an ideal goal has been reached at any particular stage of religious life. Certain results attained may be exceptionally valuable, but according to a genuinely developmental conception of life these attainments cannot be called completely ideal and absolute. In fact such terms are not consonant with the notion of vital growth. From this point of view all objective items are merely the product of certain religious activities on the part of individuals who may attempt to make their attainments serviceable for future generations by labeling these results "ideal" and "absolute." But the only ideal which true development knows is the necessity of constantly striving to produce a genuine religious life in each new generation which shall not only emulate the past but shall endeavor to transcend all previous so-called ideals. Even to say that certain past attainments have not yet been transcended does not alter the situation. It is still, and always will be, the business of a truly developmental and vital religion to strive, nor can any limit be fixed beyond which it may be said that striving becomes useless. This does not imply a depreciation of the past, but only the abandonment of the Platonic Absolute in favor of a strictly empirical criterion for estimating the worth of religious values.

Another mode of thinking, which received a strong impetus from Herder and Schleiermacher, which was adopted by Ritschl, and which has become widely prevalent, especially among the so-called modern "liberal" theologians, has exerted an important influence upon the definition of Christianity's nature. Although representatives of this view commonly hold to some form of belief in an Absolute, they do not attach primary worth to philosophical formulation of dogma, but place chief stress upon personal religious experience. They define Christianity mainly as a type of experience realized within the community of believers. While absolute identity of experience for all members of the community cannot be affirmed, there is supposed to be a common element sufficiently representative to constitute the essence of Christianity, and to furnish a basis for belief in its distinctiveness and finality.

Schleiermacher advocated essentially this position when he defined religion as a "feeling of dependence," a consciousness of the individual's relation to Deity. Christianity, however, he regarded as a genuine product of the human spirit rather than a new divine insert into life. Man has been so created that spiritual growth is a fundamental law of his constitution; in fact, all spiritual life has its ground in the creative purpose of God, who by hidden laws effects a revelation of himself, now dimly, now brightly, through the medium of earthly individuals but supremely in the person of Jesus. Thus even Jesus' God-consciousness is fundamentally a personal attainment on his part, reached through the normal exercise of his own spiritual personality. Similarly believers, while availing themselves of historical means of grace, must find the essential content of religion in a personal experience of God, worked out in accordance with the inherent capabilities of the individual. The help which comes from without does not create religion, but only stimulates and brings to fruitage powers already latent in man.

On this interpretation Christianity is developmental, but only in a restricted sense of the term. There is development in the personal attainment of experience, yet this experience is conditioned by an original supernatural endowment bestowed upon humanity at creation. Moreover, the perfect embodiment of the God-consciousness in the person of Jesus is a norm for determining the true character and content of experience. Thus, ultimately, Christianity is supernaturally conditioned and is made to conform to an objective criterion, so that the process of growth pertains only to the working-out of these given data in the religious life of the individual and of the community. Furthermore, Schleiermacher paid little attention to the historical career of Christianity. He generally ignored the influence of varying local conditions and contemporary thinking as possible factors influencing religious experience in successive periods of history.

To Ritschl[1] the need of treating Christianity in a more strictly historical fashion appealed more strongly. This seemingly was an inheritance from his earlier training in the Tübingen school. He followed Schleiermacher, however, in defining religion as man's sense of dependence upon God. Christianity more specifically is the religion in which the God-consciousness is most truly realized because of the revelation of God in Christ.

[1] See particularly his *Die Entstehung der altkatholischen Kirche* (Bonn, 1857).

Ritschl sought to correct the strong individualism of Schleiermacher by emphasizing the significance of the community, the church, which constitutes the visible kingdom of God, but he followed Schleiermacher rather than Baur in defining the distinctive features characterizing the historical life of the community. For him the significant thing in its history was not a conflict of ideas issuing in doctrinal postulates, but a type of experience which remained essentially uniform in content from the time of Jesus and the apostles on. In this fundamental respect there was unity between Paul and the primitive Palestinian believers, and this same original feature was also held to be preserved in the early Catholic church, though it was gradually obscured by degenerating influences from the contemporary heathen world, particularly in the realm of philosophical speculation. Thus for Ritschl, as for Schleiermacher, Christianity was in no fundamental sense developmental; there was no vital interaction between essential Christianity and contemporary life during the course of history.

Between Ritschl and the modern "liberals," as represented for example by Harnack,[1] there is no radical difference of view regarding Christianity's nature. Harnack insists that the historian nowadays must show how one thing has grown out of another, he recognizes that religion too is no ready-made structure but a genuine growth, and he finds Christianity not only to have been subject to change in the past, but to be in a

---

[1] Cf. his *Lehrbuch der Dogmengeschichte* (Freiburg, 1886–90, 1894–97³), English tr., *History of Dogma* (London, 1896); *Christianity and History* (London, 1907); *Das Wesen des Christentums* (Leipzig, 1900), English tr., *What Is Christianity?* (New York, 1901).

state of constant development. Yet "essential" Christianity is something quite distinct from the totality of these varying historical phenomena commonly summed up under the general designation "Christianity." A restricted section of the whole is chosen as kernel while the remainder is declared to be only husk, and the principle of selection is determined by defining this "essence" in terms of a particular type of individual experience, the consciousness of fellowship with God, the believer thus repeating Jesus' experience of God's fatherhood and man's sonship. This ethical-religious element formed the heart of Jesus' message and constitutes the kernel of Christianity in every genuine stage of its career.

Since this essence is *ex hypothesi* a distinctively Christian possession, the influence of contemporary life upon primitive Christianity becomes a question of only minor importance. While environment does, in a general way, affect personal experience, the source of a truly Christian experience is God as mediated by the historical Jesus whose personal influence is perpetuated by believers. As Harnack puts it, "at the end of the series of messengers and agents of God stands Jesus Christ. They point back to him, and it is from him that has sprung the river of life which they bear in themselves as their own."[1] The tributaries which empty into this river are either so small as to have no appreciable effect, or else their impure waters only discolor the original stream, and necessitate the work of filtration. Thus Christianity is essentially static and quantitative rather than developmental, and the problem of its

[1] *Christianity and History*, p. 44.

relationship to contemporary life practically drops out of sight.[1]

The so-called Modernist movement within Roman Catholicism also places much emphasis upon Christian experience, though not confining its scope so narrowly as many "liberal" Protestants do. The collective Christian consciousness and the doctrine of divine immanence are basal in the Modernist's definition of Christianity. It is primarily an affair of the human spirit in fellowship with the immanent God of Christian faith, and so is largely developmental in character. In contrast with the traditional Catholic view, primitive Christianity is not regarded as a perfect robe to be further unfolded but as a vital organism constantly expanding into new stages of life; and, as opposed to the Protestant notion of deterioration, every stage in this development is held to be part of a legitimate and necessary growth.[2] Christianity at first was a religion of spiritual simplicity, "formless and undogmatic," which spread over the Roman world, "adapting itself to the mentality and spiritual education of every region

[1] Similarly Mezger, *Die Absolutheit des Christentums und die Religionsgeschichte* (Tübingen, 1912), makes the untranscendable nature of Christian experience as revealed in Jesus the guaranty of Christianity's absoluteness. Christian development pertains to the more perfect realization of fellowship with God, but this type of experience is not subject to change, and can never be transcended, nor does it owe its genesis to evolutionary forces. In other words, Christianity is ultimately a canonical experience, and everything else that goes into the making of its history is of secondary moment if not, indeed, really spurious.

[2] See Loisy, *L'Évangile et l'église* (Paris, 1903, 1908⁴), English tr., *The Gospel and the Church* (London, 1903).

and borrowing from each the elements most suited for its own further development."[1]

Yet by a kind of dualism Christianity from the start is found to contain a static element which remains unaffected by development. To cite the Modernist *Programme*, "everything in the history of Christianity has changed—doctrine, hierarchy, worship; but all these changes have been providential means for the preservation of the gospel spirit which has remained unchanged through the ages."[2] There is "a religious experience which once evoked by the preaching of Christ has remained substantially the same thing under all its successive embodiments."[3] Since this immutable essence constitutes the fundamental and distinctive thing in primitive Christianity, the Modernist does not need to be concerned primarily with the question of environmental influences. They have no vital bearing upon Christianity's ultimate genesis and essential character, but pertain only to its later expansion.

This survey of opinion shows how generally Christianity has been defined in static and quantitative terms. At one time it is said to be identical with an ecclesiastical

[1] *The Programme of Modernism* (New York, 1908), pp. 79 f.

[2] P. 92.

[3] P. 77. Cf. also Loisy, *The Gospel and the Church*, p. 171: "Setting aside all theological subtleties, the Catholic church, as a society founded on the gospel, is identical with the first circle of the disciples of Jesus if she feels herself to be, and is, in the same relation with Jesus as the disciples were, if there is a general correspondence between her actual state and the primitive state, if the actual organism is only the primitive organism developed and decided, and if the elements of the church today are the primitive elements grown and fortified, adapted to the ever-increasing functions they have to fulfil."

organization, which is attested by mechanical revelation or approved by practical tests of efficiency. Again, it is a fixed system of doctrine, whose finality is established by appeal either to a scriptural canon, or to a certain form of metaphysical speculation. Finally, it is a specific type of religious experience, either narrowly restricted in content, or else made broad enough to include different varieties. Even when the notion of development is introduced to account for changes in the course of history, a certain immutable and historically unconditioned "essence" appears at the outset, or emerges in the process of growth. This forms the primal element in Christianity's constitution, and is the ultimate ground of its distinctive character as a religion. The student of Christian origins is, therefore, mainly concerned with this initial and fundamental essence. The question of contemporary influences is wholly secondary, since it relates only to the later history of this given original and never to its primary constitution. All phenomena fall into two categories, namely, original or borrowed, genuine or spurious, essential or unessential.

It is becoming more and more difficult to maintain the legitimacy of these distinctions. Any effort to fix upon an irreducible minimum of genuine "essence" can succeed only by setting up some quantity of experience, or belief, or practice as essential, while all other features are denominated unessential. But this is a doubtful procedure. In the first place, instead of defining Christianity comprehensively, attention is centered upon certain restricted phases of the whole. Even if it were possible to ascertain with perfect certainty a given sum of items possessed in common by all Christians, it would still be quite unfair to neglect all other features which may have been equally important and essential at certain periods and within particular circles. To affirm, for example, that the essential elements of Christianity in the first century were only those items which believers of that day have in common with the "liberal" theologian of the twentieth century, is to eliminate as unessential to first-century believers their realistic eschatology, their belief in demons and angels, their vivid supernaturalism, their sacramentalism, their notion of the miraculous content of religious experience, and various other features of similar importance. Certainly primitive Christianity cannot be perfectly understood without taking full account of these items, and one may fairly question the legitimacy of any interpretation which does not make them even "essential" to Christianity's existence in the first century.

Furthermore, the customary distinction between genuine and spurious is likely to prove misleading. It assumes that a sharp line can be drawn between what we know to have been original with a certain group of persons like, say, Jesus and the apostles, and constituent items from other sources. But this rigid distinction is not always possible, not even in the case of Jesus himself. He and his followers all lived in vital contact with specific environments and their religion was the outcome of personal reaction upon their several worlds of reality. Not only is it thus impracticable to distinguish between "genuine" and "spurious" in their religion, but the attempt to do so leads to a false inference. It is a mistake to assume that only those items were genuine which chanced to be strictly novel, while those which can be proved to be old or secondary are therefore spurious. Everything was genuine in so far as it was the expression of genuine conviction and experience on their part, and answered a real religious need of their time. Similarly in later times reaction upon new data produces different phases of religion whose genuineness, however, cannot be impugned merely on the ground either of newness or of want of newness. All items which answer the actual demands of any age constitute genuine factors in its religious life. Only when one assumes that a specific set of data from a particular group of individuals can be justly said to embrace everything belonging to real religion, may all other items be called spurious. But this, both practically and theoretically, is a very precarious assumption.

An even more serious difficulty connected with defining Christianity as a static essence is the fact that any such definition deals with certain products or objective characteristics of this religious movement rather than with its real life. It is true that Christian persons for nearly nineteen hundred years have been contributing toward a rich fund of historical data on the basis of which we may describe various phases of their religious activity. They have established organizations, formulated doctrines, and defined the content of their experience in order to conserve and legitimize for the benefit of others the results of their own religious living. Their work in these respects certainly has its value, yet no given quantity of excerpts from these data can be said to constitute "Christianity" in the ultimate sense of that term. Such things will at best be only products—perhaps in some instances merely by-products—of the great vital religious movement as a whole. In order to understand the real genesis and the peculiar genius of the Christian movement we must penetrate beneath these historical remains to the vital forces by which they were produced and sustained from age to age.

In this fundamental and comprehensive sense Christianity is coterminous with the actual religious living of individuals and communities who from generation to generation have inherited the Christian name and made the religious attainments of former Christians a part of their own world of objective reality. Historical Christianity is a result of this religious living and must of necessity show a variety of features corresponding to different conditions of life at different times and in different localities. A quantitative definition of this religious movement must, if it is to be comprehensive or even representative of the whole, be true to the totality of past historical phenomena and must accurately anticipate all future variations. A statement which includes only a certain selected "essence," or which sets limits to the possibilities of future development, is in reality only a partial definition of certain phases which have appeared in the historical career of the movement. Christianity can be ultimately and comprehensively conceived only in the developmental sense, as the product of actual persons working out their religious problems in immediate contact with their several worlds of reality, the process being renewed in the religious experience of each new generation.

CHAPTER II

THE IMPORTANCE OF ENVIRONMENT FOR CHRISTIAN ORIGINS

A developmental conception of Christianity's nature carries with it important implications for a genetic study of the new religion's early history. If the movement is understood to have been from the outset an affair of real life, the variant factors entering into the making of life in that day will naturally have much to do with fashioning the historical phenomenon which we commonly term primitive Christianity. In that case any effort to understand the real inner constitution of this new movement must be based upon a careful study of the vital forces dominating the first believers' immediate environment. Must the student of Christian origins relate the new religion thus closely to its contemporary world?

The problem of origins is a comparatively simple one when Christianity's nature is defined statically. Then a particular quantity of instruction, especially communicated to certain individuals and passed on by them to their successors, constitutes the substance of the new religion. It is a quantity of revelation uniquely and authoritatively mediated through specified agencies. One has only to define the proper channel of revelation in order to learn the secret of Christianity's being. If an ecclesiastical organization is vested with this divine authority, the pronouncements of the church regarding the origins of religion are final. If a canon of Scripture is made the norm for testing revelation, the New Testament version of the rise of Christianity can be accepted without reserve or supplement. If the writers of the New Testament books are thought to be interpreters who do not always report tradition completely and infallibly, the divine deposit of truth may yet be found in the teaching of prominent persons like Paul or Jesus. Christianity is still essentially a gift from heaven, granted to certain select individuals. At stated times in the past God has determined to make himself known to specific persons who, in turn, have left to posterity definite instructions to be observed by all later generations who would be truly religious. Thus the initial force which brought the new religion into being and the power by which it is at present maintained act from without and guarantee its other-worldly character.

This emphasis upon externalism is out of harmony with a thoroughly vital conception of religious development. According to the latter notion, communion with God was not in the past arbitrarily conditioned by special displays of the divine initiative, nor is it to be obtained at present by any one set of specific prescriptions. It is available for every individual on a strictly empirical basis. Therefore spiritual attainments are conditioned by one's surroundings, they are colored by the characteristics of one's personality, and they are measured by the vigor of one's religious activity. The content of experience will vary according to individual circumstances and will be variously expressed in the language of different persons. Since experience is not externally and mechanically mediated, variation does not invalidate its content nor does uniformity guarantee its normativeness.

Consequently Christianity may quite properly embrace different types of religious attainment in accordance with variations in environment and personality.

From this point of view the primary activity which called the Christian movement into existence was not the *ab extra* insertion of some other-worldly quantity of ritual, doctrine, or ethical instruction into the realm of human experience, but an outburst of spiritual energy on the part of Jesus and his followers striving after new and richer religious attainments under the stimuli of a new and more suggestive environment. It was only natural, from the standpoint of ancient psychology and metaphysics, that those attainments should have been portrayed in the language of externalism; but from the modern standpoint they must be estimated in terms of various individuals' response to their religious environment, their direct reaction upon their own peculiar world, and their personal conquests in the realm of spiritual experience.

The importance of becoming familiar with the early Christians' world as a means of understanding their life is coming to be more fully appreciated by students of Christian origins. In the first place, the language in which the New Testament books are written is now regarded as a distinct product of Graeco-Roman times. This language is Greek, but it is not the Greek of Plato or Xenophon either in its style or in its vocabulary. Centuries of life under new conditons had produced a language which was in some respects new. Old words underwent a change in meaning; new words were coined, syntactical usage changed, and new standards of literary style were established. This new world-speech—the *koine* (κοινή)—is the product of post-classical times and can be properly understood only in the new setting. Formerly it used to be supposed that the New Testament contained a large number of *hapax legomena*, and that the New Testament writers had been forced to create this unique vocabulary in order to express their new religious ideas. Similarly other words apparently had in their New Testament setting a significance not exemplified elsewhere in Greek literature. But in the great majority of instances these unusual words have since been found in the everyday speech of that age. Thus we are brought to realize the necessity of reading the New Testament books primarily in the light of linguistic usage in the first century of our era.[1]

The political and social background of early Christianity is also largely a Hellenistic product. Even within Palestine the conditions under which Jesus and his followers lived were quite directly the result of contact with the outside world. It was this force which had caused the Maccabean rebellion, and the

[1] The literature on this subject is already voluminous. A few representative books are Thumb, *Die griechische Sprache im Zeitalter des Hellenismus* (Strassburg, 1901); Deissmann, *Bibelstudien* (Marburg, 1895) and *Neue Bibelstudien* (*ibid.*, 1897), English tr., *Bible Studies* (Edinburgh, 1901), also *Licht vom Osten* (Tübingen, 1908, 1909[2]), English tr., *Light from the Ancient East* (New York and London, 1910); J. H. Moulton, *A Grammar of New Testament Greek* (Edinburgh, 1905, 1906[2]); Radermacher, *Neutestamentliche Grammatik* (Tübingen, 1911). For periodical literature, being mostly a survey of recent books, see Witkowski, "Bericht über die Literatur zum Koine aus den Jahren 1903–6," *Jahresbericht für Altertumswissenschaft*, CLIX (1912), 1–279; Deissmann, "Die Sprache der griechischen Bibel," *Theologische Rundschau*, XV (1912), 339–64; Stocks, "Das neutestamentliche Griechisch im Lichte der modernen Sprachforschung," *Neue kirchliche Zeitschrift*, XXIV (1913), 633–53 and 681–700.

subsequent political and social problems of Jewish life
were solved under the influence of constant pressure
from without. The existence of such parties as Sadducees, Pharisees, and Zealots, the presence of the tax-
collectors and the exaction of the tribute money, the
policing of Jerusalem with foreign soldiers and the
Roman control of the high-priesthood, the establishment of synagogues where the service was conducted
in the Greek language—these are a few indications of the
extent to which foreign forces had affected conditions of
life even in Judaea; while for the Jews of the Dispersion
this sort of influence was necessarily much greater.

The early Christians soon found themselves in even
closer touch than the Jews had been with gentile life.
When they broke with the synagogue, as they were soon
forced to do, and when the membership of the community
became largely gentile, the background of their life and
thinking became increasingly non-Jewish. Their cultural status in general was that of the society in which
they had been reared, the activities of their everyday
life were determined by contemporary economic conditions, in fact their whole world of reality with all its
complicated relationships was the Graeco-Roman world
of the first century A.D. In so far as these relationships
affect the religion of individuals—and such influence is
always more or less pronounced—it is important that the
contemporary political, social, and cultural situation
should be taken into account in studying the beginnings
of Christianity.

Still more important for our present study is the
religious setting which the Graeco-Roman world furnished for the life of the early Christians. It is easy,

however, to overlook the importance of this background. Until within comparatively recent times the nature of Christianity has been so defined as practically to exclude the notion of important contemporary religious relationships for the early Christians, and the subject has accordingly been very generally neglected.

We do not always realize that Christianity arose in a "very religious" world. Its ultimate triumph leaves moderns with the impression that it has always been the same dominant and self-sufficient religion which it seems to be in our day. Even when the existence of its original competitors is recognized, their popularity and strength may be greatly discounted. The religions of the Roman Empire in the first century A.D. were not so completely decadent as has often been imagined. This was in reality a period of remarkable religious activity in which various types of faith spread themselves over the Mediterranean world. The strength and extent of Judaism at that time, both in Palestine and in the Diaspora, are a well-known fact. The Gentiles also were hardly less religious in their own way than were the Jews. Paganism offered men the help of many different deities with a variety of doctrines and ceremonies designed to meet the needs of different classes of worshipers. Religion was a subject of general interest. It occupied a large place in the life of the common man, it was discussed by poets and philosophers, and even the state claimed to be established upon a religious basis.

Christians, instead of being among the first advocates of religion to enter this territory, were really among the last. Consequently they were brought into immediate contact with other faiths, a contact so close and so long continued that it at once suggests the probability of important genetic relationships between the new religion and its contemporaries. However extensively the former may seem to abound in original features, one must recognize that in childhood it was rocked in a Jewish cradle and that it grew to maturity in a gentile home. Its Jewish connections are admittedly extensive, but at an early date the new movement was transferred to gentile lands. Long before the first century closed the chief centers of Christian activity had moved from Palestine to Syrian Antioch, Ephesus, Corinth, Rome, and possibly to Alexandria. All these places were strongholds of other religions, with which Christians were thus living in close contact during the impressionable period of youthful life in the new faith.

Nor did the contemporary religions fade away quietly before the new propaganda. On the contrary, they offered a stout resistance. Although Christians vigorously proclaimed the utter worthlessness of any religion except their own, their hearers were by no means ready to accept this interpretation of the situation. It would be a grave mistake to suppose that the adherents of all other faiths were generally dissatisfied with their past religious history. Just as Yahweh retained the allegiance of his chosen people, so the pagan deities had not only loyal followers but in some instances also energetic missionaries. We must not think that the Christian evangelists cultivated purely virgin soil, for in reality they worked fields already occupied by formidable competitors. Opposition came first from the Jews and then from the Gentiles, and continued in force for several generations. Certainly at no time within the first century could it be said that the new religion had so completely displaced other faiths, or had so thoroughly isolated itself, as to make their influence an item of no possible consequence for its own life.

Since Christian missionaries were thus forced to compete for a place in occupied territory, they were not at liberty to create all religious data *de novo*. Their audiences were composed of people who had already worked out an extensive religious vocabulary, who gave much attention to the observance of stated rites, and who thought in terms of certain generally accepted ideas. While the Christian preachers could not have won converts without proclaiming the newness and superiority of Christianity, still their prospects for success would seemingly have been slight had they not used the terminology which was familiar to their hearers and shown that the new religion, however novel and self-sufficient it might claim to be, conserved and enhanced the values of the old. The latter could not be totally ignored in actual practice if Christianity was to meet, as its advocates manifestly intended it should, the same practical religious demands which its predecessors had—inadequately, according to the Christian view—aimed to satisfy. Under these circumstances it was necessary for the Christian preacher to state his message in the religious language and thought-forms of the age. While he doubtless had no intention of deliberately borrowing from foreign sources, he certainly did not have ready at hand in Christian tradition the full solution of these practical problems. It was his task to make adjustments to new situations. This pragmatic necessity may easily, though quite unconsciously, have resulted for Christians in the enrichment of experience and the evolution of ideas and practices under the influence of contemporary religions.

This possibility is further supported by the fact that Christianity did not start out full grown, but developed some of its important characteristics in response to the exigencies of expansion. At first the Christian community seemed to think of itself chiefly as a messianic company of orthodox Jews, but Jewish rejection of its messianic teaching forced the development of an independent organization. The practical demands of gentile missions also compelled a change of attitude toward the Jewish ceremonial law, a change to which some Palestinians strenuously objected. But the gentile forces prevailed. And ultimately the realistic Jewish eschatology, so dominant in the early days, had to be recast and the religious values which it embodied restated, to correspond with the actual course of history and the more stable circumstances in which gentile Christians found themselves.

Furthermore, the membership of the churches in these formative days must have consisted mainly of converts from other faiths. Christianity was not yet old enough to have trained up men from youth within its own communion. At first very little attention seems to have been given to the children, doubtless because it seemed improbable that they would have time to grow to manhood before the end of the world should come. The importance of bringing them up within the church was later realized, but the procedure apparently was contrary to apostolic practice, since tradition sought to justify the innovation by recalling that Jesus had overridden

the apostles' views when he said, "Suffer the little children to come unto me; forbid them not, for of such is
the kingdom of God."[1]   Yet in all probability during the
first century many members of Christian communities—
until the last quarter of the century certainly a large
majority—had previously been adherents of other
religions, and it is quite unlikely that their past would
be completely obliterated in making the transition from
one communion to another.   The effect of past training
was evident in the case of Palestinians like James and
his conservative associates in Jerusalem, as well as in the
case of Hellenists like Stephen, Paul, and Apollos.   That
the situation would be similar among gentile converts is
intrinsically most probable.   When they espoused the
new movement they must of necessity have brought with
them a certain intellectual, moral, and religious heritage
which would thus become a vital part of developing
Christianity.

These conditions must have been very significant for
the origins of the new religion.   Since its advocates
lived in a world already full of competing religions, since
they were in close contact with other faiths and even
contended with them for territory already occupied,
since many aspects of developing Christianity were
determined under the pressure of these conditions, and
since the membership of the Christian communities was
drawn largely from other communions, the importance of
consulting the religious situation in the contemporary
Graeco-Roman world is self-evident.

Does it follow that Christianity was not in truth a
new religion but only a recasting of religious data already

[1] Mark 10:14; Matt. 19:14; Luke 18:16.

present in the ancient world? This has sometimes been affirmed. Yet no serious historian cares to deny that a new religious awakening began with the preaching of John the Baptist, that its scope was enlarged and its force accelerated through the work of Jesus, and that in the century following his death the new movement grew rapidly in numbers until its sway extended far beyond its original Palestinian home. That the movement was new in the formal sense of being another religion among others already in existence is a generally recognized fact. Not only was it one among others, but in a relatively short time it almost completely supplanted all competitors. Though the popular faiths and the philosophies of the day endured for a few generations, they ultimately disappeared. Judaism indeed maintained an independent existence, but only under the shadow of intense opposition and in remote places. Within a few centuries Christianity became not merely the most prominent but virtually the only recognized religion of the Mediterranean world. This success is sometimes thought to prove its absolute independence of all environmental relationships; had it not been a strictly new creation it could not have routed all opponents so thoroughly, nor could it have answered so adequately the various religious demands of that day.

This, however, is not the only possible interpretation of the data. May not Christianity's phenomenal success have to be ascribed in large measure to the skill with which zealous missionaries like Paul—who strove to become "all things to all men" that he might save some—adapted themselves to contemporary conditions? In no other way is it possible, we are sometimes told, to explain how a movement begun by a small Jewish sect could expand so widely and rapidly, could add so many new features in the process of expansion, and could meet the needs of so many different types of people. Its champions, particularly on gentile soil, are credited with having possessed a real genius for adopting and readjusting current religious values, thus fortifying their cause with the more vital and permanent elements of contemporary faiths. So Christianity has been explained as a collection of ancient myths, an appropriation of current rites, and a combination of already existing religious ideas, without any essentially new features. In its most extreme form this type of interpretation can even dispense with the historical Jesus, since his personal activity is no longer necessary to account for the origin of Christianity.

This disposition to ignore the significance of historical personalities, and to attach undue importance to ideas and rites, may easily be overstressed in recognizing the importance of environment for the genesis of a religious movement. Jesus' personal activity, as well as that of his disciples, forms an indispensable factor in the origin of Christianity.[1]   Yet can their work be called "new" if they did not obtain the main content of their religion by means of formal revelation and if at the same time their thought and activity were molded and influenced by surroundings?   On a static definition of Christianity's nature this question would be answered negatively, for then newness must be measured by the quantity of absolutely new dogmas, ethical ideals, or ecclesiastical rites produced.   But a vitally developmental conception

[1] See Case, *The Historicity of Jesus* (Chicago, 1912).

of Christianity's character finds the new religion's distinctiveness in its devotees' fresh attainment of religious experience through personal religious living. Not only the content of the experience, and the doctrines or rites based upon it, but also the use which Christians make of their spiritual energy in their efforts to answer the religious demands of their age constitute, in the last analysis, the uniqueness of Christianity.

While a forceful personality like Jesus or Paul will naturally be in many respects distinctive in the realm of religion, we must guard against assuming that original features are necessarily, merely in virtue of their new-ness, more valuable than appropriated items. When religious values are tested by the criterion of vital efficiency, the question of novelty and unique origin is not primarily important. If it were possible to duplicate many experiences of the Christians in the lives of their predecessors or contemporaries, and if the majority of the ideas they advocated and the rites they observed should be found to have been already current in earlier times, the Christian movement would still retain its significance because of the way in which its exponents co-ordinated their religious activity with the life of their day. While their experience may not always have been absolutely "new," it was a fresh and vital spiritual attainment on their part. Such attainment was, to be sure, conditioned by past religious training and contemporary ideas, but it also represented the results of a new reaction upon given objective data. Similarly the ideas and rites employed to objectivize, evaluate, and convey to others the content of experiential religion may for the most part have existed already in the contemporary world, but these things took on a new significance in the Christians' own thinking when made to function anew in their solution of vital religious problems. In this sense "old" and "new" may be equally valuable and equally germane to early Christianity.

The fundamental worth of Christianity lay in the manner in which its advocates ministered to the vital religious needs of the time, not in the assumption that the methods and tools employed had never been used before. On first thought, we may be disposed to infer that they must have used new tools else they could not have accomplished their great task, but is this a necessary assumption? Historical investigation may show that they generally employed tried instruments and customary methods, adopting new ones only when the old failed to serve their purpose. Even then they need not have assumed the rôle of inventor; they may quite as likely have made a new selection from existing materials. In any case, the uniqueness of the Christians' work lay fundamentally in their vital experience and vigorous activity rather than in any creation of a new body of quantitative data.

Hence the need to study their life in the light of environment. Here they found their religious problems; these problems were worked out through reaction upon this environment; it supplied the materials for use in the construction of their religious thinking, and it furnished stimuli for their richest spiritual developments. This does not mean that there was no originality in Christianity, for it does not ignore the creative activity of those forceful personalities who were responsible for starting the new movement on its way and who added

from time to time momentum to its life. They indeed
felt themselves divinely guided in the work of giving the
world a new religion, but their conviction had been
attained, and continued to receive new impulse and
power, through a strong spiritual reaction upon their
immediate world of reality. Their faith was born and
grew to maturity amid conflicts fought out in the arena
of real life. As this scene of action was at first distinctly
Jewish, but soon became mainly gentile, the early
Christians' relation both to their Jewish and to their
gentile environment is one of the primary facts to be
reckoned with in a study of Christian origins.

This problem, particularly on the side of gentile connections, has as yet received a relatively small amount
of serious consideration. In describing the rise of Christianity much stress has been placed upon the personal
contributions of Jesus and the apostles. Their peculiar
significance for the founding of the new religion may to
some extent justify this procedure, yet even here the
environmental problem at last forces itself to the front.
While literary criticism of the Gospels has greatly clari-
fied Jesus' historical figure, the exact determination of
even the earliest source documents yields only certain
more or less primitive versions of Jesus' words and deeds.
Neither these documents, nor the Jesus whom they
portray, produced Christianity in the first instance;
Christians—or different circles of Christians—produced
the documents, describing Jesus as seen from their
point of view and interpreted in terms of their special
problems. The incentives prompting communities or
individuals to produce documents, and the influences
which guided them in the selection and revision of

materials, are the ultimate factors in the situation a knowledge of which conditions all genuinely historical study. Hence the historicity of all tradition must be judged ultimately in the light of believers' immediate surroundings.[1]

Moreover, if complete information regarding Jesus' life and teaching could be obtained this would not fully disclose the origins of Christianity, if the latter is a vital growth rather than a static quantity. As a historical movement, it arose out of what early believers made of Jesus and his teaching, not through the mere preservation of a deposit which he committed to them for safe-keeping. Their heritage from him may have been one of the most significant objective factors upon which they reacted—though historical study cannot take this statement to be simply axiomatic—yet it is to their own vital activity that we must look for the real secret of Christianity's life. Their activity was prompted, not by one agent, but by a host of stimuli which intermingled to produce the various phenomena of Christianity. In short, its origins must ultimately be read in the light of the many determining factors supplied by the entire contemporary life.

The history of early Christianity has often been written—and well written—from the standpoint of the

[1] Regard for environment is also fundamental for interpretation of the Gospels as a whole, as well as for other New Testament writings. It is a mistake to imagine that the Gospels have served their entire purpose for the historical student when he has sifted from them a set of excerpts which are thought to represent Jesus accurately. On the contrary, they are throughout excellent testimonials to the growing life of the new religion, and, in turn, can be interpreted accurately only from the standpoint of their own historical origin.

inner history of the community,[1] without special reference to the influence of other surroundings upon the lives
of believers.   The inner life of the new society is unquestionably a very important phase in the history of the
new religion.   The energy which this sense of community
life developed, the growing consciousness of a distinctive mission, the formulation of a common doctrine, the
establishment of ecclesiastical organization and ritualistic observances, and the production of a body of religious
literature are all valuable items in the story of Christianity's origin.   But if the lives of Christians were
temporally conditioned and if their contact with environment was really a vital one, as we have come to believe,
the story of their career is not complete until the various
genetic forces which acted upon their lives have been
taken into account.   In this way only shall we truly
understand the real inner life of the community itself.
In the genesis of early Christianity the contribution
received from Jesus, and the forces which were generated
within the inner circle of the first believers, formed significant items, but all these things were blended into
one effective whole under the pressure of forces supplied
by the immediate world in which Christians lived.

Consequently the primary problem in a study of
Christian origins is not to ask how many static items
other religions may have contributed toward the composition of a quantity of doctrine, conduct, or ritual

[1] E.g., Weizsäcker, *Das apostolische Zeitalter der christlichen Kirche*
(Tübingen, 1886, 1901³), English tr., *The Apostolic Age of the Christian
Church* (New York, 1892, 1899²);   McGiffert, *A History of Christianity
in the Apostolic Age* (New York, 1897, 1899²);   Ropes, *The Apostolic
Age in the Light of Modern Criticism* (New York, 1906); Achelis, *Das
Christentum in den ersten drei Jahrhunderten* (Leipzig, 1912); *et al.*

said to constitute the "essence" of Christianity. This latter statement of the problem not only rests upon a misconception of Christianity's real nature, but does equal injustice to other faiths which were also ultimately vital and developmental rather than static and quantitative existences. The genetic relation between religious movements with constantly changing vital connections cannot be adequately estimated simply on the basis of a series of similarities or differences in dogma and ritual. It is not at all inconceivable that similar items may have been produced independently, or may have had but a very remote common ancestry; while differences which may seem on the surface radical may be only regional or temperamental variations of items which are genetically closely akin. It is exceedingly difficult if not impossible to determine genetic kinships by any atomistic procedure, which touches only the surface of the problem. The deeper currents of actual life must be fathomed before one can trace the truly genetic relationships of religious movements in any age.

The atomistic method, which has been used by some students in defense of the complete originality of Christianity and by others to prove its totally secondary character, is open to other serious objections. It too easily permits the hypostatizing of ideas or rites, thus treating them as though they have a real existence apart from the life of the people by whom they are cherished. We must not forget that ideas function only when entertained by persons and reinforced by environmental stimuli; they have no power apart from these social relationships. When isolated and pushed into the center of the stage, the discussion which revolves about them too readily becomes a mere academic debate. "Ideas" cannot really be compared in any truly genetic sense until they have been connected in a vital way with the actual soil and the particular atmosphere which nourished their life.

In line with the tendency to hypostatize ideas, it has also become customary to make a sharp distinction between the *term* used to describe the idea and the *content* of the idea. Thus items in Christianity designated by the same terms as similar items in other faiths are yet found to be sufficiently unique to allow the supposition that only the *form* is borrowed while the *idea* is wholly original.[1] Whether this separation of form from content is to be made as sharply in real life as in our academic discussions may be fairly doubted. Certainly ideas have an exceedingly tenuous existence apart from the phrases embodying them, though it is inevitable that different people should stamp their individuality upon the ideas they entertain and the words they employ. But it is quite another thing to assume that the early Christians, when using terms already current among their religious contemporaries, first emptied the language of its common meaning and then filled it with a new content. Even had they done this, how would the people to whom they were speaking know what had happened? Conceding that the Christians knew the meaning generally attaching to current religious terminology,

[1] This argument is frequently advanced in such treatises as Clemen, *Religionsgeschichtliche Erklärung des Neuen Testaments* (Giessen, 1908), English tr., *Primitive Christianity and Its Non-Jewish Sources* (Edinburgh, 1912), also *Der Einfluss der Mysterienreligionen auf das älteste Christentum* (Giessen, 1913); Bonhöffer, *Epiktet und das Neue Testament* (Giessen, 1911); Kennedy, *St. Paul and the Mystery-Religions* (London, 1913).

and finding that it was used by them without definition of a change in meaning, normal procedure must assume that they—apart from individualistic variations—moved in the same thought-world as their contemporaries.

Yet another danger attending the method of itemized comparisons lies in the tendency to isolate ideas or persons from the totality of their historical environment. For example, instead of setting a New Testament writer into vital relation with his entire surroundings as a means of understanding his thought, an effort is made to expound his thinking as an independent entity. We are sometimes told that the interpreter's first duty is to define the exact meaning of a New Testament author before placing him into relation with his contemporaries. The non-Christian religions are, naturally, treated in a similar manner. When the content of two contemporary religions has been thus independently defined, each having been studied *in vacuo*, we might almost say, then the two entities are compared, with a view to observing genetic relationships. The fundamental fallacy of this procedure lies in supposing that any historic faith, or any particular exponent of that faith, can be fully understood without reference to the great vital *milieu* which environment supplies. An interpretation of religion, whether Christian or non-Christian, which does not proceed from a close examination of, and a sympathetic touch with, the total surroundings in which its adherents lived cannot be truly historical in the fullest sense of that term.

Finally, the real question at issue in a study of Christian origins is not whether certain items in the new religion can be classified as "original" while others may be only "derived." If Christianity were fundamentally a static quantity of data it might be desirable at the outset to maintain the originality of these items in order to defend the new religion's right to exist. But the situation is very different when its real nature is defined in terms of the activities of actual persons whose spiritual experience was vitally linked with a definite social and religious environment. In their case everything may be called "original," in so far as it was a product of their own personal religious reaction upon their several worlds of reality; and everything may be said to be "derived," in the sense of being the immediate product of this reaction upon data supplied by history or by immediate environment, and interpreted under the impulsion of stimuli furnished by the actual world in which believers lived.

Even mystical items of spiritual attainment cannot be exempted from these realistic connections. The early Christians actually found God in contemporary life, as well as in history and personal experience. Their age equipped them with a psychology and a metaphysics which frequently measured the highest religious values in terms of ecstasy, miracle, revelation, and externalism in general. These things in turn became a means of arriving at the heights of spiritual experience. While we may without hesitation affirm that such experience was often truly original, a new creation in the lives of believers, it cannot be hypostatized and treated as though it were an isolated entity having some existence apart from the actual conditions in which it was shaped and by which it was sustained. The founders of Christianity, like Christians in subsequent times, found God through contact with their own world, employing the agencies and responding to the stimuli furnished by their immediate surroundings.

In other words, Christianity was not at the outset, nor did it ever become, primarily an abstract quantity of doctrine, ethics, or ritual. Christians produced dogma, defined rules of conduct, and established ritualistic observances, but these were secondary to the vital activity of actual Christian persons. A new generation might be greatly influenced by the static items which it received from its ancestors, yet it chose, interpreted, and supplemented these according to its own needs and in response to the vital demands which its own experience furnished. Its objective historical inheritance formed only a part of its total world of reality, and so constituted only one phase in its religious life. Thus the advocates of the new religion had from the start vital social relationships, and many important factors entering into the making of their faith from age to age must have been supplied by their contemporary world, a knowledge of which is therefore essential to any thorough understanding of Christian origins.

The following survey of the evolution of primitive Christianity is made with special reference to the religious setting of believers. We shall not be chiefly concerned to discover just what items in the New Testament may be called "original" and what may be called "derived." Our task is broader and more fundamental. It is to study the early Christians' career in the light of their own vital reaction upon their immediate environment as they worked out their religious problems in New Testament times.

CHAPTER III

THE MEDITERRANEAN WORLD IN NEW TESTAMENT TIMES

The territory about the eastern Mediterranean had been occupied successively by a variety of civilizations before the Christian era. The fertile Nile valley, the regions watered by the Tigris and the Euphrates, the Iranian plateau, the highlands of Asia Minor, the coast lands of Phoenicia, the shores of the Aegean, and distant Italy, all made from time to time their respective contributions to the life of antiquity. Each of these civilizations shows distinctive characteristics corresponding to different climatic conditions and physical environments. Varying physical features, constituting natural barriers to unification, resulted in emphasizing tribal distinctions and in arousing national hostilities. Instead of developing a common world-culture on the basis of friendly intercourse between different peoples, one nation or another sought in turn to crush all rivals and to impose its own civilization upon the foreigner. Not until the political control came to be exercised by some one authority sufficiently strong to dominate the entire territory and sufficiently tolerant of different nationalities to allow all peoples a fair measure of equal rights, could anything like a common world-culture be established.

This goal had been at least partially attained in New Testament times. Under Alexander the Great all the country from Greece on the west to the Indus on the east, from the Black Sea and the Caspian Sea on the north to the Indian Ocean, the Persian Gulf, and Egypt on the south had been made one kingdom. Alexander had not aimed simply at conquest; he sought to establish both political and national unification by a process of fusion. The success of his work is demonstrated by the degree of uniformity and the extent of common intercourse which continued to show itself in this territory in spite of the political disruption following Alexander's death. Later, Rome continued the process of unification in the western part of Alexander's empire. The Roman dominions at the end of Trajan's reign (117 A.D.) included all of Europe northward as far as Britain, the Rhine, and the Danube; in the East, Asia Minor, Armenia, Mesopotamia, Assyria, Babylonia, Syria, Palestine, and Arabia Petraea; in the South, Egypt and the entire North African coast lands. Though Roman authority was never firmly established east of the Euphrates, still communication with the Farther East was maintained for commercial purposes. In the first century of our era there was comparatively free intercourse between all parts of that ancient world resulting in a fusion of its various elements such as had not been possible in any previous period of history.[1]

---

[1] The ancients themselves had become much interested in the study of geography, as a work like Strabo's shows (English tr. by Hamilton and Falconer, 3 vols., London, 1913). For modern treatises see Smith, *Dictionary of Greek and Roman Geography* (London, 1854); Bunbury, *A History of Ancient Geography among the Greeks and Romans* (2 vols., London, 1879); Ramsay, *Historical Geography of Asia Minor* (London, 1890), and article "Roads and Travel (in the New Testament)" in Hastings' *Dictionary of the Bible* (extra vol., New York, 1904); G. A. Smith, *Historical Geography of the Holy Land* (14th ed., New York, 1908); Hogarth, *The Nearer East* (New York, 1902); Forbiger, *Handbuch der alten Geographie* (3 vols., Leipzig, 1844–48; 2. Aufl., Hamburg, 1877);

To what part of this territory did the early Christians belong? Tradition places their first assembly in Jerusalem, although Jesus' own activity, according to Mark at least, had been chiefly in Galilee. Even if the first important gathering of believers was in Jerusalem where the mother-church remained until shortly before the fall of the city in 70 A.D., Christians in general by no means confined themselves to this narrow territory. No one set of geographical or climatic surroundings conditioned the entire life of all Christians in New Testament times. There were, of course, Christians at Jerusalem who probably remained in that particular vicinity all their lives, but others who were greatly in the majority were scattered about the Mediterranean in different localities, many of them frequently changing residence as they moved with the shifting currents of life. The New Testament data alone furnish ample evidence of this cosmopolitan character of the new movement. Christians were already in the outlying districts of Palestine when Paul persecuted the new faith, and after his conversion he propagated the same teaching in Arabia, Syria, Cilicia, Asia Minor, Macedonia, and Greece. But Paul was only one—though the principal one about whom the writer of Acts cares to tell Theophilus—of many others who had adopted this new religion and continued to preach it in their travels.

Kiepert, *Lehrbuch der alten Geographie* (Berlin, 1878), English tr., *A Manual of Ancient Geography* (London, 1881); Jung, *Grundriss der Geographie von Italien und dem Orbis Romanus* (München, 1887, 1897²); Götz, *Die Verkehrswege im Dienste des Welthandels* (Stuttgart, 1888), pp. 312–514. Murray's *Handy Classical Maps*, edited by Grundy, are convenient for use. For the present study those of "The Eastern Empires," "The Roman Empire," and "Asia Minor" will be found most valuable.

Harnack[1] has made a list of places where Christians, or Christian communities, can be traced in New Testament times, and it is both astonishingly large and of wide geographical range. It includes the chief cities of Syria and Asia Minor as well as important centers in Macedonia, Achaia, and Italy. The failure of any New Testament writer to mention Africa is probably a mere accident, for the prominence of Christianity there in the second century suggests an early planting. While it may be very possible that Paul never carried out his intention of going to Spain,[2] it is not improbable that other Christians in their travels had already reached that point. Early Christianity as represented in the New Testament is no mere local product, but a widespread religious movement embracing individuals from different places and from among different peoples.

Since historical Christianity of New Testament times is a product of Christians' activity within the Graeco-Roman world as a whole, it becomes necessary to examine the chief characteristics of this civilization as a background for the study of Christian origins. But the specific situation in the first century A.D. cannot be understood in isolation from the history of the immediately preceding period. In order to set the world of the New Testament age in its proper perspective some account must be taken of the main cultural forces brought into prominence by the work of Alexander the Great, carried forward under his successors (the "Diadochi"),

---

[1] *Mission and Expansion of Christianity in the First Three Centuries* (New York, 1908[2]), II, 91 ff.; translated from the German, *Die Mission und Ausbreitung des Christentums in den ersten drei Jahrhunderten* (Leipzig, 1906[2]).

[2] Rom. 15:24, 28.

and their descendants (the "Epigoni"), and perpetuated
without any very extensive transformations in Roman
times.

Alexander's work marks the beginnings of a new epoch
in ancient history. The type of culture which flourished
in this period is commonly designated "Hellenistic,"
in contrast with the earlier "Hellenic" civilization of
Greece proper. Formally speaking, we may say the
Hellenistic age opened when Alexander of Macedonia
set out upon his conquest of Asia in the spring of
334 B.C. His defeat of Darius at the battle of Issus
in 333 B.C. and again at Arbela in 331 B.C. brought
an end to Persian rule in western Asia.[1] Though the
conqueror's own career was a short one—he died at
Babylon in 323 B.C.—Macedonian rulers continued to
govern the chief portions of Alexander's divided empire
until Rome appeared upon the scene, finally taking over
Macedonia in 148, Greece in 146, Syria in 64, and
Egypt in 30 B.C.

Thus Macedonian rule disappeared. From this time
on the controlling authority of the Mediterranean
world was Roman. But in fixing dates we must not
think that any section of humanity's life can be sharply
isolated from its immediate context. The Hellenistic

[1] The year 338 B.C. is commonly made the beginning of the Hellenistic
age, since this is the date of Philip's victory at Chaeronea after which the
Diet of Corinth elected him στρατηγὸς αὐτοκράτωρ of the Greek forces.
After Philip's assassination in 336 Alexander was given the same appointment, but it required nearly two years to establish himself firmly in this
position, by quelling disturbances in various quarters, and administering
to his opponents in Greece a crushing defeat at Thebes. Not until the
spring of 334 had he really completed the foundation upon which the new
Hellenism was to be reared. To be sure, the initial stages of the movement were much earlier, earlier even than the battle of Chaeronea.

age has many clearly distinguishable antecedents both in Greece and in the conquered lands, for the establishment of Roman dominion did not mean the obliteration of the previous civilization. In fact the distinctive characteristics of Hellenistic culture remained very largely unchanged under the Roman emperors. Consequently the surroundings of Christians in New Testament times were virtually Hellenistic, even though in the more formal sense the world of that day was Roman.

This Graeco-Roman age has often been termed a decadent period in history, and therefore its importance has usually been greatly underestimated. When judged according to classical Hellenic standards the culture of Hellenistic times does at first sight seem quite inferior. This later age produced no poets to vie with Aeschylus, Sophocles, or Euripides; no philosophers who compete for first place with Socrates, Plato, or Aristotle; and no historian whom we read by the side of Herodotus, Thucydides, or Xenophon; yet, in contrast with Hellenism proper, "Hellenicism," if we may use this rare though much-needed word, produced a distinctive culture whose significance for the history of human progress is none the less worthy of attention because it does not chance to be a mere replica of classical Hellenism.

The political events of this period form a long and complicated story which can here be traced only in broadest outlines.[1] The brilliant military career of Alexander has been recorded by several ancient historians. One of the

[1] Some attention is usually given to this period in the standard histories of Greece, of which Holm, *Geschichte des Griechenlands bis zum Ausgange des sechsten Jahrhunderts vor Christus* (Berlin, 1836), English tr., *A History of Greece* (Vol. IV, New York, 1899), and Beloch, *Griechische Geschichte*, III, 1 (Strassburg, 1904), 260–556, and the same author's

most critical and accurate extant accounts is by Arrian, a Greek writer of the second century A.D. Of the source materials at his disposal the author employed chiefly a work by Ptolemy and another by Aristobulus. Both these persons had accompanied Alexander, the former being the founder of the Egyptian kingdom after Alexander's empire fell to pieces. As both works were compiled after their hero's death and by two persons of such prominence, Arrian believed their narratives to be generally trustworthy where their accounts agreed,

"Griechische Geschichte seit Alexander" in Gercke and Norden, *Einleitung in die Altertumswissenschaft*, III (Leipzig, 1913²), are among the best. Books dealing specifically with the Hellenistic age are: Droysen, *Geschichte des Hellenismus* (3 vols., Gotha, 1836–42, 1877–78²), the latest edition of which is a French translation, *Histoire de l'hellénisme* (Paris, 1883–85), made under the direction of Bouché-Leclercq; Mahaffy, *The Story of Alexander's Empire* (London, 1887), *Greek Life and Thought from the Age of Alexander to the Roman Conquest* (New York, 1887, 1896²), and *The Progress of Hellenism under Alexander's Empire* (Chicago, 1905); Niese, *Geschichte der griechischen und makedonischen Staaten seit der Schlacht bei Chaeronea* (3 vols., Gotha, 1893–1903); Kaerst, *Geschichte des hellenistischen Zeitalters* (2 vols., Leipzig, 1901–9). The situation in Roman times may be studied in Hertzberg, *Geschichte Griechenlands unter der Herrschaft der Römer* (3 vols., Halle, 1866–75); Marquardt, *Römische Staatsverwaltung*, being Vols. IV (Leipzig, 1881²), V (*ibid.*, 1884²), and VI (*ibid.*, 1885³) of *Handbuch der römischen Alterthümer* by Marquardt and Mommsen; Mommsen, *Römische Geschichte* (Vol. V, Berlin, 1894⁴), English tr., *The Provinces of the Roman Empire from Caesar to Diocletian* (2 vols., New York, 1887); Colin, *Rome et la Grèce de 200 à 146 avant Jésus-Christ* (Paris, 1905); Mahaffy, *The Silver Age in the Greek World* (Chicago, 1906) recast from the same author's *Greek World under Roman Sway* (New York, 1890); Hahn, *Rom und Romanismus im griechisch-römischen Osten bis auf die Zeit Hadrians* (Leipzig, 1906); Thieling, *Der Hellenismus in Kleinafrika: Der griechische Kultureinfluss in den römischen Provinzen Nordwestafrikas* (Leipzig, 1911). For accounts of this period among the ancient historians see Polybius, iv f., and xviii–xxxiii; Diodorus, xvii–xx; Livy, xxxi–xlv; and Appian, ix–xii.

but where they disagreed he selected what appeared to him the more creditable and more worthy of preservation. No modern work can supplant this conscientious account by a biographer who has sufficient admiration for his hero to write appreciatively and yet possesses a remarkably keen sense of loyalty to truth. The author's attitude throughout is well described in his closing words: "In relating the history of Alexander's achievements there are some things which I have been compelled to censure but I am not ashamed to admire Alexander himself. Those actions I have branded as bad both out of regard for my own truthfulness and at the same time for the good of humanity. For this reason it was not without the agency of God that I myself undertook the task of writing this history." Here Arrian shows the effects of the strongly ethical and religious training he had received from Epictetus, a training which seems to have inculcated intellectual accuracy among its moral and religious precepts.[1]

Alexander's career was as strikingly brilliant as it was brief. He moved his army, thirty to forty thousand strong, across the Hellespont in the spring of 334 B.C. First he visited the site of ancient Troy, performing religious ceremonies and going forward on his mission in the spirit of the ancient Homeric heroes. Though a Persian fleet held the Aegean, he seemed to have no fear

---

[1] Plutarch's *Alexander* is also important. Though not so lengthy as Arrian's account it is more interesting as a character sketch. Plutarch's information was doubtless also derived mainly from the works of Ptolemy and Aristobulus, whose writings unfortunately are no longer extant. A great many ancient historians wrote about Alexander, e.g., Diodorus, xvii. For fragments from many sources see Müller, *Scriptores rerum Alexandri Magni* (Paris, 1877).

of being cut off from his base in Macedonia. In fact, it soon became evident that he intended to conquer so thoroughly the whole territory about the eastern Mediterranean that the fleet would be effectually isolated from the Persian land forces and thus would be rendered comparatively harmless. Accordingly Alexander did not follow up his victories over Darius first on the banks of the Granicus in 334 and again at Issus in 333. Instead of pursuing the Persians inland he proceeded to take possession of Syria and Egypt.

He passed the winter of 332–31 in Egypt. While here he founded Alexandria, which was destined to become the chief commercial city of his empire as well as a most important center of culture in later times. At this time Alexander displayed again his usual attitude of deference toward the religion of the conquered peoples. The joy with which the Egyptians received him as their deliverer from the rule of the less sympathetic Persians is reflected in the tradition of his visit to the oracle of Ammon in the oasis of Siwah where the oracle is said to have informed him that he was a son of the god, though there is much variant ancient tradition on this subject.[1] Josephus[2] reports a similarly favorable attitude of Alexander toward Jewish religion. While Josephus can hardly be called an unbiased authority on this subject, it would have been perfectly consistent with Alexander's attitude toward other foreign faiths for him to have treated Jerusalem with favor even to the extent of offering a sacrifice in the temple.

[1] Cf. Arrian, iii. 4; vii. 29; Plutarch, *Alexander*, 27; Diodorus, xvii. 51; Strabo, xvii. 1. 43; Livy, ix. 18.

[2] *Ant.*, XI, 8.

The conqueror was now ready for his eastern expedition. He set out in the spring of 331 and passing through Syria and Mesopotamia he arrived at the Tigris River which he crossed September 20. Here the Persian forces made their last stand, but the Macedonians won an easy victory. Alexander did not pursue Darius immediately, but turned south to take possession of the rich Babylonian lands. Having gathered wealth here and at Susa, where the Persian kings had stored vast treasures, he ascended into the plateau of Iran. Here he captured the royal city of Persepolis and with it a great store of treasure. Pursuing the fleeing enemy he traversed Media, passed through the Caspian gates into the regions of Hyrcania, southeast of the Caspian Sea, and by forced marches with a few chosen followers finally overtook the fleeing Persians. He at last captured the dead body of Darius, slain by his companions and guarded only by his faithful dog.[1] The body was buried with kingly honors at Persepolis. The countries of Media and Parthia were placed under the rule of Alexander's appointees and he pushed his way on toward India.

He came into the valley of the Kabul in the winter of 330–329,[2] and the next spring crossed the Hindu-Kush range, entering Bactria. The summer of the next year found him in India where he passed over the Indus and established his dominion in the Punjab. His army refused to accompany him farther east, so he turned southward, following the Indus to the sea. In the

---

[1] Aelian, *De natura animalium*, vi. 25.

[2] According to the common dating, but some scholars say 329–328, e.g., Hogarth, *Philip and Alexander of Macedon*, pp. 296 ff.

meantime a fleet was prepared which was sent to explore the sea route from India to Babylonia, while Alexander with the last of his forces set out in October to make the journey by land. After a weary march through the desert of Gadrosia the various parts of the army came together again in the Carmanian territory lying north of the mouth of the Persian Gulf. On reaching Susa in the spring of 324 Alexander took some time to adjust the affairs of government throughout his widely extended dominions. The next spring he moved to Babylon and made preparations for exploring the water route from Babylonia to Egypt. Incidentally he also planned to conquer Arabia, which was reported to be a land of wealth. All was in readiness for the expedition when Alexander fell sick and died in June, 323 B.C.

With the death of Alexander the political unification which had been established began to crumble. It had been his custom to appoint governors like the Persian satraps over different provinces of the empire. This custom was continued, and an effort was made to maintain unity by setting up Alexander's infant son, and also his imbecile brother, Philip Arrhidaeus, as joint kings under the regency of Perdiccas, a distinguished general of Alexander's army. But this arrangement proved wholly inadequate for the complicated situation. The ease with which certain cities like Rhodes, and districts like Pontus, which had never been thoroughly conquered by the Macedonians, broke away from the central control, the existence of jealousies among the leading personages in the government, and an ambition on Perdiccas' part to possess himself of the entire empire precipitated internal warfare which ultimately resulted in a threefold division of the whole territory. In Macedonia the Antigonids ruled, claiming authority also over Greece and Thrace. The Seleucid rulers inherited the Asiatic dominions, and the Ptolemies established themselves in Egypt.

The Antigonid kingdom arose only after a hard struggle. Antigonus Cyclops, one of Alexander's generals, had been made governor of Phrygia in 333, and on Alexander's death Lycia and Pamphylia were added to his territory. He assumed the title of king in 306, though he had not yet established himself in Macedonia. After his death in 301 his son Demetrius took up the fight and set himself upon the Macedonian throne in 294. From that time on the descendants of Antigonus[1] ruled, with a few interruptions, the ancient kingdom of Macedonia until it was dismembered by Rome in 168 and finally converted into a Roman province in 148 B.C.

In general the Asiatic dominions of Alexander passed into the hands of Seleucus, a Macedonian who had distinguished himself in the Indian campaign. He was made chiliarch after Alexander's death, and two years later, satrap of Babylonia. The defeat of Antigonus Cyclops at Gaza in 312 was so important for the authority of Seleucus that this has become the generally accepted date for the beginning of Seleucid rule. He did not at once gain control of western Asia, but he asserted his power effectively in the East. Not until the death

[1] The Antigonid line, with approximate dates, consists of Antigonus Cyclops (323–301), Demetrius I (301–283), Antigonus Gonatas (283–239), Demetrius II (239–229), Antigonus Doson (regent 229–221), Philip V (221–179), Perseus (179–168). Tarn, *Antigonos Gonatas* (Oxford, 1913), gives an account of the most important representative of this house.

of Antigonus in 301 did Syria come under Seleucus'
authority. On gaining this territory he founded the city
of Antioch on the Orontes, making it the capital of his
empire. Later he subdued the greater part of Asia
Minor and was about to establish himself in Macedonia
when he was assassinated. The history of the Seleucid
rulers is a troubled one. They were at war now with
one enemy and now with another. They were almost
constantly competing with the Ptolemies for the control
of Palestine and with the Antigonids, or with native
rulers, for the control of Asia Minor. In the East
they were perpetually troubled by uprisings of native
princes whom they were frequently unable to dislodge
from power. Furthermore, internal troubles so hastened
the disintegration of their authority that Antiochus XIII
was incapable of offering serious resistance to Pompey,
and Syria was constituted a Roman province in 64 B.C.[1]

The situation in Egypt was, on the whole, a more
stable one. Ptolemy, son of a Macedonian nobleman

---

[1] The Seleucid rulers may be listed as follows: Seleucus Nicator
(312–281), Antiochus I Soter (281–262), Antiochus II Theos (262–246),
Seleucus II Callinicus (246–227), Seleucus III Soter (227–223), Antiochus
III the Great (223–187), Seleucus IV Philopator (187–176), Antiochus
IV Epiphanes (176–164), Antiochus V Eupator (164–162), Demetrius I
Soter (162–150), Alexandar Balas (150–145), Demetrius II Nicator
(145–140 and 129–126), Antiochus VI (145–143), Tryphon (143–138),
Antiochus VII Sidetes (138–129). After this the line of succession is
hopelessly confused, rival claimants maintaining themselves con-
temporaneously. One line traced its descent from Antiochus VII and
another from Demetrius II. Important books on this period are Frölich,
Annales compendiarii regum et rerum Syriae (Wien, 1750); Gardner,
Coins of the Seleucid Kings of Syria in the British Museum (London, 1878);
Babelon, *Rois de Syrie, d'Arménie et de Commagène* (Paris, 1890); Bevan,
The House of Seleucus (2 vols., London, 1902); Bouché-Leclercq, *Histoire
des Séleucides* (Paris, 1913).

named Lagus, became satrap of Egypt after Alexander's death. His task in governing this territory
was much less difficult than that of Antigonus or
Seleucus, hence he was able to develop extensively
the commercial possibilities of his dominions. This
condition of affairs continued with his successors,
whose wars were mainly for the purpose of controlling the commerce of the eastern Mediterranean. For
this very reason it was inevitable that the Romans,
who had crushed the Carthaginians in order to control the West, should also covet Egypt. But the
Ptolemies in general were not aggressive rulers, they
became willing allies of Rome, and their power had
been greatly weakened at an early date by domestic
strife. Consequently, Rome removed its more dangerous enemies in Macedonia and Asia before deposing
the Ptolemaic dynasty and converting Egypt into a
province in 30 B.C.[1]

[1] The rulers of the Ptolemaic dynasty are: Ptolemy I Soter I (323–
285), Ptolemy II Philadelphus (285–246), Ptolemy III Euergetes I
(246–221), Ptolemy IV Philopator I (221–204), Ptolemy V Epiphanes
(204–181), Ptolemy VI Philometor (181–145), Ptolemy VII Euergetes
II (145–116), Ptolemy VIII Soter II (116–108 and 88–80), Ptolemy
IX Alexander I (108–88), Berenice (80), Ptolemy X Alexander II
(80), Ptolemy XI Philopater II Philadelphus Auletes (80–58 and 55–51),
Cleopatra (51–30), Ptolemy XII Philopator III (51–47), Ptolemy XIII
Philopator IV (47–44), Ptolemy XIV Caesar (51–30). Of the extensive
literature on the Ptolemies, cf. Champollion-Figeac, *Annales des
Lagides* (Paris, 1819); Letronne, *Recueil des inscriptions grecques et
latines de l'Égypte*, etc. (Paris, 1842, 1848); Mahaffy, *The Empire of
the Ptolemies* (London, 1895), and *A History of Egypt under the
Ptolemaic Dynasty* (New York, 1899); M. L. Strack, *Die Dynastie der
Ptolemäer* (Berlin, 1897); P. M. Meyer, *Das Heerwesen der Ptolemäer
und Römer in Aegypten* (Leipzig, 1900); Bouché-Leclercq, *Histoire des
Lagides* (4 vols., Paris, 1903–7); Steiner, *Der Fiskus der Ptolemäer*
(Leipzig, 1913).

Under the early emperors[1] Roman rule was firmly established in the East as far as the Euphrates and the borders of Arabia. While various native rulers were permitted to exercise a measure of autonomy, as for example the Herods in Palestine, Rome ruled with a strong hand and was much more successful than Alexander's successors had been in preserving peace. Never before in the history of that ancient world had people known for so long a period the same measure of political unity and stable government as that given to them by the Roman emperors in the first century of the Christian era.

This process of unification, which had been going on intermittently since the time of Alexander the Great, resulted in a new and distinct type of world-culture. The dominant item in it was, however, Greek, for Macedonia had become quite thoroughly Hellenized before becoming a world-power. Philip of Macedon had brought the Athenian philosopher Aristotle to Pella to become the tutor of his son Alexander, and when the latter went upon his eastern expedition he took along scholars to gather information of all sorts from the new country. Even before Alexander's day the Macedonians had come to admire Greek literature and art. The Macedonian kings who imported the culture of Greece into their court affirmed that they themselves were Greeks, for their ancestors, so they said, had originally migrated

[1] A list of the early emperors may prove useful for future reference: Augustus (27 B.C.–14 A.D.), Tiberius (14–37), Gaius Caligula (37–41), Claudius (41–54), Nero (54–68), Galba (68–69), Otho and Vitellius (69), Vespasian (69–79), Titus (79–81), Domitian (81–96), Nerva (96–98), Trajan (98–117), Hadrian (117–38), Antonius Pius (138–61), Marcus Aurelius (161–80, with whom Verus was associated from 161–69).

from Argos to Macedonia.[1] Nor is Alexander alone responsible for the dissemination of Greek culture in antiquity. Previous to his time Asia Minor, Italy, Phoenicia, Egypt, and even countries farther inland, such as Persia, had received cultural influences from Greece. But with Alexander the expansion became much more general and assumed many totally new forms.

This new expansion of Hellenism meant a very substantial transformation of Hellenism itself. In the first place the ancient conception of the city-state as the political unit gave place to the notion of world-empire under monarchical rule. The thought of kingship had early become repugnant to both Greeks and Romans. The former had never been able to present for any extended period a united front against Persia, for the very reason that there was no central authority within Greece itself. The Greeks needed a king. The conception of a pan-Hellenic movement began to take shape in the days of Xenophon and Isocrates. The former in his treatise on the education of Cyrus tacitly praises the monarchical ideal, and Isocrates definitely advocates with all his trained eloquence that the Greeks unite under Philip of Macedon for the triumph of Greek power. But no one could have anticipated the success which was to attend Alexander. Although the free Greek city still retained a place within the empire of Alexander and his successors, it never could be restored to its full former glory. With the exception of a few of the stronger and wealthier cities, freedom meant only a measure of autonomy subject to the will of the monarch.

[1] Herodotus, v. 20 and 22; viii. 137; ix. 45.

The Romans were destined to undergo a similar experience. A republican form of government was adequate so long as the city of Rome was practically the nation, and while constant warfare against common foes fostered loyalty to the state. But the conquest of the Roman legions added so many distant provinces to the kingdom that the republic inevitably gave way to the empire with one ruler who was virtually an absolute monarch. Though he bore only the title of emperor, Augustus was as much a king as any of the oriental potentates had been. In the case of both Greeks and Romans the triumph of the monarchical idea was in reality a triumph of orientalism.

The cultural consequences of this new unification are very significant. One of its most important effects is to be seen in the cosmopolitan currents which the new order of things set in motion. Greek exclusiveness and disdain for foreigners were displaced by a degree of toleration and respect. Not only did artisans and merchants from the Orient invade every Greek city of importance, bringing with them their own culture, but Greeks themselves traveled into foreign lands where they learned that the foreigner could not be simply dismissed with the epithet "barbarian," and that the "world" (οἰκουμένη) could no longer be thought to coincide with the boundaries of ancient Hellas. Alexander had founded Greek cities at numerous points in his new empire, and since many of these places were important commercial centers Greek inhabitants became closely associated with peoples of other nationalities. In fact, it was always Alexander's policy to bring about as thorough a fusion as possible between Greeks and natives.

This policy also had its marked effect upon the Orientals. Their culture was not ruthlessly suppressed by the conqueror but, on the contrary, it was given a new and less restricted field of activity. The stability of Greek rule enabled the Asiatics to exhibit and pursue unmolested their industrial and commercial genius, while their adoption of the Greek language made them at home in all parts of the world where they were generally free, however, to maintain as much of their national individuality as they might choose. But this very freedom of intercourse, which resulted in a large infusion of Greek ideas and manners of life, naturally tended to obliterate national distinctions and to issue in a strongly syncretistic form of culture. The Orient became Greek, though not in the classical sense; it was not Hellenic but Hellenistic.

When Roman domination displaced Greek rule the situation did not greatly change. The cultural forces of the period continued to follow the lines laid down in the previous age. Rome did not crush the civilization of its conquered peoples any more than Alexander had done, and the stable government it established only permitted fusing tendencies to work all the more effectively. Hellenistic manners gained so substantial a place among Romans themselves that their culture had become largely Hellenistic in the first century A.D. Even in the time of Horace it could be remarked that captive Greece took her fierce conqueror captive and introduced her arts into rustic Latium.[1]

The component factors in this new Graeco-Roman culture are far too numerous to be listed in detail in this

[1] *Epistles*, ii. 1. 156.

connection.[1] Our primary interest is in the religious status of society, but the latter cannot be correctly understood except in relation to the total cultural situation. At that time society was greatly diversified in character, both because of the mixture of nationalities and on account of wide differences between individuals' stations in life. There was a very distinct court life from the time of Alexander on, which was not always wholly bad in spite of its many reprehensible features. At an early date the Macedonian kings had brought Greek culture to their courts, to which Alexander later added many oriental adornments. His successors were sometimes men of letters, or at least they were interested in the literary and scientific pursuits of the day. In addition to the cities of Greece, where men of culture still

[1] Some useful works, in addition to those of a more general character cited above (p. 53, note 1), dealing with this side of the Graeco-Roman world are Hausrath, *Neutestamentliche Zeitgeschichte* (4 vols., München, 1868 ff.), English tr., *A History of New Testament Times* (4 vols., London, 1895); Hatch, *The Influence of Greek Ideas and Usages upon the Christian Church* (London, 1890); L. Friedländer, *Darstellungen aus der Sittengeschichte Roms in der Zeit von Augustus bis zum Ausgang der Antonine* (3 vols., Leipzig, 1888–96), English tr., *Roman Life and Manners under the Early Empire* (4 vols., New York, 1908–13); Dill, *Roman Society from Nero to Marcus Aurelius* (New York, 1904); Geffcken, *Aus der Werdezeit des Christentums* (Leipzig, 1904, 1909²); Wendland, *Die hellenistisch-römische Kultur in ihren Beziehungen zu Judentum und Christentum* (Tübingen, 1907, 1912²); Staerk, *Neutestamentliche Zeitgeschichte* (Leipzig, 1907, 1912²); Deissmann, *Licht vom Osten* (Tübingen, 1909²), English tr., *Light from the Ancient East* (New York, 1910); Wilamowitz-Moellendorff und Niese, *Staat und Gesellschaft der Griechen und Römer* (Leipzig, 1910); Fowler, *Social Life at Rome in the Age of Cicero* (New York, 1909); Tucker, *Life in the Roman World of Nero and Saint Paul* (New York, 1910); A. Bauer, *Vom Griechentum zum Christentum* (Leipzig, 1910); T. C. Hall, *Historical Setting of the Early Gospel* (New York, 1912); Baumgarten, Poland, und Wagner, *Die hellenistisch-römische Kultur* (Leipzig, 1913).

assembled, Antioch in Syria and Alexandria in Egypt—
particularly the latter—formed seats of learning supported chiefly by royal patronage.

But the work of the court philosopher or *littérateur* was
not the only factor, nor even the chief factor, in stamping
the influence of the ruler upon the life of the people.
The poorest subject in the empire felt directly or indirectly the weight of supporting the monarchical institution, although he may never have witnessed a royal
procession. While the payment of taxes was a burden,
yet not all peoples in the empire resented this imposition
so seriously as did the Jews. In fact, many persons so
appreciated the stability of Roman rule and others
were so hypnotized by its splendor that not a few were
ready to hail the emperor as a savior and god. Even
those who clung to the ancient forms of worship naturally
found themselves phrasing their religious thinking in
terms of imperialism. Thus the court, which embodied
the monarchical principle so overwhelmingly in these
days, exerted a most powerful and permeating influence
in the Graeco-Roman world in New Testament times.

In addition to the court, with its favorites and officials
scattered over the empire, there was a large class of
fairly prosperous citizens who had made their own
way in the world. The Hellenistic age with its enlarged
arena for action gave great opportunity for the development of individualism. In the small city-state the
citizen lived for the state, but a world-empire was too
large and depended too little upon individual support
to call forth the personal loyalty and service which had
been so manifest in former times. The whole world
was now the sphere of action for the individual, his

primary motive for activity being his own personal welfare. Not a few citizens of the empire profited by the opportunity thus opened to them.

While this was distinctly a commercial age, still it was an age of intellectualism. Naturally it was less idealistic than classical Hellenic culture had been, for realism is a normal accompaniment of individualism. Plato philosophized for philosophy's sake, but the Stoics, who were in the ascendency in Hellenistic times, philosophized for man's sake. The various sciences—geography, astronomy, mathematics, mechanics, medicine—were divorced from philosophy where they had originally belonged and were given an emphatically empirical bent. Not even oratory, literature, and religion escaped. Rhetoric was cultivated primarily as a means by which the individual earned a livelihood; the poets wrote not to exalt an abstract ideal but to please the court; historians became realistic also, gathering facts by accurate research instead of recording fanciful legends;[1] and, as for religion, the type most in demand was the one which gave the individual the most positive and realistic assurances of his own personal salvation. This whole tendency toward individualism and realism was part of the spirit of the

[1] For the extensive Greek literature of the period see von Christ, *Geschichte der griechischen Litteratur*, 2. Teil (München, 1911–12[5]); Croiset, *Histoire de la littérature grecque* (Vol. V, Paris, 1899); Susemihl, *Geschichte der griechischen Literatur in der Alexandrinerzeit* (2 vols., Leipzig, 1891–92). For Latin writers see the standard histories of the literature, e.g., von Schanz, *Geschichte der römischen Litteratur* (München, 1907–12[3]), or Teuffel, *Geschichte der römischen Literatur*, particularly Vol. II (Leipzig, 1910[6]), English tr., from the 5th German ed., *Teuffel's History of Roman Literature* (2 vols., London, 1891–92). A good general survey is given by various authors in "Die griechische und lateinische Literatur und Sprache," *Kultur der Gegenwart*, I, 8, 3 (Leipzig, 1912[3]).

age[1] which produced a class of industrious, self-reliant, and often prosperous citizens.

An age of competitive individualism in producing its successful class also begets a class of failures. The "survival of the fittest" in society does not mean elimination, but rather distress, for the unfit. This was eminently true of the Graeco-Roman world, where destitute people were to be found in great numbers, particularly in all the large cities. The ranks of these unfortunates were augmented by vast numbers of slaves, though the latter were often more favored in having a sure support from some good master. Slaves who were sometimes skilled laborers, tradesmen, or educators frequently obtained their freedom and became wealthy citizens,[2] but at other times these freedmen merely swelled the numbers of the needy proletariat who eked out a living with difficulty in the overcrowded centers of population.[3] This proletariat was exceedingly complex. The pressure of

[1] It is quite possible that these tendencies had begun to appear before Alexander's day (cf. Corssen, Über Begriff und Wesen des Hellenismus," *Zeitschrift für die neutestamentliche Wissenschaft*, IX [1908], 81–95), but they certainly received a great stimulus in Hellenistic times.

[2] It is of such that the aristocratic Horace writes (*Epode*, iv):

> Howe'er, proud of your cash, Rome's streets you range,
> Your breed, mere fortune cannot change.

[3] Cf. Beloch, *Die Bevölkerung der griechisch-römischen Welt* (Leipzig, 1886); E. Meyer, "Die Bevölkerung des Altertums," *Handwörterbuch der Staatswissenschaften*, II (Jena, 1909), 898–913. On the subject of slavery see Wallon, *Histoire de l'esclavage dans l'antiquité* (3 vols., Paris, 1879²); Schneider, *Zur Geschichte der Sklaverei im alten Rom* (Zürich, 1892); E. Meyer, *Die Sklaverei im Altertum* (Dresden, 1898); Calderini, *La manomissione e la condizione dei liberti in Grecia* (Milano, 1908); Buckland, *The Roman Law of Slavery* (Cambridge, 1909); Kautsky, *Der Ursprung des Christentums* (Stuttgart, 1908), pp. 26–69; Steinmann, *Die Sklavenfrage in der alten Kirche* (Berlin, 1910).

competition caused artisans, tradesmen, and laborers to change residence frequently, and the freedmen, who as slaves had been imported from some remote part of the empire, added another heterogeneous element to the already complex society. The total result was a fusion of many nationalities within the population, particularly in the large cities. Tacitus says,[1] speaking of Rome, that it was the place into which abominations from all parts of the world flowed together and prospered. A similar complexity in the life of the masses might have been observed, though perhaps in a less degree, at many places in the Mediterranean world.

This chaotic and unfortunate condition of society did not pass entirely unheeded by people of that age. The compulsion of common needs drew various classes of persons together in gilds, social groups, and religious societies.[2] Even the rulers concerned themselves with the situation. In Rome, for example, Augustus had taken measures to restrict the extent of manumissions in order that the helpless element of society might not be increased any more than possible. The political authorities, even if not prompted by humanitarian motives, sought as a police measure to restrain the growth of this element in the population and to provide means, such as the free distribution of corn, for alleviating its distresses. The Cynic-Stoic preachers ministered less materially to contemporary needs, but they aimed to give a more permanent relief by teaching men to endure

[1] *Annals*, xv, 44.

[2] Cf. Poland, *Geschichte des griechischen Vereinswesens* (Leipzig, 1909); von Pöhlmann, *Geschichte der sozialen Frage und des Sozialismus in der antiken Welt* (München, 1912), particularly II, 415 ff.; Troeltsch, *Die Soziallehren der christlichen Kirche* (Tübingen, 1912), pp. 15-178.

hardship unfalteringly. Religion also with a vast number of cults and rites offered its consolations and promises to needy humanity, groping its way through what seemed to be a very dark and hostile world.

What, finally, was the contemporary religious situation? The Hellenistic world produced no single religion distinctive to itself, unless Christianity be called such. This age was content for the most part to inherit and transform religious legacies from the past. These inheritances were drawn from a variety of sources with the result that religious life exhibited great complexities. But the fusion of diverse elements was never so complete and general as to produce any unified result which could be called the one dominant religion of the time. Consequently, the religious life of that day can be best understood by fixing attention upon some of its more prominent constituent factors and characteristics.[1]

This religious syncretism was as complex as society itself. Every nationality which contributed to the making of Hellenistic life had something to do with determining the religious character of the new society. When Asia was conquered by the Macedonians the latter had no fixed national faith to impose upon the foreigner, but already in Asia and Egypt various religions had become firmly established and continued to hold their ground even before the conqueror. Indeed, it was the Orient which supplied the new culture with some of its most important religious features. This was quite as true of conditions under the Romans as under the Macedonians. The former brought with them no one dominant national faith to supply the religious needs of all

[1] For details see below, chaps. vii–ix.

those peoples whose political needs were so often met by Rome. While the Romans were teaching their governmental science to the Orientals the latter were teaching their religions to the Romans.

The religious forces of the Graeco-Roman world of New Testament times are so varied that they almost defy even the most general classification. There were many survivals from ancient seats of culture, such as Egypt, Babylonia, Persia, Palestine, Greece, and Rome, while many local faiths native to different groups of people still persisted. Among these survivals from earlier times we are doubtless most familiar with Judaism, but the disproportionately large place it occupies on our horizon is due to the fact that it has been the object of our continued attention while other religious movements within that world have been generally ignored. There were in reality a great many religions which, in conformity to the cosmopolitan spirit of the age, no longer remained within former national boundaries but became in varying degrees world-movements. When the Egyptian, the Babylonian, the Persian, the Syrian, the Greek, or the Roman carried his religion to a foreign city the deities, as would be expected, often lost many of their local characteristics. Nor was the traveler averse to hearing about other gods if they could offer him new hopes or greater satisfaction for the yearnings of his soul. Indeed, he often encountered ardent missionaries who affirmed that their own peculiar faith was alone worthy of allegiance. These conditions made the period one of great religious unrest.

Although this syncretism is exceedingly complex, exhibiting various blendings of historic elements, still we can distinguish in it certain main tendencies. There is, first, the nationalistic type of religion. Formerly, many of the local historic faiths had also been national, but with the downfall of the local government which the deity was supposed to protect, and with the elimination of national boundaries by the foreign conqueror, the local deities often lost their national character. The relation between the god and the worshiper became more exclusively a personal one, in keeping with the strongly individualistic tendencies of the time. Even though the national ideal was sometimes retained, as was conspicuously the case with the Jews, when the religion was transplanted to foreign soil, the national emphasis was subordinated to the personal. In general we may say that the people of the Graeco-Roman world had given up the search for a god that could save a nation and were looking for a deity who could save an individual, or a group of individuals set apart as the nucleus of a new society which was conceived to be other-worldly in its essential character. Yet the notion of humanity's solidarity produced a new national ideal stimulated by the unity of empire. Thus emperor worship became a substitute for the national religions of former times. This is a distinct phase of Graeco-Roman religions, which, though embodying earlier elements, was largely a product of this age and had great significance for the life of the time.

A second item in these complex religious developments may be termed the religion of philosophy. This was the faith of the educated and thoughtful, but it showed many variations corresponding to different types of philosophy then current. Platonism had some vogue, though it was less popular in the first century A.D. than in later times when revived in the form of neo-Platonism. The influential philosophies in the first century were more truly Hellenistic products. The two most important schools, each of which had its own distinctive religious significance, were the Epicureans and the Stoics. The former were significant religiously chiefly for the criticisms they leveled against traditional notions, while the latter, with their Cynic kinsmen, stood out uniquely as the exponents of a monotheistic faith infused with a vigorous ethical idealism.

A third type may be termed the mystery-religions. These were cults of particular deities worshiped by certain groups of people, who had been formally initiated into the society of devotees. After observing prescribed religious rites and witnessing at initiation certain symbolic performances termed "mysteries,"[1] they became members of the society and believed that their hope of a blessed immortality was secure. This type of religion was widely current in the Graeco-Roman world in pre-Christian times. Some of the best known of these cults were those of Demeter and Dionysus in Greece and Thrace; Cybele and Attis in Phrygia; Atargatis in Cilicia; Aphrodite and Adonis in Syria; Ashtart and Eshmun (Adon) in Phoenicia; Ishtar and Tammuz in Babylonia; Isis, Osiris, and Serapis in Egypt; and Mithra in Persia. Apart from the Demeter cult, which had become especially localized at Eleusis, these religions often traveled far from their native land, following the current of syncretistic life in Graeco-Roman times. With the exception of Mithraism, they were located in

[1] Herodotus, ii. 171.

various places about the Mediterranean world a century or more before the opening of our era.

Numerous popular superstitions were also rife in this age and so must be noted among its religious characteristics. Many persons consulted oracles and practiced divination. They believed in demon possession, cultivated the art of exorcism, and were in fact the victims of vast numbers of superstitious fears and practices. This was true not only of the lower classes, but of many others beside, not even exempting the Roman emperors. Suetonius' *Lives of the Caesars* gives many illustrations of this fact. Perhaps it was fear of physical harm only which made Augustus flee to the cellar and caused Caligula to hide under his bed whenever a severe thunderstorm arose, but it was certainly crass superstition that led Augustus, on account of a dream he once had, to attire himself as a beggar on a certain day of the year and solicit alms in the street.

The Graeco-Roman world was not without theological reflection also. There were certain persons who emphasized metaphysical speculation as the *summum bonum* of religion. This interest was not necessarily embodied in one special movement, but showed itself in various quarters and within different religious circles. It dealt with such problems as the nature of the soul, the character of its relationship to the body on the one hand and to the deity on the other, the process by which the relationship might be readjusted for the soul's welfare, and the ultimate disposition of both body and soul. The relation between the deity and the individual was often defined in terms of mystical union, more or less realistically conceived according to the cultural status or personal bias of the interpreter. Such theological speculations seem to have thriven best in the Orient, but they became widely diffused in the Graeco-Roman world. In Pythagoreanism and Orphism, in many of the mystery-cults, in early Gnosticism, and even in Stoicism they had made their influence felt in one form or another already in pre-Christian times.

Such was the world in which the early Christians lived. Their association with the ancient faiths which had survived to that day, and their contact with those religious tendencies which were more especially distinctive of Hellenistic times furnished the setting for their lives and defined many of the great religious problems which they sought to solve.[1] The lines along which these

---

[1] The foregoing survey of religious conditions is so brief that it may well be supplemented by further references to literature. On the various national religions which formed the background of the Hellenistic age one may consult *Lehrbuch der Religionsgeschichte* (edited by Chantepie de la Saussaye, 2 vols., Tübingen, 1905³); G. F. Moore, *History of Religions* (New York, 1914), or Toy, *Introduction to the History of Religions* (New York, 1913), where representative works are listed. For ancient Egypt see Steindorff, *Religion of Ancient Egypt* (New York, 1905); Wiedemann, *Die ägyptische Religion* (Berlin, 1909²), also article "Religion of Egypt" in Hastings' *Dictionary of the Bible* (extra vol., New York, 1904); Erman, *Die ägyptische Religion* (Berlin, 1905, 1909²), English tr., *A Handbook of Egyptian Religion* (London, 1907); Breasted, *Development of Religion and Thought in Ancient Egypt* (New York, 1912).

Of the many workers in the field of Babylonian and Assyrian religion see especially Jastrow, *Religion of Babylonia and Assyria* (Boston, 1898), a long article on the same subject in Hastings' *Dictionary of the Bible* (extra vol.); also *Aspects of Religious Belief and Practice in Babylonia and Assyria* (New York, 1911), *Die Religion Babyloniens und Assyriens* (Giessen, 1905–12) and *Hebrew and Babylonian Traditions* (New York, 1914). Cf. also King, *Babylonian Religion and Mythology* (London, 1899); Dhorme, *La religion assyro-babylonienne* (Paris, 1910).

Persian religion is treated by Jackson, "Die iranische Religion," in Gieger und Kuhn, *Grundriss der iranischen Philologie*, II (Stuttgart,

surroundings influenced the evolution of early Christianity must now be given more detailed consideration.

1904), 612–708; J. H. Moulton, *Early Zoroastrianism* (London, 1913) and *Early Religious Poetry of Persia* (Cambridge, 1911); Tiele, *The Religion of the Iranian Peoples* (London, 1912) and *Geschiedenis van den Godsdienst in de oudheid tot op Alexander den Groote*, II (Amsterdam, 1902).

In addition to such reference works as Farnell, *Cults of the Greek States* (5 vols., Oxford, 1896–1909) and Gruppe, *Griechische Mythologie und Religionsgeschichte* (München, 1906), the more recent studies on Greek religion are Jane Harrison, *Prolegomena to the Study of Greek Religion* (Cambridge, 1903, 1908²) and *Themis* (Cambridge, 1912); Farnell, *The Higher Aspects of Greek Religion* (New York, 1912); and Murray, *Four Stages of Greek Religion* (New York, 1912).

Roman religion has been treated in several standard works. Among the latest are Carter, *The Religious Life of Ancient Rome* (Boston, 1911); Fowler, *The Religious Experience of the Roman People* (New York, 1911); Wissowa, *Religion und Kultus der Römer* (München, 1902, 1912²). The last-named work is rich in reference to the literature.

The religion of other parts of the Mediterranean world and the syncretistic developments of Graeco-Roman times have not been studied so generally and comprehensively. In addition to the works to be cited below in connection with special topics, see Cumont, *Les religions orientales dans le paganisme romain* (Paris, 1906, 1909²), English tr., *Oriental Religions in Roman Paganism* (Chicago, 1911), and *Astrology and Religion among Greeks and Romans* (New York, 1912); Reitzenstein, *Poimandres* (Leipzig, 1904) and *Die hellenistischen Mysterienreligionen* (Leipzig, 1910); Otto, *Priester und Tempel im hellenistischen Aegypten* (2 vols., Leipzig, 1905–8); Glover, *The Conflict of Religions in the Early Roman Empire* (London, 1909); Schmidt, *Kultübertragungen* (Giessen, 1910); Toutain, *Les cultes païens dans l'empire romain*, I, ii (Paris, 1911).

For literature on Judaism see below, chap. iv, *passim;* and on Buddhism in its relation to Christianity, p. 194, n. 2.

CHAPTER IV

THE EARLY CHRISTIANS' JEWISH CONNECTIONS

Among the ethnic faiths which had survived in the Mediterranean world of the first century A.D., Judaism was the one with which Christians at the outset were most intimately associated. The relationship was closest in Palestine, but it was not confined exclusively to this territory. Christian preachers even in gentile lands must have been in almost constant contact with Jews, who were scattered widely over the Roman empire.

In Palestine, however, the association was particularly close. The antecedents of the Christian movement in the first period of its career were all Jewish, and in the main also Palestinian. While we must not assume that life within Palestine in pre-Christian times might not already have received important contributions from without, we may affirm that the earliest Christians derived their chief religious heritage directly from their Palestinian environment. This supplied to them the initial religious forces later fused into that new movement which in time came to be differentiated from Judaism, and to be distinguished by the name "Christianity." It was the life of Palestine that furnished the chief problems with which the first Christians were concerned; it was this background which gave them John the Baptist and Jesus, from whom they derived so much; and it was Judaism which had provided them with religious training from earliest childhood. The general persistence of Jewish features within primitive

Christianity was a perfectly natural consequence of existing conditions.

It is not necessary at this point to give a detailed account of first-century Judaism. While there are still many unsolved problems in this field, in general it is familiar ground today, or may easily be made such by consulting some of the many valuable treatises upon the subject. For our present purposes a brief survey of the more prominent features in the Jewish religion of the first century A.D. will suffice.[1]

The political history of the Hebrew people had much to do with shaping the development of their religion. At one time or another they had been subject to every important political power that had arisen in that ancient world. The Egyptians, the Babylonians, the Assyrians,

[1] Some of the more important works on the subject are: Grätz, *Geschichte der Juden*, III (Leipzig, 1905–6⁵); Keim, *Geschichte Jesu von Nazara*, I (Zürich, 1867), English tr., *History of Jesus of Nazara* (London, 1876); Toy, *Judaism and Christianity, A Sketch of the Progress of Thought from the Old Testament to the New Testament* (Boston, 1890); Schürer, *Geschichte des jüdischen Volkes im Zeitalter Jesu Christi* (3 vols., Leipzig, 1901–9⁴; see especially I, 4 ff., for literature), English tr., *History of the Jewish People in the Time of Jesus Christ* (New York, 1891); O. Holtzmann, *Neutestamentliche Zeitgeschichte* (Tübingen, 1895, 1906²); Mathews, *History of New Testament Times in Palestine* (New York, 1899, 1910²); Thackeray, *The Relation of St. Paul to Contemporary Jewish Thought* (New York, 1900); Bousset, *Die Religion des Judentums im neutestamentlichen Zeitalter* (Berlin, 1903, 1906²); Oesterley and Box, *Religion and Worship of the Synagogue* (New York, 1907); Fairweather, *The Background of the Gospels, or Judaism in the Period between the Old and the New Testaments* (New York, 1908); Felten, *Neutestamentliche Zeitgeschichte, oder Judentum und Heidentum zur Zeit Christi und der Apostel* (Mainz, 1910); H. J. Holtzmann, *Lehrbuch der neutestamentlichen Theologie* (Tübingen, 1911²), I, 27–159; Bertholet, *Die jüdische Religion von der Zeit Esras bis zum Zeitalter Christi* (Tübingen, 1911); Juster, *Les Juifs dans l'empire romaine, leur condition juridique, économique et sociale* (2 vols., Paris, 1914).

the Persians, the Macedonians, and the Romans all exercised, at different times, dominion over Palestine. In addition to this pressure of foreign influence from without the Jews themselves pressed out into the life of the surrounding peoples. They had established important colonies in Egypt and Babylonia at an early date, and in Graeco-Roman times they were so numerous in every land that Strabo remarks, if Josephus reports him correctly, "It is difficult to find a place in the habitable earth that has not admitted this tribe of men and is not possessed by them."[1]

In spite of both foreign oppression and residence in foreign lands, the Jews in a remarkable degree preserved intact their national individuality. This was due primarily to the strong nationalistic character of their religion. They believed that in days of old Yahweh had chosen them to be a peculiar people whom he would one day exalt to a position of primacy among the nations. Political reverses had not shattered their hopes, for their prophets had declared that these misfortunes were a consequence of the people's sin and not a denial of the Deity's power. He was still the God of Israel and would ultimately fulfil his promises when his people had shown themselves worthy of his favor, consequently the ruling motive in life was to learn and to do his will. Loyalty to this ideal and the consequent isolation it involved set

[1] Josephus, *Ant.*, XIV, vii, 2. See further on the dispersion of the Jewish people, Harnack, *The Mission and Expansion of Christianity*, I, 1–18; T. Reinach, article "Diaspora" in the *Jewish Encyclopedia* (New York, 1903), IV, 559 ff.; Schürer, *Geschichte*, usw., III⁴, 1–188, English tr., *History of the Jewish People*, II, ii, 220 ff., and article "Diaspora" in Hastings' *Dictionary of the Bible*, extra vol., pp. 91–109; Juster, *op. cit.*, pp. 179–209.

the Jews apart as a distinct people, whether in Palestine or among the Gentiles.

The three chief institutions used for realizing their ideal were the temple, the synagogue, and the Scriptures. The temple, while it stood, was the central sanctuary, serving as a focal point for the maintenance of the national faith. This was the visible dwelling of Yahweh, and all loyal Jews contributed regularly toward its support. The synagogue was in many ways a much more important institution, for it furnished a local rallying-point for the life of particular communities. Every Jew, no matter how far removed from the Holy City, longed to visit the Jerusalem temple at least once in his lifetime, but this hope, often long deferred and sometimes never realized, would alone hardly have been vital enough to preserve the unity of the scattered nation. The synagogue was really the institution which kept alive the national faith. Hence the destruction of the temple did not materially affect the religion of the Jewish people as a whole.

Their sacred writings were the chief means by which the Jews believed they could learn to do God's will. This was the one source of authority from which rules were derived for the direction of every phase of conduct. From the day of birth until the day of death the life of the true Jew was ordered according to the divine instruction, expressed or implied in the Torah, the "Teaching" in which God had revealed his will to his chosen people. But already in the first century A.D. these books were ancient documents and so had to be expounded in order to be understood and made available for guidance in daily living. This necessity

produced the scribe, who played a very important part
in the making of later Judaism. The exposition of the
Scriptures involved the task of finding therein rules
for conduct in every sphere of activity, incentives for
the cultivation of moral character, materials for the
construction of religious doctrine, and stimuli for the
enrichment of religious experience. These three great
institutions—the temple, the synagogue, and the Torah
—made the Jews a unique people, distinguishing them,
whether in Palestine or in the Diaspora, from all their
contemporaries.

Though the Jews were thus distinct from other
peoples, their own life had many complexities. The
popular notion, that Judaism in the first century was a
uniform system of barren legal observances, is not true
to facts. Like all real life it was subject to specific
environmental forces, which produced a variety of tendencies even in the realm of religion. In the first place,
politics had exerted a strongly determining influence
upon the Jews from times of old, but in the Graeco-
Roman period new problems arose producing distinct
parties such as Sadducees, Pharisees, and Zealots.
Strife between these rival parties had a marked effect
upon religion as well as upon the destiny of the Jewish
state. Society also was complex and diversified. Some
persons were hospitable to foreign manners, while others
were bitterly hostile. The population included prosperous citizens as well as those who lived in great poverty.
Even in matters of religion there were many variations.
The Torah was expounded differently by different rabbis,
who had their respective followers; the national hope
was variously interpreted in different circles; and even

ritual observances were made the subject of divergent opinions, as the Essene movement alone shows.

The conditions under which the Jewish people lived, particularly from the Exile on, had tended to diversify their interests. Upon many of their numbers influences from Babylonia and Persia had been acting vigorously for a long time. Greek influences also became very powerful among certain circles a century or more before the Christian era, and under the Romans the pressure of these and other foreign forces continued to be felt. These influences were not simply political; they were also religious, and stimulated a religious reaction on the part of the Jewish people. As the circumstances varied so the reaction varied, resulting in the formation of different sects within Judaism and the advocacy of various opinions on matters of religion. It is not at all improbable that the reference of II Esdras 14:46 to the seventy esoteric books, in addition to the twenty-four in common use, correctly represents different lines of religious interest, such as we see, for example, in the Essenes and in the Zadokite sectaries. One who supposes that Judaism in New Testament times was a thoroughly unified system of doctrine, ritual, or conduct must have observed but very superficially the actual conditions of life in that age.

Yet this diversity was mainly a matter of emphasis. Members of different parties were none the less Jews because they found their special interests leading in different directions. A Philo or a Josephus may have lived in a very different world of reality from that of a Judaean rabbi, but they all admired alike their ancient religious heritage and were equally ready to undertake, each in his own way, the task of its defense. Each used data from the past and under the stimulus of his own peculiar environment worked out an interpretation answering to his own needs. Some persons dwelt upon the legalistic features of the ancient faith, others found their inspirations in the older prophets, others meditated on the teachings of the sages, others elaborated the apocalyptic imagery suggested in Daniel, and others exalted the national ideal of an earthly prince. The environment also varied. In some circles the horizon was narrow, extending only to the limits of a local Jewish community, in others a new impetus to religious thinking had been supplied by contact with Babylonia or Persia, while in still others the new stimulus had come in from the Graeco-Roman world. Yet with all this variety in point of view and environment there was no thought of disloyalty to Jewish tradition. Since all these variations arose in response to vital conditions, they did not tend to disintegrate but really served to strengthen the life of Judaism.

The early Christians were in close touch with Judaism in many of its varied phases. While a very close connection between the two religions is generally admitted, the nature of the relationship is not always clearly defined. The fact of extensive common possessions on the part of Jews and early Christians no longer calls for demonstration, nor are the main lines of agreement in serious need of restatement; but the genetic character of the relationship is a question of primary importance, particularly for our present study. Was Christianity connected with Judaism in a vital way, or did the connection consist merely in the common possession of a quantity of static items of theological speculation or traditional customs which were ultimately to be discarded in order that the new religion might be free to express itself according to its own original constitution?

The abundant use of the Old Testament in the New seems to prove that the old and the new religions were intimately related at the outset, yet there is also ample evidence that the breach between the two was both wide and deep even before the close of the first century A.D. According to the New Testament representation, Jesus was in almost constant conflict with the scribes and Pharisees who finally brought about his death, Stephen was stoned by the Jewish mob at the instigation of religious leaders who were zealous for the traditions of the fathers, Paul after his conversion was persistently persecuted by his own countrymen, and the antagonism between Jews and Christians grew more and more bitter as time advanced.

In view of this early and continued hostility, how is it possible to think of a close genetic kinship between the two religions? Among Christians the prevailing method of maintaining this connection has been to pass over later Judaism as a perversion of ancient faith and to connect the religion of Jesus and the apostles most closely with that of the old Hebrew worthies. The fulfilment of messianic prophecy in the person of Jesus is the main link connecting the old and the new orders. He was the redeemer whom God, from the day Adam and Eve were driven out of Eden, had appointed to deliver mankind and had foreshadowed in all the prophets. In addition to the fulfilment of messianic predictions, the more truly spiritual and ethical elements of Old Testament religion are also said to be genuinely perpetuated within Christian circles only, and the Mosaic legislation is believed to have reached its only correct interpretation and application among members of the new community. So the argument runs, in the traditional Christian apologetic.

Furthermore, Christians early discovered, by means of the exegetical methods then in vogue, many Old Testament passages to indicate that God had intended Christianity to supplant Judaism. On this hypothesis, Jews, in the interim between the Old and New Testaments, had become blind to the intent of prophecy, had lost the spiritual vision of the ancients, and had converted the teaching of Moses and his successors into a deadening casuistic legalism. Therefore God rescued the treasures of revelation from degradation at the hands of the Pharisees and committed them to the care and keeping of Christians. The fall of Jerusalem and the dispersion of the homeless people were cited as further proof that God had withdrawn his favor from the descendants of his chosen people and had transferred his affections to Christians alone.[1]

The correctness of this deprecatory estimate of Judaism in relation to the origin of Christianity has often been called in question. Naturally the Jews have always

[1] To cite a typical statement of this opinion, Origen (*Cels.*, II, 8) says: "For it is indeed manifest that when they beheld Jesus they did not see who he was, and when they heard him they did not understand from his words the divinity that was in him and which transferred God's providential care, hitherto exercised over the Jews, to his converts from the heathen. Therefore we may see that after the advent of Jesus the Jews were altogether abandoned and possess now none of what were

protested against this interpretation of their history. They will not concede that they have perverted the faith of their fathers, nor do they believe that they have been abandoned by God. On the contrary, they still claim to be his chosen people and the custodians of the divine oracles. A recent defender of their position says: "The Jew still believes that the mission of Israel is a real living power in the world of today. To live the true Jewish life is the highest ideal he knows. He has learnt from the prophets and from history that Israel has been chosen to be a 'light to the Gentiles,' but he has also been taught that the light of Israel is God."[1]

Likewise from the standpoint of history the traditional view of Christianity's relation to contemporary Jewish religion has been subjected to several criticisms. Among other things, we are told that the character of Judaism in Jesus' day has usually been misrepresented. Many of the Gospels' unfavorable statements regarding the Pharisees are said not only to be untrue but to have been prompted by Christian hatred of Jewish opponents. Just as Christians think the Talmud gives a grossly distorted picture of Jesus and his followers—when it does not utterly ignore them—in order to serve the interests of Jewish antagonists, so many Jews see

considered their ancient glories, so that there is no indication of any divinity abiding amongst them. . . . . For what nation is an exile from their own metropolis, and from the place sacred to the worship of their fathers, save the Jews only? And these calamities they have suffered because they were a most wicked nation which, although guilty of many other sins, yet had been punished so severely for none as for those that were committed against our Jesus."

[1] G. Friedlander, *Hellenism and Christianity* (London, 1912), p. x.

in the Gospels a similar bias against the Pharisees.[1]
Not only are the sweeping charges made against them
in the New Testament said to be false, but as a class the
Pharisees are declared to have been exponents of a
genuinely spiritual religion, while Judaism as a whole
in Jesus' time was not so utterly devoid of vital spirituality as its critics have frequently affirmed.   This opinion,
so stoutly defended by Jews,[2] has of late found sup-
porters even within Christian circles.[3]

[1] Among recent expressions on this point, Montefiore's is one of the
more moderate.   Commenting on Mark 7:9–13, he says that the usual
interpretation, which makes the Pharisees and scribes set duty to the
temple above obligation to parents, is "in flat contradiction to the law
as laid down by the Mishnah, as commented on by the Talmud, and
as universally accepted and interpreted by all the Jewish codifiers."
Furthermore, "the truth is that the rabbis taught a tremendous respect
and reverence for parents.   In this matter they are perfectly sound;
indeed on family relations they are keener than Jesus" (*Synoptic Gospels* [New York, 1909], I, 164 ff.).

[2] We should expect "orthodox" Jewish apologists to insist on the
ideal character of Judaism in every stage of its history.   But even
"liberal" Jews, who give more attention to historical considerations,
find themselves compelled to disagree at various points with such
Christian expositions of Judaism as Weber's *System der altsynagogalen
palästinishen Theologie* (Leipzig, 1880;   2. Aufl., *Die Lehren des Talmud*,
1886;   3. Aufl., *Jüdische Theologie auf Grund des Talmud und verwandter
Schriften*, 1897); Schürer's *Geschichte des jüdischen Volkes*, usw., particularly the chapter on "Das Leben unter dem Gesetz," II, 545–79,
English tr., *History of the Jewish People*, etc., II, ii, 90–125; or Bousset's
Religion des Judentums.   For recent "liberal" Jewish defense of the
"spiritual" character of Pharisaism, see Montefiore, *op. cit.*, also
Origin and Growth of Religions (London, 1892, pp. 465–552), *The Relig-
ious Teaching of Jesus* (New York, 1910); Schechter, *Some Aspects of
Rabbinic Theology* (New York, 1909); Horodezky, "Zwei Richtungen
im Judentum," *Archiv für Religionswissenschaft*, XV (1912), 99–136;
Abelson, *The Immanence of God in Rabbinical Literature* (New York,
1912) and *Jewish Mysticism* (London, 1913).

[3] E.g., Hart, *Hope of Catholick Judaism* (Oxford, 1910), thinks the
idea of hope with the Jews has always been fundamentally and consciously a personal trust in God; and Herford, *Pharisaism: Its Aim and
Method* (New York, 1912), defends most vigorously the spirituality

In the second place, the Christian claim for unique originality in the teaching of Jesus and the apostles has often been denied by Jewish critics. The main content of personal religion as depicted, for example, in the Sermon on the Mount, is said to offer no features of importance not already current in the teaching of the rabbis. On its ethical and spiritual side the New Testament as a whole is found to be mainly a fruit of Pharisaic Judaism. That which differentiates it from Judaism, making it inferior and false from the Jewish point of view, is its doctrine of Jesus' messiahship with its accompanying belief in his supernatural personality. When these items have been set aside the spiritual and ethical residuum of New Testament religion is declared to be only an appropriation from contemporary Judaism.[1]

A disposition on the part of certain modern scholars to find Christianity's "essence" in Jesus' teaching

of the Pharisees: "Why should not the Christian be glad to own that the Jew, even the Pharisee, knew more of the deep things of God than he had supposed, and after a way which was not the Christian way, yet loved the Lord his God with heart and soul and strength and mind— yes, and his neighbor as himself?" (p. 333).

[1] Among older works the following are representative: Nork, *Rabbinische Quellen und Parallelen zu neutestamentlichen Schriftstellen* (Leipzig, 1839); Grätz, *Geschichte der Juden;* Grünbaum, *Die Sittenlehre des Judenthums* (Mannheim, 1867; 2. Aufl., Strassburg, 1878); Rodrigues, *Les origines du Sermon du Montagne* (Paris, 1868); Duschak, *Die Moral der Evangelien und des Talmud* (Brünn, 1877); Schreiber, *Die Principien des Judenthums verglichen mit denen des Christentums* (Leipzig, 1877). Cf. more recently G. Friedlander, *The Jewish Sources of the Sermon on the Mount* (London, 1911). Christian interpreters have often sought illustrative materials in later Jewish writings but have not thought the New Testament to be secondary, e.g., J. Lightfoot, *Horae hebraicae et talmudicae in quatuor Evangelistas* (Leipzig, 1684); Schöttgen, *Horae hebraicae et talmudicae in universum Novum Testamentum* (Dresden and Leipzig, 1733); Meuschen, *Novum Testamentum ex Talmude et antiquitatibus Hebraeorum illustratum* (Leipzig, 1736);

regarding spiritual sonship to God and love to one's neighbor raises more sharply than ever the problem of originality in this phase of New Testament religion. When the uniqueness of the new movement is not found in its christological and soteriological doctrines, but in the superiority of its ethical-religious ideals, an inferior estimate is readily implied for this side of Jewish religion in Jesus' day. But Jewish scholars strenuously object to this implication. Even when they admit that Jesus was a remarkable teacher possessed of keen spiritual insight, they still claim him as a true son of Israel. His greatness is but additional evidence for the greatness of their ancestral faith, so that Judaism and "essential" Christianity are at the outset practically identical. The acceptance of this conclusion leads Montefiore to remark that "in future Christianity and Judaism will be able to shake hands over the Sermon on the Mount and the fundamental elements in the moral and religious doctrine of Jesus." Adopting Wernle's view[1] that what is crucial in Jesus is "trust in God, purity of heart, compassion, humility, forgiveness, aspiration—this and nothing else," and that he who does the will of God as thus expressed in the Sermon on the Mount is "Jesus'

Wettstein [Wetstenius], *Novum Testamentum Graecum* (Amsterdam, 1751–52); T. Robinson, *The Evangelists and the Mishna* (London, 1859); Siegfried, *Analecta rabbinica* (Jena, 1875); A. Wünsche, *Neue Beiträge zur Erläuterung der Evangelien aus Talmud und Midrasch* (Göttingen, 1878); Bennett, *The Mishnah as Illustrating the Gospels* (Cambridge, 1884); Herford, *Christianity in Talmud and Midrash* (London, 1903). E. Bischoff, *Jesus und die Rabbinen* (Leipzig, 1905), contends for Jesus' absolute originality.

[1] *Sources of Our Knowledge of the Life of Jesus* (London, 1907), pp. 162 f. (translated from the German, *Die Quellen des Lebens Jesu* [Tübingen, 1905, 1913²]).

mother and sister and brother." Montefiore believes that "there have been very many Jewish mothers and sisters and brothers of Jesus all these long years from Jesus until now."[1] Christianity, then, began as a new awakening within Judaism, a revival and elaboration of the more distinctly ethical and spiritual aspects of prophetic religion. Thus Christianity is connected with Jewish religion through the medium of the ancient prophets, as Christians have so generally maintained, but this bond of union is ethics and not christological dogma.

The Judaism with which Montefiore thus identifies "essential" Christianity is itself an "essence" of prophetism, which he thinks had fallen into decay until revived by Jesus. But Jewish writers of a more "orthodox" type reject this supposition and affirm that contemporary rabbinism itself preserved the very elements which Christian authors like Harnack and Wernle find to have constituted the "essence" of Christianity.[2] Even though nothing of a notable character is discerned in the religion of Jesus, the breach between him and the Pharisees, who are taken to represent the best in contemporary Judaism, is found to have been far less serious

[1] *Synoptic Gospels*, I, cvii f.

[2] For Jewish reaction upon Harnack's *Das Wesen des Christentums* see "L'Esprit du Christianisme et du Judaisme," by "M. L.," *Revue des études juives*, LI (1905–6), 191–216, and LII (1906–7), 1–23, where the principal literature on the subject is noted. For monographs see Bäck, *Das Wesen des Judentums* (Lamm, 1905); Eschelbacher, *Das Judentum und das Wesen des Christentums* (Berlin, 1905); Güdemann, *Jüdische Apologetik* (Glogau, 1906); Bergmann, *Jüdische Apologetik im neutestamentlichen Zeitalter* (Berlin, 1908). Brief excerpts from many writers are given in de le Roi's *Neujüdische Stimmen über Jesum Christum* (Leipzig, 1910).

than the Gospel writers assume. In fact, his death, for which the New Testament makes the Pharisees chiefly responsible, is said to have been brought about by the political rather than the religious authorities. The blame should be placed upon the Sadducean high priest and the Romans, and not upon the Pharisees with whom Jesus was in essential harmony.[1] According to this interpretation the Christian movement did not become noticeably differentiated from Judaism until after Jesus' death when certain of his followers began to preach his messiahship, to reverence him as God, and to proclaim his speedy coming in judgment. These features are conceded to have been new—in so far as they were not borrowed from heathen sources—but the ideals and content of personal religious living within

[1] This opinion has been held by Jews of various schools since the publication of L. Philippson's *Haben wirklich die Juden Jesum gekreuzigt?* (Berlin, 1866). For its more recent advocacy see Hirsch, *The Crucifixion from a Jewish Standpoint* (New York, 1892, 1908[2]); Drucker, *The Trial of Jesus from Jewish Sources* (New York, 1907); Montefiore, *Synoptic Gospels*, I, 345 ff.; Klein, *Är Jesus en historisk personlighet?* (Stockholm, 1910); Chwolson, *Über die Frage, ob Jesus gelebt hat* (Leipzig, 1910). Büchler, *Das Synedrion in Jerusalem*, usw. (Wien, 1902), posits two sanhedrins in Jerusalem, one a body of priestly authorities connected with the temple and the other the Sanhedrin proper, composed of scribes and rabbis. It was the former assembly which condemned Jesus. The French Protestant scholar, Goguel, finds two trials narrated in the Gospels, one conducted by the Jews and the other by the Romans. The latter alone is historical. Pilate had consulted the Sanhedrin merely to make sure that his extreme action against Jesus would not be resented by that body. The Sanhedrin had taken no initiative in the matter, nor had it any real part in carrying out Pilate's program. Later he threw the responsibility upon the Jews, and this idea was elaborated in Christian polemic against them (*Juifs et Romains dans l'histoire de la passion* [Paris, 1911]). For further literature see Juster, *Les Juifs dans l'empire romain*, II, 137 f.

the new community are thought to have been supplied
by contemporary Judaism. Hence bitter antagonism
toward the Jews, although prominent in the New Testament account of Jesus' life, must belong historically
to a subsequent period. It cannot have been the attitude of Jesus, or of the earliest Christians, who are
assumed to have had no thought of a break with Jewish
religion.

Moriz Friedländer, a Jewish writer of the "liberal"
school, offers a still different interpretation of the genetic
relationship between the two religions. Although he
does not trace the line of succession through orthodox
legalism, he still gives the new movement excellent
Jewish connections. At the beginning of the Christian
era the Jews of Palestine, he believes, comprised several
distinct and rather sharply differentiated classes such
as Pharisees, Apocalyptists, Essenes, 'Am-ha'arets,
and Minim. Heterogeneous elements, represented for
instance by the Wisdom writers and the Therapeutae,
were likewise discernible in Hellenistic Judaism. Since
the Pharisees are assumed to be a distinctly separate
class of bigoted nationalists and rigid formalists, genuine
Hebrew faith can have been truly perpetuated only
outside these official circles, and it is from these extra-
official sources that the true Jewish heritage of Christianity is derived. Genetically it was most closely akin
to the 'Am-ha'arets,[1] who were the pious people of the
land and who were, therefore, opposed to the Pharisees.

[1] The rôle of the 'Am-ha'arets in the first century A.D. is very
uncertain. Cf. Schürer, *Geschichte*, usw., II, 468 f.; Büchler, *Der
galiläische 'Am ha-Aretz des zweiten Jahrhunderts* (Wien, 1906); Montefiore, *Synoptic Gospels*, I, lxxvi.

The connection with Essenism was also close. These tendencies were represented in the movement of John the Baptist, they were perpetuated by Jesus, and so formed the basis of the Christian movement. Formerly Friedländer located the transition from Judaism to Christianity in Hellenistic lands, but in his *Synagoge und Kirche* he definitely fixes upon Perea as the place of Christianity's birth.[1]

The idea of connecting primitive Christianity with certain Jewish sects instead of with the main line of Palestinian Judaism had already been advocated before Friedländer wrote. In the early eighteenth century the English Deist Toland wrote a treatise entitled *Nazarenus, or Jewish, Gentile and Mahometan Christianity*, in which he made primitive Christianity an Ebionite movement beside which the Pauline movement later arose.[2] The name Ebionite was suggested by the mention of a Jewish-Christian heresy bearing that title in certain of the Church Fathers.[3] A century after Toland another English writer, Thomas DeQuincey, suggested that

[1] Note particularly his *Zur Entstehungsgeschichte des Christentums* (Wien, 1894), *Das Judentum in der vorchristlichen griechischen Welt: Ein Beitrag zur Entstehungsgeschichte des Christentums* (Wien, 1897), *Geschichte der jüdischen Apologetik als Vorgeschichte des Christentums* (Zürich, 1903), *Die religiösen Bewegungen innerhalb des Judentums im Zeitalter Jesu* (Berlin, 1905), and *Synagoge und Kirche in ihren Anfängen* (Berlin, 1908).

[2] This division of early Christianity into an Ebionite and a Pauline school resembles the antithesis "Petrine" and "Pauline" made by Baur. On Toland as a forerunner of the Tübingen school see Patrick, "Two English Forerunners of the Tübingen School: Thomas Morgan and John Toland," *Theological Review*, No. LIX (1877), pp. 562–603.

[3] E.g., Irenaeus, *Haer.*, I, xxvi, 2; Hippolytus, *Haer.*, VII, 35; Origen, *Cels.*, V, 61. The word "Ebionites" (אֶבְיוֹנִים) signifies poor people.

Christianity was a perpetuation of Essenism. This notion had begun to be used in the first half of the nineteenth century as material forming the basis for fanciful lives of Jesus, his skill at miracles being ascribed to wisdom derived from early association with the Essenes, under whose direction he was assumed to have conducted his public activity.[1] This type of interpretation is now confined almost exclusively to writers who deny outright the historicity of Jesus. These Jewish sects, which are sometimes said to be largely influenced by non-Jewish ideas, are thought to furnish sufficient vitality to account for the origin of the new religion.

What is to be said of the view, so generally held by Christians and so commonly denied by Jews, that Christianity at the start had essentially no relation to contemporary Judaism? While Jewish opinion is often discounted—for Judaism as well as Christianity may have its zealous apologists—it is an undeniable fact that the early Christians were closely associated with Jews, were indeed Jews themselves, and so are likely to have been as truly obligated to their immediate environment as they were to ancient prophetism. While members of the primitive community may have been distinctly original in many respects, and may have drawn freely upon the Old Testament, it does not follow that they were not intimately related to the religious situation which produced them, and upon which they in turn reacted most immediately in their efforts to measure up to contemporary religious demands. Their problems were not merely their own personal concern, but were

[1] See Case, *Historicity of Jesus* (Chicago, 1912), pp. 32–34, for literature on this subject.

framed if not indeed answered with reference to the
pressing demands of the day. Under these circumstances early Christianity in Palestine must be set into
much closer relation with contemporary Judaism than
some interpreters of Christian origins have been accustomed to allow. The supposition of Christianity's
unique independence is tenable only on the hypothesis
that Judaism at this time was, in the estimation of early
Christians, utterly devoid of all religious values. But
this conclusion is far from self-evident, and a closer study
of primitive Christianity raises grave doubts regarding
its validity.

On the other hand, the historical conditions are not
satisfied by the disposition, manifest among some Jewish writers, to deny all distinctiveness to the new
religion. Had nascent Christianity been only a composite of excerpts from Judaism there would have been
no room for that display of creative personal leadership
so characteristic of the new movement, nor would the
conditions have been such as to bring about sharp
antagonism between the two religions. The latter
phenomenon is particularly striking. Though the
evangelists may have overstressed its prominence in
the time of Jesus, it cannot be doubted, quite apart from
any dispute as to who was immediately responsible for
Jesus' death, that he was unacceptable to many Jews.
It would have been absurd for the Gospel writers in
their anti-Jewish polemic to make Jesus so eminently
persona non grata to the Jews of his day if exactly the
contrary relationship had been the historical fact.
Granting that the notion of hostility may be overemphasized by the evangelists, we are still forced to

believe that it had some basis in fact.[1] And the same
situation is seen in the experience of the primitive community. While the early believers did not immediately
break with their ancestral faith there was something
about them which aroused the hostility of their Jewish
brethren. Even if the description in Acts is held to be
historically uncertain at many points, there can be no
reasonable doubt about the bitter hostility of the Jewish
leaders both before and after Paul's conversion.[2] When
the Gospels were written it is perfectly evident that the
cleft had become so wide between the Christians and
their Jewish kinsmen that hope of ever bridging the
chasm was beginning to be abandoned. Little as the
early Christians may have desired to break with the
faith of their fathers, there was something sufficiently
distinctive about them to invoke Jewish hostility and
to force separation.

Yet this enmity does not imply the complete lack of all
connection between the two religions, nor must we conclude that this relationship can have been maintained
only through the medium of Jewish sects. It would
not be inherently impossible to suppose that Christianity grew out of a Jewish sectarian movement with which
John the Baptist and Jesus were allied. The difficulty
with this hypothesis is the impossibility of finding
substantial historical evidence for the existence of any
sect which has sufficient likeness to Christianity to be
reasonably called its source. Essenes, Zealots, Therapeutae, and the like, all fail to meet the requirements.

---

[1] Cf. I Thess. 2:15. Paul is likely to have been accurately informed
on this point, however much one may suspect the statements of later
writers.

[2] Gal. 1:13; I Cor. 15:9; Phil. 3:6.

If one could assume the existence of a well-defined sect of Messianists in pre-Christian times it might be made the special source of the new movement, but apart from Zealot enthusiasts—with whom the early Christians are certainly not to be reckoned in spite of the fact that Jesus apparently was condemned on the charge of being a messianic pretender—there is no intimation that such a sect existed *as a sect*. The early Christians' connections are with contemporary Judaism as a whole, and not with some incidental phase of that religion.

Among Christian scholars, F. C. Baur was one of the first to recognize a real point of attachment between primitive Christianity and contemporary Judaism, yet he accepted as historical the New Testament representation of a sharp antagonism between the two religions. How was it possible for Christianity to have real Jewish connections and at the same time to be strongly anti-Jewish? Baur solved this problem by positing two conflicting divisions within Christianity itself. One was a Jewish party led by Peter and his associates in Jerusalem where legalism was emphasized in agreement with strictly Jewish principles, and the other was a Hellenistic party established by Paul in his fight for freedom from the law.[1] This did not mean that Jerusalem Christianity was not fundamentally different from Judaism, or that Paul, on the other hand, was entirely free from Jewish influences. Since Baur was

[1] Of Baur's many works see especially "Die Christuspartei in der corinthischen Gemeinde," *Tübinger Zeitschrift für Theologie*, Heft. 4 (1831), 61–206; *Paulus, der Apostel Jesu Christi* (Stuttgart, 1845, 1866–67²), English tr., *Paul the Apostle* (Edinburgh, 1873–75); and *Vorlesungen über neutestamentliche Theologie* (herausgegeben von F. F. Baur, Leipzig, 1864). Cf. above, p. 13.

not so much interested in explaining how Christianity arose out of Judaism as in accounting for the early transition of the new religion from the Jewish to the gentile thought-world, he concerned himself for the most part with but one item in Christianity's Jewish connections. That was the position of the ceremonial law as related to the doctrine of redemption. In contrast with Paul's gospel of freedom, the Petrine community still adhered to the Mosaic ordinance of circumcision as a necessary accompaniment of faith. Apart from this main difference the two parties had much in common, and even the conservatives seem, in Baur's thought, to represent a religion which is quite distinct from Judaism. When compared with the Pharisees, Jesus is found to have been unique in his emphasis upon ethical inwardness and personal piety. To some extent the early community did, indeed, obscure his teaching by dragging it down to their lower spiritual level, yet their new religion was primarily a heritage from Jesus and so transcended all immediate Jewish connections. Although Paul was the first to make a formal break with Judaism he was but carrying to a logical issue what was already implicit in Jesus' own teaching and what was fundamental to the Jerusalem community's faith in Christ.[1]

[1] Since Baur is often thought to have divided primitive Christianity into two sharply differentiated parties, one being emphatically Jewish and the other distinctly Greek, it may be well to note how closely he follows the traditional view of Christianity's essential independence of contemporary Judaism, and how truly a unit both the Petrine and the Pauline parties are in this respect. He says: "In dem Apostel Paulus war zuerst der wesentliche Unterschied des Christentums vom Judentum, die Unmöglichkeit, auf der Grundlage des Judentums das von Christus

Baur's recognition of a cleft within early Christianity has given direction to the main lines of much subsequent discussion. Taking their cue from him, some interpreters divide Jewish Christianity itself into two sections, the former representing the chief apostles who stood quite aloof from Judaism except for the matter of circumcision, and the latter being a body of Judaizers who adhered tenaciously to hereditary customs and beliefs.[1] While the primitive apostles kept the "pure" gospel in the foreground, to that extent being in harmony with Paul, the Judaizers remained so seriously entangled with Jewish religion that they were scarcely worthy of the name Christian, and so ere long fell back into the Jewish fold. By this method the Christianity of the first believers as a whole is made to transcend Judaism, it derives its main content directly from Jesus, distinctly contemporary Judaism exerts no essential influence upon the new faith, and its Jewish heritage is really only the Old Testament religion.

Another line of development from Baur makes Paul its point of departure. His breach with the Palestinian

erworbene Heil sich zuzueignen, zum bestimmten Bewusstsein gekommen." Yet Paul did not create this distinction, "nur hat er bloss für das Bewusstsein ausgesprochen, was an sich, principiell und tatsächlich, oder *implicite* schon in der Lehre Jesu enthalten war." The same thing was true of the "Petrine" Christians, although they "überhaupt noch keine Ahnung davon hatten, welcher Keim eines tiefgehenden Zwiespaltes mit dem Judentum in ihrem Glauben an Christus verborgen lag" (*Vorlesungen*, usw., pp. 128 f.).

[1] A characteristic defense of this position may be seen in Sorley, *Jewish Christians and Judaism* (Cambridge, 1881), or Hort, *Judaistic Christianity* (London, 1894). Hoennicke, *Das Judenchristentum im ersten und zweiten Jahrhundert* (Berlin, 1908), takes essentially the same position, though believing the breach between Paul and the primitive apostles to have been more serious.

church is thought to be much more fundamental than Baur supposed, for the principle of universalism, which Baur allowed to be *implicit* with the first apostles, is now conceded to Paul only. The gulf separating him from the Jerusalem community is made so wide that he virtually becomes the founder of the new religion on gentile soil. It still has Jewish connections, but these are most immediately with the Judaism of the Diaspora in which Paul had been reared, rather than with the Palestinian *milieu* in which Jesus and the first disciples lived. The central item of Paul's gospel is found to be his conception of universal redemption made possible through the death of Christ. This notion is an expansion of universalistic tendencies already begun by Hellenistic Jews, but in its Christian form it is a distinctly Pauline creation. In comparison with the legalistic and nationalistic ideal of the Jerusalem community, the preaching of the new doctrine is to all intents and purposes the beginning of a new religion.[1] While it has specific Hellenistic Jewish connections at the outset, they are only peripheral and are easily dismissed by later generations who wish to restate Paul's religion in terms of Greek thinking.

Several objections may be urged against this mode of interpretation. To make Paul and his immediate associates the sole founders of gentile Christianity is a doubtful historical procedure. The New Testament is so

[1] This view has been most recently advocated by Wrede, *Paulus* (Tübingen, 1904), English tr., *Paul* (Boston, 1908). But the main lines of the representation were already present in the works of Tübingen scholars such as Holsten, *Zum Evangelium des Paulus und Petrus* (Rostock, 1868) and *Das Evangelium des Paulus* (Berlin, 1880, 1898²); Pfleiderer, *Der Paulinismus* (Leipzig, 1890²), English tr., *Paulinism* (London, 1891²). This is also one of the crucial points at issue in the much-debated Paul-and-Jesus controversy.

deficient in its description of gentile missionary work,
except as carried on by Paul and his colaborers, that one
all too easily forgets to take account of similar work on
the part of those who did not come within the range of
Paul's immediate influence, or who did not work under
his supervision. While he and his companions were
vigorously pushing forward the evangelization of one
section of the Graeco-Roman world other laborers were
cultivating other fields, and contributing effectively
toward the world-expansion of the new religion. We
learn from one of Paul's letters that an important church
had been established at Rome, and the fame of its faith
had become world-wide, without any assistance from
Paul.[1] When Paul was working the territory to the
northeast of the Mediterranean the others were carrying
the propaganda to the West and probably to the South.
Sometimes even in the East Paul was anticipated and
helped by laborers from other fields.[2] History has not
fully recorded the activities of persons who are mentioned in the early part of the Book of Acts, but who
drop out of sight as soon as Paul takes the center of the
stage. Did their missionary labors cease as suddenly as
the story of their career breaks off in Acts? That is
hardly probable. In fact, various hints to the contrary
may still be gleaned from the New Testament. Paul
speaks of the missionary methods of Barnabas, Peter,
and the Lord's brethren as well known to the Christian
community in Corinth.[3] The variety of our New Testament literature all of which is written in Greek and so
is more or less directly a product of gentile Christianity,

[1] Rom. 1:8-15.

[2] Acts 18:24 ff.; 19:1; cf. 18:2.   [3] I Cor. 9:4-6.

the widely scattered places in which we find the new religion at the end of the New Testament period, and the slight extent to which so-called Pauline views manifest themselves in the Christian literature of the second century, all go to show that gentile Christianity was not a peculiarly "Pauline" creation.

Furthermore, Paul never conceives his work to be the establishment of a new religion as compared with that which he had previously persecuted, and to which he had been converted on the road to Damascus. He may show independence when defending his apostleship, or when advocating the liberties of the gentile converts, but he derives his apostolic credentials from the same source as do his predecessors,[1] and he does not even claim to have been original in creating the notion of justification by faith.[2] When he preaches the coming of an apocalyptic Messiah in the person of the crucified Jesus, who had been raised from the dead and elevated to a position of dignity in heaven—an item which he unquestionably makes fundamental in his gospel—is he not distinctly "Christian" rather than Pauline, and Christian too in the "Jewish" sense? Since Paul emphatically affirms that there is only one gospel which he and all others share alike, that is, the gospel of faith in this heavenly Messiah, perhaps the legalistic controversy did not in the long run cut so deep as the later Tübingen scholars have been wont to assume.

This brings us to a consideration of eschatology, as demonstrating the close and vital relationship between the early Christians and their Jewish contemporaries. The Jewish expectation of the heavenly Messiah whose

[1] I Cor. 15:8 f.; Gal. 2:8.   [2] Gal. 2:14 ff.

coming will bring the present evil age to a close and
result in the establishment of a new order of existence,
though only vaguely suggested in the Old Testament, is
held to have been a prominent item in the Judaism of
Jesus' day.   Until within the last half-century very little
notice has been taken of this side of Judaism, but of
late it has been much emphasized.[1]   When the early
Christians preached the coming of the heavenly Messiah
who was to bring all evil to an end and set up a new
kingdom in righteousness, they were, it is said, not

[1] A beginning in this direction was made by Dillmann, *Das Buch
Henoch* (Leipzig, 1851), and Hilgenfeld, *Die jüdische Apokalyptik* (Jena,
1857).   The study was furthered by Colani, *Jésus-Christ et les croyances
messianiques de son temps* (Strassburg, 1864); Vernes, *Histoire des idées
messianiques depuis Alexandre jusqu'à l'empereur Hadrian* (Paris, 1874).
At present this subject has an extensive literature dealing with both
Judaism and Christianity.   Jewish views are expounded in various
treatises on Judaism (see above, p. 79), e.g., Schürer, *Geschichte*, usw.,
II, 609–51, English tr., *History of the Jewish People*, II, ii, 126–87; Volz,
Jüdische Eschatologie von Daniel bis Akiba (Tübingen, 1903); Bousset,
Die Religion des Judentums, pp. 233 f.; Gressmann, *Der Ursprung der
israelitisch-jüdischen Eschatologie* (Göttingen, 1906); Lagrange, *Le messia-
nisme chez les Juifs* (Paris, 1908); Bertholet, *Die jüdische Religion*,
pp. 133 ff., 435 ff.   A comparative study of Jewish and Christian views
is made by Charles, *Eschatology, Hebrew, Jewish and Christian* (New
York, 1899), and Mathews, *The Messianic Hope in the New Testament*
(Chicago, 1905).   Recent studies on Jesus and on Paul devote considerable attention to this element in early Christianity, e.g., J. Weiss, *Die
Predigt Jesu vom Reiche Gottes* (Göttingen, 1892, 1900[2]); Baldensperger,
*Das Selbstbewusstsein Jesu im Lichte der messianischen Hoffnungen seiner
Zeit* (Strassburg, 1888, 1892[2], 3d ed., of first part, *Die messianisch-
apokalyptischen Hoffnungen des Judentums*, 1903); Brückner, *Die
Entstehung der paulinischen Christologie* (Strassburg, 1903); H. J. Holtz-
mann, *Das messianische Bewusstsein Jesu* (Tübingen, 1907); E. F. Scott,
The Kingdom and the Messiah (New York, 1911); Schweitzer, *Geschichte
der paulinischen Forschung* (Tübingen, 1911) and *Geschichte der Leben-
Jesu-Forschung* (Tübingen, 1906, 1913[2]), English tr., *The Quest of the
Historical Jesus* (New York, 1910).

deriving their message simply from Jesus, but were phrasing their estimate of him in the familiar terminology of contemporary Jewish apocalyptic. So far as this phase of doctrine is thought to be central in early Christianity —and it is now so regarded by many interpreters—the new religion proves to have had substantial and immediate connections with later Judaism.

Much can be said in favor of this opinion. The presence of this type of messianic hope in late Judaism is attested both in the first century before and in the first century after the opening of the Christian era.[1] The extant literary evidence is, to be sure, not so extensive as one could wish, yet the existence of this type of hope is well attested. Nor is there any uncertainty regarding the strong resemblance between these Jewish expectations and the early Christians' picture of their coming Messiah. Readjustments are made to suit the Christian situation, but still the gospel portrait of the heavenly Son of Man to come on the clouds in glory,[2] the description in Acts of the appointed Messiah whose coming awaits the restoration of all things,[3] the Pauline Messiah to be revealed in judgment,[4] and the reigning Messiah of the Apocalypse, all hark back most distinctly to the apocalyptic conceptions of later Judaism. Quite apart from the much-debated question of Jesus' own idea of his messianic program, it is perfectly clear that his disciples after his death evaluated his personality by means of this current Jewish coinage.

[1] E.g., Enoch, IV Ezra, Baruch, etc.; cf. Schürer, *Geschichte*, usw., III, 263 ff. For texts see Charles, *Apocrypha and Pseudepigrapha* (Oxford, 1913).

[2] Mark 8:37; 13:24 ff.

[3] Acts 3:20 f.   [4] I Cor. 1:8 f.; 4:5, etc.

If Paul and his predecessors reared the superstructure of their faith upon a Jewish type of messianic hope re-worded in terms of belief in Jesus' resurrection, exaltation to lordship, and imminent Parousia, and if other Christians besides Paul and his companions were also propagating the same faith in gentile lands, no reasons remain for following the later Tübingen scholars in finding Christianity's Jewish connections chiefly in the Diaspora. It may be quite true that the new religion was freshly influenced by Judaism in gentile territory, where the gospel was, in the first instance, often proclaimed in connection with the synagogue assemblies, and from which it doubtless drew converts. These persons who had been reared in a Hellenistic atmosphere, retained after their conversion, as would be expected, many religious values which their past experience had supplied. But a similar situation existed earlier in Palestine. Certainly Christianity had distinctly Jewish features before it became an extra-Palestinian propaganda, and, since many of the earlier missionaries had themselves been Palestinians, Christianity even on gentile soil cannot have been very different from that of the primitive community. Changes, of course, took place with the passage of time and the rise of new situations. But so far as Jewish influence is concerned, conditions in the Diaspora were not so very different from those of Palestine as to call for extensive readjustment in Christianity's Jewish relationships in gentile lands.

Much less are we able to believe that gentile Christianity was a new creation by Paul. To what extent he was original, or how far he adopted Greek or Graeco-

Jewish ideas in working out the logic of the redemptive scheme, is another question. Whatever answer one may give to this, the fact remains that Paul and his predecessors shared alike in this fundamental item of common Christian belief. He and they had identically the same recipe for obtaining salvation: a confession of Jesus' messianic lordship on the basis of a belief that God had raised him from the dead.[1] Also the consummation of salvation was, both for him and for them, to be accomplished by Jesus' return in judgment. Differences in details ought not to be allowed to obscure these central elements in their common faith.

Another school of interpreters finds Christianity's Jewish connections to have been relatively insignificant for the genesis of the new religion, particularly when it became a gentile movement. This independence is not ascribed to the Christians' possession of new christological doctrine, or to their unique religious experience, as some earlier interpreters have often insisted. Nor is this credited to Paul's doctrine of universalism, as the later Tübingen scholars affirmed. The new movement is thought to have been independent of Judaism because it had so generally taken up from its gentile environment Hellenistic features of a non-Jewish character. Even the messianism of the primitive community is thought to have had a comparatively insignificant place under the new conditions. Since the success of Christianity outside of Palestine is credited largely to the appropriation of items from the contemporary gentile world, this view implies, even if it does not explicitly

[1] Rom. 10:9.

affirm, that Christianity on gentile soil was only remotely connected with Judaism.

Not all representatives of this so-called *religionsgeschichtliche* school hold identically the same opinions on the question of Christianity's genetic relation to Judaism. Non-Jewish elements are sometimes said to have come in directly through Palestinian connections where syncretistic influences are thought to have been at work even before Christianity arose.[1] Under these conditions the genetic relation between the two religions is really close and vital in so far as Judaism at that time was actually syncretistic. But other adherents of the *religionsgeschichtliche* school attach much less importance to contemporary Jewish faith, and derive the foreign elements of Christianity from the believers' first-hand contact with the Hellenistic world. This procedure results in a separation of gentile Christianity from Palestinian Christianity similar to that made by Tübingen scholars, although a very different explanation is given for the necessity of the separation.

The view in question appears most fully worked out in Bousset's recent volume, *Kyrios Christos.*[2]   Accord-

[1] E.g., Gunkel, *Zum religionsgeschichtlichen Verständnis des Neuen Testaments* (Göttingen, 1903, 1910²).

[2] Bousset, *Kyrios Christos: Geschichte des Christusglaubens von den Anfängen des Christentums bis Irenaeus* (Göttingen, 1913); cf. also Heitmüller, "Zum Problem Paulus und Jesus," *Zeitschrift für die neutestamentliche Wissenschaft*, XIII (1912), 320–37; Böhlig, "Zum Begriff Kyrios bei Paulus," *ibid.*, XIV (1913), 23–37. Reitzenstein, *Poimandres* and *Die hellenistischen Mysterienreligionen;* Böhlig, *Die Geisteskultur von Tarsos* (Göttingen, 1913), and similar studies in contemporary Hellenistic religions furnish a basis for this type of interpretation. J. Weiss, *Das Urchristentum* (Göttingen, 1914), though freely employing data supplied by the *religionsgeschichtliche* school, is more reserved in breaking Christianity's Jewish connections.

ing to this interpretation the primitive Christians shared the current eschatological form of the Jewish messianic hope, the distinctive Christian feature being the identification of Jesus with the apocalyptic Son of Man. The next stage of development is seen in the early Hellenistic community with its center probably at Antioch in Syria. While it was not without Jewish connections, its most distinctive characteristic was neither Jewish nor primitive Christian in origin, but purely Hellenistic. This distinctive item was reverence for Jesus as Lord (Κύριος, *Kyrios*). From being a religion of faith in a coming Messiah, Christianity has now become the cult of the present Lord. Thus the *Kyrios* cult becomes a powerful rival of primitive Christian eschatology, and is destined to push it quite completely into the background.[1] Paul represents a further stage in this course of development, he being entirely

[1] "Der Menschensohn wird so ziemlich vergessen werden und als eine unverstandene Hieroglyphe in den Evangelien stehen bleiben, dem im Kulte gegenwärtigen Kyrios gehört die Zukunft" (Bousset, *op. cit.*, p. 125). J. Weiss states the matter more cautiously and probably more accurately: "In dem starken Hervortreten dieses Namens (*Kyrios*) vor dem Messiastitel kündigt sich nun auch eine sehr bemerkenswerte sachliche Verschiebung gegenüber der Urgemeinde an. Mit dem Zurücktreten des nationalen Moments trat auch das eschatologische wenn auch nicht in die zweite Linie, so doch ein wenig aus der vordersten Stellung zurück. Das Verhältnis zu dem erhöhten Kyrios behielt natürlich seine eschatologische Perspektive; die Parusie Christi blieb ein äusserst wichtiges Moment, namentlich für die aus dem Judentum gekommenen Gemeindeglieder. Aber für die Mehrzahl der Heidenchristen war doch hiermit eine neue *Gegenwarts-Religion* gegeben; damit war ein Gegengewicht gegen die vorwiegend eschatologische Religion der Urgemeinde vorhanden; . . . . der himmlische Herr war immer da und bot alles, was man brauchte, schon jetzt in reichster Fülle. So kommt es, dass an Stelle des grossen Weltendramas immer mehr der individuelle Vorgang der Erlösung des Einzelnen in den Vordergrund trat" (*Das Urchristentum*, I, 128 f.).

removed from contact with the Palestinian Christians. It was the Hellenistic community only that he had persecuted, and it was this circle alone which later furnished him all his historical data about Christianity. Thus the new religion for Paul was, from the first, the worship of a present Lord—a *Kyrios* cult—rather than a Judaeo-Christian belief in an eschatological Messiah. In post-Pauline times Christianity's Jewish connections grew still more remote and of less vital significance for the existence of the new religion.

In how far is this type of interpretation valid? While it may have been a perfectly normal thing for Christians in a gentile atmosphere to phrase their religion in the language and spirit of the gentile world, it is still a question whether advocates of the new faith, like Paul and his Hellenistic Jewish predecessors, did so soon break with their past religious heritage. That Paul was a product of gentile Christianity is perhaps nearer to the truth than was the Tübingen view that he was its creator. At least he and his immediate associates were neither the first nor the only missionaries in gentile lands, but that gentile Christianity before Paul and Paul himself were so remotely related to the Christianity of Palestine as Bousset affirms, and hence so far removed from Judaism, is more doubtful.

This opinion is open to one of the chief objections urged against the Tübingen view, namely, it passes too lightly over the eschatological features in Paul's letters. It was perhaps only natural, in view of Schweitzer's recent one-sided use of eschatology to explain everything in Paul,[1]

[1] Cf. his *Geschichte der paulinischen Forschung* (Tübingen, 1911), English tr., *Paul and His Interpreters* (London, 1912).

that the pendulum should swing to the opposite extreme, but in avoiding the Scylla of Schweitzer has not Bousset become involved in the perils of Charybdis? Whatever else Paul may have included within the horizon of his religious world, he certainly did retain and make prominent a Christianized form of the Jewish apocalyptic hope. He admonished the Thessalonians to prepare for the end of the world, which was coming suddenly as a thief in the night.[1] The Corinthians are exhorted to suspend judgment upon their fellows since they are all alike waiting for the revelation of Jesus when every man's work will be tested by the fire of the final judgment day. The interim is so short that marriage is discouraged, and those who are questioning regarding the resurrection of the dead are told of the Parousia of Christ when he is to conquer death and complete the work of restoration by giving over the newly established kingdom to the Father.[2] The Romans are warned that the night is far spent and the day at hand when all shall stand before God's judgment seat, and the Philippians are encouraged to go on to perfection until the day of Jesus Christ, confident that the Lord is at hand.[3] Paul endures his present afflictions as a missionary the more cheerfully because of the prospect of reward in this coming day of judgment. The Thessalonians are to be his joy and crown of glorying "before our Lord Jesus at his coming"; and his sufferings on behalf of the Gentiles, being "a sweet savor unto God," he gladly bears as "light afflictions" in comparison with the "eternal

[1] I Thess. 1:10; 3:13; 4:15–18; 5:2, 23.

[2] I Cor. 1:7 f.; 3:13; 4:5; 15:23 ff.; 16:22; II Cor. 5:10.

[3] Rom. 13:12; 14:10; Phil. 1:6, 10; 4:5.

weight of glory" which is to be his when he stands in
the judgment and there presents the fruit of his missionary labors.[1]

On the whole would it not be more truly descriptive
of Paul's attitude to call his religion a "Christ" (Messiah) cult rather than a "Lord" (*Kyrios*) cult? It is
very true that Paul makes much of Jesus' lordship over
the community. Christians are those who "call upon
the name of the Lord"; to be saved one must "confess
with the mouth that Jesus is Lord," and "the Lord is
the Spirit," whose presence in the believer is the very
cornerstone of the Christian life. Yet in all this there
is no disposition on Paul's part to minimize Jesus'
function as Messiah, or to discount the supreme significance of that moment in history when Jesus will
appear in messianic splendor bringing the present evil
age to an end, establishing an eternal kingdom in righteousness, and at last handing over to God the perfected
product of his messianic work. At best the present
lordship of Jesus over the community is only a make-
shift, a temporary expedient to bridge over the time
until the day of judgment breaks, manifesting the ultimate triumph of Jesus as Messiah and establishing the
dominion of God forevermore.

Furthermore, for Paul "Lord" is only a title for
Jesus, while "Christ," though originally a title, has come
to be practically a proper name co-ordinate with the
name Jesus, consequently "Christ" identifies the individual himself and does not merely describe one of his
attributes. Therefore it is not surprising that Paul

[1] I Thess. 2:19 f.; I Cor. 9:23–27; 15:31; II Cor. 2:14 ff.; 4:14–17;
Rom. 8:17; Phil. 2:16.

uses this term more frequently than "Lord."[1] Also in the rites of the cult, "Lord" does not predominate over the term "Christ," although Bousset seems to assume that it does. In speaking of baptism, for instance, he says that in the Pauline age this rite was performed in the name of "the Lord Jesus," the name and the Spirit being the effective factors in the sacrament.[2] But if we state the matter in Paul's language it is Christ rather than Lord which is most frequently associated with the baptismal rite. When writing to the Galatians he insists upon the adequacy of the religion of faith in "Christ Jesus," reminding his readers that all who have been "baptized into Christ have put on Christ" and so are all one "in Christ Jesus."[3] They now have membership in the "Christ Jesus" religion, which is superior to all rivals. Speaking of the labels by which the different parties in Corinth have designated themselves, Paul asks the schismatics, "Is the Christ divided?"[4] Has

---

[1] Including Colossians and Ephesians, but not the Pastorals, the figures for Pauline usage are approximately as follows: Χριστός alone, 206 times (77 times with the article); Χριστὸς Ἰησοῦς, 56 times; Ἰησοῦς Χριστός, 20 times; Κύριος alone, referring to Jesus (though whether used of Jesus or of God cannot always be positively decided), 139 times; Κύριος Ἰησοῦς, 16 times; Κύριος Ἰησοῦς Χριστός, variously combined, 61 times; Ἰησοῦς alone, 15 times but 143 times combined with other terms. Thus for individual words, Χριστός occurs 343 times; Κύριος, 216 times; Ἰησοῦς, 168 times.

[2] *Kyrios Christos*, p. 101; cf. Wernle, *Die Anfänge unserer Religion* (Tübingen, 1904², p. 176; *The Beginnings of Christianity*, I [New York, 1903], 247 f.), who says that the word Christ had a strange sound for Greek ears and on that account Paul used Κύριος instead, introducing it "als Aequivalent für Messias in die offiziellen Bekenntnisformeln."

[3] Gal. 3:26–28.

[4] I Cor. 1:11–13. Although Paul writes ὁ Χριστός, the article is probably simply anaphoric, so that Paul is not using Christ as a title, but in the dynamic personal sense to emphasize the fact that the Corinthians individually and collectively belong to Christ (cf. I Cor. 3:23).

Paul been crucified for you, or have you been baptized into the name of Paul?" Since this question must be answered negatively there is no logical place for schism. All are members of the "Christ" into whom they have been baptized. Similarly, jealousies which are prone to arise through the exercise of different spiritual gifts are to be avoided by exalting the notion of the community's unity, all having been baptized in one Spirit, into one body, and having drunk the same spiritual drink, that is, "the Christ."[1] Again, the Israelites in the wilderness were "baptized into Moses," but their real spiritual drink was "the Christ."[2] Over against the "Moses" religion, bringing it to completion, stands the "Christ" religion with its seal of baptism "into Christ." In arguing for the distinctiveness and adequacy of the new religion, Paul reminds the Romans of the supreme significance of their having been baptized "into Christ." For as Christ was raised from the dead by the glory of the Father so they live a new life unto God "in Christ Jesus."[3] Even if the statement that the Corinthians had been washed, sanctified, and justified "in the name of the Lord Jesus Christ" is a reference to baptism, as seems probable, still the term "Christ" is not displaced but is merely supplemented by the title "Lord," and the immediate context goes on to emphasize that the Christian life should be one of purity because Christians now are members of "Christ."[4]

Paul does speak of the Lord's table and the Lord's (κυριακόν) Supper, but the religious significance of the

[1] I Cor. 12:12 f.   [2] I Cor. 10:1-4.

[3] Rom. 6:1-11; also Col. 2:11 f. speaks of being buried with "Christ" in baptism.

[4] I Cor. 6:11-15.

rite consists in bringing the communicant into fellowship with the blood and the body of "the Christ,"[1] and the dynamic significance of "the name" which Phil. 2:9 ff. is taken to illustrate[2] does not inhere in the name Lord, but rather in the name Jesus, the dynamic quality of which—the name being equivalent to the person—produces confession of "Jesus Christ's" lordship.[3] There is really quite as much reason to believe that the religion of Paul, and of the Hellenistic community he represents, was a "Christ" cult as that it was a "Lord" cult. We do not mean to deny the importance attached to confession of Jesus' lordship. We would only affirm that Jesus and Christ were the terms used to identify specifically that powerful personage who had primary significance for the community's life, while the thought of Jesus' lordship was a secondary, though indeed an important, notion. Christians spoke of the Lord "Jesus Christ," while other religionists spoke of the Lord "Serapis," and others of the Lord "Caesar." In this general sense each was a *Kyrios* cult—a fact which Bousset seems to be entirely correct in emphasizing—but a more truly descriptive definition must set in the foreground the specific, divine potency about which the faith of the community centers and from which the rites derived their significance. This is, respectively, Caesar, Serapis, or Jesus Christ. On this point Paul expresses himself explicitly: "there are many gods and

[1] τοῦ Χριστοῦ (I Cor. 10:16).

[2] Bousset, *Kyrios Christos*, pp. 106 f.

[3] We ought to remember that what Paul really said was, "God hath exalted him and given him the name that is above every name in order that in the name of Jesus every knee should bow . . . . and every tongue confess that Jesus Christ is Lord." See below, p. 158, n. 3.

many lords, but for us there is one God, the FATHER
. . . . and one Lord, JESUS CHRIST."[1] This centrality
of the Christ name, though adjusted to a new setting,
shows a close genetic kinship between the new propaganda on gentile soil and its earlier exponents in Palestine. Both Paul and the Hellenistic Christians who
preceded him were not only advocates of a Jewish-
Christian apocalyptic hope, but they alike employed
the Jewish term "Christ" (Messiah) to designate the
object of their faith.[2]

Even the notion of Jesus' lordship is likely to have
been already an item in the faith of the Palestinian
community.[3] When Paul teaches gentile converts the
prayer "maranatha,"[4] he would seem to be perpetuating

[1] I Cor. 8:5 f.

[2] The persistence of this name in gentile territory is further attested
by the name "Christianity." The founder of this religion is also known
to outsiders, e.g., Tacitus, Suetonius, Pliny, Josephus, as "Christ,"
and the world at large seems for some time to have thought Christianity
a Jewish sect.

[3] The evidence for this conclusion is given in detail in the article
"Κύριος as a Title for Christ," *Journal of Biblical Literature*, XXVI
(1907), 151–61; see also Bacon, *Jesus the Son of God* (New Haven, 1911),
pp. 53–77; and J. Weiss, *Christus: Die Anfänge des Dogmas* (Tübingen,
1909), English tr., *Christ, the Beginnings of Dogma* (London, 1911),
pp. 45–55, and *Das Urchristentum*, I, 25 ff. (but also 127 ff. and 351 ff.).

[4] μαραναθα (I Cor. 16:22; *Did.* 10:6; cf. Rev. 22:20) is a trans-
literation of מָרַנָא תָא, meaning "Our Lord, come!" This is the more
probable reading, though מָרַן אֲתָא, "Our Lord has come," or "is
coming" (*perfectum propheticum*), is possible. It is conceivable that
the full form אתא may have been an imperative (cf. ܐܬܐ in Syr. Sin.
Mark 10:21; Luke 16:2, etc.), but Paul would probably have transliter-
ated this εθα or ιθα. For אירתא as an imperative, sometimes vocalized
with ṣere and sometimes with ḥireq, see Dalman, *Grammatik des jüdisch-
palästinischen Aramäisch* (Leipzig, 1905²), pp. 356 f. It seems preferable, therefore, to read מָרַנָא תָא. Its meaning is more natural to

terminology which had already become stereotyped in the Aramaic-speaking community at Jerusalem. But this Bousset will not concede. He will allow that the Palestinians did pray *maranatha*, but he says they only meant "Our Teacher, come!" The word *mar* may have been used of a professional teacher in Jesus' day, but it certainly was used in a great many other connections, some of which seem much more appropriate to the primitive Christians' enthusiastic hope and prayer for the coming of their heaven-exalted Messiah than would be indicated by the sober ejaculation, "Our Teacher, come!" They were calling for the coming of one whose authority had been demonstrated by a resurrection from the dead, one who had been appointed to conduct the great assize at the end of the present age, one whose triumph over death gave him primacy among angelic spirits and established him as the champion of the forces of good over against Satan and his hosts. When they called him *Marana* they surely would have used the word to connote those higher phases of authority with which it was so commonly associated in their day and their environment.[1] They were really praying

Paul's situation. The older form of the suffix **נ**א is attested in Paul's day and vicinity by the **מראנא**, used of King Aretas in the Nabatean inscriptions (*CIS*, II, 199 and 206). **תא** is also a regular form of the imperative (cf. Dalman, *op. cit.*, pp. 152, n. 3, and 357, n. 1; also the familiar **ׯ** of Syr. Sin., e.g., Matt. 5:24; Luke 18:22; John 1:46; 4:16; 11:43; see also Nöldeke, *Göttingische gelehrte Anzeigen* [1884], p. 1023; and Zahn, *Einleitung in das Neue Testament*, I [Leipzig, 1908³], 216 ff.).

[1] The term was one of wide application among Semitic-speaking peoples to denote different degrees of authority from that of the owner of property to that of God in his capacity as ruler of the universe. It was also very commonly used to designate the authority of the king in

for the coming of the Lord of the new kingdom; otherwise it is altogether improbable that they would have
prayed at all for his advent.[1]

Paul's interest in, and connection with, the Jews and
the Jewish Christians of Palestine is shown in a number

contrast with his subjects who were "servants." But it was not a
proper name for God, as the Septuagint Κύριος might mislead us to
suppose, nor was it a current surrogate for יהוה. Jewish Christians
would therefore feel no hesitation about using it of Jesus, for it would
imply no rivalry with Yahweh. To be sure, Yahweh is מרה מלכין and
מרא שמיא (Dan. 2:47; 5:23), in the sense that he possesses supreme
authority, and if Jesus spoke in Aramaic the words assigned to him in
Matt. 11:25; Luke 10:21 he probably said מרא דשמיא וערא. But
מרא was used equally freely of various grades of authority, as Onkelos
attests, although it was apparently a favorite term in Aramaic for describing the authority of kings. In the Zenjirli inscriptions Tiglath-pileser is
מרא רבעי ארקא and מראי. In the Nabatean inscriptions of the first
century A.D. Aretas is מראנא (*CIS*, II, 199, 201, 205 f., 208 f., 350).
The people of Palmyra address Ba'al Shamin as מרא עלמא; their
favorite prince is מרן and מרחון, and the Roman emperor is קסר מרן.
It would be perfectly appropriate and natural for the Aramaic-speaking
Christians of Palestine to call the exalted Messiah מרן in this elevated
sense, as a person who now occupied a position of special authority in
the realm of spirits.

[1] The only positive argument which is urged against this use of מרן
in the primitive community is the absence of Κύριος in the earliest stratum
of synoptic tradition. But this argument rests upon too many uncertainties to carry much weight. The absence of the term from this
tradition may merely show good historical perspective on the part of
the writers who knew that the word had not been applied generally to
Jesus during his earthly life. They do not represent that "Christ"
was a common designation for the earthly Jesus. Yet we can hardly
doubt that in their own circle he was commonly spoken of as the "Messiah." He was the humble "Jesus" while on earth, he is now the community's "Lord" in the realm of spirits, and also "Messiah" to be
revealed at the end of the age. Paul, too, on referring to tradition
received from his predecessors, uses "Lord" or "Lord Jesus" as though
it were a common designation in these earlier circles, e.g., I Thess.
1:6; 2:15; 4:15; Gal. 1:19; I Cor. 6:14; 7:10, 12, 25; 9:5, 14; 11:23,
26 f.; Rom. 4:24.

of other ways. He affirms his own Jewish ancestry most emphatically.[1] He longs for the conversion of the Jews, and believes that this ideal will finally be realized.[2] He visited Jerusalem several times and regarded it a matter of real importance that he should win the approval of the Jerusalem church in his gentile missionary work. It gave him no slight satisfaction to be able to say that the Judaean Christians on hearing of his missionary work in Syria and Cilicia gave glory to God for him who had once persecuted them.[3] And he gathered from his gentile fields the collection for the Palestinian Christians with as much zeal and fidelity as he would have displayed in making the appointed contribution to the temple had he remained within the Jewish fold. Paul seems to have believed that the new religion had a close genetic kinship with Judaism, but above all that Christianity on gentile soil was genetically the very same religion as Christianity in Palestine. Paul regards it the crowning act of his labors in the East to be able to requite in small measure the Jerusalem Christians for supplying to the Gentiles the true religion.[4] Although he had

[1] II Cor. 11:22; Rom. 11:1; Phil. 3:5.

[2] Rom. 9:1 ff.; 11:1 ff.

[3] Gal. 1:21, 24. The assertion that Paul never persecuted Judaean Christians (Bousset, *op. cit.*, p. 92; see also Mommsen, "Die Rechtsverhältnisse des Apostels Paulus," *Zeitschrift für die neutestamentliche Wissenschaft* [1901], 81 f., and Heitmüller, "Zum Problem Paulus und Jesus," *ibid.*, XIII [1912], 377), rests mainly upon the remark of vs. 22: "I was unknown by face to the churches of Judaea." But the context does not bear out so general an inference. All Paul says is that he made no personal visit to those churches *while he was working in Syria and Cilicia* (ἔπειτα ἦλθον . . . . ἤμην δὲ ἀγνοούμενος); cf. also J. Weiss, *Das Urchristentum*, I, 136, n. 1.

[4] Rom. 15:26–28.

not received his commission from the Jerusalem apostles, he had received no new commission in comparison with theirs, and although the first period of his Christian career had been spent in Damascus and Arabia, he reckoned his evangelizing activity territorially as beginning at Jerusalem.[1]

So in general the New Testament writers believed that their religion, although it possessed new and truer items, had a substantial foundation in Judaism. It was also a unit in itself, notwithstanding the diversities of Christian activity in scattered fields. While the New Testament is so largely a gentile Christian book, it uniformly attests the consciousness of a close genetic kinship with Judaism. When the Gospels were written the Old Testament was used as a source book for messianic prophecy and for Christian instruction generally. John the Baptist and Jesus were represented as working almost exclusively in a Jewish setting, the first disciples were believed to have been closely attached to Judaism, the new propaganda was said to have been carried on frequently in connection with the synagogue. Paul himself not only thought Judaism the true ancestor of the new religion, but looked for the speedy reconciliation of these two estranged kinsmen. The author of Matthew, in spite of his anti-Jewish polemic, emphatically affirmed both Jesus' loyalty to the law and the permanent character of that institution.[2] The third evangelist, in proving to Theophilus the validity of the new faith, closely associated its origin and early history with Jerusalem.[3] And so anti-Jewish a writer as John

[1] Rom. 15:19.   [2] 5:17-19.
[3] Cf. Acts 1:8 ff.; 2:1 ff.; 8:14 ff.; 9:26-30.

approvingly reported Jesus to have said that "salvation is of the Jews."[1]

The early Christians and their Jewish kinsmen certainly had much in common religiously. This common possession was not merely a legacy from the Old Testament, it was also a heritage from the religious life of later times. Nor did it consist primarily in the adoption of ideas and customs which were essentially foreign to the real nature of the new religion, with the consequence that these things had to be dismissed before the new movement could realize its universal destiny. On the contrary, it carried its rich Jewish heritage to the Gentiles and, though extensive transformations took place in the course of time, Christians continued to feel that their religion had a substantial Jewish background. In this feeling they were unquestionably correct.

Yet we cannot set apart a definite quantum of early Christian doctrine or ritual, labeling it "Jewish" in contrast with other items which are distinctively "Christian"; nor can we restrict the Christian's debt to Judaism within one particular sphere. This is because the relationship between the two religions was one of life and so was subject to much variation. The connections were as numerous and varied as were the individuals in whose career these relations actually existed and found expression. The religious lives of different persons amid different surroundings and with different types of experience all went into the making of the new religion's history. Some persons had absorbed into the fiber of their religious life one type of Jewish influence and some another, according to

[1] 4:22.

individual tastes and circumstances. Other members of the new community had received their training from earliest childhood within Jewish circles, and so owed that ancient faith a much larger debt than they could possibly realize. A similar situation was true of those who had been proselytes to Judaism before adopting Christianity. Of others, who came under Jewish influence only indirectly through contact with Christian converts from Judaism, or through the use of Jewish books within the new community, the heritage from the Jews was doubtless less extensive but no less real. As these varied relationships were a matter of actual life, Christianity's Jewish connections in New Testament times must be admitted to have been vital in character as well as wide and varied in extent.

CHAPTER V

THE BREACH BETWEEN CHRISTIANS AND JEWS

The relation between the first Christians and their Jewish kinsmen was so close, and the two had so much in common, that the rapid development of bitter hostility between them demands detailed explanation.

The Jews seem to have taken the initiative in forcing separation. The early group of disciples described in the Book of Acts apparently had no thought of severing traditional religious connections, or of establishing any movement outside the pale of Judaism. Is this representation of Acts historical? It is true that the writer was desirous of assuring Theophilus that the new religion had the full authority of antiquity, therefore primitive Christianity was given the best of Jewish credentials and was allowed to become a gentile propaganda only after Jews had consistently rejected the gospel. From this representation one might infer that Acts had overrated the attachment to Judaism. Yet this accusation would hold only for the formal side of the relationship, since the author was himself convinced that the new faith by its very nature was destined from the beginning to become universal and so to be independent of the old. This led him to make the connection between the two formal rather than essential. The characters who work out this historical transition often move upon the stage like figures performing mechanically, and arriving at a result which surprises no one because the outcome had been fully anticipated. Hence the intrinsic possibility that the relation to Judaism, though less official and formal, was in reality more genuine and natural than Acts represents.

Furthermore, Paul's account of the situation in which his liberalism was a stumbling-block to many Palestinian Christians also suggests that their attitude was a conservative one. They observed diligently the customary religious conventions and were so true to the ancestral faith that the thought of carrying the gospel of the Messiah into Samaria, or into gentile territory, dawned upon them only gradually, and the legitimacy of the procedure was admitted only hesitatingly. Loyalty to the religion of their fathers is one of the best-attested characteristics of the first Christians. The message they preached was intended by them primarily if not exclusively for Israelites, and its fulfilment was to be the perfect realization of Israel's long-deferred hope. Thus they had no desire to break with Judaism, and did not even think of themselves as a separate sect. They were the true Judaism, bringing to every Israelite the message of the coming Messiah.

Their hopes were doomed to disappointment. Their kinsmen so generally refused to agree with them, and indeed so vigorously opposed them, that they were early forced into a position of isolation. It cannot have been long before vigorous measures were taken to suppress their activity. The Book of Acts gives no explicit information about the date of the early persecution, but it was in full swing when Paul's conversion took place, perhaps only a year, or at most within three years, after Jesus' crucifixion. Nor did opposition cease with Paul. On the contrary, he himself now became the object of persecution directed against the new propaganda on both gentile and Palestinian soil.[1] Too much must not be inferred from the idealistic statement of Acts 9:31 to the effect that the church throughout all Judaea and Galilee and Samaria had peace after Paul's hand was stayed. While the narrative is henceforth interested mainly in the opposition encountered by Paul, there are still some indications that even in Judaea the Christian situation continued to be precarious. On one occasion James, the brother of John, was put to death and Peter barely escaped a similar fate.[2] According to one tradition, accepted as authentic by several scholars, John also suffered martyrdom at this time.[3] When Peter removed from Jerusalem, James seems to have become the chief personage in the mother-church. A definite date for this event cannot be fixed. Eusebius reports Clement of Alexandria to have said that Peter, James, and John were not covetous for honor and so chose James for the head of the community after Jesus' ascension.[4] It is possible, perhaps probable, that Herod's persecution (44 A.D.) resulted in Peter's leaving Jerusalem, so that James henceforth was looked upon

[1] Cf. I Thess. 2:14 f.; II Cor. 11:24, 32 f.; Acts 9:23, 29.

[2] Acts, chap. 12.

[3] See de Boor, "Neue Fragmente des Papias," *Texte und Untersuchungen*, V, 2 (Leipzig, 1888), pp. 167 ff.; Badham, "The Martyrdom of St. John," *American Journal of Theology*, III (1899), 729–40, VIII (1904), 539–54; Schwartz, "Ueber den Tod der Söhne Zebedaei," *Abhandlungen der königlichen Gesellschaft der Wissenschaften zu Göttingen*, Neue Folge, VII, No. 5 (Berlin, 1904); Bousset, *Die Offenbarung Johannis* (Göttingen, 1906), pp. 34–49; Moffatt, *Introduction to the Literature of the New Testament* (New York, 1911), pp. 601 ff., where other literature is cited.

[4] *HE*, II, 1.

as leader of the community.[1] Clement of Alexandria
preserves a fragment in which Peter says that the
apostles had been instructed to preach to Israel twelve
years, after which time they were to go forth to the
world.[2] This may have been about the length of time
spent by the apostles in their most strenuous activities
to evangelize their own countrymen, an effort yielding
such meager results that they now sought members
for the new messianic kingdom in other lands. According to Josephus, James, the Lord's brother, also fell a
victim to Jewish hatred in the year 62 when the Sadducean high priest Ananus had him stoned along with
others for breaking the law.[3] This is a very strange
charge to bring against James who elsewhere in tradition figures as a staunch supporter of the law.[4] Josephus
says that the fairer-minded Jews, probably meaning
Pharisees, protested against Ananus' conduct, but
Hegesippus makes the scribes and Pharisees directly
responsible for James's death.[5] Certainty on this point
is not now attainable; we can only say that James met
death at the hands of the Jews. Finally, the withdrawal
of the Jerusalem Christians to Pella during the war
against Rome (66–70 A.D.)[6] severed forever any lingering
bonds of sympathy between the two faiths and showed
how completely even the most Jewish Christians had
lost their concern for the nation's preservation. This

[1] Acts 12:17; 15:13; 21:18; Gal. 1:19; 2:9.

[2] *Strom.*, VI, 5, 43.   [3] *Ant.*, XX, ix, 1.

[4] Cf. Gal. 2:9; Acts 15:13.

[5] According to Eusebius, *HE*, II, 23.

[6] Eusebius, *HE*, III, v. 2 f.; Epiphanius, *Haer.*, XXIX, 7 (Migne,
XLI, col. 401), and *De mensuris et ponderibus*, 15 (Migne, XLIII, col.
261).

rapid sketch makes it clear that Jewish opposition to Christianity had been constant, though varying in intensity at different periods, from an early date both in Palestine and in the Diaspora.

What was the ground of this opposition? There is nothing to indicate that it was a continuation of that conflict between Jesus and the Pharisees which is so prominent in the Gospels. The disciples were not opposed because they had been followers of the Crucified One; they incurred hostility on account of their own estatic, pneumatic, dynamic conduct. The details given in the early chapters of Acts may, it is true, be somewhat idealized under the influence of subsequent interpretation. Since this book, like the former treatise by the same author, was doubtless composed for the purpose of strengthening Theophilus' faith,[1] and since the author's own faith was surely strong enough to surmount many difficulties which a lack of first-hand information might occasion, it becomes necessary in a strictly historical inquiry to deal critically with his narrative. He certainly employed genuine historical tradition when it was available, and he not improbably used oral or even documentary source materials in the composition of the Acts as he did in the writing of his Gospel.[2] But the discovery of these sources by a process of literary analysis, though never so successful, does not supply the ultimate criterion of historical

[1] Luke 1:3 f.; Acts 1:1.

[2] Luke 1:1–3. One of the most recent and most successful attempts at analysis is Harnack's *Die Apostelgeschichte* (Leipzig, 1908), English tr., *The Acts of the Apostles* (New York, 1909). For a survey of the literature see Moffatt, *Introduction to the Literature of the New Testament*, pp. 268 ff.

accuracy. This must be sought in a critical estimate based upon internal indicia, tested on the one hand by comparison with the Jewish background of the early community, and on the other by data from Paul's letters.

Notwithstanding these difficulties, it is still possible to determine the chief factors in the situation which brought about the early Christians' separation from Judaism. There are various indications to show that it was in the first instance their own pneumatic activity which gave offense to the Jews. The new movement had begun in ecstasy. Paul explicitly affirms that his new faith, as well as that of his predecessors, rested upon a vision-experience of the risen Jesus. These ecstatic phenomena had occurred in the case of Cephas, of the Twelve, of a company of approximately five hundred persons, of James, of all of the apostles, and finally of Paul himself.[1] Henceforth they identified the heavenly Jesus with the expected heavenly Messiah of Jewish apocalyptic. The notion of a unique spiritual endowment was naturally associated with this new faith in the risen Jesus. The Messiah himself in Jewish thinking was to possess a special pneumatic equipment.[2] Isaiah's description of the messianic king upon whom the spirit of Yahweh was to rest, "the spirit of wisdom and understanding, the spirit of counsel and might, the spirit of

---

[1] I Cor. 15:5 ff.

[2] See Bousset, *Die Religion des Judentums*, pp. 452–58, and Volz, *Der Geist Gottes* (Tübingen, 1910), pp. 87 ff. For the prominent place which the idea of the Spirit occupied first in Jewish religion and then in Christianity, see further Gunkel, *Die Wirkungen des heiligen Geistes* (Göttingen, 1888, 1908²); Weinel, *Die Wirkungen des Geistes und der Geister* (Freiburg, 1899); Wood, *The Spirit of God in Biblical Literature* (New York, 1904).

knowledge and of the fear of Yahweh,"[1] had been freely applied by later Jewish writers to the apocalyptic Messiah. Thus in En. 62:2 the elect one is seen seated upon the throne of glory of the Lord of spirits and the spirit of righteousness is poured out over him.[2]

His subjects were also to share in this pneumatic equipment, either by way of preparation for his coming or else as part of their inheritance in the messianic blessing. Joel recounts among the special acts to be performed by God before the day of judgment an outpouring of the Spirit upon all flesh, so that the sons and daughters of Israel should prophesy, their old men should dream dreams, and their young men should see visions.[3] In the Testament of Judah, section 24, it is said that the heavens will open over the Messiah, pouring down upon him the blessings of the Spirit from the Holy Father, and the Messiah himself will pour out the spirit of his grace upon his subjects who will become truly his sons.

---

[1] Isa. 11:2; cf. 42:1; 61:1 ff. Christian tradition made extensive use of this notion in defending its doctrine of Jesus' messiahship while on earth (see Mark 1:11 and parallels; John 1:33; Luke 1:80; Acts 10:38; Gospel according to Hebrews; Jerome, *Com. Isa.* 11:2).

[2] See further En. 49:1-4; Pss. Sol. 17:42; 18:8; Test. Levi, 18.

[3] Joel 2:28 ff.; cf. Zech. 12:10. The prophet Joel seems to make these phenomena merely premonitory signs of the coming of the messianic age, but the author of Acts, according to the usual interpretation, uses the prophecy to describe the character of the messianic community itself. While such freedom in use of Scripture was characteristic of that period, it may be that the early Christians were in reality still looking to the future for the true messianic age, consequently the charismata were for them a fulfilment of the prophecy in its original sense. As later Christian thinkers gradually changed the messianic emphasis from the future to the lifetime of Jesus, they came to treat charismata as less anticipatory and more as an actual realization of the messianic blessings.

Similarly the Zadokite sectaries believed the Anointed One mediated a knowledge of the Holy Spirit.[1]

The ecstatic experiences which established faith in Jesus' resurrection and exaltation to messianic dignity, the current idea of the Messiah's own unique spiritual endowment, and the expectation of an unusual demonstration of charismatic activity among men, either as an anticipation of the end or as a participation in messianic blessings, lead us to expect that the first disciples would assign a large place to the activities of the Spirit in their new life.

The probability of this supposition is further confirmed by the central position which is given to the Spirit in Christianity as expounded by the New Testament writers. This power is active in connection with the birth and childhood of both John the Baptist and Jesus.[2] Jesus is initiated into the work of his public ministry by a special spiritual endowment at baptism;[3] his conduct is sometimes determined by the dictates of the Spirit;[4] his numerous encounters with demons demonstrate that the Holy Spirit, which took up its abode in him at baptism, is superior in power to Satan, the prince of evil spirits, and his demonic representatives upon earth;[5] and blasphemy against the Holy Spirit as its power is manifest in the work of Jesus is the one unforgivable sin.[6]

[1] Schechter's edition, Text A, II, 13.

[2] Mark 1:18, 20; Luke 1:15, 35, 41, 67, 80; 2:25 f.

[3] Matt. 3:16 f.; Mark 1:10 f.; Luke 3:21 f.; John 1:33a; Acts 10:38.

[4] Matt. 4:1; Mark 1:12; Luke 4:1, 14; cf. John 3:34.

[5] Matt. 12:25 ff.; Mark 3:23 ff.; Luke 11:17 ff.

[6] Matt. 12:32; Mark 3:29; Luke 12:10.

Christians themselves are similarly endowed for carrying on the work begun by Jesus. At the beginning of his career it is affirmed that he will baptize his followers with the Spirit,[1] a promise fulfilled according to the Fourth Gospel on the day of his resurrection, but at Pentecost according to Acts.[2] Henceforth believers' lives constantly display the workings of the Spirit; in fact, the Book of Acts might be called a history of the activities of the Holy Ghost.[3] Throughout Paul's epistles the indwelling of the Spirit is the ground and inspiration of the entire Christian life.[4] Indeed it might be said that Christianity as described by the various New Testament writers is in general a religion of the Holy Spirit. This entire situation prepares us to believe that Christians from the first were pre-eminently pneumatic individuals.

When and how did the first believers receive their special spiritual equipment? It is a noteworthy fact that the New Testament offers no one stereotyped formula for obtaining this endowment. Jesus himself received it immediately after baptism,[5] and John the Baptist declared that Jesus would administer a baptism of the Holy Spirit to his disciples.[6] In Acts this promise was fulfilled in a miraculous demonstration at Pentecost,

[1] Matt. 3:11; Mark 1:8; Luke 3:16; John 1:33*b;* Acts 11:16.

[2] John 20:22; Acts 2:1 ff.

[3] E.g., 1:2, 5, 8; 2:1 ff.; 4:8, 31; 5:3, 32; 6:3, 5, 10; 7:51, 55; 8:15 ff., 29, 39; 9:17, 31; 10:44-47; 11:15-17, 24, 28; 13:2, 4, 9, 52; 15:8, 28; 16:6 f.; 19:2, 6; 20:23, 28; 21:4, 11; 28:25.

[4] To cite only a few representative passages, Rom. 8:1-17; I Cor. 2:10-16; 14:1 ff.; II Cor. 3:17 f.; Gal. 3:2-5.

[5] Matt. 3:16; Mark 1:10; Luke 3:22; John 1:33*a.*

[6] Matt. 3:11; Mark 1:8; Luke 3:16; John 1:33*b;* Acts 11:16.

while in the Gospel of John Jesus exhaled the Spirit upon his followers on the evening of the day he rose from the dead.[1] Of later converts, some became pneumatic on hearing the preaching of the gospel;[2] others received the gift as Jesus did in connection with baptism;[3] on other occasions the desired endowment was obtained by the laying on of hands.[4] To determine from this complicated situation how the early believers obtained their first consciousness of spiritual equipment is not an easy task.

Apparently Paul connected his unique pneumatic endowment most immediately with his conversion experience. Although he subsequently had frequent visions and revelations, his ecstatic experience on the road to Damascus was the one outstanding event in his life which marked the beginning of his career as a spiritual individual.[5] Those who became Christians in response to Paul's preaching passed through a similar experience, if we may take the Galatian situation to be typical. The apostle exhibited before the eye of his audience Jesus crucified,[6] and as his hearers exercised faith in the redeeming work of the Messiah as portrayed by Paul, they received the charismatic endowment which enabled them to work "miracles." Paul does not say that the spiritual equipment of the new convert was fully attained at this particular moment; in fact, he frequently intimates that the new life was to be cultivated and increased by various means, but conversion was the

[1] 20:22.

[2] Gal. 3:2; I Thess. 1:6; Acts 10:44–48; 11:15.

[3] Acts 2:38; cf. I Cor. 12:13.   [5] Gal. 1:15 f.; 2:20.

[4] Acts 8:14–17; 9:17; 19:2 ff.   [6] Gal. 3:1–5; cf. I Cor. 2:2.

initial stage in the Christian's career as a pneumatic
person.

It is conceivable that the first disciples also associated
the beginnings of their pneumatic life with those ecstatic
experiences in which they had seen the risen Jesus.
There were significant Jewish precedents for positing
an activity of the Spirit in connection with vision and
ecstasy. The ecstatic activity of King Saul was ascribed
to the presence of the Spirit of God, and the same cause
produced a similar phenomenon in the case of messengers
whom Saul sent to arrest David.[1] But the most striking
Old Testament illustration is to be found in Ezekiel.
His prophetic career opened with a wonderful vision
of the heavenly glory of God. When he fell face down-
ward upon the ground God spoke to him out of heaven
and the Spirit straightway entered into him, setting
him upon his feet. Henceforth his whole life was pervaded by demonstrations of a pneumatic character.
The Spirit repeatedly "entered into" him or "fell
upon" him, commanding him to speak or transporting
him from place to place.[2] When the first Christians
saw Jesus in his resurrection glory, the feeling of assurance and elation which took possession of them at that

[1] I Sam. 10:10; 19:20-24.

[2] See, e.g., 2:2 ff.; 3:12, 24; 8:3 ff.; 11:1, 5, 24. Christian tradition
made extensive use of these ideas: cf. the bright light and the voice in
connection with Paul's conversion (Acts 9:3 ff; 22:6 ff.; 26:12 ff.; cf.
Ezek. 1:28; 2:1 ff.); the opening of heaven above Jesus at baptism, the
descent of the Spirit, the voice, and the subsequent impulsion of the
Spirit (Mark 1:10 ff. and parallels; cf. Ezek. 1:1; 2:2 ff.; 3:12-24);
the career of the evangelist Philip (Acts 8:29, 39 f.); or Jesus' statement
in the Gospel according to the Hebrews: "My mother, the Holy Spirit,
took me by one of the hairs of my head and carried me off to Mount
Tabor" (cf. Ezek. 8:3).

time would most surely have been interpreted in terms of pneumatic endowment, if, indeed, the Spirit was not credited with making the vision possible. This for a Jew would be the natural way to explain such experiences.

In the opening chapters of Acts the pneumatic endowment of the disciples is depicted in a most formal manner. The company of believers assemble in the upper room where they perfect the organization and wait for Pentecost when the new movement is to be equipped by the promised outpouring of the Holy Spirit, and is thereby to be started officially on its world-conquering career. This is the formal beginning of the new religion, and the event quite appropriately takes place on the very day which commemorated the giving of the law, the birthday of the old religion which the new is intended to supplant. Just when Pentecost came to be celebrated in this special way is not perfectly clear,[1] but the author

---

[1] For a similar comparison between Christianity and Judaism see Gal. 4:29 f.; Heb. 2:2-4; 12:18-24. According to Benzinger, article "Pentecost" in the *Encyclopedia Biblica*, III (New York, 1902), it was not until after the fall of Jerusalem that the Feast of Pentecost was observed as a commemoration of the giving of the law. The reason for this opinion is the silence of Philo and Josephus. The writer of the article "Pentecost" in the *Jewish Encyclopedia*, IX (New York, 1905), says: "The traditional festival of Pentecost as the birthday of the Torah, when Israel became a constitutional body and a distinguished people, remained the sole celebration after the exile" (p. 593). This interpretation of the giving of the law seems to have been current in Philo's day, whether or not it was connected with Pentecost. He protests against its crassness, but does not deny the miracle. God did not utter a voice, "for he is not like a man in need of a mouth and of a tongue and of a windpipe, but as it seems to me he at that time wrought a most conspicuous and evidently holy miracle, commanding an invisible sound to be created in the air, more marvelous than all the instruments that ever existed. . . . . A rational soul filled with clearness and distinctness, which fashioned the air and stretched it out and changed it into a

of Acts, or his source, was certainly acquainted with this custom and used it in his interpretation of Christianity's origin. The forty days of waiting by the disciples are the same as Moses' period of preparation in Sinai;[1] the thunder and lightning, with the voice of God coming from the midst of the fire, correspond to the roaring sound and tongues of flame in Acts;[2] and the proclamation of the gospel in different languages repeats the midrastic representation of the manner in which the law was promulgated from Sinai, when seventy voices proclaimed it to as many different peoples, but all save Israel rejected. This type of interpretation was perfectly natural to Christians after they had attained their consciousness of independent solidarity and had begun to make their propaganda a world missionary movement.

Even if the details in Acts are somewhat idealized, as seems most probable, this first Pentecost after Jesus' death may still have been unusually significant for the disciples. It probably was the occasion of their return to Jerusalem, if, as many interpreters think, they had fled when Jesus was put to death. Possibly they needed no incentive for returning other than a desire to observe

kind of flaming fire, and so sounded forth so loud and articulate a voice like a breath passing through a trumpet, so that those who were at a great distance appeared to hear equally with those who were near to it" (*De decalogo*, 9). Again, "A voice sounded forth from out of the midst of the fire, which had flowed from heaven, a most marvelous and awful voice, the flame being endowed with articulate speech in a language familiar to the hearers, which expressed its words with such clearness and distinctness that the people seemed rather to be seeing than hearing it" (*ibid.*, 11).

[1] Exod. 24:18.
[2] Exod. 20:18 ff.; Deut. 5:4 f.; 33:2 f.; Ps. 68:8.

the feast,[1] but those who had already come to believe
in Jesus' resurrection and messiahship may have been
expecting some unusual demonstration on his part at
this time. Their hope of his speedy coming in glory
will, at the latest, have begun to take shape the moment
their faith in Jesus' resurrection and exaltation became
established. Pentecost was an occasion which might
easily have stimulated this hope. In general, a feast
season brought together a large company and was a time
of renewed expectation when messianic pretenders
easily took advantage of the excitability of the multitude. This feast doubtless was remembered as the time
when the Jews, after the death of Herod the Great, had
made one of their most vigorous protests against the
Roman authority, and when the people zealously gave
their lives in the cause of liberty.[2] The desire for freedom was so deep-rooted in their faith that various leaders
successfully assumed for a time the rôle of deliverer.
The large attendance at Pentecost would bring together

[1] According to the Fourth Gospel, the Last Supper was not the
observance of Passover, but was an ordinary meal on the previous evening. The events of the next day prevented the disciples from keeping
the Passover, hence they might return a month later to observe this
feast as prescribed by Num. 9:9–11. Others insist that the disciples
lingered expectantly in the vicinity of Jerusalem and did not witness the
appearances of the risen Jesus first in Galilee. So Frey, *Der Schluss des
Marcus Evangeliums und die Erscheinungen des Auferstandenen* (Leipzig,
1913); cf. also J. Weiss, *Das Urchristentum*, I, 9 ff.

[2] Josephus, *Ant.*, XVII, 10; *War*, II, 3 f. In addition to the notion
that Pentecost marked the beginning of Israel's career as a separate
people, according to Jubilees various other significant events occurred
on that date, e.g., the covenant with Noah regarding eating blood, the
covenant between Jacob and Laban, and renewal of the blood covenant
with Abraham and Moses. It was a fitting season for the establishment
of a new order of things.

former followers of Jesus, who thus renewed their acquaintanceship. Those who had come to believe in his resurrection and exaltation found here a favorable opportunity for the propagation of their new faith. Now that Jesus had been elevated to a position of authority in the realm of spirits earthly messianic aspirants could no longer appeal to his followers. They looked for an other-worldly demonstration of divine power, a real sign from heaven to effect the deliverance of Israel. Pentecost with all its peculiar associations might very easily stimulate their expectations, and mark some fresh experiences in their ecstatic life.

Preaching was naturally one of the earliest forms of activity undertaken by the reassembled believers. Their consciousness of spiritual equipment easily suggested the work of the prophetic preacher. In the Old Testament Moses was credited with expressing a wish that all Yahweh's people, like Eldad and Medad,[1] might become prophets through receiving the Spirit. The exercise of this gift by the seventy elders, as well as by the bands of prophets with which Saul was connected,[2] was probably a display of ecstasy not essentially different from speaking with tongues described by Paul in the fourteenth chapter of I Corinthians. Similar phenomena in the life of the new community would be only a natural outcome of their Jewish inheritance interpreted in the light of their recent experiences. But the great prophets of Israel, in addition to being ecstatics, had uttered a divine message of warning or of consolation in different crises of history. They proclaimed so vigorously the advent of the days of visitation and

[1] Num. 11:29.   [2] I Sam. 10:5 ff.

recompense against Israel that one might say "the prophet is a fool, the man that hath the spirit is mad, for the abundance of thine iniquity."[1] And again, "The Spirit of the Lord Yahweh is upon me, because Yahweh hath anointed me to preach good tidings to the meek, he hath sent me to bind up the broken-hearted, to proclaim liberty to the captives, and the opening [of the prison] to them that are bound, to proclaim the year of Yahweh's favor and the day of vengeance of our God."[2] These and many similar passages in their Scriptures furnish Christians ample guidance for the prophetic interpretation of their mission as believers in the risen and exalted Jesus.

The office of "prophet," like that of "apostle," had become an established institution in Paul's day. Ability to prophesy was specifically a "spiritual" gift,[3] but in contrast with tongues, prophecy was an intelligible utterance tending toward the edification, exhortation, and consolation of believers, while for the unlearned and unbelieving it was intended to produce a conviction of sin, a fear of judgment, and worshipful recognition of God's presence with Christians.[4] Paul gives no intimation that this work of the prophet was a new thing on gentile soil. In fact, the spiritually endowed man of God, calling sinners to repentance, exhorting backsliders to renew their allegiance to the Deity, comforting the faithful, and announcing the future program of the Almighty, was a characteristically Jewish figure from the time of the ancient prophets to the days of John the Baptist and Jesus.

[1] Hos. 9:7.
[2] Isa. 61:1 f.; cf. Luke 4:16 ff.
[3] I Cor. 12:10, 28.
[4] I Cor., chap. 14.

It is quite true that Judaism in post-exilic times became largely a book religion and so gave less prominence than formerly to the prophet; still the Jewish people were constantly involved in embarrassing political circumstances which called forth champions of righteousness, liberty, and hope, who did a work very similar in spirit to that of the earlier prophets. In taking up this same duty the leaders of the primitive Christian community found in their new pneumatic equipment and in their belief that Jesus had triumphed over death an additional incentive for assuming the prophetic rôle. Now they were better qualified than any of their predecessors had been to disclose the details of the coming deliverance. The risen Jesus of their faith supplied the needed center about which a new interpretation of the messianic hope could revolve.

The preaching activity of the first Christians was probably the initial cause of Jewish opposition, yet the new movement as a whole may at first have seemed quite harmless. The private life of Christians, even on its ecstatic side, is not likely to have occasioned offense, nor would public preaching necessarily involve opposition. Freedom in the expression of opinion was not only characteristic of synagogue life, but the appearance of various teachers and preachers, especially at feast seasons, was a phenomenon to which the Jews by this time had become well accustomed. Neither would a type of teaching which concerned itself with the national hope, offering a brighter prospect and demanding as its condition renewed devotion to God, necessarily be offensive. Even the prediction of the imminent kingdom to be ushered in by divine intervention must have been an acceptable notion to large numbers of Jews. These general characteristics of the Christian movement were too closely in line with much that was characteristic of Judaism at this time to occasion any serious break between the first disciples and their immediate religious environment.

The ground of separation must be sought in other and more distinctive characteristics of the disciples' life. In general, preaching of Jesus' messiahship with the consequent implications for conduct and doctrine was the chief occasion of Jewish hostility. This phase of Christian teaching assumed different aspects. Just how much blame was placed upon the Jews for the death of Jesus is not clear from our sources of information, but at the outset probably not a great deal. The disciples at first are not likely to have approached their hearers with those severe upbraidings of later times when the situation had been aggravated by a persistent rejection of belief in the messiahship of the risen Jesus as well as by the bitter persecution of those who defended this faith. Then the crime of the Jews, and the consequent doom awaiting them as punishment were portrayed in vivid colors. But in earlier times Jesus' death seems to have been viewed more as the result of misunderstanding than as a crime.

In Paul's day, when the relationship between the two movements had become very strained, the Jews' hostility to Jesus was one of the many performances done "to fill up their sins always,"[1] yet they will hardly have been wiser, in Paul's thought, than the evil angelic powers who were ultimately responsible for the event, yet who did it in ignorance.[2]   Furthermore, the wrong,

---

[1] I Thess. 2:15 f.   [2] I Cor. 2:6–8.

great as it was, could be righted, and Paul was still hopeful that it would be when his kinsmen who had a zeal for God, but not according to knowledge, should accept Jesus as the coming Messiah.[1] Earlier believers will naturally have judged still more leniently,[2] particularly since the death of Jesus was now understood to be the indispensable link in the chain of events leading up to his final manifestation in messianic glory. The idea that his executioners had condemned him through ignorance was complementary to the disciples' own failure adequately to perceive the messianic character of his work previous to his resurrection. As they excused themselves on the ground of short-sightedness so they probably would be disposed to excuse, for a similar reason, those who had crucified Jesus.

Much less would they at the outset think of upbraiding the Jews for failure to recognize the messianic claims of the earthly Jesus. Since his personal followers had been so tardy in this respect and had not arrived at any full appreciation of his messiahship—for this is the representation of the earliest tradition—until they attained their resurrection faith and received the accompanying outpouring of the Spirit, it would be manifestly absurd for them to charge outsiders with deficiency of belief. Failure to believe that Jesus was the *coming* Messiah, not doubt about his messiahship while upon earth, was the main complaint which the early preachers would have to urge against their Jewish hearers. This was a criticism of the Jews for rejecting the Christian preachers' assertions about Jesus, and not an accusation against them for rejecting Jesus' teaching about himself.

[1] Rom. 9:30—10:4; 11:25-32.   [2] Cf. Acts 3:17; 13:27.

This latter phase of criticism doubtless developed at an early date, as the disciples' own mission was interpreted primarily in terms of prophetic preaching. But they seem at first to have placed chief stress upon Jesus' career as a prophetic teacher. Our custom of distinguishing two types of primitive gospel tradition, sayings and doings, while misleading if used too rigidly, does serve to designate two main interests prominent among the framers of early tradition. The non-Markan source materials employed in common by Matthew and Luke are mainly of the "saying" type. Jesus' work finds its climax in the assertion that the poor have the gospel preached to them and that that man is blessed who does not stumble at this interpretation of Jesus' mission.[1] Similarly in Acts, chap. 3, Jesus is the martyr-prophet whom God had promised to raise up from among the people of Israel, and who by his message should bless them in turning them away from their iniquities. This portrait is evidently primitive, being derived from one of the sources employed by the author of Acts. It certainly is not a picture such as a later writer would create on the basis of the much more elaborate representation of Jesus in his earthly messianic career described by Mark and incorporated into the Third Gospel. In the earlier picture Jesus, like the first disciples, is a prophet of the coming kingdom with a message of moral reform and renewed consecration to God, a message with which Jewish audiences had, in a general way, long been familiar.

None of these circumstances is likely to have brought Jews and Christians into very bitter conflict, though

[1] Matt. 11:5 f.; Luke 7:22 f.; cf. 4:16 ff.

the way for a serious breach was certainly being made
ready. Even when believers came to place more stress
upon the evidences of Jesus' right to messianic reverence
during his lifetime, and when they, having thus established their own faith, could more consistently blame
others for rejecting these credentials, there was still
but little inducement for Jews to do more than turn
a deaf ear to the Christian preachers' accusation. It
was not a custom among the Jews to persecute messianic
claimants; they left that work to the foreign ruler who
was always on the watch to anticipate any messianic
agitation which might arise. The Jews, for the most
part, were anxious and expectant, more concerned
with the credentials of any proposed Messiah than
with his suppression. While they rejected Christians'
advocacy of Jesus' claims, the main proof of these
claims, even for the disciples, was an affair of the
future. Hence Jewish unbelievers could easily rest
satisfied, so far as the simple affirmation that Jesus
had been or was yet to be the Messiah was concerned,
with demanding a sign from heaven. They would
believe when they should see Jesus fulfilling the Messiah's rôle by coming in glory. The disciples' assertions were doubted, but they did not necessarily call
for persecution. It was easy to tolerate these extrem-
ists whose numbers cannot have been large in spite of
Acts' idealized multiplication of church members,[1] while
they remained loyal to traditional Judaism, and proclaimed with only slightly varying details the realization of a religious hope, the cherishing of which was

[1] Cf. Brun, "Etwa 3000 Seelen Act 2, 41," *Zeitschrift für die neutestamentliche Wissenschaft*, XIV (1913), 94–96.

regarded by many Israelites to be the world-mission of their nation.

The phases of the Christian propaganda which aroused more vigorous opposition were, according to Acts, three-fold. There was first an arrest of the disciples on the charge of performing a miracle by unlawful means, a suspected violation of the Deuteronomic injunction against the practice of magic.[1] Again, it was the disciples' reverence for, and proclamation of, Jesus raised and exalted at God's right hand, which gave further offense—perhaps seeming to Jews to endanger, if not actually to deny, the monotheistic faith which they so zealously guarded.[2] In the third place, there are intimations that Christians were persecuted because they had criticized the Jews for being untrue to the ancient faith, the edge of the criticism being turned against the Christians by charging them, falsely says Acts, with laxity toward the temple and the religious customs established by Moses.[3]

---

[1] Acts 3:6, 12–16; 4:7 ff.; 5:16–18, 40; Deut. 18:9 ff.

[2] Acts 4:33; 5:28 ff.; 7:54–58; cf. 1:23; 4:1–3.

[3] Acts 6:1—7:53. A fourth point, closely akin to the last, at which Christians are supposed to have made themselves intolerable in the eyes of the Jews, is often said to have been their laxity toward legalism, due to an inherent universalism in their faith received from Jesus, latent in the life and teaching of the primitive community, and brought to new and extended expression in the career of Paul. The validity of this hypothesis is, as we have discovered (see above, pp. 101–3), not so certain as has commonly been supposed, and so far as Acts is concerned, there are only vague hints that this feature was present in primitive Christianity (Acts 1:8). Here the representation is that the gospel goes to the Gentiles because of Jewish rejection of Jesus' messiahship, not because its universalistic features called forth hostility. This situation is as true of Paul in Acts' account as of other Christian preachers (Acts 8:1; 9:22 ff.; 13:46; 18:6; 22:19–21; 26:19–21; 28:25–28).

These different items stand variously blended and combined with other data in the Book of Acts. Hence it is not easy to ascertain the exact degree in which they represent the actual facts in the history of the early Christian community. As for the hostility aroused by miracle activity, one might suspect that the wonderful deeds of the apostles were largely an idealization on the part of the narrator, carrying over into Acts the miraculous element in the Gospels. That the narrative does contain much idealization cannot plausibly be denied.[1] Furthermore, if Jesus were allowed to work miracles so freely as the Gospels represent, it is scarcely probable, we might say, that the first disciples would be sharply opposed on this ground. This problem cannot be solved from the data of Acts alone. Appeal must also be made to the distinctive characteristics of the first Christians' life, to their Jewish antecedents, and to the testimony of Paul.

The Christians' consciousness of special pneumatic endowment, with the accompanying ecstatic element in their life, forms a natural background for the practice of mighty works. The notion that an individual especially favored by the Deity was on that account possessed of extraordinary powers, not only finds a place in the religious psychology of primitive peoples everywhere, but is characteristic of certain types of believers in practically all ages. The Spirit-filled man of the Old Testament freely displayed miraculous abilities.[2] When God took of his Spirit from Moses, who himself performed various mighty works, and endowed

[1] E.g., 2:43; 5:15 f.
[2] See Volz, *Der Geist Gottes*, pp. 33 ff.

the seventy elders,[1] they at once became ecstatic prophets.[2] When the Spirit of Yahweh came mightily upon Saul he, along with the bands of wandering prophets, exhibited a miraculous ecstatic frenzy.[3] The mysterious man of God from Judah who spoke against Jeroboam was attested by signs and even the presence of his dead body miraculously restrained the natural impulses of the lion whose ferocity ceased with fulfilling the divine command to slay the prophet.[4] Elijah, the man of God *par excellence*, was a miracle-worker from the outset,[5] and Elisha who received the firstborn's portion of his master's spirit immediately exhibited his new endowment by means of a miraculous parting of the waters of the Jordan.[6] Elisha in turn sought at his death to convey the prophet's divine potency to Joash the king by placing his hands upon the king's hands, but the king proved to be a very poor medium of ecstatic frenzy.[7]

When the early Christians associated their ecstatic life with the idea of special spiritual endowment, and when they interpreted their mission in terms of prophetic preaching to prepare Israel for the imminent advent of the Messiah, it was only natural that they should expect for themselves displays of the divine favor similar to those shown to Moses, Elijah, and Elisha— prophets who had been raised up to save Israel in past crises, none of which could, however, equal in importance the crisis now imminent.   The heroic age was about to

---

[1] Exod., chaps. 8–12; 14:21 ff.; 15:23 ff.; Num. 16:29–35; 17:5 ff.

[2] Num. 11:25.   [5] I Kings 17:1.

[3] I Sam. 10:6 ff.; 19:23 f.   [6] II Kings 2:9–15.

[4] I Kings 13:4 f., 28.   [7] II Kings 13:14–19.

dawn with unparalleled splendor, and the disciples were its forerunners. At first they may have thought the end so near that the work of Elijah, who was to return and prepare Israel for the coming of the great and terrible day of Yahweh had been intrusted to their hands.[1] Elijah had been the greatest of the miracle-working prophets, and the preparatory work preceding the end of the age might well be expected to show these same characteristics.

Thus far we have been dealing mainly with mere possibilities. Paul's letters supply a more certain historical basis. He speaks as though the working of miracles was generally recognized to be a fundamental feature of early Christianity. In his list of significant persons within the church, apostles stand first, prophets second, teachers third; in his list of important activities the gradation arranged in the descending scale runs, miracles (δυνάμεις), gifts of healings, helps, guides, varieties of tongues.[2] The leading personalities in the

[1] Mal. 4:5 f. Just what early Christians actually did with this prophecy is not clear. In some circles John the Baptist's work was, by implication at least, identified with that of the promised Elijah (Matt. 3:4; 17:9-13; Mark 1:6; 9:11-13). Yet opinion was not unanimous. Matt. 11:14 makes the identification subject to one's willingness to believe it. The Gospel of Luke says John came "in the spirit and power of Elijah" (1:17), and this evangelist seems more reluctant than Mark and Matthew to identify John with Elijah. Other tradition affirms, or makes John himself affirm, that he is not Elijah (Acts 13:24 f.; John 1:20; cf. 1:21, 25; 6:14; 7:41 f.). There were two main considerations affecting early Christian interpretation of this subject: (1) fluctuation of opinion regarding the time of Parousia, and so doubt as to when Elijah was to return, and (2) the necessity of meeting problems raised by the presence of John's movement side by side with the Christian movement. But as neither of these problems had become acute in the earliest period, it is doubtful whether the first Christians discussed the question of John's relation to Elijah.

[2] I Cor. 12:28; cf. vss. 8 ff.

community would, of course, display the most important
activities, hence the appropriateness of citing as evidence
of his apostolic authority the "miracles" which were
wrought in connection with his preaching in Corinth.[1]
He often refers to the dynamic display (δύναμις) which
attended his work generally. His gospel came to the
Thessalonians not simply as a spoken message, but as a
convincing miraculous manifestation of pneumatic
activity.[2] The Corinthians had been evangelized in
the same manner,[3] and Paul reminds the Romans that
throughout his entire missionary career Christ wrought
through him for the conversion of the Gentiles, not only
in preaching, but also in signs and wonders performed
by the dynamic of the Holy Spirit.[4]

Did Paul claim this ability for himself alone? Apparently not, for other Christians, in the Pauline
churches at least, had this spiritual power. Among the
diversity of charismata displayed in Corinth some
persons exercised gifts of healings (χαρίσματα ἰαμάτων)
while others worked miracles (δυνάμεις), though these
several gifts were the endowment of the same Spirit
in every instance.[5] Thus the fundamental condition
of wonderful works is spiritual equipment, shared by

[1] II Cor. 12:12: "Truly the signs of an apostle were wrought among
you in all patience by signs [σημείοις] and wonders [τέρασιν] and
miracles [δυνάμεσιν]." The same language is used in Acts 2:22 to
defend the uniqueness of Jesus: ἄνδρα ἀποδεδειγμένον ἀπὸ τοῦ θεοῦ εἰς
ὑμᾶς δυνάμεσι καὶ τέρασι καὶ σημείοις. Also the lawless one to appear
before the end will be similarly equipped by Satan (II Thess. 2:9).

[2] I Thess. 1:5.

[3] I Cor. 2:4 f.   [4] Rom. 15:18 f.; cf. 1:16.

[5] I Cor. 12:9 f., 28. Here Paul seems to be guarding against the
gentile notion of polytheistic spirits.

the community as a whole and expressing itself in miracles where and when God wills. Similarly, when Paul wishes to give the Galatians a sure criterion for deciding the superiority of his gospel over that of the Judaizers he asks only one question: "Was it by works of law or by hearing of faith that you received the Spirit?" And then repeating the question, he sets in the foreground as a recognized item of Christianity's superiority the miraculous activities which spiritual endowment effected: "Does he who supplies you with the Spirit and works miracles among you do so because of your obedience to the law, or because you are obedient to the gospel of faith?"[1] The same display of miracles, so strikingly manifest in Paul's own career as to attest his very apostleship, is also to be found among other believers, owing to the primary fact that the new religion is characterized by a special outpouring of the Spirit.

What was true of the Pauline communities need not necessarily have been true of others. Yet it is equally unsafe to conclude offhand that the Pauline churches were essentially distinctive in these fundamental matters. Paul emphasizes the idea of uniformity among his own churches,[2] and he not infrequently cites the example or

---

[1] Gal. 3:3, 5. It is possible, so far as the mere wording of the passage goes, to affirm that Paul is here referring simply to his own performance of miracles while among the Galatians. But such an interpretation is quite unnatural; it certainly was God, or the exalted Christ, who supplied the Spirit and also made possible the working of miracles, and since the primary endowment is not confined to Paul there is no real reason for restricting the latter to him. In fact, if this restriction were made, his argument would lose its natural force.

[2] Cf. I Cor. 4:17; 7:11; II Cor. 12:13.

authority of his predecessors, thus implying substantial agreement with them.   His reference to the "churches of Judaea" shows that they were not only treated with respect but were regarded as in a measure normative among Gentiles.   This was the source from which all authoritative words of Jesus must have been ultimately derived,[1] and Paul was careful to note that the Palestinian church approved of his work among the Gentiles.[2] The Judaean churches were models for the Thessalonians[3] and if Paul's own authority seemed insufficient to the Corinthians, they were reminded that "the churches of God"—perhaps those of Judaea are especially in mind—had no such custom as the things for which certain disturbers in Corinth were agitating.[4]

It was important that the gentile communities should be conscious of their essential agreement with earlier Christians, for the latter were universally admitted to be the first heirs of the new salvation.   If Paul's churches differed from those founded by other leaders, his converts naturally would be fearful lest they should inherit only an inferior place in the new kingdom.   Doubtless his enemies preyed upon this fear, not only affirming the inferiority of the churches Paul founded, but also reflecting unfavorably upon his apostolic credentials.   Apropos of this crucial question he said to the Corinthians: "Even if I am nothing, as my opponents affirm, yet in no one thing did I fall behind those who are called pre-eminently apostles.   In my work among you the tokens of the apostle were accomplished persistently

---

[1] I Cor. 7:10, 12, 25; 9:14; 11:23; I Thess. 4:15.

[2] Gal. 1:22; 2:1 ff.

[3] I Thess. 2:14.   [4] I Cor. 11:16; cf. 11:2; 14:33.

in signs and wonders and miracles. What then is there in which you were made inferior to the rest of the churches—unless it be the fact that I did not burden you with supporting an apostle?"[1] This reference to the apostle's support, taken in connection with I Cor. 9:5, shows, if this were not already clear, that Paul has in mind the leaders of the original Palestinian community, "the rest of the apostles, the brothers of the Lord and Cephas." Thus miracles seem to have been generally accepted as the supreme test of validity for the pillar apostles and their communities. In this incidental way Paul clearly testified to the working of miracles in the early Christian movement in consequence of the ecstatic life which had been awakened by the Christian's consciousness of special pneumatic endowment.[2]

But Paul does not explicitly define "miracles," nor does he say how these phenomena were effected. His readers were so familiar with these things that explanations were quite unnecessary. At present the actual situation can only be inferred by deduction from certain incidental statements. Paul seems to distinguish between gifts of healings (χαρίσματα ἰαμάτων) and workings of miracles (ἐνεργήματα δυνάμεων), the latter being the greater endowment, and both being ultimately accomplished through the possession of the Spirit whose genuineness is attested by the acknowledgment of Jesus' lordship.[3] It is sometimes said that Paul merely used

[1] II Cor. 12:11-13.

[2] Cf. Gal. 3:3-5. The Judaizers in their stress upon legalism naturally minimized the ecstatic phase of primitive Christianity, emphasizing instead those items in which Christianity was most in conformity with contemporary Judaism.

[3] I Cor. 12:1-10, 28-30.

miracles as a general term of which gifts of healing formed a specific class. While the two things are doubtless closely akin, they certainly are set into two separate categories and are treated as two distinct phases of spiritual activity.[1] Why he should have listed them separately and what real distinction he made between them, he does not explicitly state.

Perhaps it was customary in that age to distinguish between healings and certain other phases of dynamic activity, such as casting out demons. To be sure, all sickness was generally thought to be the work of hostile demonic powers, and any sort of healing was thus a triumph over demons. Yet there was one type of malady, differing from ordinary physical ailments, in which the presence of the demon was more realistically displayed. This was demon possession *par excellence*. In such cases special means were employed to cast out the demon, or to ward off dangers with which demons might threaten an individual. The more ordinary sicknesses were often treated in a quite different way. Thus in Tobit[2] the gall of the fish is preserved to be used in anointing and healing blind eyes, while the heart and liver of the fish are useful for exorcising a demon. Josephus[3] seeks to establish the superiority of Solomon over all the ancients and particularly over the Egyptians by affirming that he provided both (1) incantations for the relief of diseases ($\tau\grave{\alpha}$ $\nu o\sigma\acute{\eta}\mu\alpha\tau\alpha$), and (2) methods of exorcism by which demons can be so thoroughly driven out that they never return. Healings and exorcisms, though both have to do with the evil effects of demons,

---

[1] $\check{\epsilon}\pi\epsilon\iota\tau\alpha$ $\delta\upsilon\nu\acute{\alpha}\mu\epsilon\iota\varsigma$, $\check{\epsilon}\pi\epsilon\iota\tau\alpha$ $\chi\alpha\rho\acute{\iota}\sigma\mu\alpha\tau\alpha$ $\acute{\iota}\alpha\mu\acute{\alpha}\tau\omega\nu$ (I Cor. 12:28).

[2] 6:8; 8:2 f.; 11:1-13.   [3] *Ant.*, VIII, ii, 5.

form two fairly distinct types of activity on the part
of the ancient wonder-worker. A great variety of
means were employed for each, but healings were frequently effected through touching or anointing.[1] Exorcisms, on the other hand, were commonly accomplished
by pronouncing sacred names and formulas of incanta-
tion. Thus the exorciser whom Josephus describes
employed a ring and a root of some plant named by
Solomon, but he completed and confirmed his work by
making "mention of Solomon and reciting the incanta-
tion which he composed." The magical papyri abundantly attest the extensive use of sacred names and
formulas in the practice of exorcism.

This general distinction between exorcisms and healings is reflected in Mark's statement that Jesus, because
of the people's unbelief, was unable to perform any
miracle ($\delta \acute{v} v a \mu \iota v$) in Nazareth except to heal a few sick
people through the laying on of hands.[2] While Jesus
frequently effects cures by means of touch,[3] more striking
wonders result from his spoken word.[4] In every case of
exorcism it is the simple word of Jesus which produces
the miracle. He taught "as one having authority and
not as the scribes" means, for Mark at least, this display of Jesus' superiority over demons—"with authority

---

[1] Weinreich, *Antike Heilungswunder* (Giessen, 1909), has shown how
widely the healing power of the hand was believed in by Greeks and
Romans. Healing by touch is illustrated in the stories of Elijah and
Elisha, is frequent in the account of Jesus' career, and is practiced in
early Christianity. See also Behm, *Die Handauflegung im Urchristentum*, usw. (Leipzig, 1911).

[2] 6:5 f.

[3] E.g., Mark 1:31, 41; 3:9; 5:23, 25, 41; 6:56; 7:32; 8:22.

[4] E.g., Mark 1:25 f.; 2:11; 3:5; 4:39; 5:13; 7:29; 9:25; 10:22;
cf. 6:41, 50; 8:6.

he commandeth even the unclean spirits and they obey him."[1] The contrast which Mark here draws between Jesus and the scribes is essentially the same as that drawn by Paul in Gal. 3:3–5 between his religion and that of the Judaizers. The former represents the new, authoritative, dynamic religion; the latter is a dead traditionalism. The circle of Christians represented by Mark commonly grouped Jesus' wonders into two main classes: those effected by touching and those accomplished by the dynamic of his personality expressing itself in speech. The latter were treated as unquestionably the more distinctive and significant, exorcism being the chief miracle in this group. Hence to accuse Jesus of casting out demons by any other means than by the divine Spirit within him was the one unpardonable sin.[2] Likewise the disciples—and here Mark had better opportunities than he had in the case of Jesus for obtaining first-hand information—performed two sorts of wonders: (1) they cast out demons, and (2) they anointed many with oil and healed them.[3]

Here perhaps is the key to Paul's classification. "Gifts of healings" represent ability to effect cures by

---

[1] Mark 1:22, 27.   [2] Mark 3:29 f.

[3] Mark 6:13; cf. Luke 10:9, 17. Just as Jesus began his career by this twofold demonstration of divine power (1:32 f.) so the disciples follow the same course. Mark seems here to assign this work to the Twelve during Jesus' lifetime, but this is perhaps idealization on the basis of their activities in the early church. Indeed, we find them toward the close of Jesus' career making an unsuccessful attempt to exorcise, the explanation of their failure being insufficient prayer (Mark 9:29). After Jesus' death his followers attained their miracle-working power by the intensity of a meditation which issued in the enthusiasm of their new ecstatic life interpreted in terms of special spiritual endowment. Thus they became equipped for healing the sick and· working

means of anointing, and the like;[1] while "miracles" are a more distinctive display of the new spiritual power with which Christians had been especially endowed. Could these latter have been, as in Mark, a display of exorcising ability? Interpreters sometimes remark that no one has yet been able to convict the apostle Paul of practicing exorcism. Are we fair to him, however, when we say "convict"? Would it not be truer to say "credit"? Certainly in his thought-world the stage is fully set for such a performance. The present evil age is dominated by Satan and his hosts.[2] He is the perpetual enemy of Christians and constantly schemes in conjunction with the demonic powers subject to him to lead astray, afflict, and destroy believers.[3] Demons are behind all idol-worship, and while the idol itself is nothing, the demon is a dreadful power whose harmful influence is to be strenuously avoided.[4] The ills of

miracles. Mark is likely to have been fairly familiar with this situation, and to have viewed the earlier history in its light. In fact, his portrayal of Jesus' miraculous career is suspiciously like that of the ideal Christian in this respect—he is first filled with the Holy Spirit, under its guidance he next encounters the prince of evil spirits, and his life henceforth is pre-eminently that of the ideal pneumatic individual who no longer fears Satan and his emissaries.

[1] Cf. Jas. 5:14–18.

[2] Gal. 1:4; I Cor. 2:6, 8; II Cor. 4:4; 6:15. For Paul's peculiar world-view, according to which the present age is ruled by demonic powers, while good powers, especially in the person of the risen Jesus and his spiritually endowed followers in whom he is realistically present, are already pitted against the evil one and his agents, see Everling, *Die paulinische Angelologie und Dämonologie* (Göttingen, 1888); Dibelius, *Die Geisterwelt im Glauben des Paulus* (Göttingen, 1909); Gunkel, *Die Wirkungen des heiligen Geistes*, pp. 57 ff.

[3] I Cor. 7:5; II Cor. 2:11; 11:14; 12:7; I Thess. 2:18; 3:5.

[4] I Cor. 10:19 ff.; cf. 6:15 ff.

life are due to Satan's activity. Paul's bodily affliction
is a messenger of Satan, which the Lord has failed to
remove in spite of Paul's efforts to have the troubler
driven away.[1] Obstreperous members of the community, when turned over to Satan, become subject to
his afflictions in this life and so suffer sufficient punishment to permit the bestowal of salvation upon them
in the next.[2] Sickness and death are the extreme forms
of punishment in this life[3] and they will hold sway until
the final triumph of Christ when the complete power
of Satan, as expressed even in death itself, shall have
been utterly abolished.[4]

Over against the powers of evil which rule the present
age stand the Lord Jesus Christ and his Spirit-filled
followers who owe their sole allegiance immediately to
Christ, though ultimately to God.[5] With the exaltation of Jesus, the outpouring of the Holy Spirit, and
the establishment of the Christian community, the dominion of Satan has received its death sentence. The
crucifixion may have seemed a temporary triumph for
the forces of evil, but in reality it was only the beginning
of the final conflict which is to result in their complete

[1] II Cor. 12:7 ff.   [2] I Cor. 5:5.

[3] I Cor. 11:29–32.

[4] I Cor. 15:25 f. Paul seems to have started out with the belief
that the Christian who had received the divine Spirit could not be
harmed by Satanic powers of sickness and death, and so would live until
the Parousia. If he failed to do so it was because he had been disobedient to God, who gave him over to the power of Satan for punishment (cf. I Cor. 5:5; 11:29 ff.; I Thess. 5:23). But as the Parousia
was delayed, death, though it still may have been due to demonic
activity, came to be regarded as the one way of immediate deliverance
from the present evil age (Phil. 1:23 f.).

[5] I Cor. 8:4 ff.

overthrow.[1] The Christians have anticipated the privileges of the new age; in fact, they already stand safely within the new kingdom.[2] Not only are they superior to all the powers of evil, but ultimately they are to preside in judgment over angels.[3] The surety of all this lies in the fact that they are equipped with the Spirit.[4] The yoke of Satan has been forever cast off, so far as the new spiritual community is concerned. Thus Christians represent the light of the new age already breaking into the darkness of the evil age; as Christmen they stand over against Satan and his demonic representatives.[5]

What then is the normal attitude of Christians toward the powers of evil? It must be one of unremitting hostility as well as one of triumphant activity. For Paul who thus believed realistically in the activity of demons on the one hand, and in the truly supernatural character of the Christian's spiritual equipment on the other, the practice of exorcism would be a perfectly normal procedure. And, indeed, the particular method employed by Paul is not only easily surmised but is quite clearly indicated in certain passages of his letters where he refers to the dynamic significance of "the Name." Christians are those who call upon the name of our Lord Jesus Christ.[6] Since God has temporarily committed all authority unto the risen Jesus he is now Lord of all. Those who believingly accept the Christian preaching regarding the exalted Jesus are saved

[1] I Cor. 1:28; 2:6, 8; 15:24–27; II Thess. 2:8 ff.

[2] Rom. 8:38 f.; Gal. 1:4; I Cor. 3:21 ff.

[3] I Cor. 6:3.   [5] I Cor. 3:16; 6:15 ff.; 10:21.

[4] Rom. 8:14–17.   [6] I Cor. 1:2.

through calling upon his name.[1]   The excommunica-
tion of disobedient members of the community also
takes place in the name, and so through the power of the
Lord Jesus.[2]   This absolute power of the name has been
granted to Jesus as a reward for his voluntary submission to God.   Wherefore God exalted him to the position of lordship in order that in the name of JESUS—
not "Lord"—all heavenly, earthly, and catachthonic
beings, whether angels, men, or demons, should become
subject to his authority.   This display of the dynamic
quality of the name of Jesus becomes in turn a complete
demonstration of the Christian contention that Jesus
had been exalted to a position of lordship second only
to that of God, the Father.[3]

That the name of Jesus was used in exorcism, as well
as for other dynamic purposes by Paul and his associates,
is a most probable inference from the above data.   Nor
is this likely to have been a novel procedure with Paul.
The notion that special virtue attached to the name of
a revered person was prevalent in the world of that day,

[1] Rom. 10:9-14.

[2] I Cor. 5:3 f.; cf. II Thess. 3:6.

[3] Phil. 2:5-11.   The name is Jesus, the title is Lord.   It may be
somewhat difficult for moderns to maintain this distinction since Lord
is so often used by us as a proper name for God.   The Septuagint did,
to be sure, use Κύριος to render the proper name יהוה, but for Greek
readers the mere name Lord cannot of itself have seemed uniquely
significant.   The term was too common a one, being applied to various
personages to denote different degrees of authority from that of the
owner of a small bit of property to that of the emperor, or of God as
ruler of the universe.   In contrast with all other lords, excepting God
alone, Jesus Christ is the individual who holds the position of unique
authority over the Christian community, and who is ultimately destined
to abolish all other authorities except that of the one true God (I Cor.
8:5 f.; 15:25-28).   See above, pp. 115 ff.

even among the Jews,[1] and it is so pervasive in New Testament Christianity that one cannot consistently make Paul alone responsible for its genesis. In fact, the use of Jesus' name in exorcism, even outside the circle of leading Christians, was gaining ground already in New Testament times, although some persons held that this was the sole prerogative of the apostolic community.[2]

It is probable, therefore, that Christians before Paul's day did assume the rôle of miracle-worker, and that they performed wonders through the power of Jesus' name. Hence the representation of Acts to the effect that this phase of Christian activity aroused at the outset sharp Jewish hostility is probably in the main true to fact. Orthodox Judaism, in Palestine at least, was sensitive upon the subject of such practices, since they so readily led to the introduction of foreign deities' names. For some time the Jewish populace had probably been favorably disposed toward this innovation, otherwise the law would not have pronounced so emphatically against it.[3]

[1] See Heitmüller, *Im Namen Jesu* (Göttingen, 1903), pp. 132 ff.: "Nach all diesem kann es keinem Zweifel unterliegen, dass der, oben namentlich mit Zügen aus der rabbinischen Litteratur gezeichnete, Glaube an den göttlichen Namen und seine Wirkungen zur Zeit des Neuen Testaments im Judentum zum mindesten längst vorhanden und wirksam war" (p. 153).

[2] Mark 9:38 (was this foreign exorcist Paul?); Matt. 7:22. Even Jewish exorcists sought to avail themselves of this new name (Acts 19:13; Tosephta, *Hullin*, II:21-23).

[3] Deut. 18:9-22; cf. Ezek. 20:26-28, 31, 39. Similarly Philo: "Moses, knowing that the act of divination co-operates in no slight degree with the errors of the lives of the multitude so as to lead them out of the right way, did not suffer his disciples to use any species of it whatever, but drove all who paid it any observance far from his everlasting constitution" (*De spec. leg.*, i=*on Monarchy*, i, 9).

This prohibition did not mean that the Jews' own sacred names might not be so employed if the pressure of circumstances required this,[1] or that their exorcists and healers did not, on occasion, smuggle in foreign names. But Christians were openly acknowledging the power of Jesus' name, which to every Jew must have seemed a direct violation of the Deuteronomic law. Christians, indeed, readily defended their position by reminding their persecutors that Moses in this very same connection had promised that God would raise up from among the Jews a prophet unto whom they were to give heed, and now this prediction had been fulfilled in the person of Jesus.[2] But outside the Christian circle the Jews did not so interpret Moses, and they instituted a vigorous persecution against those who did.

The crime of the Christians lay not simply in breaking a commandment of the law. This new faith in Jesus' name rested upon a belief in his resurrection and exaltation to heavenly dignity which placed him on the plane of divinity, and so must have seemed to unbelievers to be a violation of monotheism. This was the fundamental reason why Christianity had been offensive to Paul, if we may trust, in the absence of more explicit testimony, the psychology of his experience as revealed in his own statements about his conversion, and the cardinal items of the new faith which he was thus led to accept. Its cornerstone was confession of Jesus' lordship based upon a belief in his resurrection, the latter

[1] Matt. 12:27. Yet the evidence that such practices had become current in Palestine in Jesus' day is exceedingly meager, whatever the situation may have been among the Jews of the dispersion.

[2] Deut. 18:15; Acts 3:22–26; 4:8–12.

being guaranteed through actual visions of the Risen One vouchsafed to certain persons prominent in the leadership of the new movement.[1] Since these things are now made central and fundamental, they doubtless were the features which incensed him most as a persecutor. He has now cast in his lot with those who call upon the Name, who regulate their lives by his power, and who believe in the triumphant lordship of Jesus soon to be revealed in glory.

When, finally, Acts represents Jews and Christians in conflict regarding the proper interpretation of Jewish tradition, the situation depicted probably does not belong to the very earliest times. Even Hellenistic Jews who adopted Christianity—for example, Paul—did not lose their respect for the temple or for Moses.[2] They were ultimately compelled, because of the inevitable breach with the Jews, to interpret anew their relationship to these institutions. But this break was not at the outset occasioned by dissatisfaction either with their ancestral religion or with their Jewish kinsmen's attitude toward the past—except as that attitude bore upon the question of belief in Jesus' messiahship. Here, as at other points, the primary cause of hostility is the Christian claim that Jesus has been raised to the divine sphere and so is worthy of reverence. Though the Book of Acts gives a long speech of Stephen arraigning the Jews for disloyalty to their religious inheritance, the context in which the speech is set—and perhaps this context was supplied by the author's source material—shows that it was against the pneumatically endowed Stephen,

[1] Cf. Gal. 1:1; Rom. 1:4; 10:8 f.; I Cor. 15:5-11.
[2] See above, pp. 118 ff.

declaring his faith in the Lord Jesus standing on the right hand of God, that the outburst of Jewish hatred was directed. In acknowledging Jesus' lordship Stephen had committed the heinous sin of blasphemy, for which stoning was an appointed means of punishment.[1]

Thus it appears that the chief incentive for vigorous Jewish hostility toward the first Christians lay in the Christians' attitude toward the risen Jesus, whom they now assigned a unique position in the world of angelic beings. And this was no mere doctrinaire matter either in the Christians' own experience, or in their relation to others. They believed Jesus occupied this new position because he had actually manifested himself in visible form to certain members of their community. Various ecstatic experiences, interpreted in terms of new spiritual endowment, were taken to indicate that a new order of things was impending if not indeed actually present. The name of the heavenly Jesus proved dynamically effective against sickness and demon-possession, thus adding strength to the conviction that Jesus now occupied a position of lordship in the angelic realm. Conviction necessarily found expression in propaganda, which gradually attracted more and more attention. At first the Jews seemed to have been rather indifferent toward these new enthusiasts. Perhaps the police authorities were the first to take action against them on the ground that they were endangering the

[1] Lev. 24:11–16. It seemed probable to the Gospel writers as they surmised what happened in the council chamber of the high priest, interpreting it in the light of their own subsequent experience, that Jesus himself had been condemned on the charge of blasphemy when he was finally induced to acknowledge his own claim to divine honors (Matt. 26:65 f.; Mark 14:63 f.; Luke 22:69).

peace.[1]   Religious opposition was also aroused by a suspicion of magical practices.   But hostility did not burst into full flame until Jews became generally aware that Christians were virtually rendering the risen Jesus divine honors, which ought, they said, to be accorded to God alone.   This was the situation which called out the activities of the arch-persecutor Saul of Tarsus who, in his zeal for the traditions of the fathers, determined to demolish the new heresy.

Christians bore persecution with great fortitude. They were not inspired by hostility toward, but by the fullest sense of community with, their Jewish kinsmen. At first they regarded it as their mission to preach to Israel alone, for Israel's interests were their only concern. They did not wish to be disinherited by their Jewish brethren nor did they for a long time cease to hope that their missionary efforts would one day prove successful. Even Paul, who had turned from Judaism to become a vigorous champion of the new movement, and who had consequently suffered great afflictions at the hands of the Jews, after years of rejection cried in anguish of heart, "I could wish that I myself were anathema from Christ, for my brethren's sake, my kinsmen according to the flesh, who are Israelites, whose is the adoption, and the glory, and the covenants, and the giving of the law, and the service of God, and the promises, whose

[1] Acts says the Sadducees were the first to arrest the Christian preachers.   The author of Acts improbably conjectures that this was because of doctrinal objections.   A messianic agitation based upon faith in Jesus' resurrection might well have aroused suspicion because of political danger, and the Sadducees who were interested in preserving order would desire to disperse any crowds that might grow sufficiently enthusiastic to create a riot.

are the fathers, and of whom is Christ as concerning
the flesh, who is over all, God blessed forever."[1]   All
Christians of Jewish descent—and at first they constituted the entire membership of the community—must
have felt that their religious inheritance was thoroughly
Jewish, that their hopes for the future rested solely
upon the fulfilment of God's promises to Israel, and that
their heavenly Messiah was the realization of a purely
Jewish hope.   Religious differences between them and
their opponents, in time greatly magnified by the heat
of controversy, cannot in reality have been regarded as
serious, so far as the great historical religious heritage
of Israel was concerned.   It would be quite unfair to
the psychology of the first Christians to affirm that
they were ever conscious of standing outside the limits
of the true Jewish faith.   In so far as appeal was
made to Gentiles it merely aimed, as in Paul's case,
to accomplish the salvation of Gentiles along with that
of Jews.

Yet Jews persistently rejected the new propaganda,
primarily because it ascribed to Jesus a dignity which in
their eyes he did not deserve.   Although this was an
impassable barrier, Christians for a long time continued
to press their cause upon Jewish hearers, and thus there
developed, as the breach widened and the Christian
movement became more strongly differentiated, the
strong anti-Jewish polemic so largely reflected in varying
stages of progress in our New Testament books.   In
the meantime many advocates of the new movement
were adapting themselves to, and drawing fresh strength
from, a new set of religious surroundings.   Otherwise

[1] Rom. 9:3–5.

their cause must soon have perished from sheer lack of adherents. Since this new environment was gentile, the further growth of the new movement must be followed in connection with contemporary religious life outside Palestine.

CHAPTER VI

THE EARLY CHRISTIANS' CONTACT WITH GENTILE RELIGIONS

When the early Christians were forced out of Judaism because of the ecstatic life which their faith in the risen Jesus produced, that fact alone would not have made it absolutely necessary for the new movement to become a gentile propaganda. It might conceivably have continued to exist in some remote place as an obscure, unorthodox Jewish sect. How did it happen that the new religion, instead of becoming thus exclusive, moved in the opposite direction even to the extent of ultimately including the entire gentile world within its horizon?

This result was not attained immediately, nor was the thought of gentile missions shared alike by all Christians. There were differences of opinion, not only regarding the method of evangelization, but also regarding the very advisability of the undertaking. Representatives of different views were so sincere in their respective convictions that each party believed itself to be in full agreement with Jesus' teaching. On the one hand, he was reported to have said that he was not sent except to the lost sheep of the house of Israel, that it was not meet to take the children's bread and cast it to the dogs, that holy things ought not to be given to the dogs nor pearls cast before swine, and that the Twelve should go neither to Gentiles nor to Samaritans, for there would not be time to complete the evangelization of Israel before the end of the world would come.[1]

In other passages the outlook is much wider. The disciples are told that they must pass through many trials in order to bear testimony unto the Gentiles; Jesus admires the faith of the heathen in contrast with the Jew's lack of faith; the end of the world is to be delayed until the Gentiles are evangelized; the natural descendants of Abraham, Isaac, and Jacob are to be rejected from the kingdom and their place is to be taken by those who come from "the east and the west"; and the disciples are finally commissioned to make disciples of all the nations. Beginning with Jerusalem they are to extend their activities through Judaea, Samaria, and unto the uttermost parts of the earth.[2] This variety of conception shows the process of development through which the early Christians passed. Whatever Jesus' own attitude may have been,[3] he certainly impressed no definite program upon the disciples, or if he did, they failed to comprehend his meaning. They worked out the problem in reaction upon their own situation and in accordance with a variety of opinions among themselves. Therefore it is not surprising that the language of Jesus should have been refracted by the atmosphere of controversy through which it passed in the Apostolic age.

But by the close of the New Testament period the notion of gentile missions had come to occupy a prominent place in the Christians' program. In fact, their program

[1] See Matt. 7:6; 10:5 f., 23; 15:24, 26; 19:28.

[2] See Matt. 8:11 f.; 10:22; 13:37–43, 47–50; 21:33–44; 22:1–14; 24:14, 34, 45 ff.; 26:13; 28:19; Acts 1:8; cf. 10:47; 11:17.

[3] Cf. Spitta, *Jesus und die Heidenmission* (Giessen, 1909).

had, to their minds, been carried well along toward completion. Mark affirmed that the gospel must be preached to the Gentiles before the end would come, yet he thought the end would come while members of Jesus' own generation were still alive.[1] Paul, who strove so hard to fulfil these preliminary conditions, believed that he had already accomplished this task "from Jerusalem and round about even unto Illyricum." Others had preached in Italy, while perhaps still others had worked in Africa, so Paul was anxious to push on to Spain in order to bring the work of world-evangelization to completion.[2] The Book of Acts is a history of missions, tracing the spread of the gospel, chiefly as preached by Paul, from Jerusalem to Rome. The remaining New Testament books, if not witnessing to immediate missionary enterprises, at least show Christianity in possession of various fields throughout the Roman empire.

Numerous forces were at work to bring about this result. In the first place the Christians had been missionaries from the start, their mission being the conversion of Israel to belief in Jesus' messiahship. The kingdom was imminent, and they were the heralds of its coming. But the advent of the Messiah awaited certain preliminary conditions, chief among which was the work of gathering members for the new kingdom. This task was in their hands, and a consciousness of the obligations resting upon them spurred them on to zealous missionary activity. In this way they hoped not only to hasten the coming of the new age, but to receive at last the "well done, good and faithful servant, enter

[1] 9:1; 13:10, 26 f.   [2] Rom. 15:18-28.

thou into the joy of thy Lord."[1]   They acted upon two fundamental convictions.   First, salvation could not be fully attained until the present evil age had been brought to an end, and secondly, no one would participate in the blessings of the messianic age who had not previously acknowledged belief in Jesus' resurrection and exaltation to lordship in heaven whence he had already come in the Spirit—or had made the Spirit's coming possible—but would come in messianic glory at the end of the age.   Under these circumstances the supreme duty of Christians was speedily to assemble the largest possible number of members for the coming kingdom.

Probably at the outset no one supposed it would ever be necessary to go outside of Israel in order to procure these citizens.   But the Jews failed to respond as generally as the Christian missionaries had hoped they would, and the kingdom's coming was delayed.   At this point the Christians were confronted by some of the most difficult problems they had to face during the first half-century in the history of the new movement.   What would be the consequences if they were not successful in converting the Jews?   This question has lost its difficulty for us since we can answer it in the light of history, but the early Christians had no such easy solution at hand.   Their hopes were from the foundation up constructed of strictly Jewish materials, and if the Jews now failed to unite in finishing the structure could the work really come to completion?   Some Christians hoped it could, even with a scanty following which they

[1] Matt. 25:21; cf. I Thess. 2:19 f.; I Cor. 9:23–27; 15:31; II Cor. 2:14 ff.; 4:14–17; Rom. 8:17; Phil. 2:6.

had gathered from among the Jews—those who were to be saved were after all only a few. Others conceived the notion of bringing in help from without; they would go out into the byways and hedges to gather guests for the messianic banquet. But this consciousness of a gentile mission was arrived at only gradually and not without many misgivings. Even Paul, who labored so strenuously in gentile fields, still looked for the climax of missionary activity to be reached through the conversion of the Jews.[1]

To be sure, Christians had good Jewish precedent for seeking converts from among the Gentiles. The missionary idea had come to expression among the Jews in the latter part of the Old Testament period, and it continued to gain strength with the growing importance of Judaism in the Diaspora.[2] But this implied no notion of breaking with Judaism, for missions to the Gentiles aimed simply at the conversion of foreigners to the Jewish faith. Experience among foreign peoples often did have a liberalizing effect upon the missionary, but he never thought of abandoning the religion of his fathers in order to establish a new religion on gentile soil.

At first Christians also assumed the same attitude, only their conception of what constituted true Judaism was phrased in the language of messianic faith. Thus Paul, epitomizing the results of his work in Thessalonica, says, "Ye turned unto God from idols to serve the living and the true God and to wait for his Son from heaven

[1] Rom. 11:25–32.

[2] See Schürer, *Geschichte*, usw., III, 150–88; Bousset, *Religion des Judentums*, pp. 60–99; Bertholet, *Die jüdische Religion*, pp. 149 ff.; Staerk, *Neutestamentliche Zeitgeschichte*, II, 41–53.

whom he raised from the dead, even Jesus, who deliver-
eth us from the wrath to come."[1] These converts had
simply adopted Jewish messianism as recast by Christians who, on the basis of their belief in Jesus' resurrection, identified him with the coming Messiah. The
Corinthians likewise were a messianic community
"waiting for the revelation of our Lord Jesus Christ,"
whose resurrection established the validity of the new
religion.[2] Similarly the "righteousness which is of
faith" is defined for the Romans in terms of the confession of Jesus' lordship, which proceeds from belief in
his resurrection.[3] Thus the Christian missionaries were
preaching the new "true" Judaism in gentile lands—
the one God, his appointed Messiah, the imminent kingdom, and the consummation of salvation at the end of
the age.

The very fact that Christianity was, at first, a spontaneous, ecstatic movement greatly facilitated the
gentile mission. If it had begun as a well-defined system of doctrine and ritual, numerous questions of detail
would have offered initial difficulties which might have
greatly hampered the activities of the new enthusiasts.
As it was, they acted first and reflected afterward.
Consequently some of their most troublesome problems
did not become acute until the new enterprise was strong
enough to survive the turmoils of controversy. It is
true that the writer of Acts seems to suppose the exercise
of a careful official supervision from the start, but the
data of Paul's letters do not bear out this hypothesis.
For some time he and Barnabas, and doubtless still

[1] I Thess. 1:9 f.
[2] I Cor. 1:7; 15:14 ff.   [3] Rom. 10:9.

other workers, had been gathering gentile converts who were "waiting for the revelation of the Lord Jesus," before any academic discussions arose regarding the methods to be employed in the mission, or the relation between Jewish and gentile converts within the same community. The Council at Jerusalem was a result and not a precursor of the Gentiles' evangelization.

When the question of the Gentiles' freedom did come up for debate Paul evolved a dialectical defense of his conduct in the form of the doctrine of justification by faith. The fact that some of his longest extant letters were written largely to defend himself and his work against opponents tends to overemphasize the dialectical side of Paul's activity. Nevertheless, it is perfectly clear that his primary concern had been to preach the risen Son of God, who was revealed to him at conversion. This, he says, was the way in which both he and Peter had been "energized" for their respective, but fundamentally common, tasks.[1] In the early days when the coming of the kingdom was felt to be near at hand, the important matter was to believe in the risen Jesus and await his Parousia. Other things—family relationships, slavery, politics, Jewish ritual, and the like—were of secondary moment on account of the "shortness of the time."[2] It greatly grieved Paul to find that some Christians were dwelling upon these minor items instead of stressing faith in Jesus Christ and cultivating the Spirit-filled life which this faith made possible. The possession of the Spirit was the practical criterion of Christianity's validity,[3] a vision of the risen Jesus was

[1] Gal. 1:16; 2:8.

[2] I Cor. 7:8–31; Gal. 5:6; 6:15.   [3] Gal. 3:3–5.

the essential thing in an apostle's equipment,[1] and to assemble a company of expectant, Spirit-filled persons, who awaited Jesus' coming in messianic glory, was the primary task of both the Jewish and the gentile missionary.

Although the Christian mission had the advantage of being a spontaneous movement, it also profited much from its Jewish connections. Notwithstanding the contempt which Greek and Latin writers often express for Jews,[2] the Jewish religion did appeal strongly to many Gentiles, even among the more cultured classes. Strabo is not alone in his admiration for Moses, though it is perfectly clear that this ancient geographer had no thorough acquaintance with the history or the literature of the Hebrews.[3] Admiration for Moses did not, however, necessarily include admiration for the Jews. This is commonly recognized in the case of the Christians, but the same thing seems to have been to some extent true of the attitude which others took toward the Jews and their religion. Moses lived far enough in the past to be idealized, hence the more attractive elements in this ancient faith could be associated with his name, while less acceptable features were regarded as later perversions for which the more ordinary Jew was made responsible. Thus Strabo calls Moses and his companions right-minded persons who established no ordinary kind of government, and whose successors followed in his footsteps for some time "worshiping God with sincerity,"

[1] Gal. 1:1, 16; I Cor. 9:1; 15:8.

[2] See T. Reinach, *Textes d'auteurs grecs et romains relatifs au Judaïsme* (Paris, 1895); Schürer, *Geschichte*, usw., III, 529–45; Stähelin, *Der Antisemitismus des Altertums* (Basel, 1905).

[3] Strabo, xvi. 2. 35–39.

but later there arose a period of "superstition" when Jewish ritualistic practices were introduced. Thus were the mighty fallen; "their beginning was good but they degenerated."

This was essentially the attitude of many Gentiles who knew Jewish religion much more intimately than Strabo did. Long before Christianity arose the Jews had translated their Scriptures into Greek, had established synagogues in their various communities scattered about the Mediterranean, and were seeking to commend their religion to the Gentiles. Their efforts were attended by a measure of success. They not only won proselytes but attracted others who admired their religion, even though unwilling to become identified with the Jewish nation. The New Testament speaks of the "God-fearers" as a distinct class who were thus attracted to Judaism.[1] They attended the synagogue service, admired the Jewish Scriptures for their antiquity, their ethical ideals, and their monotheistic faith, but hesitated at adopting the Jewish ritual and casting in their lot with the Jewish race. To admire the ancient religious heritage of the Jews was one thing, but to

---

[1] They are designated φοβούμενοι τὸν θεόν (Acts 10:2, 22, 35; 13:16, 26), σεβόμενοι τὸν θεόν (Acts 16:14; 18:7; cf. 13:43, 50; 17:4, 17; Josephus, *Ant.*, XIV, vii, 2). Their exact standing in Judaism is a matter of dispute. It has been affirmed that they were the talmudic "proselytes of the gate," a view which Schürer formerly held, but later abandoned completely in favor of the opinion that they were in no sense reckoned among proselytes. See Schürer, *Geschichte*, usw., III, 172 ff.; Porter, "Proselyte" in Hastings' *Dictionary of the Bible*, IV (New York, 1903); Lake, *The Earlier Epistles of St. Paul* (London, 1911), pp. 37 ff. It is certain that these persons were, for the New Testament writers, not full-fledged Jews, but Gentiles who sympathized with the Jewish religion.

become a full-fledged member of the Jewish community was quite another. Many Gentiles refused to take this latter step, although they were sympathetic toward the Jews' religion.

The Christians offered these "God-fearers" an easy solution for their problem. If they would join the Christian movement they might not only share the full blessings of the ancient religion without the hindrances involved in attaching themselves strictly to the Jewish community, but they would also participate in new blessings which Judaism was utterly incapable of conferring. Since many of the earlier Christians were themselves Jews, they began their preaching in connection with the synagogue where they sometimes won converts directly from Judaism, but their greatest success seems to have been among the "God-fearers." The crop for which the soil had been prepared and planted by the Jews was harvested by the Christian missionaries, consequently it is not surprising that Jewish hostility toward Christians should have been quite as bitter in gentile lands as in Palestine.

In preaching directly to Gentiles, Christians also availed themselves of much preliminary work already accomplished by Jewish apologists.[1] This feature of the Christian propaganda is more pronounced in the second and third centuries, yet in the New Testament period Christian preachers certainly employed current Jewish methods of approaching Gentiles. In the first

---

[1] See Geffcken, *Zwei griechische Apologeten* (Leipzig, 1907); M. Friedländer, *Geschichte der jüdischen Apologetik als Vorgeschichte des Christentums* (Zürich, 1906); Krüger, *Philo und Josephus als Apologeten des Judentums* (Leipzig, 1906); Schürer, *Geschichte*, usw., III, 545–53.

place, they used the Jewish Scriptures in the Greek translation which had been made, not only for the convenience of Greek-speaking Jews, but probably also with some intention of commending their religion to outsiders.[1]   These ancient writings could not be used without interpretation, but here again the Jews had set an example which Christians followed and extended.[2] The criticisms which Jewish preachers leveled against idolatry were also taken over by Christian missionaries.[3] On the whole the new religion even in gentile lands had much in common with Judaism and profited greatly by the preliminary evangelistic work which had been carried on by the Jews.

Yet Christians were compelled to establish an independent movement because of the central position which the risen Jesus occupied in their preaching.   While some converts were won from among the Jews, others from among proselytes to Judaism, and others from the God-fearers, the real success of the new religion depended upon the ability of its advocates to draw followers directly from the gentile world.   Though we now have no means of determining the exact numbers, these apparently constituted the majority of the membership in most of

[1] Doubtless many Jewish scholars had come to feel it their duty to write in Greek in order "to profit them which are without" (Prologue to Eccles.).   See Bertholet, *Die jüdische Religion*, pp. 478 ff.

[2] See Case, "The Scribes' Interpretation of the Old Testament" and "The New Testament Writers' Interpretation of the Old Testament," *Biblical World*, XXXVIII (1911), 28–40 and 92–102.

[3] See Wernle, "Altchristliche Apologetik im Neuen Testament," *Zeitschrift für die neutestamentliche Wissenschaft*, I (1900), 42–65; E. F. Scott, *The Apologetic of the New Testament* (New York, 1907), pp. 110–45; J. Weiss, *Das Urchristentum*, I, 162 ff.

the churches outside of Palestine in New Testament times. The Galatian converts are clearly Gentiles for whose "liberty in Christ" Paul is contending;[1] the Thessalonian converts had previously been idol-worshipers;[2] it was not easy to persuade the Corinthians to sever their former connections with idolatry or to abandon the heathen vices in which "some" of them had been steeped;[3] Paul evidently thought there was a large gentile constituency among the Christians at Rome;[4] the Ephesians had formerly been "Gentiles in the flesh;"[5] and the Pastorals are interested in training teachers for the Gentiles.[6] Other parts of the New Testament also have a prevailing gentile outlook. The Gospel of Mark shows many signs of having been intended for this class of readers.[7] Although there is a strong Jewish interest in Matthew,[8] yet the rejection of Jews and the reception of Gentiles into the kingdom is a favorite theme with this author.[9] The writings of Luke, though less

---

[1] Gal. 1:16; 2:2 ff.; 3:8 ff.

[2] I Thess. 1:9; cf. 2:16; 4:3–7.

[3] I Cor. 8:1 ff.; 6:9–11; 10:14 ff.; 12:2.

[4] Cf. Rom. 1:13–16; 2:8–16; 3:9, 29 f.; 9:22–31; 11:11 ff.; 15:7–13.

[5] Eph. 2:11; 3:1, 6, 8; 4:17; cf. Col. 1:27.

[6] I Tim. 2:7; 3:16; II Tim. 1:11; 4:17.

[7] E.g., 3:17; 5:41; 7:2–4, 11, 19, 34; 10:46; 12:18, 42; 13:3; 14:2, 32; 15:34, 42, where an explanation is given of some Jewish word, custom, or situation for the benefit of gentile readers.

[8] This is shown in the stress placed upon the fulfilment of Old Testament prophecy (1:22; 2:15, 17, 23; 4:14; 8:17; 12:17; 13:14, 35; 21:4; 27:9), in the representation that Jesus worked particularly for the benefit of the Jews (10:5 f., 23; 15:24; 19:28), and in the definition of Christianity as a completion of the ancient religion (5:17–20; 23:3*a*, 23*b*; 24:20).

[9] See above, p. 167, n. 2.

bitter toward Jews, clearly regard Christianity's mission to be world-wide.[1]   In the Fourth Gospel the transition from Jews to Greeks already takes place during Jesus' lifetime.[2]

In appealing directly to Gentiles, Christians were brought into immediate contact with other religions beside Judaism.   At first the dominant environmental influence affecting them had been solely Jewish.   But when the missionary enterprise came to be directed chiefly toward Gentiles the varied religious phenomena of this new world brought new factors into their lives. A convert from the circle of "God-fearers," or even from among Jewish proselytes, might bring into Christianity some religious heritage from his earlier training in a gentile faith.   But when converts were made directly from a Greek audience, and when the membership of the Christian community received larger and larger accretions from this source, contact with gentile religions became a very significant fact for the history of the new propaganda.   While this transition was made gradually, in the case of some Christians it occurred at a relatively early date.   Almost from the beginning of his Christian career Paul worked in gentile surroundings, and presumably several of his contemporaries shared a similar experience.   Certainly by the middle of the first century Christianity had become very generally a gentile missionary enterprise, and consequently the fresh environmental influences which contributed to the growing life of the new movement have to be sought in the religious atmosphere of the gentile world.

[1] Cf. Luke 2:31 f.; 3:6; 4:24–27; 24:47; Acts 1:8, etc.
[2] Cf. John 12:20, 32.

To what extent did these new surroundings affect the life and thinking of Christians in New Testament times? On this question there have been, and still are, various shades of opinion. One might at first sight question whether it was at all possible for the early missionaries in view of their belief in Christianity's superiority to admit into the new religion any influences from the surrounding gentile world. Undoubtedly they felt themselves to be the advocates of the only true religion, particularly when opposed by Jews and Gentiles. Notwithstanding Paul's very substantial Jewish heritage and his continued reverence for the religion of his fathers, when opposed by Jews he sharply criticized them for their rejection of Jesus and pronounced doom upon so much of their religious activity as did not allow itself to pass over into Christianity.[1] Similarly Paul's formal criticism of the gentile religion was thoroughly condemnatory, in spite of his disposition at other times to give Gentiles favorable consideration.[2] In his more antagonistic moods, the wisdom of the Greeks was set aside as utterly worthless and doomed to destruction; while the popular religion of the gentile world was condemned for its immorality, its senseless idolatry, and its demoniacal character.[3] Other Christians may not have held views identical in all respects with Paul's yet in the main his opinions probably are fairly representative, particularly in the estimate of paganism made by

[1] I Thess. 2:15 f.; Gal. 3:19–29; Rom. 3:9–20; 9:31 ff.

[2] E.g., Rom. 2:14 f.; 3:29 f.

[3] See Rom. 1:18–32; I Cor. 1:18–25; 2:8; 6:9; 8:4; 10:20; 12:2; II Cor. 4:3 f.; Gal. 1:4; 4:8 ff.; I Thess. 4:5; II Thess. 1:7; Eph. 2: 2 f., 12; 4:17 f.; 5:8, 16; 6:12; Col. 1:21; 2:13, 18.

Christians who had previously been trained in Judaism. Those who had received their early training in some gentile religion were perhaps in the formal sense just as antagonistic to it as Paul was to his ancestral faith, though in reality the gentile convert would owe, as Paul did, a very substantial debt to the religion of his fathers.

Sweeping condemnations were to be expected under the circumstances, for formal criticism must in the nature of the case be wholesale. No competing religious movement could, as such, be allowed favorable comparison with Christianity. Since all other religions are held to be erroneous in principle and inferior in practice, the Christian critic does not stop to note items of value amid masses of alleged error. But it would hardly be safe to conclude from this doctrinaire attitude of the critic that valuable elements were not recognized on occasion, or that many such values were not actually absorbed by Christianity. Rarely does a victor fail to profit from contact with, and conquest over, a competitor, even though the latter's possessions are, in the heat of conflict, pronounced quite worthless. We know, for example, that Paul's formal criticism of the Jews did not deter him from retaining so much of Judaism as seemed to him valuable and suitable to the purposes of his new propaganda. Nor did his condemnation of the Gentiles prevent him from recognizing that they might please God by living according to the dictates of conscience.[1] Christians who had been converted from paganism would certainly not have been less favorably disposed toward Gentiles, while normal obligations to the past would, in their case, have been similar to Paul's debt to Judaism.

[1] Rom. 2:14 f.

Opposition to other faiths as systems of religion did not necessarily prohibit a practical appropriation of worthy aspirations, noble ideals, or useful ideas from the contemporary religious world.

Moreover, Christianity was, for some time, not so fully developed that its advocates were primarily concerned with details of apologetic, minutely differentiating their faith from all others. While they doubtless felt themselves to be distinctive in many particulars, they did not at the outset propound an elaborately worked-out scheme of doctrine and a fully organized ecclesiastical system. Their interests revolved about certain central items, such as Jesus' resurrection, impending judgment, and believers' spiritual endowment. The full content of religious living, and the details of organization and dogma, which were ultimately to characterize the new society, resulted from a process of gradual growth in which the genealogical connections of new features seem at first to have attracted little if any attention. Under these conditions influences from the contemporary religious world were easily possible since they would operate for the most part unconsciously, being inherent in the religious fiber of converts from other faiths, or gradually absorbed from the atmosphere of the mission field. Belief in Christianity's superiority would not necessarily prevent such a course of development.

These conditions were not materially changed, even when we recognize that Christians felt themselves divinely guided in the establishment of the new religion. The thought of a formal and completed revelation was hardly prominent enough in the consciousness of the first missionaries to constitute a totally impassable barrier between them and their contemporaries. Before the New Testament Canon was definitely fixed the conception of revelation was much more elastic than in the later period. In fact, its very content was the product of experience. Judaism was believed to offer a genuine historic revelation which supplied certain items of the new faith, but it did not furnish, at least not in the thought of Paul, a complete equipment for Christianity. This task had not been accomplished even by Jesus himself. Since certain gaps remained to be filled in by believers from their own experience, they courageously set about this undertaking, in all good conscience accounting themselves worthy on the ground of their belief in Christ and in response to necessities arising in the course of their work, to equip the new faith with all features needful for the proper expansion of its life.[1] This work, to be sure, was done under God's direction, but the result was a matter of immediate experience, its character and content being determined by the religious impulses of living Christians. Since their convictions were a product of actual life, and since their experiences matured under the pressure of new problems arising out of the peculiar circumstances in which they found themselves, we must guard against reading into the thinking of early believers the views of later generations who so objectivized and hardened the conception of revelation as to make it the historically unconditioned source of all details in organization, ritual, and dogma, which emerged with the gradual growth of the Christian society. At first revelation was not defined so formally nor was it made so exclusively a thing of the past as to

[1] I Cor. 7:25, 40.

preclude the possibility of the Christians' own vital reaction upon, and obligation to, their immediate religious environment, even on gentile soil.

The possibility of receiving influence from this source was enhanced by the Christians' habit of assuming that their religion was the legitimate heir of all goodness which had previously existed in the universe. If Judaism or paganism held anything that seemed estimable, this without further ado was credited in Christianity's favor. Paul believed that not only his pre-Christian career, but the entire Old Testament dispensation and the whole course of past history had been ordered with reference to the establishment of Christianity, and consequently formed a proper part of its history in so far as Paul was able to make these things fit into his scheme of thinking. When appropriated religious values were recognized, the supremacy and uniqueness of Christianity were thought to be adequately guarded by affirming that these items had been rescued from their false setting in Judaism or paganism and had been restored to their divinely intended position in the new religion. Although both contemporary Judaism and contemporary paganism might be scathingly condemned, Christians still could highly esteem as their own proper possession items which a gradual process of vital growth had brought to them from these sources.

This method of reasoning became quite general among the early Church Fathers. Justin Martyr after his conversion retained his high estimate of Greek philosophy by affirming that Heraclitus, Socrates, and many Stoics were virtually Christians because they had been enlightened by the Logos, later to be more perfectly revealed

in the person of Christ.[1]   Athenagoras said that Greek
poets and philosophers possessed an "affinity with
the afflatus from God,"[2] and Tertullian called Seneca
"frequently ours."[3]   Clement of Alexandria defended at
length the partial inspiration of the Greek philosophers
and poets;[4] and Origen allowed that many philosophers
were in harmony with God's law in that they declared
the one who created all things to be God.[5]   Lactantius
believed that no sect of paganism was so erroneous and
no philosopher so vain as not to see something of the
truth.[6]   Augustine affirmed that "the very thing which
is now called the Christian religion existed among the
ancients even from the creation of mankind, yet not
until Christ himself came in the flesh did the true
religion, which already existed, begin to be called
Christian."[7]

This appreciation of the Gentiles quickly turned into
sharp criticism when opponents used the similarities
between paganism and Christianity to argue that the
latter lacked originality and so must be secondary and
inferior in character.   Christians did not deny the
existence of similarities, but they declared that the
Christian features of paganism were not indigenous.
They had been pilfered from Moses and the prophets
either directly or else through the intermediate activity
of evil demons who wished to forestall Christianity.

[1] *Apol.*, i. 5, 46; ii. 8, 10, 13.

[2] *Apol.*, vii.   [3] *De anima*, xx.

[4] *Strom.*, i. 2, 4 f., 13, 17, 19; v. 13; vi. 8.

[5] *In Genesim Homilia*, xiv. 3; cf. *Cels.*, vi. 1 ff.

[6] *Inst.*, vii. 7.

[7] *Retract.*, I. xiii. 3 (Migne, XXXII, 603); cf. *Conf.*, vii. 9 and 13 f.

Justin, recognizing the parallels which Greek writers of antiquity furnished for such Christian ideas as the activity of the Logos in creation, the incarnation of the Logos, the virgin birth, the miracles of Jesus, his divine sonship, the rites of baptism, and the Lord's Supper, stoutly affirmed that the ancients had learned these things from the wisdom of the Hebrews where Christianity was fully prefigured.[1] Tertullian similarly explained the origin of pagan rites, which seemed to anticipate those of Christianity, and he also declared the Old Testament to be the fountain from which all poets and sophists had drunk, their wisdom being but an imitation of the prophets.[2] Clement of Alexandria accused the Greeks of plagiarizing from the more ancient wisdom of the Hebrews, Plato even being a debtor to Moses.[3] Pagans, on the other hand, charged Christians with unscrupulously appropriating their sacred rites and held that their religion contained all the essentials of Christianity. Augustine complains that the Phrygian priest endeavored to seduce Christians by saying that "the bonneted one [of Attis] is himself a Christian."[4]

In more recent times discussion has followed the same general lines. One class of writers, discovering extensive similarities between Christianity and paganism, exploits them for Christianity's detriment—a method

[1] *Apol.*, i. 23, 54 f., 59, 62, 66; *Dial.*, 78.

[2] *De corona*, 15; *Ad haer.*, 40; *De jejunio*, 16; *Apol.*, 47.

[3] *Strom.*, i. 21–29; v. 14.

[4] "Et ipse pilleatus christianus est" (*In Joannis Evangelium tractatus*, vii. 6 [Migne, XXXV, 1440]). For this type of controversy between Christians and pagans see Cumont, "La polémique de l'Ambrosiaster contre les païens," *Revue d'histoire et de littérature religieuses*, VIII (1903), 423–36.

of procedure in vogue since the days of Celsus at the
latest.[1]   Even when this type of study is not deliberately derogatory in aim, it nevertheless frequently
results in denying the possibility of any substantial
originality with the Christian religion. Since all its
constituent factors are derived from a variety of contemporary sources, the new religion can be only a
reassembling of items from paganism. Sometimes
current philosophical notions are thought to constitute
its chief ingredients; other writers draw more extensively
upon ancient mythology to explain its origins; others
place stress upon pagan cults, making Christianity the
perpetuation under a new name of earlier forms of
worship.   Thus the new religion is essentially paganism
redivivus.[2]

[1] Origen, *Cels.*, i. 2, 4, etc.

[2] Works of this sort are numerous and widely varied in character, e.g.,
Le Christianisme dévoilé (published anonymously in 1767); Volney, *Les
ruines* (Paris, 1791); Dupuis, *Origine de tous les cultes* (3 vols., Paris,
1794); Richter, *Das Christentum und die ältesten Religionen des Orients*
(Leipzig, 1891); Gfrörer, *Kritische Geschichte des Urchristentums* (2 vols.,
Stuttgart, 1831–38); Hennell, *An Inquiry concerning the Origin of Christianity* (London, 1838); Havet, *Le Christianisme et ses origines* (4 vols.,
Paris, 1871–84); Bosc, *La vie ésotérique de Jésus de Nazareth et les origines
orientales du Christianisme* (Paris, 1902); Whittaker, *The Origins of Chris-
tianity* (London, 1904, 1909[2]); Promus, *Die Entstehung des Christentums*
(Jena, 1905 [a pseudonymous brochure]); Vollers, *Die Weltreligionen in
ihrem geschichtlichen Zusammenhange* (Jena, 1907), pp. 122 ff.; Kautsky,
Der Ursprung des Christentums (Stuttgart, 1908); Maurenbrecher, *Von
Nazareth nach Golgatha: Eine Untersuchung über die weltgeschichtlichen
Zusammenhänge des Urchristentums* (Berlin-Schöneberg, 1909) and *Von
Jerusalem nach Rom* (Berlin-Schöneberg, 1910); Carus, *The Pleroma: An
Essay on the Origin of Christianity* (Chicago, 1909); S. Reinach, *Orpheus:
Histoire générale des religions* (Paris, 1909), chaps. viii f.   Here belong
also the various works denying the historicity of Jesus, which may be
found listed by Case, *The Historicity of Jesus*, chap. ii, or Schweitzer,
Geschichte der Leben-Jesu-Forschung, chaps. xi, xii, xxii.

In contrast with this attitude, other interpreters recognize, as did the patristic writers, that there are many parallels between early Christianity and gentile religions, but these parallels are not thought to lessen Christianity's uniqueness. They are not regarded as contributions to its content but foreshadowings of its coming, and as such they become proofs of its divine authority. They are dim prophetic anticipations which enhance its value as revelation, "for its glory lies, not in its having relation to nothing which went before itself, but rather in its having relation to everything, in its being the middle point to which all lines, some consciously, more unconsciously, were tending and in which all centered at the last."[1] This has been a favorite theme with Christian apologists who, like Eusebius in his *Praeparatio evangelica*, thought they could see in the religious bankruptcy of the pagan world evidence that the time was ripe for the dawn of Christianity. Every real religious yearning of those times was a sign of Christianity's coming, for not until the new, truly revealed faith became known could any religious desire ever be really satisfied.

[1] Trench, *Christ the Desire of All Nations, or The Unconscious Prophecies of Heathendom* (London, 1846; New York, 1866). In a similar vein are Pressensé, *The Religions before Christ* (Edinburgh, 1862); Spiess, *Logos spermaticos* (Leipzig, 1871); Hicks, *Traces of Greek Philosophy and Roman Law in the New Testament* (London, 1896); Jeremias, *Babylonisches in Neuen Testament* (Leipzig, 1905), pp. 2 f.; Radau, *Bel, The Christ of Ancient Times* (Chicago, 1908); Mills, *Our Own Religion in Ancient Persia* (Chicago, 1913). The same principle, though emanating from a very different conception of revelation, was employed by Tindal, *Christianity as Old as Creation, or The Gospel a Republication of the Religion of Nature* (London, 1730). This so-called "Bible of Deism" defined truly revealed Christianity as the religion of Nature or Reason, consequently it must be as old as creation.

Another type of opinion is far more conservative in admitting any real parallelism between gentile religions and Christianity. At least in all its essentials Christianity is held to have been distinctly original. These interpreters, whose position has already been defined,[1] do not think of "essential" Christianity as the religious life of various people in different times and circumstances, but as a selected quantity of religio-ethical teaching, which is believed to have emanated from Jesus. Hence only in secondary matters could other faiths make any contribution to the new religion. Many of the supposed similarities between it and its contemporaries are, from this point of view, found to be of a purely external and unessential character. Foreign influences are sometimes allowed to come in through Judaism, but otherwise New Testament religion was only slightly, if at all, influenced by contemporary gentile faiths. In later times the process of paganization went on within the ancient Catholic church,[2] but this simply meant a corruption of the earlier faith, which is found to be essentially original in most parts of the New Testament.[3]

[1] See above, pp. 19 ff.

[2] Cf. Priestley, *History of the Corruption of Christianity* (Birmingham, 1782); Lewis, *Paganism Surviving in Christianity* (New York, 1892). Soltau, *Das Fortleben des Heidentums in der altchristlichen Kirche* (Berlin, 1906), carries the process of corruption well back into the New Testament where he finds large importations from heathendom, although he defines "essential" religion in terms of Jesus' ethics.

[3] The literature on Christianity's relation to non-Jewish religions is cited very fully by Clemen, *Religionsgeschichtliche Erklärung des Neuen Testaments* (Giessen, 1909), English tr., *Primitive Christianity and Its Non-Jewish Sources* (Edinburgh, 1912), and *Der Einfluss der Mysterienreligionen auf das älteste Christentum* (Giessen, 1913). Further illustrations of this general position are Bonhöffer, *Epiktet und das Neue Testa-*

When we view Christianity as the religious life of real persons, the problem of their relation to environment cannot be settled so easily. Those interpreters who think they have discovered the secret of the new religion's origin by assembling a collection of similar ideas or practices from the contemporary world forget that these things could not function anew in society until they had been embodied in the lives of vigorous personalities. However many items Christians may have taken over from gentile religions, the fact of personal leadership is one of the most prominent features of the new society. In other words, there would have been no Christianity had not the data which are said to have been appropriated from the religious environment been subjected to a personal reaction on the part of individuals whose experience was sufficiently distinctive to lead them to believe that they were advocates of the only true religion.

On the other hand, one can hardly nowadays take seriously the hypothesis that features of other religions, later reproduced in Christianity, were merely foreshadowings of a future revelation. This explanation is too formal and unreal to be linked with a vital conception of Christianity's character. Such an interpretation can be true only in the sense that Christians in response to, or under the tutelage of, a gentile environment evolved

ment (Giessen, 1911); Nösgen, "Der angebliche orientalische Einschlag der Theologie des Apostels Paulus," *Neue kirchliche Zeitschrift*, X (1909), 231–83; Allo, *L'Évangile en face du syncrétisme païen* (Paris, 1910 ["Christianity is not a syncretism but a synthesis"]); Heinrici, *Hellenismus und Christentum* (Berlin, 1909) and *Die Eigenart des Christentums* (Leipzig, 1911); Kennedy, *St. Paul and the Mystery Religions* (London, 1913).

an interpretation of religious experience along the lines
and in the language of the thought-world which constituted for Gentiles the realm of greatest reality.
That this process actually did go on, and that it contributed very fundamentally to the character, strength,
and usefulness of the new religion in the Greek world,
is coming to be recognized more and more fully as a
result of historical investigation into the origins of Christianity.

In the third place, to deny this vital relationship
between Christians and their gentile surroundings, or
to affirm that this environment could only contribute
secondary and detrimental features, is to ignore the
religious character of that contemporary world and at
the same time to stress only one phase of primitive
Christianity's varied life. Highly as Christians may
have prized the religio-ethical teaching of Jesus, represented, for example, by the Sermon on the Mount, this
teaching did not furnish the sole and perhaps not the
chief driving force of the new religion as proclaimed
either in Jewish or in gentile territory. Faith in the
Risen One, the new ecstatic life which accompanied this
faith, escape from the present evil world, assurance of
blessedness in the world to come, these were the central
notes in the new propaganda. These data, arising out
of the early believers' experience, called forth in the first
instance by the stimuli which their Jewish surroundings
supplied, later served as focal points for gathering up
and enriching the religious activities, convictions, and
aspirations of gentile converts. But the process was not
purely one-sided; it was one of both give and take. The
Gentiles accepted Christianity with the conviction that

it offered them the best means of realizing the total desiderata in religion, but the Christian missionary did not create *de novo* the religious sense of gentile converts, much as he may have quickened it by means of his new message. They already cherished longings of a religious character, they had capacities and means for acquiring religious experience, they possessed definite standards for estimating religious values, and they had reached varying degrees of attainment in the cultivation of religious living. All this formed the basis for the cultivation and interpretation of their religious experience as Christians, and so it became an integral factor in the growing life of the new religion.

Christianity's close contact with paganism has often been recognized, but chiefly in the period subsequent to the New Testament; or when the new religion has been allowed any real relationships with its gentile environment, these have commonly been found in classical Greece and Rome rather than in the popular contemporary religious life.[1] The further task, the problem of the so-called *religionsgeschichtliche Schule*, is to relate the Christianity of New Testament times

[1] E.g., Uhlhorn, *Der Kampf des Christentums mit dem Heidentum* (Stuttgart, 1874, 1899⁶), English tr., *Conflict of Christianity with Heathenism* (New York, 1886); Renan, *The Influence of the Institutions, Thought, and Culture of Rome on Christianity* (London, 1880), also *Histoire des origines du Christianisme* (Paris, 1862 ff.); Keim, *Rom und das Christentum* (Berlin, 1881); Hatch, *The Influence of Greek Ideas and Usages upon the Christian Church;* von Arneth, *Das classische Heidentum und die christliche Religion* (2 vols., Wien, 1895); Allard, *Le christianisme et l'empire romain de Néron à Théodose* (Paris, 1897²); Harnack, *Die Mission und Ausbreitung des Christentums*, usw.; Duchesne, *Histoire ancienne de l'Église* (3 vols., Paris, 1906–10), English tr., *Early History of the Christian Church* (London, 1909).

to its immediate religious environment in the popular life of the Graeco-Roman world.[1]   The extent to which this contact with gentile religions affected the development of the new movement can be ascertained only by studying more particularly the Christians' career in relation to the chief religious forces dominating their gentile surroundings.   This environment was, as we have earlier had occasion to observe, a highly syncretistic one.   While many survivals from earlier times persisted within the Graeco-Roman religions of this period, none of the older ethnic faiths exerted so immediate an influence upon Christians as did Judaism.   The influence of other ancient national religions, if at all significant for the career of Christianity, was mediated mainly through Judaism, or through the syncretistic life of the gentile world.

[1] Until within comparatively recent times philologists rather than theologians have been most interested in this field of inquiry, e.g., Eichhorn, Usener, Dieterich, Wünsch, Reitzenstein, Frazer, Cumont, *et al.* A partial application of these materials to the study of Christian origins was made by Pfleiderer, *Das Christusbild des urchristlichen Glaubens in religionsgeschichtlicher Beleuchtung* (Berlin, 1903), English tr., *Early Christian Conception of Christ* (New York, 1905).   Further works which employ the *religionsgeschichtliche* method either in part or in full are, in addition to some already mentioned above (pp. 66 and 108 f.), Brückner, *Der sterbende und auferstehende Gottheiland in den orientalischen Religionen und ihr Verhältnis zum Christentum* (Tübingen, 1908); Heitmüller, *Im Namen Jesu,* and *Taufe und Abendmahl bei Paulus* (Göttingen, 1903), also *Taufe und Abendmahl im Urchristentum* (Tübingen, 1911); Conybeare, *Myth, Magic, and Morals: A Study of Christian Origins* (London, 1909); Jacoby, *Die antiken Mysterienreligionen und das Christentum* (Tübingen, 1910); see also various volumes in Lietzmann's *Handbuch zum Neuen Testament* (Tübingen, 1906 ff.).   A sympathetic summary of literature is given by Bousset, "Die Religionsgeschichte und das Neue Testament," *Theologische Rundschau,* VII (1904), 265–77, 311–18, 353–65; also Emerton, "The Religious Environment of Early Christianity," *Harvard Theological Review,* III (1910), 181–208.

In so far as these foreign items came in through Judaism they constituted an integral part of the early Christians' Jewish heritage, and so do not concern us at present. Also within gentile circles contact with these earlier faiths would hardly be direct, even though their influence survived. It would be mediated more particularly by the special religious activities which the peculiar life of the Hellenistic age had called into being. This was, in the main, probably true even of the religious heritage received from Greece and Rome, to say nothing of the more remote and ancient civilizations. Hence, instead of attempting at the outset to discover the particular items in Christianity which were derived from, say, Egypt,[1] Babylonia,[2]

---

[1] For the view that Egyptian religion had influenced the Hermetic books, and, through these, Christianity, see particularly Reitzenstein, *Poimandres: Studien zur griechisch-ägyptischen und frühchristlichen Literatur* (Leipzig, 1904); Mead, *Thrice Greatest Hermes, Studies in Hellenistic Philosophy and Gnosis* (3 vols., London, 1906); Petrie, *Personal Religion in Egypt before Christianity* (London, 1909). Zielinski, on the contrary, doubts any strong Egyptian influence in this literature ("Hermes und die Hermetik," *Archiv fur Religionswissenschaft*, VIII [1904-5], 321-72, and IX [1906], 25-60).

[2] Babylonian influence on Christianity is a much-discussed subject. It is affirmed in various degrees by Schrader, *Die Keilinschriften und das Alte Testament* (Berlin, 1903³), pp. 377 ff.; Gunkel, *Schöpfung und Chaos in Urzeit und Endzeit* (Göttingen, 1895) and *Zum religionsgeschichtlichen Verständnis des Neuen Testament* (Göttingen, 1903, 1910²); Jeremias, *Babylonisches im Neuen Testament* (Leipzig, 1905); Jensen, *Das Gilgamesch-Epos in der Weltliteratur* (Strassburg, 1906), *Moses, Jesus, Paulus: Drei Varianten des babylonischen Gottmenschen Gilgamesch* (Frankfurt a.M., 1909); Zimmern, *Zum Streit um die "Christusmythe": Das babylonische Material in seinen Hauptpunkten dargestellt* (Berlin, 1910). For criticisms of the pan-Babylonists' contentions see Kugler, *Im Bannkreis Babels* (Münster i.W., 1910), and Toy, "Pan-Babylonism," *Harvard Theological Review*, III (1910), 47-84.

Persia,[1] or India,[2] we shall consider the life of the early Christians in relation to certain religious phenomena which were more especially distinctive of Graeco-Roman times.

[1] Stave, *Über den Einfluss des Parsismus auf das Judentum* (Haarlem, 1898), discusses at length the question of Persian influence upon Judaism and thus indirectly upon Christianity. See further Böklen, *Die Verwandtschaft der jüdisch-christlichen mit der parsischen Eschatologie* (Göttingen, 1902); Moffatt, "Zoroastrianism and Primitive Christianity," *Hibbert Journal,* I. (1903), 763–80, and II (1904), 347–59; Jackson, "Zoroastrianism and the Resemblances between It and Christianity," *Biblical World,* XXVII (1906), 335–43; Mills, *Avesta Eschatology Compared with the Books of Daniel and Revelations* (Chicago, 1908) and *Our Own Religion in Ancient Persia.*

[2] Several writers have stoutly maintained a Buddhistic influence upon the New Testament. Among the more sober advocates of this opinion are Seydel, *Das Evangelium von Jesu in seinen Verhältnissen zu Buddha-Sage und Buddha-Lehre,* usw. (Leipzig, 1882) and *Die Buddha-Legende und das Leben Jesu nach den Evangelien* (Weimar, 1897[2]); Van den Berg van Eysinga, *Indische Invloeden op oude christelijke Verhalen* (Leiden, 1901); Edmunds, *Buddhistic and Christian Gospels* (2 vols., Philadelphia, 1902, 1908–9[4]); Garbe, *Indien und das Christentum: Eine Untersuchung der religionsgeschichtlichen Zusammenhänge* (Tübingen, 1914). Others assert Buddhism's debt to Christianity, e.g., Hopkins, *India, Old and New* (New York, 1901), pp. 122 ff.; Wecker, "Christlicher Einfluss auf den Buddhismus," *Theologische Quartalschrift,* XCII (1910), 417–57 and 538–65. Doubt about any mutual influence is expressed, for example, by Lehmann, *Der Buddhismus als indische Sekte, als Weltreligion* (Tübingen, 1911). The various views on this general subject are conveniently summarized and critically estimated by von Hase, *New Testament Parallels to Buddhistic Literature* (New York, 1907), and Faber, *Buddhistische und neutestamentliche Erzählungen* (Leipzig, 1913).

CHAPTER VII

THE RELIGIOUS SIGNIFICANCE OF EMPEROR-WORSHIP

The national religions of antiquity commonly cherished a belief that the gods were especially interested in their followers' political welfare. This interest was usually thought to find its expression in certain mutual relations existing between the deity and the ruler. The king was in some sense God's representative, either being of divine descent or else divinely chosen and endowed for the exercise of sovereignty. This belief is exemplified in the history of the Egyptians, the Babylonians and Assyrians, the Hebrews, and also among less well-known peoples of that ancient Orient. It persisted as long as the various nations maintained any semblance of independence or continued to hope for a restoration of former glory.

The Macedonian conquest was a severe shock to the national ideals of the conquered peoples. Alexander, to be sure, did not abolish native religions, nor was he even as hostile toward them as some earlier conquerors had been. But the essential unification of nations which followed his work and which was still further advanced by the Romans hastened the necessity, which had to some extent already begun to manifest itself in the Persian period, for abandoning the national emphasis in religion. This meant, for those ancient religions which survived in Hellenistic times, the severance of political ties and the substitution of a personal emphasis. This development is most familiarly illustrated in the history of the Jews who held long and tenaciously to national expectations but were finally compelled to abandon them except as a vague and distant hope.   One of the prominent items in the early Christians' success was their decision to forsake the narrow national ideals with which they began their propaganda.

Yet the political status of people always has some significance for their religion.   This fact was as true of the Graeco-Roman period as of earlier times.   The consciousness of political stability and human solidarity resulting from unification of empire inevitably affected the religious life of many persons in the first century A.D. If the Macedonians and the Romans had possessed some one strong national faith of their own this would naturally have become the official religion of their respective régimes.   But this was not the case.   The conquerors were not without religion, but it was not sufficiently developed and distinctive to become the dominant faith of a world-empire, at least not without undergoing important transformations.   Moreover, the foreign policy of the conquerors, in religion as in other things, was rarely one of superimposition, consequently the national side of religious feeling in the Hellenistic age sought a new channel of expression.   This was found in the worship of the ruler.

Christians in New Testament times did not greatly concern themselves with Roman politics,[1] yet they preached an emphatically imperial type of religion.   The dominant note in their message was the approaching

---

[1] But Weinel, *Die Stellung des Urchristentums zum Staat* (Tübingen, 1908), finds the Christians' attitude to have been more deliberately hostile.

kingdom to be ushered in by a heaven-sent ruler, Jesus the Messiah, who had already, while on earth, demonstrated his fitness for this new task. Instead of the visible political order the Christians substituted a spiritual order—in fact, a dual spiritual order. At present the kingdom of evil with Satan at its head was in the ascendancy, but this condition of affairs was nearing an end. The new kingdom of righteousness, the earnest of which believers had already experienced, was to be ushered in at an early date by the Parousia of the Lord Jesus Christ. At first this faith did not necessarily involve any hostility toward Rome, for the latter was merely a temporary phase of the present order which was rapidly to pass away. But as Christianity grew to be a gentile missionary movement, it came into competition with emperor-worship, and ultimately this initial rivalry was displaced by bitter hostility. This latter stage of development did not reach its climax until after New Testament times, but Christians from the first were confronted by emperor-worship as one of the important religious phenomena of their environment. Hence the propriety of asking what significance the imperial cult, already established throughout Mediterranean lands, had for the evolving life of Christianity—the new imperial religion.

Emperor-worship in the New Testament period was the climax of a long line of development in the political and religious history of that ancient world.[1] The

---

[1] See Beurlier, *De divinis honoribus quos acceperunt Alexander et successores ejus* (Paris, 1890) and *Le culte impérial, son histoire et son organisation depuis Auguste jusqu'à Justinien* (Paris, 1891); Boissier, *La religion romaine*, I (Paris, 1892⁴), 109–86; Hirschfeld, "Zur Geschichte des römischen Kaisercultus," *Sitzungsberichte der Königlich-Preussischen*

genetic connections between varying phases of this phenomenon in different countries and at different times
are not always clear, but its early appearance and
increasing importance in the Graeco-Roman world
are beyond question.   According to the usual view, worship of the emperor was a spontaneous evolution from
Greek hero-worship which gathered to itself in the
process of growth oriental features such as the separateness of the sovereign, his divine equipment or descent,
and the notion of his mission as a world-savior.   Other
interpreters make the oriental elements primary, tracing the genesis of the custom to the newly arising conception of empire which the Greeks learned from the
Orient and passed on to the Roman.[1]   For the New
Testament student, however, it is of greater consequence
to understand the composite elements which had gone
into the making of emperor-worship, as it existed in

Akademie der Wissenschaften (1888), 833–62; Krascheninnikoff, "Über
die Einführung des provinzialen Kaiserkultus im römischen Westen,"
Philologus, LIII, Neue Folge VII (1894), 147–89; Kornemann, "Zur
Geschichte der antiken Herrscherkulte," *Klio: Beiträge zur alten Geschichte*, I (1901–2), 51–146; Heinen, "Zur Begründung des römischen
Kaiserkultus: Chronologische Übersicht von 43 v. bis 14 n. Chr.,"
ibid., XI (1911), 129–77; Beloch, *Griechische Geschichte*, III, i, 47–51
and 368–77; Deissmann, *Licht vom Osten*, pp. 243–87, English tr., *Light
from the Ancient East*, pp. 342–84; A. Bauer, *Vom Griechentum zum
Christentum*, pp. 53–92; Gruppe, *Griechische Mythologie*, pp. 1499–1519;
Toutain, *Les cultes païens dans l'empire romain*, I, i, 19–179; Wendland,
Die hellenistisch-römische Kultur, pp. 123–27 and 142–51; Wissowa,
Religion und Kultus der Römer, pp. 338–48.

[1] So Kaerst, *Geschichte des hellenistischen Zeitalters*, II, i, 374–426,
who thinks the source of the practice to be "von oben her."   That is, the
king is worshiped in the first instance as the exponent of the monarchical
idea, the embodiment of the divine rule upon earth. See, on the contrary, E. Meyer, "Alexander der Grosse und die absolute Monarchie."
Kleine Schriften (Halle a.S., 1910), pp. 283–332.

the first century A.D., than to decide which of these items was genetically primary.

The notion of a unique relation between the king and the deity was very ancient and widespread. From remote antiquity Egyptian rulers had been regarded as the incarnation of a god whose name they bore in their official title. The ruler's coming into the world was the rising of the sun-god in the east and his death was the setting of the sun in the west. He did not suffer the fate of ordinary mortals at death, but went by a royal road to dwell with Re forever, the gods greeting him upon his arrival as an imperishable glorious being. Although the king in ancient times seems never to have been made the object of worship, the notion of sovereignty was thoroughly religious in character, and the king's conduct was ordered according to rigidly prescribed ritualistic requirements.[1]

Likewise among the Babylonians and Assyrians the king occupied a unique though quite different position. The name of Sargon I has the determinative *ilu*, which signifies that he was himself a god or that he bore a divine name, and his son Naramsin is expressly designated "god."[2] Gudea of Lagash refers to himself as a child of the goddess Gatumdug and prays to her: "I have no mother, you are my mother. I have no

[1] See Moret, *Du caractère religieux de la royauté pharaonique* (Paris, 1902).

[2] Cf. Thureau-Dangin, *Revue d'Assyriologie*, IV (1897), 76. The determinative *ilu* before Hammurabi's name is now generally taken to signify only that the first part of his name is that of a god, and not that the king himself is divine; cf. Ungnad, *Zeitschrift für Assyriologie*, XXII (1909), 8. For the legend of Sargon's divine descent see Gressmann's *Altorientalische Texte und Bilder zum Alten Testamente* (Tübingen, 1909), I, 79.

father, you are my father . . . . in the sanctuary you bore me." Other ancient Babylonian kings affirm that they were nourished by a goddess with holy milk.[1] But evidence that the king was ever deified outright as in Egypt is very meager, and even the claim to divine sonship is said to be less in evidence in later times. Radau thinks that the Babylonians' hesitation in ascribing deity to their kings is due to Sumerian influence, which dulled the original Semitic notion that the king is always the Son of God, "nay, even a god himself."[2]

However this may be, the monarch is still distinguished by the unique relation between himself and the gods, a relation which implies, even when it does not explicitly affirm, divine descent. He is always their favorite, they instruct him for the discharge of his duty, and he is in general their agent in the exercise of his functions as sovereign. A few sentences from the prologue to Hammurabi's Code will illustrate this attitude: "When the lofty king Anu, king of Anunnaki, and Bel, Lord of heaven and earth, who determines the destiny of the land, committed the rule of all mankind to Marduk, the chief son of Ea; . . . . when they pronounced the lofty name of Babylon . . . . and in its midst established an everlasting kingdom whose foundations were as firm as heaven and earth, at that time Anu and Bel called me, Hammurabi, the exalted prince, the worshiper of the gods, to cause justice to prevail in the

[1] E.g., Ennatum, Entemena, Lugalzaggisi. For references see Lietzmann, *Der Weltheiland* (Bonn, 1909), pp. 48 f.

[2] Radau, *Early Babylonian History* (Oxford, 1900). On the relation of Sumerians and Semites see E. Meyer, *Abhandlungen der Königlich-Preussischen Akademie der Wissenschaften, Philosophisch-historische Classe* (1906), III, 1–125.

land, to destroy the wicked and the evil, to prevent the strong from opposing the weak, to go forth like the sun over the black-headed race, to enlighten the land, and to further the welfare of the people. Hammurabi, the governor named by Bel am I, who brought about plenty and abundance . . . . who rejoiced the heart of Marduk, his lord, who daily served in Esagila, of the seed royal which Sin begat, who filled the city Ur with plenty, the pious and suppliant one . . . . the exalted one . . . . the divine city king, wise and intelligent . . . . the lord adorned with scepter and crown whom the wise God Ma-ma has clothed with complete power."[1]

Among the Hebrews also kingship had a distinctly religious character. The ideal monarch who possessed a special endowment of the spirit became the Son of God through divine anointing and was henceforth Yahweh's vicegerent upon earth. When the succession of rulers failed in Israel, or when the actual kings fell short of the divine standard, the ideal itself was not abandoned but was projected far into the future. One day a prince would arise who would be endowed with a full measure of the Spirit and would establish over all the earth a kingdom of righteousness—an accomplishment to be effected through "the zeal of Yahweh of hosts."[2] In the process of time the conception of the sovereign's divinity was so extended in some circles of thought that God himself was the only monarch whose authority was to be recognized;[3] or his true representative was to be a

[1] Harper, *The Code of Hammurabi* (Chicago, 1904), pp. 3 ff.

[2] Isa. 9:7; cf. 11:1 ff.

[3] The Zealots affirmed that God was their only ἡγεμόνα καὶ δεσπότην, and they refused to call any man δεσπότης (Josephus, *Ant.*, XVIII, i, 6).

pre-existent heavenly being who would descend to earth
to destroy evil and set up the eternal kingdom of God.

Thus the idea of rulership had an emphatically religious
content, the king being either God himself or his especially equipped representative.   Politics were primarily
a concern of the gods, and the king exercised a divinely
delegated authority as the vicegerent of heaven rather
than the representative of men.   He possessed God-given
endowments which set him apart from ordinary mortals,
yet he was not the object of his subjects' religion, not
even in Egypt, where he was believed to be the very incarnation of the sun-god.   On the contrary, his religious
position was much more nearly that of the ideal religious
person, officiating in the ritual in an exemplary manner
on important occasions.   Even the Pharaonic deity-king
was not free from the necessity of strict ceremonial
observances.   It was not the figure of the ruler which
gave the monarchical idea its unique religious significance in the Orient; it was rather the monarchical
position which made the ruler significant.   Everything
rested upon the fundamental notion that monarchy was
a divine institution, a heaven-sent boon to mankind.
The ruler's position was unique because he represented
the gods rather than the people.   He received laws from
heaven which he communicated to his subjects, they
rendered him obedience resembling in kind that which
they gave the deity, but they formally worshiped only
the mighty gods who ruled over both the monarch and
his subject.   This notion of the divine status of the
monarchical idea continued down to Graeco-Roman
times and formed an important item in the early Christians' religious environment.

Greece and Rome originally presented a very different situation. Their conception of government was fundamentally democratic; it was the people rather than the gods who were primarily responsible for the national weal. Rulers were revered for their own attainments, their right to divine honors depending upon their own display of prowess. Gods were made in the image of great men, and men who had proved themselves superior in bravery, or generous in bestowing benefits upon their fellows, were at death elevated to the rank of divinity and worshiped accordingly. A few illustrations will suffice to remind us of the important rôle which hero-worship played among the Greeks, and also its bearing on the later practice of worshiping the monarch.

Herodotus often refers to the custom of honoring heroic men and founders of cities with religious rites. When Miltiades died the Chersonesians, because he had built a wall to ward off the attacks of their enemies, sacrificed to him "as is usual to a founder" and instituted games in his honor.[1] Sometimes the custom was observed in obedience to instruction received from the oracle. This was the case with the Phocaeans who, on gaining possession of Hyela, established sacred rites to Cyrnus as a hero.[2] Also to Xerxes' giant friend Artachaees, who was buried at Acanthus, the Acanthians "in obedience to an oracle offered sacrifice as to a hero invoking him by name."[3] Philippus, son of Butacides, "on account of his beauty" was honored with a shrine upon his sepulcher and was propitiated with sacrifices.[4] Thucydides[5] records another good illustration. Brasidas,

[1] vi. 38. [3] vii. 117.
[2] i. 167. [4] v. 47. [5] v. 11.

leader of the Spartan forces stationed in Amphipolis, was slain in a bold but successful sally against the Athenians. He was buried at the public expense, a fence was built about his tomb, offerings were made to him as a hero, he was honored with games and annual sacrifices, and he was called the founder of the settlement, his memory supplanting that of Hagnon who had formerly been so honored.

These pragmatic tests for determining one's right to religious honors were not confined exclusively to heroic deeds. Philippus, as we saw, was revered because of his beauty, but Herodotus says this procedure was quite exceptional. Persons who had shown remarkable wisdom, or who had displayed poetical skill, also became objects of reverence. Already in the fifth century B.C. Empedocles had been honored by his followers as a god, Protagoras was said to have been the son of Apollo, Aristotle erected an altar to Plato, and later we find a cult of Homer in Alexandria. The Greek mind readily employed religious categories to express its reverence for distinguished personalities. This was not merely a disposition of the populace; it was also true of the educated. The divine was recognized in the human, so that the divinity and pre-existence of the human soul were easily attainable ideas. The political theories of Plato and Aristotle, constructed on this type of anthropology, made the ideal ruler a veritable divinity among men, ruling without regard to law because "he himself is the law." Thus Greek thinking arrived, though by a different road, at a conception of rulership essentially more despotic than that of the Orientals. The fundamental difference was that in the Orient theology had been the determining factor in the religious interpretation of monarchy, while in Greece the point of departure was anthropology. The Greek theory of monarchy started with man and made of him its god; the oriental notion started with God and made the monarch in his image. Both of these tendencies survived until Christian times and were employed by the missionaries in defining their notion of both the new kingdom of God and the monarchical functions of Jesus.

The process of fusing these two conceptions began with the career of Alexander the Great. He probably learned from Aristotle the Platonic conception of the ideal republic with its man-god king, and he held in high esteem the memory of ancient heroes. One of his first acts on crossing the Hellespont was to visit Troy in order to pay his respects to the heroes of that conflict before starting out on his own mission of conquest. After arriving in Egypt he visited the oracle of Zeus-Ammon, where tradition says he was pronounced by the priest to be a son of the deity. Strabo reports various traditions to the same effect. The long-silent oracle of Apollo among the Branchidae revived in Alexander's time and the Milesian ambassadors carried back to Memphis numerous answers of the oracle regarding Alexander's descent from Zeus and his future victories. The Erythraean prophetess had also affirmed Alexander's divine descent.[1] Then came the further display of his prowess in the East, where he surrounded his person with the splendors of the Persian court and added to the amazement of his generation the conquest of nearly the whole of the then known world.

[1] Strabo, xvii. 1. 43.

The death of Alexander's favorite companion, Hephaestion, called forth clearly Alexander's own ideas on the subject of hero-worship.   He at once sent messengers to the temple of Zeus in Egypt to inquire whether it was permitted to offer sacrifices to Hephaestion as a god.   On learning that this could not be done, but that his dead friend might be honored as a hero, Alexander ordered chapels erected to him and insisted that a reverence very closely akin to that shown the gods should be paid to Hephaestion.[1]   Alexander's zeal in this matter was so great that he wrote Cleomenes, governor of Egypt, "If I find the sacred rites and chapels of the hero Hephaestion well completed I will not only pardon you any crimes you may have committed in the past, but in the future you shall suffer no unpleasant treatment from me, however great may be the crimes you commit."   As Cleomenes had little interest in religion, but was much addicted to "crimes" for which he might suffer severely when Alexander discovered them, the inducement which Alexander held out to him reveals the king's insight into human nature as well as his willingness to sacrifice the welfare of the living for the honor of the dead.

Whether Alexander ever claimed divine honors for himself is a disputed point,[2] but he certainly accepted such without protest.   The Ionians, probably during his lifetime, out of gratitude for the liberty he had won for them, dedicated a sacred grove to him above Chalcideis and celebrated, probably on his birthday, yearly games in his honor.[3]   Greece proper was doubtless less apprecia-

[1] Arrian, *Anabasis*, vii. 14, 23.   [3] Strabo, xiv. 1. 31.
[2] See Kornemann, *op. cit.*, p. 58, n. 4.

tive of Alexander's services, for he had figured as their conqueror before he started upon his eastern career. But the Greeks of the mainland so far overcame their prejudices by the year 323 that shortly before Alexander's death messengers were sent to him wearing golden wreaths upon their heads and offering him a golden crown, thus signifying that they accorded him divine respect.[1] His Stoic biographer, Arrian, excuses Alexander's acceptance of these compliments on the ground that it was a concession to the customs and thinking of the conquered peoples, and so was justifiable as a practical governmental policy. But the Hephaestion incident alone shows that the notion of deification was so deeply ingrained in Alexander's own thinking that suggestions of his divinity during his lifetime probably did not seem to him wholly vain, particularly after he had come into closer touch with the Orient and had learned the religious significance it attached to the monarch. If Alexander had come to feel that he was the instrument of heaven in the establishment of world-empire,[2] it would not be difficult for him to take seriously the religious formalities connected with his name, although such reverence had commonly been reserved for Greek heroes until death.[3]

A cult of Alexander sprang up immediately after his death. Ptolemy, who gained possession of the dead

---

[1] Arrian, *Anabasis*, vii. 23.   [2] So Plutarch, *Alex.*, 1.

[3] Lysander is an exception if Duris, who is the source of Plutarch's information, is reliable (*Lysander*, 18), but Duris belonged to the Hellenistic age when the worship of living rulers had become fully established, and he may have read the earlier history in terms of later thinking. See Diodorus, xvi. 20, 92, for suggestions that Dion of Syracuse and Philip of Macedon had shared heroic honors while still alive.

king's body, carried it to Egypt, ultimately interring it in Alexandria where a temple was reared to Alexander's memory and sacrifices were offered to him as a hero.[1] Eumenes affirmed that Alexander had appeared to him in a dream and indicated his wish still to be the leader of the people. Eumenes accordingly erected a beautiful tent as a symbol of the dead king's presence. Within it was a throne with royal accouterments and before it an altar for burnt offerings. Instead of the images of ancient deities only, which had been used by Alexander in stamping his coins, Alexander's own image with the horns of the god Ammon appears upon the coinage. It would seem that an Alexander cult was generally popular with his successors, particularly in Asia and Egypt. While this reverence doubtless bore the character of Greek hero-worship, it is also probable that the disposition Alexander had felt to worship Hephaestion as a god would find actual expression in the worship of Alexander. According to Suidas, Antipater alone of the Diadochi thought it sacrilege to call Alexander "god."

It was not long before his successors and their descendants applied to themselves in their capacity as sovereign similar notions. After Alexander's death worship of the living ruler soon became an established practice. The custom grew rapidly in Egypt and Syria. It appeared sporadically among the Greeks, but it made little headway in Macedonia. At first it was a spontaneous outburst of Greek gratitude or flattery, as when the city of Scepsis in 311 B.C. consecrated a sacred inclosure to Antigonus, erected him an altar, and set up his statue. In 307 the Athenians, in gratitude for

[1] Diodorus, xviii. 28.

deliverance from the Macedonians, called Demetrius and his father Antigonus "savior-gods," built them an altar, established a feast in their honor, and chose a priest for the new cult.   Three years later the Rhodians, in recognition of the assistance Ptolemy had given them against Demetrius, built Ptolemy an altar and established a yearly feast in his honor.

Deification of the living monarch did not appear immediately in Egypt, but when once the custom began it was carried much farther than in Greece.   When Ptolemy I died, his son Ptolemy Philadelphus declared him to be a new god, "Ptolemy Soter," and established a yearly festival to be celebrated on the king's birthday. Ptolemy and Alexander were now honored side by side, the worship of each becoming a state cult.   When Philadelphus' mother, Berenice, died in 279, she was at once deified and her cult was joined to that of her husband.   The two were worshiped as "savior-gods" (θεοὶ σωτῆρες).   In 271 the sister-wife of Philadelphus died and she too was immediately apotheosized as "Aphrodite Arsinoe Philadelphus."   Her worship became a state cult in Alexandria, and probably also in Arsinoe.   Then came the significant transition from the deification of the dead to the deification of the living ruler.   Philadelphus was given a place beside his sister-wife and the cult of the living king and the dead queen was officially recognized, the two being worshiped under the designation "brother-gods" (θεοὶ ἀδελφοί).   On the Rosetta Stone the fifth Ptolemy, then reigning, is called a god, sprung from a god and a goddess, just as Horos is a son of Osiris and Isis.   An inscription on the wall of the temple at Edfu referring to the eighth Ptolemy says, "Horos of Edfu, the god Api, lord of heaven, who flames in the horizon, he beholds his house, he knows his beloved son, King Ptolemy Soter Philometor, he establishes him upon his throne forever."[1] From the time of Philadelphus on, the Ptolemaic rulers receive official deification from the priest, they are associated as temple companions with certain of the ancient deities, and become the deities' representative—a new Aphrodite or a new Dionysus—upon earth. In addition to "savior-gods" and "brother-gods" we meet also "benefactor-gods" (θεοὶ εὐεργέται), "philopator gods" (θεοὶ φιλοπάτορες), "manifest gods" (θεοὶ ἐπιφαναί), and so on down to Roman times.[2]

Syria experienced a similar evolution. On the death of Seleucus I, his son Antiochus consecrated to him in Seleucia a sacred grove with a temple and gave him, as cult title, the name "Zeus Victor" (Ζεὺς Νικάτωρ). Antiochus I was hailed as savior by different communities, he was honored with games, and at death he was deified as Apollo Soter (Apollo savior). With Antiochus II, who assumed the cult surname "Theos" (god), worship of the living ruler became established within the Seleucid empire as well as in Egypt. The origins of the practice among the Seleucids are less well known, though its existence, not in the form of a centralized system like that prevailing in Egypt but as a provincial cult established in different satrapies of the empire, is a well-attested fact. Among the official sacral surnames taken by different rulers to illustrate their divinity were the terms "Kallinikos" ("gloriously triumphant," an epithet of Hercules),

---

[1] Cited by Mahaffy, *Empire of the Ptolemies*, pp. 239 ff.

[2] For details see Kornemann, *op. cit.*, pp. 67 ff.

"Soter" (savior), "Philopator" (father-lover), "Theos Epiphanes" (god manifest), "Nicator" (victor), "Theos Nicator" (god victor), "Epiphanes Dionysus" (manifest Dionysus), and probably in later times "Eusebes" (pious). Thus the Seleucids claimed to be, in the fullest sense, god manifest in the flesh. Their right to divine honors was not determined by a priestly decree as in Egypt, nor by the disposition of any community to institute religious ceremonies in their honor. It proceeded directly from the ruler himself in his capacity as god-king. He was "theos" in virtue of his monarchical position. This was the Hellenistic notion with which the Jews came into sharp conflict in Maccabean times and it was the conception which had prevailed for centuries in the lands where Christianity was first preached as a gentile missionary movement.

Rome first appeared in eastern politics chiefly as the liberator of the Greeks. The Roman general, Flamininus, after his defeat of Philip V of Macedon, was greeted by the assembly at the Isthmian games in the year 196 B.C. as savior, and the city of Chalcis rendered him divine honors. He was placed beside Apollo with an appropriate temple and priesthood. In the years following, Roman generals and governors were similarly honored on various occasions by the Greeks. Beside them was placed, as a personification of the new political power, the goddess Roma, who took a position similar to that of the divine queen in the Orient. This goddess, who was a new religious creation of the East, had a temple erected to her first at Smyrna in the year 195 B.C., and other temples soon sprang up at different places. The prowess of Rome in the East was greatly

augmented in the first century B.C. by the brilliant
military career of Pompey. He was greeted as a god
by an inscription over the city gate through which he
passed into Athens, and in honor of his success against
Mithradates he was given a position beside the deified
Alexander. When Julius Caesar pursued the illustrious
Pompey to the East and defeated him at the battle of
Pharsalus in 48 B.C., it was Caesar's turn to receive the
compliments of the Greeks. This is attested by an
Ephesian inscription in which the Greek cities of Asia
honor him as "god manifest, son of Ares and Aphrodite,
and common savior of human life." In still other inscriptions he is designated "benefactor," "founder,"
"savior," and "the god and dictator and savior of the
world."[1]

On his return to Rome various honors of an unusual
sort were bestowed upon him which marked the first
stages in the development of emperor-worship in the
West. His triumphal chariot was placed before the
statue of Jupiter, and his statue was erected upon the
Capitol with an inscription in which he is called a demi-
god.[2] A little later his statue was set up in the temple of
Quirinus and bore the inscription "to the invincible
God." Although many similar honors were bestowed
upon him in his lifetime, an official cult of Caesar was not
established in Rome until after his death. On the second
of August in the year 44 B.C. Octavian erected in the
temple of Venus a statue to Caesar with the inscription
Divo Julio, and on September first Antony applied to
the Senate to set apart a day for making yearly supplica-

---

[1] For references see Heinen, *op. cit.*, pp. 130 f. and 132, n. 3.

[2] Dion Cassius, xliii. 14. 6; Suetonius, *Julius Caesar*, 76.

tion to the new god.   The deification of Caesar, as well as the name *Divus Julius*, was fixed by law January first, 42 B.C.   From this time on worship of the ruler, deified after death when the Senate so decreed, became a legal institution even at Rome itself.   These new divinities were *divi* rather than *dei*, that is, they were men raised to the rank of gods rather than incarnations of ancient deities, but in the popular feeling they were often quite as truly reverenced as were the ancient deities.   Moreover, they were sometimes credited with pre-existence, divine parentage, and miraculous birth.

The cult of the living ruler, however, did not gain ready recognition in the city of Rome, but it was widely prevalent in the provinces.   Even Antony, who claimed to be descended from Hercules, had been greeted as Dionysus at Ephesus and Athens, an Egyptian inscription called him god and honored him as Osiris, and Cleopatra erected a temple to him in Alexandria, but it seems to have been completed as a temple of Octavian.[1] The worship of Octavian, in association with the goddess Roma, was widely established, particularly in the East, In the year 29 B.C. he had permitted the Romans of the province of Asia and Bithynia to erect a temple in Ephesus to the goddess Roma and the divinity Julius Caesar. But to the Greeks of this province he gave permission to dedicate a temple to Roma and to himself.   Thus he openly permitted Roman citizens to worship the dead ruler, whose apotheosis had been authoritatively confirmed, but this restriction was not imposed upon Greeks.

This reserve was part of Octavian's care not to offend the democratic spirit of the Roman people.   Even after

[1] Heinen, *op. cit.*, p. 142, n. 1.

the establishment of the empire in 27 B.C., when the
Senate conferred upon him the cognomen "Augustus,"
he still preserved his tactful and cautious attitude.
Suetonius[1] says that within Rome he positively refused
any such divine honors as were abundantly bestowed
upon him in the provinces, and, melting down all the
silver statues that had been erected to him, he made
tripods for Palatine Apollo. He abhorred the title
lord, and was greatly offended once at a play when he
was addressed as "just and generous lord." Yet all
this did not prevent an unauthorized deification of the
living Augustus from establishing itself in popular belief,
nor do we hear of any systematic punishments being
imposed upon those who transgressed his professed
wishes in these matters. At several places in Italy his
cult is known to have existed before the emperor's
death,[2] though to what extent the personnel of the
worshipers was Roman or foreign can hardly be determined.

Augustus' long and prosperous rule was particularly
conducive to the growth of emperor-worship, which
was in reality popular appreciation expressed in terms
of religion. Josephus[3] says the temple Herod built to
Augustus at Caesarea was remarkable for its size and
beauty. In it was a Colossus of the emperor not inferior
to that of Jupiter Olympus after which it was modeled,
and also one of Roma, the equal of that of Juno at Argos.
These temples with their official priests and stated

---

[1] *Augustus*, 52 f.

[2] For localities see Heinen, *op. cit.*, p. 175, and L. R. Taylor, *Cults of
Ostia* (Bryn Mawr, 1912), p. 46, n. 2.

[3] *Ant.*, XV, 9; *War*, I, 21.

ceremonials existed in relative abundance, especially in eastern lands, during the lifetime of Augustus. Of the many complimentary inscriptions to him expressing appreciation in religious terms, we may cite a portion of the decree making his birthday the official beginning of the year. The date is about 9 B.C. In part it reads: "Since Providence which orders all of our life, introducing esteem and distinction, adorned our life most perfectly by granting us Augustus whom she filled with virtue for the benefit of mankind, sending him to be a savior for us as well as for our descendants, bringing all wars to an end and setting up all things in order, when Caesar appeared he fulfilled the hopes of those who pointed forward to him, not only excelling previous benefactors, but leaving to future generations no hope of surpassing him. The birthday of the god [Augustus] was for the world the beginning of the good tidings [gospels] because of him."[1] On various occasions he is styled "savior of the Greeks and of the whole inhabited earth," "savior and benefactor," "savior and founder," "savior and God," "son of God, god Augustus, overseer of every land and sea." In Egypt he was called "god of gods," "father of the gods," "son of the sun," "beloved of Ptah and Isis." The official apotheosis of Augustus after his death only further confirmed his worship which was already prevalent throughout the greater part of his empire, especially in those regions where Christianity first gained a hearing a generation later.

Conditions under Augustus' successors continued to favor the practice of emperor-worship. The cult of

[1] Dittenberger, *Orientis Graeci Inscriptiones Selectae* (2 vols., Leipzig, 1903–5), II, 50 ff. (No. 458).

Augustus attained wide vogue, not only in the East but also in the West.[1] The decree of the Senate on September 17, 14 A.D., elevating the deceased emperor to a place among the gods of the state, under the title *Divus Augustus*, met with general approval. In fact, a man of Praetorian rank affirmed under oath, according to Suetonius,[2] that he had visibly witnessed the ascent of Augustus' spirit from the funeral pyre to heaven. Tiberius heartily approved of the apotheosis of Augustus, but assumed a reserved attitude on the subject of his own right to divine honors. In defending his action in permitting the people of Asia to build him a temple he cited the example of Augustus, who had given similar permissions in his lifetime, but Tiberius declared that it was not his intention to be generally apotheosized throughout the provinces.[3] Evidently he was not absolutely opposed to such honors and he clearly intimated that he aspired to deification after death. Josephus says that Caligula exercised at first a similar self-restraint, but later grew so conceited in his possession of power that he made of himself a god.[4] Claudius practiced moderation, refusing all excessive honors,[5] but one of Nero's first acts was to have Claudius apotheosized. When Tiridates visited Nero, first in Naples and then in Rome, Dion Cassius[6] states that this Parthian prince bowed himself before the emperor, saying, "O

---

[1] Tacitus, *Annals*, i. 78.   [2] *Augustus*, 100.

[3] Tacitus, *Annals*, iv. 37 f.

[4] *Ant.*, XVIII, 7. See further Dittenberger, *Sylloge Inscriptionum Graecarum* (3 vols., Leipzig, 1898–1901), I, 567 ff. (Nos. 364 f.), and Paton and Hicks, *The Inscriptions of Cos* (Oxford, 1891), p. 281 (No. 391).

[5] Suetonius, *Claud.*, 12.   [6] lxiii. 1–5.

Lord, I . . . . am thy slave, I am come to thee, my God, worshiping thee even as I worship Mithra." Vespasian figures in tradition as a supernatural personality through an experience in the temple of Serapis in Alexandria, and also by his performance of miracles which was a mark of the "divine majesty and authority" with which he had been endowed as emperor.[1]   To cite again from Suetonius,[2] Domitian assumed divinity for himself first by recalling his divorced wife with the proclamation that he called her to his *pulvinar*, which was the technical name for the consecrated bed on which the images of the gods lay.   He also instructed his procurators when issuing orders in his name to say "Our lord and god" thus commands.

It would be superfluous to cite further data to show how thoroughly habituated the people of the Graeco-Roman world had become to the custom of attaching religious significance to the person of the ruler.   Nor are we to imagine that this was always merely empty flattery.   In some instances, it is true, political causes were the primary agency at work, but some rulers, such for example as Augustus, evoked a genuine appreciation which could find its proper expression for many of their subjects only in terms of religion.   Public opinion was not controlled by official apotheosis but by popular sentiment.   Suetonius' remark[3] that the people fully believed in the divinity of Julius Caesar seems to imply

[1] Suetonius, *Vesp.*, 7; cf. Tacitus, *Hist.*, iv. 82. 2; Josephus, *Ant.*, VIII, ii, 5.

[2] *Domit.*, 13.   See also Hiller von Gaertringen, *Inschriften von Priene* (Berlin, 1906), p. 147 (No. 229).

[3] *Julius Caesar*, 88.

that other deifications decreed by the Senate were not always so readily accepted. In that age it was easy to ascribe divinity, or even outright deity, to a ruler who, like Julius Caesar or Augustus, called forth popular enthusiasm and admiration. Such persons were worshiped with genuine religious feeling, while the cult of a less popular ruler would be observed in a more perfunctory manner.

The cult of both the living and the deceased emperor was well established in the life and thinking of vast numbers of people, particularly in the eastern provinces where gentile Christianity passed through the early stages of its development. Indeed, the Christians of Palestine must have been quite generally familiar with this pervasive religious phenomenon of their day, since it had called forth Jewish protests on various occasions. Christians as well as Jews doubtless opposed the imperial cult, but in so far as it had shaped the channels for religious thinking, and put into circulation a coinage for estimating religious values, it would inevitably exert some influence upon the trend of Christianity's development. Converts to the new religion had learned ways of thinking in connection with emperor-worship which they doubtless found useful in their effort to define the character of the new kingdom and to formulate a fitting religious interpretation of the person of its ruler.

What were some of the more prominent phases of imperial religion which lent themselves most readily to the service of Christians in their gentile missionary propaganda? One of these items was the general desire for deliverance from present evils by seeking the aid of a heaven-sent helper.[1] This longing for a savior had come to be associated with emperor-worship at an early date. The conception itself was ancient, but it blossomed with peculiar vigor in the thinking of the gentile world in the Graeco-Roman period.

Its antecedents are to be seen even in ancient Egypt. Perhaps as early as 2000 B.C. the Egyptian prophet, Ipuwer, laments the deplorable conditions into which Egypt has been plunged by bad government. Blood is everywhere, commerce and industry are ruined, justice no longer reigns, and the people are like wandering sheep without a shepherd. Then the prophet describes the ideal ruler for whom he longs, a savior-king "who brings cooling to the flame. It is said he is the shepherd of men; there is no evil in his heart. . . . . Where is he today? Is he sleeping? Behold, his might is not seen."[2] On the other hand, in seasons of prosperity the Egyptian monarch is lauded for saving the people from distress and mediating to them the divine help. In the royal inscriptions Rameses II is thus addressed: "We come to thee, Lord of heaven, Lord of earth, Re, life of the whole earth . . . . giver of breath unto the nostrils of all, making all the gods live, pillar of heaven, support of earth . . . . our king, our lord, our sun, by the words of whose mouth Atum lives . . . . Pharaoh, who makes all men live when he has shone

[1] See Lietzmann, *Der Weltheiland*, and Zimmern, *Zum Streit um die Christusmythe*.

[2] See H. O. Lange, "Prophezeiungen eines ägyptischen Weisen, usw.," *Sitzungsberichte der Königlich-Preussischen Akademie der Wissenschaften* (1903), I, 601–10; A. H. Gardiner, *The Admonitions of an Egyptian Sage* (Leipzig, 1909); Breasted, "The Earliest Social Prophet," *American Journal of Theology*, XIV (1910), 114–16.

upon them."[1]   Again Merneptah is praised as the divinely sent protector of Egypt's peace: "Great joy has
come in Egypt, rejoicing comes forth from the towns
of Tomeri [Egypt].   They converse of the victories
which Merneptah has achieved among the Tehenu:
'How amiable is he, the victorious ruler, how magnified
is the king among the gods, how fortunate is he, the
commanding lord; sit happily down and talk or walk,
or walk far out upon the way, for there is no fear in the
heart of the people.   One comes and goes with singing
and there is no lamentation of mourning people.   The
towns are settled again anew; as for the one that
ploweth his harvest, he shall eat it.   Re has turned
himself to Egypt.   He was born destined to be her
protector, the king Merneptah.'"[2]

Similar conceptions are found in Babylonia and Assyria.   The Babylonian notion of the period of distress,
followed by an age of divine relief, is portrayed in the
mythology, especially in the story of Creation.   Tiamat
and her associates represent the terrors of the evil age
over whom the divine king, Marduk, triumphs, ushering
in the new age of salvation.   But in actual life men found
themselves still subject to unfavorable circumstances,
consequently they ascribed periods of distress to an
evil régime, while rulers who established more favorable
conditions were hailed as divine deliverers.   Thus they
describe conditions under the wicked king: "War and
strife will not cease from his kingdom.   Under his rule
men will devour one another, people will sell their children for money, the lands will fall together in disorder,

[1] Breasted, *Ancient Records of Egypt* (Chicago, 1906), III, 108.
[2] *Op. cit.*, p. 263.

the husband will leave his wife and the wife will leave her husband, the mother will bar the door against her daughter, the possession of Babylon will come to Subartu [Mesopotamia] and Assyria, the king of Babylon will bring out the property of his palace . . . . to the prince of Assyria."[1] Standing in sharp contrast with this prophecy against the wicked king of Babylon is a letter to the Assyrian king, Asurbanipal, from one of his courtiers: "Shamash and Adad have through their infallible oracle destined my lord the king for his royal rule over the lands: 'favorable reign, days of justice, years of righteousness, copious rainfall, mighty freshets, favorable market prices.' The gods are well disposed, fear of God is abundant, the sanctuaries are overloaded. The great gods of heaven and earth have announced regarding my lord, the king: 'Old men will leap for joy, children will sing, women and maidens will joyfully devote themselves to the duty of wife, they will give life to sons and daughters.' Animal life multiplies. My lord the king has bestowed life upon him whose sins had destined him for death; they who were many years in prison, thou hast set free. They who were sick many days have been restored to health; the hungry became satisfied, the impoverished became fat; the naked became clothed with garments."[2] Asurnasipal's prayer to Ishtar shows the same consciousness of a divine saving mission on the part of the ruler: "But thou, O Ishtar, mighty princess of the gods, in the lifting up of

[1] Ungnad, in Gressmann's *Altorientalische Texte und Bilder zum Alten Testamente*, I, 75 f.

[2] Harper, *Assyrian and Babylonian Letters* (Chicago, 1892), Part I, No. 2, pp. 2 f.

thine eyes didst thou teach me, and didst desire my rule.
Thou didst take from out of the mountains and didst
call me to the threshold of the peoples, thou didst preserve for me the scepter of the temples until the becoming
old of mankind.   And thou, O Ishtar, didst make great
my name, and thou hast granted unto the faithful salvation, mercy."[1]

The resemblance of these ideas to certain features
of the so-called messianic hope of the Hebrews is apparent.[2]   The prophets lament the evils which befall
the people under the rule of a wicked monarch, and
they paint an ideal picture of that age when the righteous
king shall reign.   The political history of the Hebrews
was such that their hope was destined to remain almost
entirely an affair of the future, but it was none the less
vividly described.   Under these circumstances the figure
of the savior-prince necessarily remained vague, but
the righteous character and divine potency of the kingdom to be established were prominent ideas.   The land
would be miraculously fruitful, the wild beasts and
domestic animals would live together in peace, the knowledge of Yahweh would fill the earth, all wars would cease,
and God's chosen king would rule forever in righteousness.[3]   These ideas, so familiar in Hebrew prophecy,
continued to thrive in later Judaism, but they need no
further elaboration in this connection.   They are dis-

[1] Brünnow, "Assyrian Hymns," *Zeitschrift für Assyriologie*, V (1890),
70, lines 25–30.

[2] On the genetic kinships of Israel's hope see Gressmann, *Der Ursprung der israelitischen Eschatologie* (Göttingen, 1905); Oesterley, *The
Evolution of the Messianic Idea: A Study in Comparative Religion* (London, 1908).

[3] Cf. Isa. 9:1 ff.;   11:1 ff.

tinct from the similar hopes of surrounding peoples just in proportion to the distinctiveness of the Israelites' history. But the elemental longing for relief from distress and the custom of looking to the Deity, or his representative, for this desired salvation are not by any means a peculiarly Jewish or Christian product.

The really important rôle which this ancient and general hope of deliverance, to be attained by the aid of a heaven-sent or divinely endowed prince, played among Gentiles just before the rise of Christianity, is best seen by turning to Rome. Among the Romans in the first century B.C. there was a growing longing for the appearance of a national deliverer who would bring wars to an end and usher in the golden age of peace. Tibullus wrote: "How happily men lived when Saturn reigned before the earth was laid open by long roads. . . . . There were no armies, no enmity, no wars, nor had the cruel smith forged the sword with ruthless art. Now under the rule of Jove slaughter and swords are incessant, now sea and land offer a thousand ways of sudden death."[1] Virgil recognizes the same situation but sounds a note of hope in his oft-quoted fourth Eclogue: "The last age prophesied by the Sibyl is come and the great series of ages begins anew. Justice now returns, Saturn reigns once more, and a new progeny is sent down from high heaven. O chaste Lucina, be thou propitious to the infant boy under whom first the iron age shall cease and the golden age over all the world arise. Now thine own Apollo reigns. While thou too, Pollio, while thou art consul, this glory of our age shall dawn and the great months begin to roll. Under thy rule all vestiges of

[1] i. 3; cf. i. 11.

our guilt shall disappear, releasing the earth from fear forever. He [the new-born child] shall partake of the life of the gods, he shall see heroes mingling with gods, and be seen by them, and he shall bring peace to the world, ruling it with his father's might. On thee, O child, the earth, as her first offerings, shall pour forth everywhere without culture creeping ivy with lady's glove, and Egyptian beans with smiling acanthus intermixed. The goats of themselves shall convey homeward their udders distended with milk, nor shall the herds dread monstrous lions. Thy very cradle shall blossom with attractive flowers. The serpent shall perish and the secret-poison plant shall disappear; the Assyrian balm shall grow in every field. But as soon as thou shalt be able to read the praises of heroes and the achievements of thy sire, and to know what virtue is, the field shall by degrees grow yellow with ripening corn, blushing grapes shall hang on the rude brambles, and hard oaks shall drip with dewy honey. . . . . Dear offspring of the gods, mighty seed of Jove, enter thy great heritage, for the time is now at hand. See how the world's massive dome bows before thee—earth and oceans and the vault of heaven. See how all things rejoice at the approach of this age. Oh, that my last stage of life may continue so long and so much breath be given me as shall suffice to sing thy deeds!"[1]

Virgil expects the dawn of this new age soon, for it is to appear while yet his friend Pollio, to whom he addresses his poem, holds the consul's office. We are left to surmise the parentage of this child who is to be

[1] For the pervasiveness of these ideas in the Augustan age see references in Wendland, *Die hellenistisch-römische Kultur*, p. 143.

the savior. But when Virgil composed the *Aeneid* he seemed to feel that his prediction was finding its fulfilment in the career of Augustus. In the sixth book of the *Aeneid*[1] Anchises reveals to Aeneas the future generations of Rome in their pre-earthly state: "This way now bend both your eyes, view this lineage and your own Romans. This is Caesar and these are the whole race of Iulus who shall one day rise to the spacious axle of the sky. This, this is the man whom you have often heard promised to you, Augustus Caesar, offspring of a god, who shall establish again the golden age in Latium, through those lands where Saturn reigned of old." And then follows a prophecy of Augustus' success, which is to be more remarkable than that of Hercules or Bacchus. Horace also in a similar vein sings the praises of Augustus Caesar,

> than whom no boon of nobler worth
> Fate or kind gods ere gave, or ere shall give
> Ev'n though the golden age upon the earth
> Once more may live again.

And further,

> Who Parthia would fear, or Scythia cold,
> Or the huge swarms that German forests breed,
> While Caesar lives to save us.

He is a "winged god who deigns to don a manly frame" who along with Jupiter is to be confessed as a "present god" come to establish Roman sway over all the earth.[2]

This cosmic feature of Augustus' saving work is none the less appreciated in the East. Evidences of this fact are relatively abundant. In addition to data cited

[1] Lines 788 ff.

[2] *Odes*, i. 2. 41 ff.; iii. 5. 1 ff.; iv. 2. 37 ff.; iv. 5. 25 ff.

above,[1] a portion of the Halicarnassus inscription will be sufficient illustration: "Now the eternal and immortal power of all nature bestowed benefactions in superabundance upon men granting to our own life's good fortune Caesar Augustus, father of his own native land, Rome divine; also patrimonial Zeus and savior of the common race of mankind, all of whose prayers Providence has not only fulfilled but even surpassed. For earth and sea have peace, cities flourish, well governed, harmonious, and prosperous, the course of all good things has reached a climax, and all mankind has been filled with good hopes for the future and good cheer for the present."[2]

Thus it is evident that Christians were not the first persons to introduce the notion of salvation into the religious thinking of the gentile world. They preached, to be sure, that there was no salvation in any other name except that of Jesus, but their contemporaries believed they themselves had been deriving saving benefits of a distinctly valuable sort from other individuals, and on the basis of this experience they had accorded these persons divine honors, worshiping them as gods while yet upon earth, or when exalted to heaven after death. We have already observed a few of the instances in which significant persons were hailed as "savior" in Hellenistic times, but the list could be much enlarged.[3] Although the salvation thus obtained belonged to this

[1] See especially the birthday decree cited above p. 215.

[2] *Collection of Ancient Greek Inscriptions in the British Museum*, Part IV, section I (Oxford, 1893), p. 63, No. 894.

[3] See Wendland, "Σωτήρ: Eine religionsgeschichtliche Untersuchung," *Zeitschrift für die neutestamentliche Wissenschaft*, V (1904), 335-53.

world, while that preached by the Christians pertained in the main to the next, the Gentiles' point of view was none the less religious in character, according to the thinking of that age. In fact, the earthly national type of religious faith was the more primitive one. Moreover, the blessings which the new religion offered were perhaps more realistic than moderns, who have grown accustomed to estimate so-called "spiritual" values in terms of vague and intangible entities, are wont to suppose. At any rate, the mere fact that Gentiles thought they were already realizing their kingdom of God on earth did not of itself make their conception any less religious than that of the Christians who looked for an other-worldly kingdom to be set up in a miraculously renovated earth.

Christians found in this particular phase of their gentile religious surroundings much that helped them in their own propaganda. They preached at the outset a Jewish type of messianic hope, centering it about the person of the risen Jesus. But the fact that the Gentiles also cherished a messianic hope of their own, centering it about the deified or semi-deific person of the ruler, greatly aided Christians in making the transition from Jewish to gentile surroundings. Perhaps the most fundamental items in the transition were, from the side of the Gentiles, the transformation of their hope from a this-worldly to an other-worldly character, and, on the part of Christians, the transformation of the national Jewish Messiah into a cosmic Savior-prince. This led Christians to place more emphasis—or at least a somewhat different emphasis—upon the person of the individual who performed saving functions than they would

have done had they remained in a strictly Jewish environment. With the Jews stress fell chiefly upon God; it
was his kingdom that was to be established, and the
Messiah was significant because he was God's agent. He
might be divine, even sent forth from heaven, but his
mission was a delegated one and his personality was
quite subsidiary in comparison with the more primary
items of God and the kingdom. This way of thinking
was in line with the main trend of oriental ideas regarding the ruler who was a god-man king. On the other
hand, the Greek notion of the man-god king placed stress
upon the ruler's personal qualifications for divine honors.
The purely Jewish Messiah was not to be an object of
worship; but Gentiles would have had the greatest
difficulty in accepting anybody as their Messiah who
did not prove himself worthy of their worship.

   Christians met this situation, whether acting consciously or unconsciously, by so defining Jesus' personality as to make it evident that he transcended all
other claimants to divine honors. That they were
able to do this meant much for the success of their cause
among Gentiles and led them to stress a number of
features which otherwise might not have become prominent in the New Testament. Among other things,
remarkable accomplishments for the sake of humanity
frequently became a basis for believing in a Greek hero's
exaltation to heaven after death. We have already
seen that the first believers arrived at their faith in the
risen Jesus in a somewhat different way, but it is questionable whether they would have so diligently expounded the wonderful earthly career of Jesus had
not the situation in the gentile missionary field stimu-

lated interest in the story of his beneficent work upon earth. Recounting the life of an individual with the special purpose of creating admiration for him, if not indeed divine reverence, was a characteristic of the Hellenistic age. Hercules, Dionysus, Orpheus, and many other heroes had attained a heavenly reward and established their right to divine honors by means of their services for mankind. Plutarch applied this idea, which had been in existence a long time before he lived, to the career of the Egyptian divinities, Isis and Osiris, who, he says, "having been translated from the rank of good divinities [δαίμονες] up to that of gods by means of their virtue, as later happened to Hercules and Dionysus, received not inappropriately the united honors of gods and divinities everywhere, both in the regions above earth and in those underground, possessing the supreme power."[1]

That actual, historical personages traveled by this road to heaven was a common doctrine, fostered especially in connection with the cult of the emperor. One of the speakers in Cicero's work on the nature of the gods[2] remarks that it had been a general custom to exalt to heaven by fame and general consent those men who have rendered the public important service. Also in Scipio's dream the same idea is given a prominent place. Service for one's country assures one a special place in heaven and the enjoyment of endless happiness, for "there is nothing which takes place on earth more acceptable to the supreme Deity who governs all this world than those councils and assemblies of men bound

[1] *Isis and Osiris*, xxvii; cf. Phil. 2:9 f ·

[2] ii. 24.

together by law which are termed states. The governors and preservers of these go from hence [i.e., heaven] and hither do they return." Further Scipio is exhorted "to cultivate justice and piety, which while it should be great toward your parents and relatives should be greatest toward your country. Such a life is the path to heaven." Virgil also,[1] in revealing the state of the blessed, points out a favored band of "those who sustained wounds in fighting for their country, priests who preserved themselves pure and holy while life remained, pious poets who sung in strains worthy of Apollo, those who improved life by the invention of arts and who by their worthy deeds made others remember them, all these have their heads encircled with a snow-white fillet." This reverential attitude,[2] which goes back to the days of Greek hero-worship, received a mighty stimulus from the career of Alexander the Great and became well-nigh universal in the Augustan age. While educated persons like Cicero, Virgil, and Horace applied it mainly in the realm of statecraft, among the populace the notion was extended to cover the whole range of any heroic individual's activity. The gospel story about Jesus' virtuous life and wonderful deeds, which reached a climax in his resurrection and exaltation, on the basis of which Christians were advocating his claims to imperial honors, naturally expanded and functioned anew when the propaganda moved from a Jewish to a gentile environment.

[1] *Aeneid*, vi. 660 ff.

[2] The prevalence of this feeling in Graeco-Roman times can hardly be overemphasized. See Wendland, *Die hellenistisch-römische Kultur*, pp. 117 f., 143 f.

In those circles where special religious significance was attached to the life of the ruler, there was naturally a disposition to find in unique displays of divine activity evidence of a connection between his person and the powers of heaven. Oracles, portents, and supernatural displays of various sorts answered this demand. From Alexander the Great down to the Roman emperors of the first century A.D., and in fact for a much longer period, these things play an important part in attesting the divine connections of the ruler. Although these phenomena were especially abundant in the imperial period, Christians could easily compete with this phase of gentile faith. To begin with, they were able to point to Jesus' resurrection as a mark of divine approval at the close of Jesus' earthly activity and they were further able in the course of time to show how God had not only foreshadowed in prophecy the career of Jesus, but had specifically indicated by a voice from heaven on different occasions that Jesus was a divinely commissioned person. At this point Christians were advantaged by having, as a part of their oriental inheritance, the notion that the sovereign was divinely delegated and equipped for his task. When they moved to gentile surroundings it was very easy to supplement the notion of divine approval with the idea of a divine display of Jesus' own unique individuality, thus answering to the current trend in Greek thinking. As an illustration in point, we may notice the different ways of referring to Jesus' miracles and resurrection. The tradition embodied in the second chapter of Acts speaks of Jesus upon earth as a man approved of God by mighty works, and wonders and signs, which God did by him. It was also God who raised him from the dead and made him both Lord and Christ.[1]   In Mark these matters are presented from a more distinctly Greek point of view, or rather from a Christian point of view which has developed in the direction of Greek hero-worship.   Jesus works miracles in virtue of his own inherent authority,[2] and his approaching resurrection is not to be so much an act of God as a display of Jesus' own power—it is not God who *raises* him, but Jesus simply *rises*.[3]

In the case of a ruler whose uniqueness was a part of his own personality rather than a merely delegated endowment, it was easy to suppose, as an adequate means of accounting for his personality, that his birth had come about in some unusual manner.   The most familiar explanation offered was that of divine parentage. In the Orient the king who represented the deity was frequently termed Son of God, a phrase which might be taken either figuratively or literally according to the setting in which it was used.   We have only to recall how generally this form of expression occurs among Egyptians, Babylonians and Assyrians, and Hebrews to realize its importance for that ancient world.   The notion that the king was a literal child of the deity was frequently made to do service in explaining how gods had procured for themselves a real representative upon earth.   In Graeco-Roman times the term "Son of God"

[1] Acts 2:22, 24, 32, 36; see also 3:15; 4:10; 10:40; 13:30 ff.; 17:31; Rom. 1:4; 4:24; 6:4; 8:11; 10:9; I Cor. 6:14; 15:3, 12 ff.; II Cor. 4:14; Eph. 1:20; Phil. 2:9; Col. 2:12; I Thess. 1:10.

[2] 1:27; 2:10, 28, etc.

[3] E.g., 8:31; 9:9 f., 31; 10:34.   Matthew, on the other hand, always uses the passive, e.g., 16:21; 17:9, 23; 20:19; 27:63 f.; Luke 9:22 says "raised," but "rise" in 18:33; 24:7.

applied to the hero-prince was of very common occurrence and served admirably to explain whence this individual derived these exceptional qualities which he had proved himself capable of displaying. Even so cautious a biographer as Arrian, when discussing the question of Alexander's parentage, hesitatingly concludes that Alexander's wonderful accomplishments set him above the category of the purely human. "It seems to me that a hero totally unlike any other human being could not have been born without the agency of the deity."[1]

Other distinguished persons beside rulers were also assigned a divine origin as a means of explaining their uniqueness. In the Augustan age Arellius Fuscus said of the astrologer, "he to whom the gods themselves reveal the future, who imposes their will even on kings and peoples, cannot be fashioned by the same womb which bore us ignorant men. His is a superhuman rank. Confidant of the gods, he is himself divine."[2] Likewise the remarkable wisdom of Jesus' contemporary, Apollonius of Tyana, was explained in popular tradition by making Proteus, the god of Egypt, the father of Apollonius. An appropriate display of miracles accompanied the birth of the child. Swans sported about the mother in the meadow, and a thunderbolt descending from heaven arose aloft again, thus presaging the wonderful accomplishments by which Apollonius was to be distinguished.[3]

[1] *Anabasis*, vii. 30.

[2] Cited by Cumont, *Astrology and Religion among Greeks and Romans* (New York, 1912), p. 148. Cf. the important function which Jesus' heavenly wisdom serves in the Fourth Gospel.

[3] Philostratus, *Life of Apollonius*, i. 5 f.

The list of persons who had been assigned divine origin before the rise of Christianity is extensive.[1] But it is the religious significance of the notion in the Augustan age and the period immediately following which has greatest importance for the history of early Christianity. Augustus not only bore the title *Divi filius*, which of itself might be only a complimentary epithet, but his divine descent was, at least for eastern peoples, a substantial part of the belief in his saving mission. Suetonius is probably reporting even popular Roman tradition, if not of Augustus' own day, certainly of a period soon after his official apotheosis, when he explains the circumstances by which Apollo brought about the supernatural generation of the child and tells of the many wonders preceding and following his birth.[2] This type of tradition was widely circulated, but nothing shows the unique religious significance attached to the emperor's birth more clearly than the Priene inscription, a portion of which has already been cited.[3] In an earlier part we read, "The birthday of the divine Caesar, which we might justly rate equal to the beginning of all creation . . . . gave another aspect to the whole world, which would truly have perished utterly had not Caesar, the common good fortune of all men, been born."

Christians embraced the opportunity thus opened to them to estimate Jesus in cosmic terms along lines already familiar to Gentiles, at the same time making his religious significance transcend that of any gentile emperor. The credentials brought forward to attest

---

[1] Cf. Petersen, *Die wunderbare Geburt des Heilandes* (Tübingen, 1909), pp. 32 ff., where other literature is cited (p. 2).

[2] *Augustus*, 94.   [3] See above, p. 215.

his divine parentage and remarkable advent into the world were more impressive than those given Augustus or any of his successors. Christians affirmed also that the birth of Jesus marked the beginning of a new era in the history of humanity, hence this day was easily made to surpass in importance the birthday of any other alleged savior. When Roman rulers like Caligula followed the example set by Seleucid kings centuries earlier and claimed that they were epiphanies of the deity, gods manifest in the flesh, they were assuming no dignity which Christians could not attach to Jesus. Not only was he "God with us," but this title could be supported by the authority of antiquity through the prophetic "Immanuel." The notion that Jesus' earthly career was a manifestation of his pre-existent heavenly glory also in time came to full appreciation among Christians, especially as the gospel moved farther away from its Jewish antecedents. Paul, although mentioning the pre-existence of Jesus, does not depict Jesus' earthly career as a glorious epiphany of deity but as a humble display of servitude. The true "epiphany" is to come when Jesus returns at the Parousia. Thus Paul estimates Jesus chiefly in the language of authority. He appears upon earth as a servant and is elevated to lordship at his resurrection. But in the Fourth Gospel the epiphany actually takes place in Jesus' lifetime when he manifests the glory which he had with the Father before the foundation of the world. It is not primarily authority as with Paul, but divine nature, which John has in mind. In so far as the emperor claimed to be the actual incarnation of deity Christians now had in the Johannine metaphysical interpretation of Jesus a new weapon for defending his supremacy. But perhaps they found this less serviceable in opposing emperor-worship than in combating certain forms of philosophical religion with which they ultimately came in contact.

In presenting Jesus to the heathen as the sovereign of the new heavenly kingdom Christian missionaries advocated a new imperial cult designed to supplant all rivals. Over against the divine Caesar, whether apotheosized at death or appearing as a deity upon earth, stood Jesus raised from the dead, exalted to lordship in heaven, having previously displayed miraculous powers upon earth, having been miraculously born or appearing as a pre-existent divine being manifest in the flesh. Jesus' authority was not less great or less divine in character than that of the most distinguished Roman emperor. Jesus was lord and his subjects were servants, which was not only the typical relation between monarch and people from ancient times in the Orient, but had become a familiar notion to the Graeco-Roman world in the Hellenistic age. Although Gentiles spoke of the emperor's visit as a Parousia for which a community made special preparation,[1] Christians could announce a Parousia of their Lord Jesus Christ which called for more strenuous preparation and which would be accompanied by a display of supernatural power and splendor such as the world had never before witnessed. It meant much for the success of Christianity that its advocates could make the transition from the national messianism of their Jewish environment to the cosmic messianism of the Graeco-Roman world. Jesus now could be seen to

---

[1] See data given by Deissmann, *Licht vom Osten*, pp. 268–73, English tr., *Light from the Ancient East*, pp. 372–78.

surpass any imperial world-savior who merely delivered
mankind from the terrors of political chaos, even though
this deliverance was thought to be in reality a concern of
the gods. Great superiority could be claimed for the
new kingdom, since it was wholly an affair of the new age
when all previous dominions would forever cease. Thus
the early Christian missionaries, by appropriating certain features of imperial messianism, made their original
Jewish conception of the national kingdom adaptable to
Gentiles, and at the same time no doubt increased its
significance for themselves. The transition from the
Jewish emphasis on the kingdom to the gentile emphasis
on the figure of the savior also pointed the direction in
which Christian thinking was destined to move in suc-
ceeding generations.

It is not surprising that emperor-worship gave way
before the new religion which not only conserved so
many values of the old but heightened the significance
of the imperial idea. Yet this triumph was by no
means immediate, nor was it accomplished without effort.
That common attitude of life which reaches out toward
a superior power for assistance found a really popular expression in the worship of the monarch who was thought
to embody the divine potency for whose help mankind yearned. One who was able or willing to satisfy
the pressing needs of helpless multitudes by restoring
peace and prosperity to the world demanded and received
worshipful obedience. His cult did not need, at least
for many persons, to be established by formal mandate,
since they naturally turned with reverential feelings
toward him, pleading for further benefactions or making
grateful acknowledgments of blessings already received.

This feeling has always been, particularly among the populace, a fundamental religious impulse. Christianity on the other hand, promised well for the future, but was meager in realistic blessings in the present.

But as time passed, a union of religion with politics proved to be an increasingly unstable foundation for the religious hopes of the Graeco-Roman world. It issued as unsatisfactorily in their experience as it had in the case of the Egyptians, the Babylonians and Assyrians, or the Hebrews. Although the Caesars continued to be adorned with complimentary epithets, their subjects realized that the Golden Age was still a long way off. There was, indeed, from time to time a general stability of affairs which made life more bearable than it had been in the days of constant internal warfare, but social conditions were far from ideal. The common man still felt that he had many enemies from which he had not been delivered, and he must have been convinced that emperor-worship offered but little promise of procuring the help he needed. Even among the higher classes there must also have been much dissatisfaction. While people stood in favor with the emperor their lot was a fairly comfortable one, but who knew what day the vicissitudes of politics might bring an order for his banishment, or his death, and the confiscation of his goods. It is not difficult to understand how another type of religion which contemplated the salvation of the individual rather than that of the nation and based its assurance upon a more exclusively divine Savior, the Lord Jesus Christ, ultimately made a far stronger appeal to many people in the Graeco-Roman world.

CHAPTER VIII

THE RELIGIOUS SIGNIFICANCE OF PHILOSOPHICAL SPECULATION

Philosophy was a distinctive product of the Greek genius. Before either the Macedonians or the Romans were known to the ancient world Greek thinkers had attacked life's problems from the standpoint of reflection, formulating ideas and methods of thinking that were destined to endure long after the kingdom of Alexander and the empire of Augustus had fallen. The temporary ascendancy of the monarchical principle in Graeco-Roman times did indeed make a marked impression upon religion, yet philosophy continued to exert an influence which steadily increased as national religions gradually disappeared.

There are wide and fundamental differences between that interpretation of religion which can be adequately expressed by the monarchical ideal on the one hand, and the philosopher's conception on the other. National faiths are concerned primarily with the good of the community and only secondarily with the welfare of the individual. He shares the common good, but only as he remains a member of the social organism which supplies him his sole "means of grace." Thus only can he avail himself of the conventicles, the stated forms of worship, and the official instruction necessary for the genesis and maintenance of religious life. The keynote of such religions is the idea of authority. The deity is pictured as a mighty sovereign dominating all creation, the validity of ritual and dogma is established by tradition, and conduct is regulated in so far as it is thought to have any religious significance by definitely prescribed norms.

The position of the philosopher is radically different. He approaches religious problems from the standpoint of the individual rather than the community. Instead of defining God in the language of authority he describes him in rational or metaphysical terms, at the same time subjecting rites and dogmas to severe scrutiny or even to open criticism. Conduct also is provided with new sanctions which emanate from personal conviction instead of being prescribed by external authorities. The philosopher may eventually strive to make his conclusions normative for others, but individual freedom is the presupposition upon which his own creative work is done.

Before attempting a more detailed estimate of the philosopher's significance for the history of religion within the Graeco-Roman world, it may be well to observe briefly the outstanding characteristics of the general religious situation upon which he reacted.

For centuries the Homeric mythology had been the orthodox theology of the Greeks, and a thinker who found himself out of harmony with traditional views might be subjected to criticism, banished, or even put to death for heresy. The experiences of Anaxagoras, Protagoras, and Socrates illustrate these possibilities. While the Greeks never had what could be called one orthodox national faith—for in religion as in politics the city was autonomous—yet in literature, art, and mythology the Olympians had become supreme during the classical period. It is not surprising that those students of antiquity who have derived their information of Greek life chiefly from its more formal literary and artistic remains should have mistakenly supposed that worship of the Homeric gods constituted the sum total of early Greek religion, or formed, in fact, the chief content of all Graeco-Roman religion before the rise of Christianity.

On the contrary, long before the Christian era many criticisms had been leveled against these ancient gods, and other media for estimating religious values had been employed in their stead. The idea of portraying deity in human form was criticized as early as the sixth century B.C. by Xenophanes, who remarked that if oxen, horses, and lions had hands with which to make images they would picture the gods as oxen, horses, and lions. In Xenophanes' own opinion there is one god, greatest among gods and men. He cannot be represented in anthropomorphic form, for he is "all sight, all mind, all ear, and without effort rules everything by thought."[1] Dissatisfaction with popular anthropomorphism manifested itself increasingly in both the classical and the Hellenistic periods. Many persons were too intelligent to take seriously this realistic feature of contemporary polytheism.

Cultured people raised even more serious objections to the Homeric mythology. Many of the Olympians' deeds were felt to be absurd, scandalous, and sometimes grossly immoral. Self-respecting men would never act so disgracefully, much less would real gods thus deport themselves.[2] But if there could be no such

[1] Diels, *Fragmente der Vorsokratiker* (Berlin, 1912³), I, 15, 23–25.
[2] Cf. Cicero, *De deor. nat.*, i. 16; Lucretius, *De rer. nat.*, i. 83 ff.

gods, how did mythology arise? Various rationalistic
explanations had been advanced in the early days of
Greek thinking. Democritus traced belief in gods to
the fear which the more terrible phenomena of nature
—thunder, lightning, earthquakes, eclipses—awakened
in men. Others said the stories about the gods were
at the outset simply legends of heroic men distorted in
order to exalt them above mortals. In Hellenistic times
it was discovered that other nations besides the Greeks
also had similar myths, and this gave rise to what might
be termed a science of mythology which sought to
equate the names and functions of various deities among
the different peoples. In certain circles the effect of this
whole line of development was to lessen greatly the
former prestige of the Olympians.

But denying the anthropomorphic gods of Olympus
did not alter the real experiences of mankind. The
world was still hostile and friendly by turns; life still
had its disappointments, its uncertainties, its calamities;
and nature was just as fickle with its frowns and smiles as
the Olympian Zeus had been. Who was now responsible
for this continued uncertainty of affairs? By some
persons the responsibility was placed upon Fortune
(τύχη). Demetrius of Phalerum, in the fourth century
B.C., assigns recent happenings in the political world to
the violence of Fortune:[1] "If some god had warned the
Persians or their king, or the Macedonians or their
king that in fifty years the very name of the Persians,
who once were masters of the world, would be lost,

[1] Polybius, xxix. 21. See, further, Cumont, "L'Éternité des empe-
reurs romains," *Revue d'histoire et de littérature religieuses*, I (1898),
435–52.

and that the Macedonians, whose name was before scarcely known, would become masters of it all, do you think they would have believed it ? Nevertheless it is true that Fortune, whose influence on our life is incalculable, who displays her power by surprises, is even now, I think, showing all mankind by her elevation of the Macedonians into the high prosperity once enjoyed by the Persians, that she has merely lent them these advantages until she may otherwise dispose of them."[1]

Other persons placed more stress upon an orderly procedure called Fate (ἀνάγκη) or Destiny (εἰμαρμένη). Events did not happen by mere chance, but conformed to a law of necessity which controlled all things. It was said to be unworthy of an intelligent man to attribute all phenomena to Chance rather than to an intelligent cause. The life of an individual might seem to contain much uncertainty but the perpetual motion of the heavens, the regularity of the stars in their courses, and the harmony of the entire universe transcended the powers of human comprehension and must be divine. Being fully complete and perfect in all its parts from all eternity, the universe itself is deity.[2] The Augustan poet Manilius in his *Astronomica*[3] contrasts the instability of historical events with the permanence of nature: "Thrones have disappeared, peoples have passed from

---

[1] The older Pliny in his *Natural History*, ii. 22, remarks that everybody everywhere throughout the world invokes Fortune only. Chance even takes precedence over God. See Wendland, *Die hellenistisch-römische Kultur*, p. 104, notes 2 and 3, for references on τύχη; also Gruppe, *Griechische Mythologie*, pp. 1498 f.

[2] Cf. Cicero, *De deor. nat.*, ii. 13, 28.

[3] i. 495 ff.; Cumont, *Astrology and Religion among the Greeks and Romans*, pp. 106–38.

dominion to slavery or from captivity to empire, but the
same months of the year have always brought up on the
horizon the same stars. . . . . Each century transforms
the features of nations, but heaven remains invariable
and preserves all its parts. The flight of time adds
nothing to them nor does age detract therefrom. Heaven
will remain perpetually the same because it has forever
been the same. As it appeared to the eyes of our fore-
fathers so will our descendants behold it. It is God, for
it is unchangeable throughout the ages."

This notion of nature's stability was an inheritance
from oriental astrology, which had become thoroughly
acclimated in the Mediterranean world before the rise
of Christianity.[1] According to Suetonius, even the
Roman emperor Tiberius abandoned the old forms of
religion and adopted astrology, being fully persuaded
that all things are governed by Fate.[2] The result of
this admiration for the heavens was a disposition to
deify not only all the heavenly bodies but also the elements—fire, air, water, and earth—as well as the phenomena of time—seasons, months, weeks, days, hours.
These deified "elements of the world" were a part of the
fatalistic natural order which bound mankind under
the laws of an inexorable necessity. While the educated man tried to find comfort in the thought of deified
nature's stable rule, to people in general it furnished no

[1] Important works on ancient astrology are Cumont, *op. cit.*, also
Oriental Religions, pp. 162–95; Bouché-Leclercq, *L'Astrologie grecque*
(Paris, 1899); Boll, *Sphaera* (Leipzig, 1903); Boll, "Die Erforschung der
antiken Astrologie," *Neue Jahrbücher für das klassische Altertum*, XXI
(1908), 103–26; Toutain, *Les cultes païens*, I, ii, 179–226; Fries, *Die
griechischen Götter und Heroen vom astralmythologischen Standpunkte
aus betrachtet* (Berlin, 1911).

[2] *Tib.*, 69.

great religious satisfactions. Inflexible destiny, differentiated into the personalized forces of nature, left the common man in bondage to powers which his experience found hostile rather than friendly. Enslaved by "elements of the world,"[1] he felt himself a mere plaything of the gods whom he worshiped, not with loving adoration, but in the agony of perpetual fear. These deities frequently became mere evil demons constantly intent upon harming mortals.

Consequently the populace often plunged into gross "superstition," as it was termed by the more intelligent,[2] who defined superstition as an unnecessary fear of deity, while true religion was a pious admiration of the gods.[3] He who did not care to worship them might ignore their existence, or at least deny their power, but even this skepticism was far less culpable than base superstition, in the eyes of many persons who themselves claimed to be truly religious. Plutarch in his treatise on *Superstition* gathers up clearly the views on this subject current among a large class of the more intelligent yet professedly religious persons. As his description tallies closely with the statements of Lucretius[4] and Cicero[5] a

[1] στοιχεῖα τοῦ κόσμου, Gal. 4:3, 9; Col. 2:8, 20. For the influence of this notion in Judaism before New Testament times see Bousset, *Die Religion des Judentums*, pp. 350 f.; or Bertholet, *Die jüdische Religion*, pp. 360, 380 f. On the subject in general see Diels, *Elementum: Zur Geschichte des Begriffes Elementum bei Griechen und Römern* (Leipzig, 1899).

[2] For data regarding superstition in antiquity see Riess, "Aberglaube," in Pauly-Wissowa, *Realencyclopädie*, I (Stuttgart, 1904); Kroll, *Antiker Aberglaube* (Hamburg, 1897); Dill, *Roman Society from Nero to Marcus Aurelius*, pp. 443–83.

[3] Cf. Cicero, *De deor. nat.*, i. 42; ii. 28.

[4] E.g., *De rer. nat.*, v. 1192 ff.

[5] E.g., *De deor. nat.*, i. 20.

century and a half before, it undoubtedly represents a
situation very common in the gentile world when Christianity arose.   He defines atheism as a state of insensi-
bility regarding things divine, brought on by an extreme
rationalistic reaction against the irrational conduct of
the superstitious persons.   Superstition, on the contrary,
proceeds from the notion that the gods are spiteful and
malignant beings—"atheism is reason deceived, superstition a passion arising out of false reasoning."   But the
latter malady is really much the worse, for it is prior to,
and in some degree justifies, doubt about the gods.
Moreover, the superstitious man, since he doubts things
which are noblest and best about the deities, would, if
consistent, also be atheistic.   He does not become such
simply because he is "far too weak-minded to think
about the gods what he wishes to think."   The atheist,
on the other hand, is so intent upon fleeing superstition
that he is carried to the opposite extreme, and misses
true religion which occupies a middle position.

The baneful character of superstition is vividly
depicted by Plutarch.   While the truly religious man
finds pleasure in festivals and banquets, ceremonies of
initiation, bacchic rites, vows, and adoration of images,
the superstitious man is filled with fear and anxiety.
He is most unhappy when approaching the shrines or
chapels of the gods, for these places are to him "the
dens of bears, the holes of dragons, the lurking-places
of the monsters of the deep."   His whole life is full of
terror, for in everything—"the sea, the air, the sky,
darkness, light, speech, silence"—he finds something
to fear.   Even in his sleep his painful notions about the
deity fill his dreams with "terrific phantoms, monstrous

apparitions, and tortures of all kinds." Should trouble befall him he finds no consolation in his religion, for he views these things as "plagues from God." Instead of seeking by natural means to remedy his ills, he refuses help lest he should seem to be fighting against the chastening of the gods. He rejects the ministry of a physician or comforter, saying, "Let me alone, my good fellow, to suffer my punishment—impious, accursed as I am, hateful to gods and demons." So he wears sackcloth or filthy rags, wallows naked in the mire, loudly confessing his sins, or performing other ridiculous actions. Nor does death release him from terror, since his imagination conjures up horrible, never-ending woes in the next world: "Deep below, the gates of hell are opened, rivers of fire and the fountains of Styx are at once disclosed. A fantastic darkness envelops all, where certain spectral forms flit about, offering frightful sight to the eye, piteous sounds to the ear. There are also judges seated and executioners in waiting, yawning gulfs and deep places crammed with all manner of evil things. Thus unhappy superstition had obtained through death an end of suffering, but has through its folly created for itself an expectation of future misery."[1]

Those who despised "superstition" were not, however, above entertaining certain notions which moderns would undoubtedly class under that name. Since necessity ruled all things, it was possible, for one who possessed sufficiently keen powers of observation, to read the future from the signs of the present. All events

[1] A summary of gentile ideas regarding punishment after death may be found in Dieterich, *Nekyia: Beiträge zur Erklärung der neuentdeckten Petrusapokalypse* (Leipzig, 1893).

proceeded in a fixed order, consequently a given series of antecedents would always indicate the same series of consequences. Even if Fate did dominate all creation it was some comfort to be able to know what was to happen, or even to undertake the paradoxical task of avoiding the anticipated decrees of destiny. Thus divination became popular again, even though the ancient oracles and many of the older forms of divination which had been so common among the Romans in former times had fallen into disuse.[1] Astrology gave new life to this whole field of activity, since it seemed quite respectable and fitting to turn to the stars for widsom. Things came to such a pass, that "people would no longer take a bath, go to the barber, change their clothes, or manicure their finger nails without first awaiting the propitious moment."[2]

Magic was very closely akin to divination. The notion of nature's uniformity, particularly as exhibited in the heavens, was the fundamental postulate from which both the diviner and the magician worked. The

[1] Von Arneth, *Das classische Heidentum und die christliche Religion*, I, 273-318, gives a concise account of the Sibyls and oracles in ancient religion. See, further, Halliday, *Greek Divination* (London, 1913). Strabo (xvii. 1. 43) remarks that the honor in which divination and oracles had been held in former times was giving way in his day (early in the first century A.D.). Romans were satisfied with "the oracles of the Sibyl and with Tyrrhenian divination by the entrails of animals, the flight of birds, and portentous appearances." Certainly this type of thinking retained its grip very firmly upon many persons. Suetonius in his lives of the Caesars revels in the narration of portentous happenings, and the Jew, Josephus (e.g., *War*, VI, v, 3), expects his gentile readers to feel the force of this sort of reasoning. The notion of portents, signs, etc., as anticipating future events was unquestionably firmly rooted in the Graeco-Roman world in the first century of our era.

[2] Cumont, *Oriental Religions*, p. 165.

latter, however, gave more attention to matters of practical efficiency, proposing not merely to reveal the workings of Fate but to provide means for averting or controlling its action. Through his acquaintance with the stars, and his knowledge of other deific powers with which men came into more immediate contact, he claimed to possess a secret wisdom which enabled him to play off one supernatural agency against another. He had learned the magic name or formula necessary to control the activity of all the powers, he could give accurate instruction about the course of action one should pursue in various contingencies, and he could furnish infallible prescriptions for averting every form of danger. These instructions were written and sold to patrons in increasingly large quantities. These books, which circulated first in the Orient and in Egypt, increased rapidly both in quantity and popularity over the whole Mediterranean world in pre-Christian times. This is probably the type of literature that Augustus collected and burned —over 2,000 volumes of it, says Suetonius.[1] The presence of such books in Ephesus in Paul's day is not at all surprising. Nor is it strange that the apostle's hearers, on becoming convinced that evil spirits could be driven off and life's ills in general could be cured through the efficacy of Jesus' name, should have been ready to destroy their magical books and adopt Paul's simpler method of averting evils.[2]

Amid this diversity of elements contributing to the complicated religious syncretism of the Graeco-Roman

[1] *Aug.*, 31.

[2] Acts 19:11 ff. For literature on magic, see Cumont, *Oriental Religions*, pp. 277 ff., notes 58, 64 f., and 72. See also above, pp. 147 ff.

world, the ancient gods of Greece lost their former
prestige. Yet they were by no means completely forgotten. Their name and fame were perpetuated in the
cultus, as well as by art and literature. Their cults
not only survived in Greece, but spread to various parts
of the Roman empire. They were transformed into the
gods of the Roman pantheon, and their names were
sometimes appropriated by cults which had been originally connected with far less distinguished divinities.
In this way the Olympians were often given the attributes or functions of other gods, and occasionally their
names were combined with those of the foreign deities.
For example, Zeus became "Zeus Oromasdes" in a
Persian atmosphere; under Jewish influences in Syria he
became "Zeus Hypsistos"; and the people of Com-
magene combined him with one of their local gods as
"Zeus Dolichaeus."[1]

Art and literature also perpetuated the Olympians'
memory. Their form had been preserved in bronze and
marble, in ivory and precious metals, by the genius of a
Phidias, a Polyclitus, or a Praxiteles. Poetic fancy also
continued to draw freely for its imagery upon the rich
mines of Homeric mythology. But anthropomorphic
mythology was no longer capable of ministering to the
deepest religious needs of the more cultured classes.
They prized its aesthetic values and tolerated it as a concession to the ignorant, but for themselves it had lost all
vital religious power. The name of Zeus, or some other
of the Olympians, was retained, but it merely served as
an image for depicting a quite new world of feeling,

[1] For this extensive fusion of gods' names and characteristics, see
Gruppe, *Griechische Mythologie*, pp. 1058 ff.

belief, and aspiration.   The shibboleths remained in the god's name and image, but the vital content of religion had greatly changed.

This change did not mean the utter abandonment of religion by educated people.   Satirists like Juvenal and Lucian did not depict the real facts, for it did not suit their purpose to portray—if indeed they appreciated—the deeper currents of spiritual life which had for centuries been moving within that ancient world.   Since Xenophanes' day dissatisfaction with traditional forms had been increasing, and more thoughtful persons had been striving to transcend the things of sense in an effort to obtain an adequate means of estimating the deepest religious experiences of the human spirit.   This attitude is well illustrated by a paragraph from Maximus of Tyre in his defense of image-worship.   Though he wrote in the second century A.D., the views he expressed are representative of a disposition which had shown itself among the educated and thoughtful centuries before. Maximus says: "God himself, the father and fashioner of all that is, older than the sun or the sky, greater than time and eternity and all the flow of being, is unnamable by any lawgiver, unutterable by any voice, not to be seen by any eye.   But we, being unable to apprehend his essence, use the help of sounds and names and pictures, of beaten gold and ivory and silver, of plants and rivers, mountain peaks and torrents, yearning for the knowledge of him, and in our weakness naming all that is beautiful in this world after his nature—just as happens to earthly lovers.   To them the most beautiful sight will be the actual lineaments of the beloved, but for remembrance' sake they will be happy in the sight of a lyre, a little spear, a chair, perhaps, or a running-ground, or anything in the world that wakens the memory of the beloved. Why should I further examine and pass judgment about images? Let men know what is divine; let them know, that is all. If a Greek is stirred to the remembrance of God by the art of Phidias, an Egyptian by paying worship to animals, another man by a river, another by a fire, I have no quarrel with their divergences. Only let them know, let them love, let them remember."[1]

How did the philosopher, who by profession addressed himself to the more serious side of life,[2] meet this complicated religious situation? His task always involves religious problems because he deals with three questions to which most religions purport to give infallible answers. The first of these is: What is reality? What is the ultimate ground of all things in the universe? For individual thinkers, particularly in Greece, the problem of being—"ontology" as we call it—was solved by scrutinizing the universe in order to discover the ultimate factors which account for its origin and disclose the secret of its continuance. This was the "physics" of the ancients, but it included both our natural science and theology.

The philosopher's second question is: Can man acquire a knowledge of ultimate reality? Are our natural senses reliable witness, or do they give us only faulty impressions of true being, a knowledge of which

[1] Cited by Murray, *Four Stages of Greek Religion*, p. 98.

[2] "Never can philosophy be praised in a sufficiently worthy manner, since he who obeys philosophy is able to pass every period of life without irksomeness" (Cicero, *De senectute*, 1). Further, "All the precepts of philosophy have reference to the conduct of life" (*De deor. nat.*, i. 3).

can be obtained only through sifting and testing the data supplied by sense-perception? The unthinking man assumes that things are in reality just what they seem to him to be, but if this were so, how could there be so many differences of opinion among individuals who all exercise the same natural faculties of sense-perception? This difference, says the philosopher, shows that our senses give us merely opinions about reality, and variant opinions at that, but not a true knowledge of ultimate being. Such knowledge then cannot be acquired by the physical senses, but only by the exercise of some higher faculty, as, for example, reason, which interprets the materials furnished by the senses. We call this the problem of "epistemology," which was for the ancient a part of "logic."

The third question relates to the philosophy of conduct. What is the thing most to be desired in life, and what are the proper means of procuring this desideratum? For the ordinary man tradition furnishes rules for the regulation of conduct and these rules are authoritatively enforced by the community. But philosophy tends to remove the hand of authority, even in the realm of ethics, thus leaving the individual free to decide for himself why one type of action is preferable to another. When external compulsions are displaced by personal convictions, ethical standards and incentives inevitably vary according to what are believed to be the ultimate realities of existence with which human life is connected.

Ontology, epistemology, ethics, these are the regions where religion and philosophy most overlap in ancient as in modern times. In the Graeco-Roman world of the first century A.D. these questions had all been vigorously

debated. Discussion had crystallized into strong conviction, and different schools had been established for the
advocacy of various opinions.[1]   Religion had answered
the ontological problem by means of its myths about
the gods, the explanation being phrased in the language
of anthropomorphism. Of physics and metaphysics in
the philosopher's sense it knew nothing, and his schema
often left scant room for the preservation of its traditions.
Religion had generally remained unconscious of the
epistemological problem since it drew upon its imagination for its picture of the unseen, accepting without
hesitation both the data of sense-perception and belief
in the reality of the supernatural. It knew nothing of
the philosopher's doubts about the reliability of sensa-
tion and felt no sympathy with his attempt to examine

[1] While acquaintance with the history of Greek philosophy in pre-
Hellenistic times, when Socrates, Plato, and Aristotle did their work,
is necessary to an understanding of the later history, a few references
to the literature of the subject must here suffice. The essential facts
may be found in any one of the following works: Benn, *The Philosophy
of Greece* (London, 1898); Ueberweg, *Grundriss der Geschichte der Philosophie des Altertums* (10. Aufl. von Prächter, Berlin, 1909 ff.), English tr.,
A History of Philosophy (New York, 1872–74); Windelband, *Geschichte
der antiken Philosophie* (3. Aufl. von Bonhöffer, München, 1912), English tr., *History of Ancient Philosophy* (New York, 1899); Gomperz,
Griechische Denker (3 vols., Leipzig, 1896–99), English tr., *Greek Thinkers*
(4 vols., New York, 1905–12); Zeller, *Die Philosophie der Griechen in
ihrer geschichtlichen Entwicklung* (3 vols., Tübingen, 1844–45, of which
there are several later editions), also *Grundriss der Geschichte der griechischen Philosophie* (Leipzig, 1883, 10. Aufl. von Lortzing, 1911).   Zeller's
works, which are most complete in the citation of original sources, have
been translated into English under various titles, e.g., *A History of Greek
Philosophy to Socrates* (2 vols., London, 1881), *Socrates and the Socratic
Schools* (London, 1885), *Plato and the Older Academy* (London, 1888),
Aristotle and the Earlier Peripatetics (London, 1897), *The Stoics, Epicureans and Skeptics* (London, 1892), *History of Eclecticism in Greek Philosophy* (London, 1883).

critically all alleged witnesses to truth. Religion had also settled the ethical problem in its own way. Its devotees were provided with prescriptions for the regulation of conduct, especially with reference to the gods. But the training of conscience, the cultivation of personal character, and the inculcation of duty toward one's fellows occupied a secondary place as compared with obedience to more formal traditional demands and ritualistic observances. The philosopher, on the other hand, starting with the personal emphasis, sometimes found himself seriously at variance with the religionist on the problem of conduct.

For first-hand knowledge of the philosophical situation in the middle of the first century B.C.—a situation which prevails in the main throughout the first century A.D.—we may go to Cicero. Although he was a Roman he took his philosophy bodily from the Greeks, devoting himself to the task of acquainting his countrymen with Greek learning. Consequently he attempted no creative work, but was mainly a summarist of other men's opinions. He strove to know the doctrines of every sect, expounding and disputing their tenets rather than affirming his own views. This also was the position of the Academy to which he professed allegiance.[1]

In opening his treatise on the gods he enumerates four schools of philosophy,[2] which are chiefly esteemed in his day. These are (1) the Epicureans, of whom the senator C. Velleius was reputed to be the ablest representative among the Romans at that time; (2) the Stoics, whose cause was championed by Q. Lucilius Balbus; (3) the Academics, represented by Cotta who also speaks for

---

[1] *De deor. nat.*, i. 5. [2] *Ibid.*, i. 6 f.

Cicero, though the latter inclines to the Stoic position in this argument;[1] and (4) the Peripatetics, who have no representative in the dialogue because they are assumed at this time to hold opinions almost identical with those of the Stoics.

These several schools are not all of equal importance for religion. The Peripatetics, who trace their origin to the Lyceum—the school of Aristotle—were not particularly influential in this period. They confined their work mostly to commentaries upon Aristotle, yet they were no longer pure Aristotelians. They had imbibed numerous elements from other sources, particularly from the Stoics, who in turn had borrowed somewhat from Aristotle. The Peripatetics perpetuated their existence as a sect until finally absorbed into neo-Platonism, but they gained no widespread popularity and seem to have made no important contribution to religious life in the early empire.

The representatives of the Academy—the school of Plato—also exerted only a minor influence upon the religion of the period. They had become vigorous champions of skepticism, not only doubting the reliability of sense-perception, but refusing to offer a substitute. They were not even sure that ultimate knowledge could be attained, and so they would venture no farther than to talk about probabilities. They also hesitated to dogmatize regarding duty, making custom, or at best practical utility, their chief norm for action.[2]

[1] iii. 40.

[2] For the early history of philosophical skepticism, which is not to be confounded with the denial of the existence of gods, see Zeller, *Die Philosophie der Griechen*[3], III, i, 478–527, English tr., *Stoics, Epicureans and Sceptics*, pp. 514–66, and Goedeckmeyer, *Geschichte des griechischen Skeptizismus* (Leipzig, 1905).

Although they traced their origin to Plato, they were really the exponents of eclecticism, embodying the skeptical principles which had been enunciated by Pyrrho of Elis (360–270 B.C.) and later by Carneades, who especially opposed the Stoics. The Academy in Cicero's day—and this was its main emphasis for the next two centuries—stood for a suspension of judgment in every debate. Its ideal was "never to interpose one's opinion, to approve only what seems most probable, to compare together different views, to see what may be advanced on either side, and to leave one's listeners free to judge without pretending to dogmatize." This school had, however, lost much of its former vigor even in Cicero's day, and he feels obliged to apologize for his professed though sometimes only half-hearted championship of its cause.[1]

While the skeptic had advocated no theories on religious questions, contenting himself with refuting the views of others, his own attitude toward traditional religion was a placidly tolerant one. His lack of genuine conviction made it impossible for him to exert any stimulating influence upon the religious life of his age. He often seems to be personally inclined to deny the existence of the gods, but he refuses to assert his opinions lest he may incur persecution. The skeptic Cotta, in Cicero's dialogue, is indeed a priest who scrupulously observes the religious rites he received from his ancestors and formally affirms his belief in the gods. He rests this belief on the authority of tradition, yet he allows that when one begins to think on the problem there are many things which cast doubt upon the gods' existence. But

[1] Cf. *De deor. nat.*, i. 3, 5.

since it is agreeable, convenient, and safe for him as a priest to believe in them, he will hold to this tenet on the basis of tradition, although his reason might lead him to the opposite conclusion. He says, "I must believe in the religion of our ancestors without any proof."[1] This blind attachment to tradition on the one hand, and lack of sincere conviction on the other, rendered the skeptic quite unfit to cope vigorously with vital religious questions.

It is to Epicureanism and Stoicism that we must look for the more serious attempts to meet contemporary religious problems. In contrast with the skeptical Academies, the Epicureans[2] were rigid dogmatists who advocated a definite creed and loyally defended it against every opponent. They affirmed the substantial reliability of the physical senses as a medium for acquiring true knowledge, and held that matter was the ultimate reality in the universe. Epicurus, who established his school at Athens in 307 B.C., was praised by his followers for penetrating into the secrets of nature and bringing forth therefrom the true wisdom for which the ages had been waiting. Especially was he lauded for liberating mankind from the despotism of traditional religious superstition. Lucretius says, "He [Epicurus]

[1] iii. 2; cf. i. 22; iii. 4.

[2] The tenth book of Diogenes Laertius, and Lucretius, *De rerum natura*, are the best extant expositions of this doctrine by the ancients. Usener, *Epicurea* (Leipzig, 1887), is the standard modern collection of Epicurus' teachings. A serviceable exposition of Epicureanism may be found in Zeller, *Die Philosophie der Griechen*[3], III, i, 363–477, English tr., *Stoics, Epicureans and Sceptics*, pp. 404–513, or Hicks, *Stoic and Epicurean* (New York, 1910), pp. 153–311. See also Wallace, *Epicureanism* (London, 1880); Trezza, *Epicuro e l'Epicureismo* (Milano, 1885); Renault, *Épicure* (Paris, 1903).

passed on far beyond the flaming walls of the world and traversed throughout in mind and spirit the immeasurable universe whence he returns a conqueror to tell us what can and what cannot come into being; in short, on what principle each thing has its powers defined, its deepest boundary mark. Therefore religion [as popularly understood] is put under foot and trampled upon in turn; his victory brings us level with heaven."[1] In positing the finality of the physical universe as perceived by the organs of sense, truth was made to consist in what one could feel, hear, see. To know how matter acted was to enter fully into the kingdom of truth.

Thus Epicurus' popularity rested upon two items, a positive and a negative. First, he answered the thinking man's craving after a knowledge of nature's secrets, and, secondly, he flatly denied the validity of popular superstition. He solved the riddle of natural phenomena by the so-called atomic theory. This type of philosophy, which had its beginnings with Democritus in the latter part of the fifth century B.C., is most elaborately preserved for us in Lucretius' well-known poem. According to Epicurean doctrine, the universe consists of two component parts: material bodies and empty space, which provides matter with an arena for action. Matter acts of itself, since there is no power from without determining its variations. This mass of corporeal substance is ultimately a vast concourse of minute particles, so small that they cannot be perceived by the senses and so compact as to be themselves indivisible. These are the atoms.

---

[1] *Op. cit.*, i. 60 ff.   Because Epicurus delivered men from the terrors of superstition, his followers were almost ready to rank him among the gods.   Cf. Cicero, *Tuscl.*, i. 21;   *De deor. nat.*, i. 16.

They have always existed, they will never cease to exist, and apart from them nothing else exists except empty space. The weight of the atoms, which are of various sizes and forms, sets them in motion. They hit each other, the lighter ones rebound, the heavier press together making solids, while others form water, fire, air, ether. As space is infinite and atoms are innumerable, the number of worlds in existence may also be infinite. The total phenomena of all existence are thus purely mechanical products of chance.

Is there any room for religion in such a philosophy? Certainly the gods of popular belief could find no place in this scheme. This was the second point which made Epicureanism attractive to many minds. The superstition of the multitudes, their fears, their absurd actions in the name of religion, their crass beliefs about the gods, these things made intelligent people appreciate the need of a religious reform. With a single stroke Epicurus wiped all this out of existence for those who adopted his philosophy. He affirmed that neither gods nor demons had anything to do with creating the world, they had no hand in its maintenance, and no power either to harm or to help human beings. Yet Epicurus did not deny the existence of gods; he merely contended, as he thought, for a purer, nobler conception of their character. He would not allow that they were in any sense mixed up with this little world of ours, hence one could not learn of their existence by observing their activities either for good or for evil in human life. Belief in their existence was therefore based solely upon the fact that mankind commonly held this conviction. It was an impression which nature herself produced, and so must be true.

Epicurus' admirers affirmed that their master was the first to use this argument, basing a conclusion upon the mind's antecedent conception—*prolepsis* (πρόληψις), as it was called—of deity's existence. While they praised him for discovering so substantial an argument,[1] his enemies declared that he ought logically to have denied outright the gods' existence, and they accused him of fearing to do this lest he should incur persecution. The justice of the charge is not wholly consistent, however, with the note of sincerity dominant in this school.

What sort of beings were the Epicurean gods, and what were their functions? Here, as usual, man made God in his own image. The highest ideal of the human life was held to be the attainment of pleasure—not mere sensual enjoyment, but a freedom from pain or disturbance of both body and mind. Above all only a peaceful mind could make life complete. The ideal wise man could smile at bodily pain when all was serene in his soul. The Epicureans' gods were, accordingly, perfectly happy beings dwelling in the ethereal regions between the innumerable worlds. They must be wholly removed from our world, for had they been in any way concerned with the affairs of men their serenity would surely have been marred. Although they were made of atoms and fashioned in human form, still they were composed of the finest sort of atoms and they abode in perfectly blissful surroundings. Worship of these deities was inculcated, not because one expected to receive aught from them, but because they were the ideal embodiment of perfect happiness. The gods do not demand worship,

[1] Cicero, *De deor. nat.*, i. 16 f. For the criticism of opponents see i. 2, 33–44; iii. 1.

indeed they have no desires in the matter, but man for his own sake needs to keep these ideals constantly before his mind.   Velleius in Cicero's dialogue says,[1] "We have no dread of those beings whom we have reason to think entirely free from all troubles themselves and who do not impose any on others.   We pay our adoration, indeed, with piety and reverence to that essence which is above all excellence and perfection."   Admiration for divine perfection formed the basal element of Epicurean worship.

The extent to which Epicureanism pervaded the Graeco-Roman world in the first century A.D. is difficult now to determine.   The school certainly maintained itself on down to the fourth century of our era.   It doubtless had a considerable following still in the first century, for no other sect stood so positively by its original tenets, refusing to yield to the eclectic tendencies prevalent in that age.   It continued to be the relentless foe of superstition, as we learn in the second century when Lucian makes the Epicureans bitter enemies of the charlatan Alexander.[2]   Probably its greatest religious significance lies in its severe protest against popular superstition, it being in this respect the precursor of Christianity.   But the Epicurean method of removing the malady proved quite inadequate for popular needs, however strongly it may have appealed to certain heroic spirits who were willing to accept the physical world at its face value and forego the natural impulse of mankind to demand help from the deity instead of being content with an attitude of pure adoration.

Stoicism filled a far larger place in the religious life of antiquity, though as a philosophy it had much in

[1] *De deor. nat.,* i. 20.   [2] *Alex.,* 25.

common with Epicureanism.[1]   Realism and materialism are fundamental principles in both schools.   The Stoic trusted the testimony of sense-perception in the main and he held the ultimate reality in the universe to be a form of matter.   Thus far he agreed with his Epicurean contemporaries.   The radical difference between the two sects lay in their respective views regarding the elemental character of matter.   Epicurus gave it merely the power of purposeless motion, consequently chance ruled everything; the Stoics endowed it with Reason (λόγος, "Word"), and so maintained that all things happen according to design.   This Reason is, to be sure, corporeal, though the lightest, most active and powerful constituent element in all existence.

There was ample room in this scheme for an elaborate theology.   Since the primary item in the universe is rational force which permeates all things, it may appropriately bear the name of deity.   Unlike the Epicurean deity, the Stoic god is inseparably linked with the world— in him we live, move, and have our being.   He may be called by many names or conceived in various capacities, but he is always the formless, divine, ethereal substance giving order to the universe, supplying life to all creation, filling the human body with an intelligent soul, and ordering all events according to one eternal purpose.   This conception of the deity's relation to the world logically nullified popular superstition just as effectively as did

---

[1] The literature on Stoicism is extensive.   In addition to Zeller and Hicks mentioned above, see Arnold, *Roman Stoicism* (Cambridge, 1911), where the important books are listed.   Bevan's recent *Stoics and Sceptics* (Oxford, 1913) is only a brief sketch.   The source materials are collected by von Arnim, *Stoicorum veterum fragmenta* (3 vols., Leipzig, 1903–5).

Epicureanism, since it made impossible the existence of any deific forces not a part of the one divine substance. When all events happen according to orderly rational design, they must be essentially good, whether they seem so or not, and there can be nothing evil in the universe except the deeds of men who neglect to live "rationally." The fundamentals of Stoic theology cannot be stated more compactly than has been done by Cleanthes, the second president of this school, in his oft-quoted hymn: "Most glorious of immortals, O Zeus of many names, almighty and everlasting, sovereign of nature, thee it is fitting that all mortals should address. . . . . Thee all this universe as it rolls circling round the earth obeys wheresoever thou dost guide and gladly owns thy sway. In thy invincible hands thou holdest as a minister the two-edged, fiery, everlasting thunderbolt under whose stroke all nature shudders. No work upon earth is wrought apart from thee, O lord, nor through the divine ethereal sphere, nor upon the sea; save only whatsoever deeds wicked men do in their own foolishness. Nay, thou knowest how to make even the rough smooth and to bring order out of disorder; and things not friendly are friendly in thy sight. For so hast thou fitted all things together, the good with the evil, that there might be one eternal law over all. . . . . Deliver men from fell ignorance. Banish it, Father, from their soul, and grant them to obey wisdom, whereon relying thou rulest all things with justice."[1]

[1] As abbreviated by Hicks in the article "Stoics" in the *Encyclopaedia Britannica*. The original text is printed in von Arnim, *Fragmenta*, I, 121 f. Complete translations are given in Hicks, *Stoic and Epicurean*, pp. 14–16, and Arnold, *Roman Stoicism*, pp. 85–87.

If we would appreciate the full religious significance of Stoicism we must note more particularly the importance it attaches to the practical side of life. Although it was commonly called a "philosophy," the leaders of the movement did not aim primarily to enrich philosophical speculation but to inculcate virtuous living. This fact appears very clearly from the circumstances of the school's origin.

A new disposition toward practical matters appeared in Greece about the middle of the fifth century B.C. with the activity of Protagoras. In contrast with philosophical disputation, which concerned itself about truth (ἀλή-θεια) or wisdom (σοφία), he proposed to pursue virtue (ἀρετή), which he defined in terms of utility. His object was to educate men to become good citizens in order that they might contribute worthily to the welfare of society. Socrates took up this notion that virtue is the chief end of existence, but he gave virtue a more distinctly moral content as well as a stronger individualistic turn. Knowledge and virtue are synonymous in his system, but knowledge is to be attained by a process of personal investigation into, and reflection upon, one's inner self. Intelligent self-mastery, combined with the effort to realize the highest attainments of which the natural self is capable in the realm of thinking and conduct, is the climax of the Socratic ideal. It is epitomized in a sentence of one of Socrates' prayers: "Beloved Pan, and all ye other gods who haunt this place, give me beauty in the inward soul, and may the outward and the inward man be at one."[1]

[1] Plato, *Phaedr.*, 279C.

A pupil of Socrates named Antisthenes, the founder of Cynicism, seized upon this notion of living true to nature. He vigorously condemned personal comforts on the ground that the amenities of civilization placed hindrances in reason's way and diverted the right operation of the will. Self-knowledge and self-realization, to be attained by means of rigid self-control, were his supreme ideal. Accordingly Antisthenes adopted a simple mode of living and cultivated a plain style of teaching with the primary object of reaching the common man, whom he wished to awaken to self-realization. He discarded the professional philosopher's garb, wearing instead a plain cloak and carrying only a staff and a wallet. The Cynic teachers' proletarian interests, the simplicity of their manner of life, their self-sacrificing service for humanity, all contributed to the school's popularity; yet its extreme asceticism, and its offenses against culture generally, greatly hindered its usefulness. Although many of its more attractive features were absorbed by Stoicism, the Cynics were still influential—perhaps more influential than we have ordinarily imagined—in the Graeco-Roman world of New Testament times. But on the side of practical living the continued influence of the Cynics is so closely associated with Stoicism that a separate treatment of the former is not necessary for our purpose.[1]

[1] Fragments from the Cynics are given in Mullach, *Fragmenta philosophorum Graecorum*, II (Paris, 1867), 261–438. For expositions of Cynicism see especially Zeller, *Die Philosophie der Griechen*[4], II, i, 280–336, and III, i, 763–76, English tr., *Socrates and the Socratic Schools*, pp. 285–337, and *Eclecticism*, pp. 288–303; Gomperz, *Greek Thinkers*, II, 139–69; Geffcken, *Kynika und Verwandtes* (Heidelberg, 1909).

The founder of Stoicism was Zeno, a Phoenician from Citium in Cyprus. He came to Athens about the year 320 B.C. perhaps on some commercial enterprise, and attended various philosophical schools, finally establishing one of his own destined to enjoy for several centuries a popularity beyond that of any rival. At first Zeno was most attracted by the practical ideals of the Cynics, represented at that time by Crates. He seems to have derived much from this source, although he soon became dissatisfied with the Cynics' crudities and turned to the Megarian Stilpo who also inculcated the Socratic ideal that virtue is knowledge, adding to it the Eleatic concept of the unity of being. But it was ultimately the Ionian materialism, as represented by Heraclitus, which Stoics found most useful in working out their philosophy. Notwithstanding the Stoics' numerous debts to other systems, their primary interests were practical rather than speculative, and it is not improbable that Diogenes Laertius[1] reports a true tradition when he says that Zeno was first attracted toward philosophical studies by reading Xenophon's Memorabilia of Socrates. The Socratic ideal of virtue, the salvation of the individual by means of self-elevation of spirit, and indifference to suffering procured through inward peace of mind were permanent characteristics of Stoic teaching.

In other respects also, Stoicism was by nature better fitted than any contemporary school to meet the demands of the age. It was itself a Hellenistic rather than a Hellenic product. Many of its greatest representatives were, like its founder, not native Greeks. Zeno's entire

[1] vii. 3.

work was done at Athens, but instead of becoming an Athenian citizen he chose still to be called Zeno the philosopher of Citium.[1]   Cleanthes was from Assos, Chrysippus was from Cilicia, Diogenes was from Seleucia, Antipater was from Tarsus—to mention only the early presidents of the school.   In these first years of its history its leaders and pupils were drawn from the Graeco-Roman world as a whole, and the movement soon came to have important centers in various leading cities such as Tarsus, Rhodes, Alexandria, and Rome.   For about five centuries it was the most influential school in the Mediterranean world.   It counted among its leaders and patrons many distinguished persons.   In connection with Tarsus alone Strabo[2] mentions as Stoic leaders, Antipater who later became head of the school in Athens, Archedemus, and two individuals named Athenodorus.   One of these Athenodori was the teacher of Cato the younger, and the other taught Augustus. Cicero, who studied under Posidonius of Rhodes, though not an outspoken champion of Stoicism, did much to make it known among the Romans where it later had distinguished representatives in the persons of Seneca, Musonius Rufus, Epictetus, and the emperor Marcus Aurelius.   No other school could so naturally reflect the realism, the cosmopolitanism, and the individualism which characterized the life of the Graeco-Roman period.

These close connections with the varied life of the Mediterranean world fitted Stoicism to become a unique power in the sphere of religion.   Although it cannot be said to have maintained its pristine purity so faithfully as did Epicureanism, the changes which it underwent in

[1] Diogenes Laertius, vii. 12.   [2] xiv. 5. 14.

the process of growth did not seriously affect its characteristics, as these appear in the more distinctly religious features of the school.

In the first place, the Stoic teacher viewed humanity religiously. In his eyes all men are not only made in the rational image of God but bear about a spark of deity—the rational soul—within their own breasts. Every man is a child of God in virtue of this rational soul within him. Hence the chief end of existence is virtuous living, which consists in conformity to the divine will. Marcus Aurelius, repeating Stoic sentiment familiar since Zeno, argues that since we are all rational beings we are all under one ethical standard and one world-law and so sharers of a common citizenship.[1] Thus the connection between man and God, as well as the common bond uniting all mankind, is the *Logos*, the divine Reason, or the "Word" as it is commonly rendered at the beginning of the Fourth Gospel.[2] Since God is thus the father of all, all men are brothers and all class distinctions are only artificial barriers to be removed by religion rather than by social revolution. Even the slave finds his deliverance in the realm of right thinking. This freedom is secured through the attainment of personal virtue, which is a conquest of the will transcending all life's disturbances. Real slaves are not made by barter but by deficiencies in character.[3] But the truly wise man who fully realizes his powers of divine rationality has little concern for outward circumstances.

[1] Marcus Aurelius, *Ad se ipsum*, iv. 4; cf. von Arnim, *Fragmenta*, I, 262; Seneca, *Dial.*, vii. 20. 5; *Epist.*, 95. 52; Epictetus, *Disc.*, i. 9.

[2] John 1:1.

[3] Von Arnim, *Fragmenta*, III. 354.

Even though he may be the lowest menial in society, in spirit he is truly free while his master may be in abject bondage to habits, conventions, desires, and worries. This subject is expounded at length in Cicero's fifth Paradox. Only the wise man is free, he who follows righteousness and rejoices in fulfilling his duty, realizing that the fortune of every man is molded by his character. All wicked men, on the other hand, are slaves, "not in the sense of bondmen who are the property of their master by purchase or by any law of the state; but if obedience to a disordered, abject mind destitute of self-control be slavery—and such it is—who can deny that all the dishonest, all the covetous, in short all the wicked are slaves?"[1] One who lives in true "harmony with nature" thereby "companies with God"[2] and cannot be in bondage to any man.

The Stoic teacher also interpreted his own mission religiously. He was neither a peddler of philosophy nor a teacher of rhetoric aiming to perpetuate a certain school of doctrine or to earn his own livelihood by entertaining the multitude. Epictetus vigorously condemns one who seeks applause or courts praise.[3] The true teacher, whom Epictetus pictures as a Cynic,[4] feels himself to be a messenger of Zeus, whose he is and whom he serves. One who attempts so great a task without the aid of God is sure to incur disaster. But success also means a career of hardship in the service of God for the benefit of one's fellow-men. He who is meditating on this calling is admonished to remember: "You are

[1] Cf. the similar remarks of Paul in Rom. 6:16.

[2] Cf. Seneca, *Epist.*, 50. 8; *Dial.*, vii. 15. 5.

[3] *Disc.*, iii. 23.   [4] iii. 22.

going to be enrolled in a combat at the Olympic games, man; not in a poor, slight contest." He must stand before the world as a God-sent example of patient endurance, "without house, without estate, without a servant, lying on the ground, without kin, and having only earth and heaven and one poor cloak." All his sufferings are interpreted as heavenly discipline which God imposes to try his mettle and prove whether he is worthy of the great conflict.

But suffering is not simply an end in itself, nor is it purely for the purpose of self-discipline. This task of preaching the Stoic gospel was undertaken for the salvation of others.[1] The world's distress and, above all, the failure of men generally to realize daily their divine possibilities filled the Stoic teacher with sympathetic longing to tell them the saving truth as he had experienced it in his own life. He would teach them how to bear burdens with fortitude and composure by forsaking their worse and rising to the true dignity of their better selves. He made his appeal to the high and the lowly alike, exhorting them to experience a new birth of the inner life by coming to a realization of their own inward power as rational beings.[2]

By both precept and example the Stoic preacher inculcated submission to the divine will as the chief end of life. Epictetus insists on keeping two rules constantly in mind: (1) good or evil is simply a matter of choice, and (2) we are to follow rather than control the

[1] See references in Wendland, *Die hellenistisch-römische Kultur*, pp. 82 f.

[2] On the Stoic doctrine of "conversion," see Arnold, *Roman Stoicism*, p. 327.

course of events decreed by God.[1] Socrates is frequently cited as the illustrious example who taught
man the great lesson of contentment with his God-
given lot in life. One ought to be able even in prison
to say with Socrates: "My dear Crito, if it thus
pleases the gods, so let it be."[2] In prosperity, in ad-
versity, or even in the presence of death this attitude
remains unchanged.[3] The Stoic would not say that he
"obeyed" God, but that he followed God heart and soul,
not because he must but because he chose so to do.[4]

The ideal relationship between individuals was interpreted by the Stoic in terms of brotherhood among men
who have God as their common father. Since the ruling
principle of the whole universe is the divine Logos (Reason) there is one rational law governing the conduct of all
men who ought to maintain both a filial attitude toward
the deity and harmonious relations among themselves.
Zeno is reported to have said in his work on the *Republic*[5]
that "love is god and is a helpmate for the safety of the
city." There is to be no spirit of retaliation among
brothers. "You say," says Epictetus,[6] "my brother
ought not to have treated me so. Very true, but he
must see to that. However he treats me, I am to act
right with regard to him, for the one is my own concern
and the other is not; I may restrain myself but I cannot control him." The four cardinal virtues to be
cultivated are Wisdom (φρόνησις, *prudentia*), Justice
(δικαιοσύνη, *justitia*), Courage (ἀνδρεία, *fortitudo*), and

---

[1] *Disc.*, iii. 10.   [2] Epictetus, *op. cit.*, i. 4.
[3] Epictetus, *op. cit.*, i. 1; *Ench.*, 5, 21.
[4] Cf. Seneca, *Epist.*, 96. 2; *Dial.*, vii. 15. 7; Epictetus, *Disc.*, iv. 1.
[5] Von Arnim, *Fragmenta*, I, 263.   [6] *Disc.*, iii. 10.

Soberness (σωφροσύνη, *temperantia*), though these were often subdivided into, or supplemented by, other terms such as faith, simplicity, gentleness, modesty, frugality.[1] It was the rule of the sincere Stoic to subject himself each day to rigorous self-examination on the way he had discharged his duty. With true religious fervor Epictetus[2] enjoins upon his pupils the verses of Pythagoras:

> Let sleep not come upon thy languid eyes
> Before each daily action thou hast scanned,
> What's done amiss, what done, what left undone;
> From first to last examine all, and then
> Blame what is wrong, in what is right rejoice.

Thus it appears that the Stoic was fundamentally religious, in the broad sense of the term, although there was a wide difference between his position and the popular faith. But the practical bent of Stoicism inclined its leaders toward the constructive task of conserving as far as possible the essence of the old faith, at the same time extending to men the benefit of the new. Consequently the Stoics sought more to purify and revitalize than to destroy popular religion. They did, however, oppose "superstition" quite as vigorously as did the Epicureans, but they proposed a very different remedy. Instead of denying the power of the gods they redefined their character, removing the element of terror and substituting the conception of a well-disposed providence. Evidence of the activity of a divine providence was seen on every hand.[3] Nature's provisions for our food and clothing, the beauties of earth and sky,

---

[1] See von Arnim, *Fragmenta*, III, 262–93 (*passim*).

[2] *Disc.*, iii. 10.

[3] The typical arguments are given in Cicero, *De deor. nat.*, ii. 29–46.

the display of intelligent purpose behind everything
in the universe compelled, according to the Stoics, a
firm belief in a ruling providence.

They likewise rejected the Homeric anthropomorphism, but retained the names of the ancient deities to
designate various forms of divine activity all of which
have their source in the one divine Reason. This irenic
attitude of the Stoics appears again in the readiness
with which they adopted astrological notions. They
felt no difficulty in affirming that the sun, the moon, the
firmament, the world itself, and all things useful to
mankind were deities, in the sense of being specific
manifestations of divine mind.[1] In line with this
development divination also was highly recommended,[2]
for it not only accorded well with their doctrine of a
beneficent providence, but had practical values which
they wished to conserve. Yet the Stoics' attitude
toward divination was very different from that of the
populace. Epictetus teaches that man has a diviner
within himself who tells him the essence of good and
evil; and when he does consult external signs his wish
ought merely to be to learn God's will and not to change
it—"You wretch! would you have anything but what is
best? And what is best except what pleases God?
Why do you, as far as in you lies, corrupt your judge and
seduce your adviser?"[3] By resorting to the allegorical
method of interpretation the Stoics also discovered a
basis of truth in ancient mythology. They had some
predecessors in this field, but it remained for them to

[1] See Cicero, *op. cit.*, ii. 21.

[2] See Cicero, *De divinatione* (*passim*).

[3] *Disc.*, ii. 7.

give allegory its classic expression,[1] thus forging a weapon for apologetic uses which was freely employed by Jews like Philo and Christians like Paul.

The Stoics held aloof from the popular forms of worship, yet they maintained a very reverential attitude toward God and emphasized the desirability of true worship. This was not to be performed in fear, because no sane man would fear a kind god whom he ought to love. "It is madness to fear the gods from whom we receive our good and happiness," says Seneca.[2] Worship was not restricted to any particular place nor was it limited to any traditional forms; it was primarily an affair of the individual's personal relationship to the deity who is present in every part of nature. By whatever names or in whatever forms the gods are recognized, "we are bound to worship and adore them, but the best, the chastest, the most sacred and pious worship is to reverence them always with a pure, perfect, and unpolluted mind and voice," according to the Stoic disputant in Cicero's dialogue on the *Nature of the Gods*.[3] To hymn their praises is apparently the supreme duty of man. The hymn of Cleanthes is a notable expression of this feeling. Similarly Epictetus, meditating on the blessing of Providence, exclaims: "Ought we not both in public and in private, incessantly to sing hymns and speak well of the deity, and rehearse his benefits? . . . . What else can I a lame old man do but sing hymns to God? If I were a nightingale I would act the part of a nightingale, if a swan the part of a swan; but since I am a reasonable creature it is my duty to praise God.

[1] See Zeller, *Stoics*, etc., pp. 354–69.
[2] *De benef.*, iv. 19.   [3] ii. 28.

This is my business.   I do it, nor will I ever desert this position so long as it is vouchsafed to me; and I exhort you to join in the same song."[1]

When the Stoic directed his gaze toward the future, he again found himself at variance with popular tradition. Of hell and its terrors he had no fear.   These morbid fancies were held to be impossible for the philosopher who did not believe in any black darkness awaiting the dead—"there is no prison house, no lake of fire or river of forgetfulness, no judgment seat, no renewal of the rule of tyrants."[2]   The fate of man's soul after death is determined by the nature of the soul's constitution. Since it is a part of the ethereal substance called the divine mind, or God, it must be immortal in the same sense that divine substance is immortal.   This fundamental notion left room for wide variations of opinion as to the different stages in the soul's career.   To be sure all were agreed—in so far as they were really Stoics— that ultimately it would be absorbed into the primal divine substance,[3] but how long would it maintain an independent consciousness and through what experiences would it pass ?   Cleanthes had maintained that all souls would continue in a separate existence until the final conflagration,[4] but Chrysippus reserved this privilege for the soul of the wise alone.   Pure Stoic learning seem-

[1] *Disc.*, i. 16.

[2] Seneca, *Dial.*, vi. 19. 4; also Cicero. *Tuscl.*, i. 16; *De deor. nat.*, ii. 2.

[3] The soul may exist a long while but it is not eternal (Cicero, *Tuscl.*, i. 31).

[4] It was generally agreed among the Stoics, Panaetius being the only exception noted, that a general conflagration would one day reduce the universe to its primal fire after which another cycle of evolution would follow, re-establishing a new world (Cicero, *De deor. nat.*, ii. 46).

ingly had little to say about the future activity of the soul, but under the influence of Pythagoreanism and Platonism on the one hand, and astral mysticism on the other, a more elaborate program appears in later writers. There is first a period of purification in which the soul passes by degrees from the lower to the higher regions, and at last, being fully purified from its stains through contact with the body, it rises to the height of heaven there to delight itself with watching the stars go round. This phase of speculation among the Stoics apparently reached its climax with Posidonius (135–51 B.C.), but it belongs genetically to a different type of philosophy, as we shall later have occasion to observe. Seneca, Epictetus, and Marcus Aurelius start Stoicism on the way back again to its original type, which faces death certainly with no fears for the future and with but slight thought of any rewards except the prospect of reabsorption into the primal divine essence.

The best known early Christian missionary to the Gentiles, in estimating the religious significance of Graeco-Roman thinking, remarks that "the world through its wisdom knew not God."[1] But when he exhorts the Romans[2] to a rational (λογικήν) service in which they present their bodies a living sacrifice holy and well-pleasing unto God, not conforming to the schema of this age but being transformed by the renovation of their mind in order that they may learn what is the good, well-pleasing, and perfect will of God, almost every phrase of his exhortation is perfectly good Stoic sentiment. It would be a comparatively easy task to assemble a long list of New Testament passages, which,

[1] I Cor. 1:21.   [2] 12:1 f.

in form or content, or both, would show striking agreements with Stoicism.[1]   These passages have furnished some interpreters convincing proof of Christianity's secondary character,[2] others have made Stoicism the borrower,[3] and still others have explained away the resemblances without finding any substantial interdependence.   At the outset the Christian movement seems to have gathered its disciples from the proletariat[4] and, as this condition of affairs probably continued for a generation or two at least, philosophical speculation within the Graeco-Roman world might naturally be thought to have relatively minor significance for the early history of Christianity.

We must remember, however, that philosophy was no longer the aristocratic thing it had been in the days of Plato.   It is not at all probable that the artisan classes

[1] See most recently Arnold, *Roman Stoicism*, pp. 408–36; cf. also Clemen, *Religionsgeschichtliche Erklärung des Neuen Testaments*, pp. 30–58, English tr., *Primitive Christianity*, pp. 41–77; H. A. Winckler, *Der Stoicismus eine Wurzel des Christentums* (Leipzig, 1879).

[2] E.g., Havet, *Le christianisme et ses origines;* Bruno Bauer, *Christus und die Caesaren* (Berlin, 1879[2]); or Steck, *Der Galaterbrief* (Berlin, 1888).

[3] I.e., the Stoicism of the first century A.D., especially as represented by Seneca, Epictetus, and Marcus Aurelius.   A spurious correspondence between Seneca and Paul had come into existence by the fourth century (cf. Jerome, *De vir. illus.*, 12), and from this it was argued that Seneca had embraced Christianity.   The view is now generally discarded by historical scholars.   For various phases of the discussion see Lightfoot's dissertation, "St. Paul and Seneca" in his *Commentary on Philippians*, pp. 270–333; Baumgarten, *Lucius Annaeus Seneca und das Christentum* (Rostock, 1895).   Zahn, *Der Stoiker Epiktet* (Leipzig, 1895[2]), and Kuiper, *Epictetus en de christelijke moraal* (Amsterdam, 1906), make Epictetus a debtor to the New Testament; but Bonhöffer, *Epiktet und das Neue Testament* (Giessen, 1911), finds no interrelationships.

[4] I Cor. 1:26.

who, in the main, constituted the membership of the early gentile churches spent any time reading Plato or Aristotle, but it is altogether likely that they were very familiar with the Cynic or Stoic popular preacher who was to be found in almost every corner of their world. Indeed this very style of discourse—the so-called Cynic-Stoic Diatribe—furnished the model for much effective Christian preaching. Some of the most striking portions of Paul's letters, which probably contain language he had become accustomed to use in his daily public addresses, display the earmarks of the familiar Diatribe style.[1]

The moment Christian missionaries began to work gentile territory and to gather converts, whether from among Jews of the Dispersion or from among the heathen, the social status of that ancient world immediately became an influential factor in the history of the Christian movement. Since philosophical speculation had become a vital part of this *milieu* in the first century A.D., it unquestionably had some significance for the evolution of early Christianity. The general protest against popular superstition also became a characteristic Christian attitude, but instead of denying the reality of demonic powers, as Epicureans and Stoics had done, Christians preached a gospel of deliverance through alliance with a new power, the risen and glorified Jesus. The fears felt by the populace on account of belief in

[1] See especially Bultmann, *Der Stil der paulinischen Predigt und die kynisch-stoische Diatribe* (Göttingen, 1910); also Norden, *Agnostos Theos* (Leipzig, 1913), which contains a wealth of material bearing upon stylistic matters and showing many striking agreements between the preaching of Christian missionaries and that of their contemporary Stoic propagandist.

demons and dread of worse terrors in the life to come were only emphasized the more strongly as Christian preachers portrayed the doom awaiting those who rejected the new gospel.

At the same time Christianity preserved the practical ideal of virtue, and the religious fervor with which the Cynic-Stoic preacher followed the lead of duty. The notion of universal brotherhood, having its basis in God's fatherhood; the idea that man has a God-given mission in life to work for the salvation of his fellow-man's soul; emphasis upon the supremacy of divine will to which all men should strive to conform; the wise man's sense of soul-freedom and his disregard for temporal things; the cultivation of positive social virtues and a spirit of loving forbearance among brothers; implicit trust in Providence; rigid self-scrutiny of one's own life; the use of allegorical interpretation as a means of conserving the religious ideas of the past; a willingness to read the will of the Deity in the "signs of the times"; the necessity of worshiping God with adoration and praise from the heart rather than in any formal manner; these are some of the things which the early Christian missionaries found already inculcated by their Cynic-Stoic predecessors and which they in turn took pains to preserve.

Yet the philosopher, however high his ideal of practical virtue might be, seemed to the Christian fundamentally lacking in a true knowledge of God. This, from the Christian point of view, was because of the philosopher's faulty epistemological theory; he erroneously supposed that by searching he could find God through his natural powers of intellect. Christians, on the contrary, believed knowledge of God to be attainable only by means of revelation.   In other words, they had adopted the epistemological theory of oriental mysticism, and this fact necessitated an interpretation of religion which was fundamentally different from that of the Greek philosopher.[1]

The Christians, however, were not the first mediators of a mystical philosophy[2] within the syncretistic life of the Mediterranean world.   Greek thinkers, by making sense-perception or mental reflection the medium for acquiring knowledge, were unable to satisfy a very general human impulse.   Shall we, in our conquest after truth, employ only the faculties of seeing or thinking, and ignore the elemental impulse of feeling?   While that, in effect, was the method of Greek philosophy, it did not prove satisfying to the majority of persons.   This defect was recognized by certain of the philosophers themselves, consequently we find them now and then yielding to the demands of emotion.

When once the emotions are allowed a place in the formation of an epistemological theory they open up a new world for religious thinking.   Metaphysics supplants physics as a medium for defining the constitution of Deity; from the beyond God comes into this world, or sends his representatives, to minister to man's need. Unless the Deity chooses thus to come, or send some communication, men must remain in utter ignorance of him. The physical and intellectual powers of apprehension, since they belong primarily to this world, are of less importance than the emotional soul, since it is readily

[1] On this point see more recently Norden, *Agnostos Theos*, pp. 83–115.

[2] On the general subject see Lehmann, *Mysticism in Heathendom and Christendom* (London, 1910).

believed to be an other-worldly element abiding temporarily in a physical body. The experiences of the present life represent only a passing phase of existence, for the essential item in personality is the soul, which looks forward to the time of its deliverance from its prison house, the body, that it may return to the heavenly abodes whence it came. An effort to insure successful deliverance from this world and safe passage into the next becomes the chief concern of religious speculation. Man alone is not equal to this task, hence the necessity of formulating a program by which divine help can be obtained. The choicest favors religion can bestow are a consciousness of present union with the Deity and the certainty of blessed immortality.

Stoicism was, of itself, quite incapable of competing with a philosophy of life which could supply these mystical features. There were, to be sure, already within the Greek world certain tendencies pointing in this general direction. These items appear in the Bacchic, the Orphic, and the Eleusinian mysteries, the Pythagorean movement, and certain features of Plato's philosophy. But this type of thinking throve especially in the East, whence it came with renewed power into the complex life of the Mediterranean world in Hellenistic times. Some of its elements, as we observed above, had been taken up by the Stoic Posidonius. Plutarch over a century later also tried to combine the heritage of Greek philosophy with mysticism, but its full religious power could hardly come to expression in the life of persons strongly addicted to intellectual pursuits in the Greek sense of the term.[1]

[1] On the presence of mysticism in the Greek world since the sixth century B.C., see Gruppe, *Griechische Mythologie*, pp. 1016–41.

When Paul declared that the world by its wisdom "knew not God," and offered his hearers "God's wisdom in a mystery" heretofore unknown but now "revealed through the Spirit,"[1] he cast in his lot with the Mystics. The new movement, much as it might seek to conserve the values of Stoicism, belonged in an essentially different religious category. Its God and man's soul were other-worldly entities, the present world offered hindrances which could be overcome only by divine help from without, and the *summum bonum* in religion was to be attained only by carrying out a divinely arranged program of redemption. In Stoicism man tried to save himself to a life of peace in this world; in Christianity he called in the aid of a God-sent deliverer who not only gave him salvation in the present but who guaranteed him a blessed immortality.

We must now inquire to what extent that ancient world was already familiar with the notion of a redemptive religion, in which man looked primarily to the Deity for deliverance from this world and for the assurance of immortal blessedness.

[1] I Cor. 2:6–10.

CHAPTER IX

HELLENISTIC RELIGIONS OF REDEMPTION

The notion of salvation is a very early and a very general one in the history of religion. It arises as soon as man becomes conscious of contact with hostile forces from whose power he seeks deliverance. He may think his enemies to be natural phenomena, such as the cold of winter which threatens him with starvation; or they may be human foes who constantly endanger his life and happiness. They may be untoward social circumstances which lay heavy burdens upon him in every hour of his existence. They may be the impersonal forces of an inexorable destiny in whose meshes he seems hopelessly entangled, or destiny may have become personalized in the form of demonic powers lurking in every shadow ready to pounce upon him any moment. Or he may regard his worst enemy to be gross materialistic existence which chokes and tarnishes his soul shut up in the prison house of the body. Again, he may lament that he has yielded to the wicked impulses of his heart and thus placed his conscience under the burden of sin and guilt. These hostile forces, acting singly or in some combination, tend to make man conscious, early in his experience, of his need of salvation.

His conception of the content of salvation naturally varies with his notion of his foes. He longs for a land of plenty with security from all invading and plundering armies; he pictures a utopia where life for everybody, and for himself in particular, will be free from distressing circumstances; he seeks to anticipate fate by providing himself with safeguards against all the demons; he looks for some means to release the soul from its prison chamber, purge it of impurities through contact with matter, and enable it to soar aloft to the ethereal regions whence it came; or, finally, he yearns for deliverance from sin and guilt, and the restoration of a pure heart, that he may fill his life with noble ethical attainments.

How is this desired deliverance to be obtained? What is the process of salvation? This question may also be answered in different ways, but the answers may be grouped into two main classes. To the first division belong all those solutions which make the attainment of salvation primarily the result of man's own action. For example, he provides himself with clothing against the frosts of winter and takes forethought concerning a sufficient supply of food. He makes himself weapons of war and builds fortresses to ward off the attacks of his enemies. He corrects social ills by reorganizing society and establishing new forms of government. He protects himself from the demons of a fatalistic world by prying into their secrets, learning their foibles, and formulating charms or other magical devices for thwarting their designs. The soul enveloped in base matter struggles though self-cultivation of its own inherent divine character to free itself from its prison house. The wicked impulses of the heart are nullified through a volitional activity of man who establishes laws for the regulation of his conduct and purges all evil out of his life. In all this man is primarily his own savior and salvation is essentially a matter of his own attainment.

The second type of answer places chief stress, not upon human effort, but upon that help which comes from without.   Man allies himself with the vital powers of nature and thus secures their aid in the maintenance of his food supply.   In his conflict with enemies he trusts in the help of a tutelary god to give his arms success. He calls upon his god to establish justice and right his social ills.   Evil demons and the forces of destiny lose their terrors for him since he is under the special care of a mightier savior-deity who is capable of carrying him safely through the vicissitudes of life.   His soul is delivered from its thraldom in matter through the help of a divine deliverer who descends to its rescue; and his success in the struggle against sin, guilt, and the power of evil desire is assured through divine aid which frees him from the bondage of the past and fills his heart with new and holy impulses. This general type of faith may be termed redemption-religion, in contrast with the former type which might be called attainment-religion.   The two types, to be sure, shade into one another.   Most religions of attainment have a place for the notion of the deity's help as a supplement to human effort, while most redemption-religions require some measure of activity on man's part.   But the general distinction is clear.   In one case it is human endeavor which stands in the foreground and conditions attainment; in the other, human effort counts only as an accessory to the redeeming work of the deity.

In the syncretism of Hellenistic times redemption-religions and attainment-religions were both current. Stoicism was a conspicuous example of the latter. Salvation pertained chiefly to the present and consisted in a freedom of soul reached through one's own efforts at self-control and self-exaltation of spirit. Man could thus save himself because at the outset he was divine— divinity tabernacled in him in virtue of the fact that he was a man. Although Stoicism had a large following, many persons still felt unable, even in the strength of their own inherent divinity, to elevate themselves into the rarefied atmosphere of Stoic serenity. The help which came from without, embodied in the person of the divine emperor, was too remote and uncertain to minister to those individual needs which came into prominence as national boundaries disappeared, leaving men in so vast a world that the older feeling of national solidarity and safety no longer remained. As a consequence of these new experiences many persons turned to a type of religion which emphasized salvation for the individual rather than for the nation, a salvation accomplished by the direct aid of Deity.

One of the most familiar means employed for the expression of this type of faith is the so-called "mystery-religions."[1] Before the beginning of our era numerous mystery-cults had become widely disseminated over the

---

[1] General works on the mysteries are few. Cumont, *Oriental Religions*, and Toutain, *Les cultes païens*, I, ii, are devoted to the Asiatic and Egyptian cults. Other treatments, sometimes only brief sketches and often concerned chiefly with Christianity as related to the mysteries, are Anrich, *Das antike Mysterienwesen in seinem Einfluss auf das Christentum* (Göttingen, 1894); Wobbermin, *Religionsgeschichtliche Studien zur Frage der Beeinflussung des Urchristentums durch das antike Mysterienwesen* (Berlin, 1896); Cheetham, *The Mysteries, Pagan and Christian* (London, 1897); De Jong, *Das antike Mysterienwesen* (Leiden, 1909); Reitzenstein, *Die hellenistischen Mysterienreligionen;* Jacoby, *Die antike Mysterienreligionen und das Christentum;* Perdelwitz, *Die Mysterienreligion und das Problem des I. Petrusbriefes* (Giessen, 1911); Clemen,

Graeco-Roman world. For several centuries they had been known among the Greeks in variant forms,[1] yet they had certain fundamental characteristics in common. Among these was a belief in immortality insured through initiation into the worship of a god or goddess who had triumphed over death and so was able to help believers to a similar victory.

The Eleusinian mysteries are the best known of these various cults which existed in Greece. Although Eleusis was a small place near Athens, at an early date these mysteries became a prominent Athenian state cult.[2] The cult seemed to owe its popularity, which it still retained in Graeco-Roman times, largely to the assurances of a blessed immortality which it professed to confer upon those who had observed the rites of initiation. The so-called "Homeric" hymn to

---

Der Einfluss der Mysterienreligionen auf das älteste Christentum; Kennedy, *St. Paul and the Mystery Religions;* Bousset, "Christentum und Mysterienreligion" and "Die Religionsgeschichte und das Neue Testament," *Theologische Rundschau,* XV (1912), 41–60, 251–77.

[1] Lobeck, *Aglaophamus* (2 vols., Königsberg, 1829), and Farnell, *Cults of the Greek States,* III, 29–393; V, 85–344, give the most complete accounts of the Greek mysteries, citing extensively from ancient writers. See also Hatch, *Influence of Greek Ideas,* etc., pp. 283–309.

[2] A great deal has been written about the Eleusinian mysteries. Besides Lobeck, *op. cit.,* pp. 1–228, and Farnell, *op. cit.,* III, 127–98, see Gruppe, *Griechische Mythologie,* pp. 48–58; Loisy, "Les mystères d'Éleusis," *Revue d'histoire et de littérature religieuses,* Nouvelle série, IV (1913), 193–225; Foucart, *Les mystères d'Éleusis* (Paris, 1914). The last-named work supersedes the same author's earlier writings, contending again for his theory that the Eleusinian mysteries are of Egyptian origin and that the chief function of the rites was to provide the soul with magic formulas for insuring its safe transit to the abodes of the blest. Quite apart from the doubtful validity of this theory, the volume contains much valuable information.

Demeter,[1] which narrates the myths connected with the cult, finally tells how Demeter the mother goddess taught to chosen persons her holy mysteries to be perpetuated for the benefit of men—"blessed is he among mortals who has seen these things! But he who is uninitiated and has no part in the sacred rites has not an equal lot in the dark gloom below." Pindar and Sophocles[2] proclaim the blessedness of the one who has witnessed the sacred rites. In experience, passing below the hollow earth, the initiate sees the goal of life as well as its Zeus-given beginning, and at death he descends to Hades confident that he will be eternally happy. Plato[3] allows that the mysteries express enigmatically the truth that one who goes to Hades uninitiated will lie in filth, while one who has been cleansed through initiation will dwell happily with the gods. In Cicero's day the Eleusinian mysteries retained the same reputation:[4] "Much that is excellent and divine does Athens seem to me to have produced and added to our life, but nothing better than those mysteries by which we are formed and molded from a rude and savage life into humanity; and indeed in the mysteries we perceive the real principles of life and learn not only to live happily but to die with a fairer hope."

To obtain initiation[5] the candidate applied to the priest in charge. In the time of Herodotus[6] only Greeks

[1] See Sikes and Allen, *Homeric Hymns* (London, 1904) for a critical edition, and Lang, *Homeric Hymns* (New York, 1899), for an English rendering.

[2] Quoted by Loebeck, *op. cit.*, p. 69.

[3] *Phaedo*, 69C.   [4] *De leg.*, iii. 14.

[5] For the details of the process see Farnell, *op. cit.*, III, 159 ff.

[6] viii. 65; cf. also Isocrates, *Paneg.*, 157.

were admitted, but later this restriction was removed and persons of any nationality were received provided they knew the Greek language in which the instruction was given to initiates. In Cicero's time "the most distant nations were initiated into the sacred and august Eleusinia."[1] But there were other preliminary requirements. Apollonius of Tyana was denied admission, if his biographer Philostratus is correctly informed,[2] because suspected of practicing wizardry, though Apollonius' reputation is saved by his prediction that the next priest will grant his request. When a candidate was received he first observed certain purificatory rites, after which he was admitted to the "Lesser Mysteries" at Agrai in February. The "Greater Mysteries" were celebrated in September and lasted several days. The ceremonies began on the thirteenth when the *epheboi* marched from Athens to Eleusis, returning the next day with the sacred relics to the Eleusinion in Athens. On the sixteenth the applicants for initiation assembled and the priest pronounced a warning to the unworthy to depart. None could be received except those who were ritualistically pure. Then followed a season of further purification in which the candidates marched to the sea to sprinkle themselves with water, and perhaps also with the blood of a slain pig. On the nineteenth all returned to Eleusis for the completion of the festival. The climactic feature of the initiation took place in the *Telesterion* (τελεστήριον), the assembly hall to which only properly prepared persons were admitted, perhaps the last preparatory act being a sacramental meal. On a stage in the middle of the hall some sort of passion-

---

[1] *De deor. nat.*, i. 42.   [2] iv. 18.

play, or religious drama, was enacted. But those who witnessed this performance were pledged to secrecy, consequently the details are very obscure. Herodotus[1] in describing the mysteries at Sais in Egypt depicts the general situation both as to this part of the mysteries and as to the necessity of secrecy. He describes the sacred precinct of Minerva behind the chapel where there "is the tomb of one whose name I consider it impious to divulge," and there is also a lake where "they perform by night the representation of that person's adventures which they call 'Mysteries' [μυστήρια]. Though accurately acquainted with these particulars, I must observe a discreet silence." He is also familiar with "the sacred rites of Demeter," yet on these he must remain silent. Nevertheless, the general import of the ceremony is clear, although the details are uncertain. The occasion was intended primarily to impress rather than to indoctrinate the audience. The teachings of this religion were conveyed to the mind through the medium of emotion aroused by visual experiences. Doctrine was inculcated by means of a scenic portrayal of symbolic action rather than by logical argumentation.

What meaning did these displays have for initiates? The whole procedure ultimately issued in an elevation of feeling, emanating from a conviction that one had peered into the divine secrets. It was said that "there is nothing greater than the Mother [Demeter] for those who have true knowledge of the divine."[2] Aristotle remarked that the initiated did not learn rules for conduct but experienced emotions and attained a certain

[1] ii. 170 f.; cf. ii. 3, 61, 86.

[2] Stobaeus, *Flor.*, 79. 13.

fitting state of mind.[1] Plutarch used the joy of the newly initiated to describe the feelings of the soul which had been purified after death.[2] These emotions were not, however, simply a temporary satisfaction; the initiate must have read in them some divine meaning as a basis for his confidence in that blessed immortality which the Eleusinian mysteries were reputed to insure. It is most probably to this item that we must look to ascertain the ultimate significance of these rites.

At this point the details have to be conjectured, but the general situation is fairly clear from the myth of Demeter and her daughter Persephone. The daughter is carried off to become the wife of Pluto, king of the lower world. The mother in grief and resentment refuses life to nature until Persephone is restored; an arrangement is made by which the latter spends a portion of the year with the mother and a portion in the nether world; the earth accordingly is given life a part of the year and is denied it a part; and Demeter before ascending Olympus with her risen daughter instructs men in her rites in order that they may attain to a blessed life after death.

The rationale of the myth is evident. It portrays the action of life in nature. Nature was dead in winter, when the mother goddess, source of all life, was grieved at the loss of her daughter; but she resumed her kindly activity in the spring and maintained life in nature until Persephone was removed again to Hades. Spring brought another release and another triumph of life over death. This victory over death, together with

---

[1] Cited by Synesius, *De Dione*, 10.

[2] *De facie in orbe lunae*, 28.

the attainment of a happy life in the next world, was the special privilege of the initiated. There certainly was some close connection between the triumph of the deity and the similar attainment of the devotee, although the manner of interpreting the relationship is now very obscure. The hierophant, we are told, delivered an address at the secret meeting when the mystery-play was staged, but what he said is largely a matter of conjecture. Lobeck made it clear that the rites were not, as had often been supposed,[1] the communication of a body of esoteric doctrines on immortality, but an appeal to emotion made by certain scenic exhibitions. If these were scenes from the experiences of Demeter and Persephone, as seems probable, the priest's words most likely dealt with the significance of these acts as a basis for the believer's hope. Persephone, carried to the realms of Hades, then restored to her mother, and the two ascending to the abodes of the gods in Olympus, are typical of the believer's future good fortune. Farnell,[2] at the end of a very cautious investigation, concludes: "These deities, the mother and the daughter and the dark god in the background, were the powers that governed the world beyond the grave: those who had won her friendship by initiation in this life would by the simple logic of faith regard themselves as certain to win blessing at their hands in the next. And this, as far as we can discern, was the ground on which flourished the Eleusinian hope."

[1] E.g., De Sainte-Croix, *Recherches historiques et critiques sur les mystères du paganisme* (2 vols., Paris, 1817²); Creuzer, *Symbolik und Mythologie* (4 vols., Darmstadt, 1810–19; 3. Aufl., Leipzig, 1837–44).

[2] *Op. cit.*, III, 197.

Whether the Eleusinian ritual was not thought to give a more realistic union with the death-conquering deity is a much-debated problem. On this point the author just cited takes a reserved position, while other interpreters find more truly sacramental features in the ritual.[1] The password in these mysteries is said to have been, "I fasted, I drank the barley-drink, I took from the sacred chest; having tasted I placed them into the basket and again from the basket into the chest."[2] This seems to imply a sacramental communion through the act of drinking and eating. Having witnessed the sacred drama, handled the holy emblems, and partaken of the sacred potion, the initiate believed himself now a partaker with the goddess in triumph over death. And it would be strange indeed if he did not regard his feeling of elation as in some sense a mystical union with the deity.

There are also indications that the Eleusinian mysteries resulted in uplifting and purifying practical life, thus supplying a present as well as a future salvation. Critics, to be sure, ridiculed these ceremonies because they seemed to condition future rewards not on ethical but on mechanical grounds. Diogenes sarcastically remarked, when asked to be initiated, "It will be an absurd thing if Aegesilaus and Epaminondas are to live in the mire and some miserable wretches who have been initiated are to be in the island of the blest."[3] But Andocides[4]

[1] E.g., Jevons, *Introduction to the Study of Religion* (London, 1896), pp. 363 ff.; Dieterich, *Eine Mithrasliturgie*, p. 164.

[2] According to Lobeck's (p. 25) reading of the sentence, which has been preserved by Clement of Alexandria, *Protr.*, ii. 21.

[3] Diogenes Laertius, vi. 2. 39.

[4] *De myster.*, 31; cf. also 125.

assumes that initiation into the sacred rites of the goddesses makes one better qualified to serve as a just judge who will punish the impious and deliver the innocent. Diodorus[1] credits the Samothracian mysteries with producing a similar effect, and Aristophanes[2] says those who have been initiated into the rites of Dionysus "lived in pious fashion as touching our duty to strangers and private people." In the second century B.C. the mysteries are credited with maintaining that "the greatest of human blessings is fellowship and trust."[3] Athens' contribution to Roman civilization is accounted by Cicero to have been "excellent and divine," but nothing was of greater value than the mysteries.[4] The Stoic Epictetus inculcates reverence for the Eleusinian mysteries which were "appointed by the ancients for the instruction and correction of life."[5] The emperor Nero, when in Athens, was afraid to attend the celebration because wicked and impious persons were warned by the herald not to approach the rites.[6] In contrast with Christianity, which took sinners to make them moral, Celsus says other mysteries received only those clean of hand and pure of soul who had lived well and justly.[7] Undoubtedly the Eleusinian mysteries, like other similar cults, exerted an elevating influence upon moral life.[8]

---

[1] v. 49. [2] *Ran.*, 455.

[3] See Farnell, *op. cit.*, III, 347, n. 185a.

[4] *De leg.*, ii. 14. [6] Suetonius, *Nero*, 24.

[5] *Disc.*, iii. 21. [7] Origen, *Cels.*, iii. 59 f.

[8] This is minimized by Rhode, *Psyche: Seelenkult und Unsterblichkeitsglaube der Griechen* (Tübingen, 1910⁵), I, 298 ff.; but Wobbermin, *Religionsgeschichtliche Studien*, usw., pp. 38 ff., successfully defends the ethical importance of the mysteries.

In the first century of our era the fame of the
Eleusinian mysteries had spread widely over the world
in which Christianity later appeared. Since they were
an official cult of Athens the rites could not be readily
established elsewhere, but similar rites were observed
at many places, either owing their origin directly to
the Eleusinian ceremonies or else having a common
parentage.[1] But the fame of the Eleusinia was so
great that persons from various and remote parts of
the ancient world visited Athens seeking initiation.
Cicero is quite right in remarking that the most distant
peoples were initiated.[2] Herodotus testified to the
great numbers of Greeks admitted in his day,[3] but by
the beginning of our era many foreigners were attracted
to these mysteries. The emperor Augustus was initiated
in 21 B.C., although he was not generally disposed
to adopt foreign religions. Yet he highly respected
the Eleusinian cult and once hearing a case in court
where the sacred rites were to be introduced in the
pleading he ordered the judges and spectators to be
dismissed while he proceeded with the trial behind
closed doors.[4] These mysteries were so renowned that
Crinagoras,[5] in the Augustan age, advised his friend
to visit Athens and see the sacred rites of Demeter,
even though he might not be able to travel anywhere

[1] On this disputed question of genetic relationship see Farnell, *op. cit.*,
III, 198 ff.

[2] *De deor. nat.*, i. 42.   [3] viii. 65.

[4] Suetonius, *Aug.*, 93. Other emperors who received initiation were
Hadrian, Verus, and Marcus Aurelius (Gruppe, *Griechische Mythologie*,
p. 1496, n. 1). Claudius even wished to transfer these mysteries to
Rome (Suetonius, *Claud.*, 25).

[5] *Anthol. Palat.*, xi. 42.

else. Seemingly the popularity of the Eleusinian mysteries had, in a sense, become world-wide by the first century of our era; nor is this surprising when we recall the demand which the social environment of that age had created in favor of a religion that could supply a personal assurance of salvation in the life to come.

The Eleusinian cult had several rivals, even in Greece, to say nothing of the numerous oriental mysteries which spread extensively over the Mediterranean world in Hellenistic times. These rival movements appear at a relatively early date in the history of Greek religion, but they seem to have had a foreign origin. Demosthenes taunts his opponent Aeschines with having assisted his mother who evidently was a traveling priestess of the Phrygian Sabazius: "You read the ritual for your mother when she conducted an initiation, and you looked after other things. At night you donned the fawn skin, you mixed the wine-bowl, you purified the candidates and wiped them off with clay and bran, then you raised them from their purification and bade them say 'I have fled an evil thing and found a better.'"[1]

The cult of Dionysus (or Bacchus) and the Orphic movement are especially worthy of notice. They had the advantage of not being a strictly state cult and so were capable of being highly developed along the lines of personal experience.[2] Their fundamental principle,

[1] Demosthenes, *De corona*, 313.

[2] Farnell, *Cults of the Greek States*, V, 85–344, and Lobeck, *Aglaophamus*, pp. 233–1104, are especially valuable for a study of the Dionysus (Bacchus) cult. Cf. also Harrison, *Prolegomena to the Study of Greek Religion*, chaps. viii–xii; Maass, *Orpheus* (München, 1895); Foucart, *Le culte de Dionysos en Attique* (Paris, 1904); Gruppe, *Griechische Mythologie*, pp. 1028–41; Quandt, *De Baccho ab Alexandri aetate in*

however, was the same as that of the Eleusinian mysteries. Their primary concern was for the devotee's future well-being; this was procured through connection with a helping deity; emotion played an important part in religious experience, and definite rites were prescribed for the realization of religious attainments.

Dionysus, originally a crude nature-deity of the Thracians, impersonated the power of life in all vegetation. In Greece he is more especially the god of the vine, and so the patron of agriculture which he is reputed to have taught to all mankind. As wine inspired the Bacchic frenzy, so the devotee who worships the power of life in nature experiences the divine possession which displays itself in the orgies of the sacred festival. Herodotus,[1] in describing the initiation of the Scythian king, Scylas, says the god "took possession" of the king—he was "maddened" by the deity. This experience of divine infilling was taken to be the earnest of a blessed immortal life. He who felt himself "full of god" (ἔνθεος), particularly when this specific deity had displayed his power of triumph over death,[2] readily believed this experience to be a foretaste of the eternal bliss awaiting the worshiper in the next world. Although these rites were subjected to criticism, as when Plato remarked that an immortality of drunkenness seemed to be thought the highest reward of virtue, yet they were generally believed to involve a real

Asia Minore culto (Dissertationes philologicae Halenses, Vol. XXI, 2, Halle, 1913); Loisy, "Dionysos et Orphée," *Revue d'histoire et de littérature religieuses*, Nouvelle série, IV (1913), 130–54.

[1] iv. 78 ff.

[2] See references in Farnell, *op. cit.*, V, 285 f.

spiritual communion with the divine. Euripides[1] probably is expressing current opinion when he says that
one who knows the mysteries "is pure in life, and revel-
ing on the mountains hath the Bacchic communion
in his soul." In fact a distinction was made between
those who merely participated in the rites and those
who realized the genuine Bacchic experience—"for
indeed they say concerning the mysteries 'Many are
the bearers of the thyrsus but the bacchanals are
few.'"[2]

Participation in the life of the god was realistically
attained by drinking the blood and eating raw the
flesh of the sacred victim in which the god was assumed
to be incarnated. Haste had to be made in devouring
the victim lest the divinity should escape, and this gave
the feast its frenzied character. The animal was sometimes a bull, a goat, or a fawn; and in earlier times even
a human being probably was devoured. This seems
to be the imagery behind a poem, doubtfully ascribed
to Theocritus, apparently written in honor of a boy
nine years old whose right to initiation is justified by
the piety of his father: "To the children of pious fathers
belong the good things rather than to those that come
of impious men."[3] Besides eating the animal, wearing
its skin as an emblem of assimilation to the deity was
also common. The frenzied worshiper, having thus
acquired the strength of the god, could dispense blessings
to others by prophesying, healing diseases, or controlling
the power of nature. In short, he who possessed the

---

[1] *Bacch.*, 75 ff.   [2] Plato, *Phaedo*, 69C.

[3] Theocritus, xxvi (*Bacch.*). 31; cf. Paul's belief in the sanctity of
the children when even one parent is a Christian (I Cor. 7:14).

divine potency which exhibited itself in ecstasy could convert the desert into a garden "flowing with milk and honey."[1]

The Graeco-Roman world was thoroughly familiar with the cult of Dionysus, which had already gained such headway among the Romans by the beginning of the second century B.C. that a strenuous effort was made to drive it out of Italy.[2] But the worship of Dionysus was so closely akin to that of other mystery-deities, and his form was so easily fused with that of Attis, Adonis, or Osiris, that it is difficult to trace independently the influence of the Dionysus mysteries. The type of religion was widely prevalent, whether bearing the name of Dionysus or that of a kindred deity.[3]

The Orphic cult[4] is only a variant form of the Dionysian, with a stronger emphasis upon theological speculation. Dionysus, who is frequently called Zagreus, plays a prominent part in the system. He is devoured by the Titans who thus absorb his essence. They are then burned up by Zeus and their ashes cast to the winds,

[1] Euripides, *Bacch.*, 143; Plato, *Ion*, 534A. See further Farnell, *op. cit.*, V, 300, n. 73.

[2] See the account of Livy, xxxix. 8–20.

[3] For the fusion of Dionysus with other gods, as well as the different Dionysi, see Herodotus, ii. 48 f.; Cicero, *De deor. nat.*, iii. 23; Tibullus, i. 8.

[4] In addition to references cited above, p. 297, n. 2, see Taylor, *The Mystical Hymns of Orpheus* (London, 1896³); Gruppe, *Die griechischen Culte und Mythen* (Leipzig, 1887), I, 612–74; Dieterich, *De hymnis Orphicis* (Marburg, 1891), reprinted in the same author's *Kleine Schriften* (Leipzig, 1911), pp. 69–110; Hauck, *De hymnorum orphicorum aetate* (Breslau, 1911); C. H. Moore, "Greek and Roman Ascetic Tendencies," *Harvard Essays on Classical Subjects* (New York, 1912), pp. 103 ff.; Diels, *Fragmente der Vorsokratiker*, II, 163–78.

but as these ashes contain the vitality of Dionysus they
become the source of divine life in all things, and particularly in the human soul.   Thus the soul by its very constitution is divine and the body is its carnal prison house
from which it is constantly seeking deliverance in death.
But death was of itself no sure deliverance.   The soul
which had not been purified by the rites of religion was
confronted by the miry pit of Hades, whence it might
be forced to return and take up its abode for further
punishment in some animal.   The purified soul, on
the other hand, inherited immortal delight.   Consequently the supreme effort of one's earthly life was to
purge the soul of bodily defilement.   This was accomplished through mystic rites, prescribed abstinences
and assimilation to the deity by means of sacrifice,
libations, and prayers.   The mystical and redemptive
character of the religion is illustrated from the Orphic
tablets.[1]   The devotee says: "I am a child of earth
and the starry heaven, but my race is of heaven (alone).
This ye know yourselves.   And lo, I am parched with
thirst and I perish.   Give me quickly the cold water flowing from the lake of memory."   Again, "Hail thou who
hast suffered the suffering.   This thou hast never suffered
before.   Thou art become God from man."   And further:
"I come a suppliant to holy Persephone that of her grace
she receive me to the seats of the hallowed.   Happy and
blessed one thou shalt be god instead of mortal."

Orphism, like Pythagoreanism which it in some
respects resembled,[2] did not maintain itself as a distinct

---

[1] Cf. Harrison, *Prolegomena to the Study of Greek Religion*, pp. 660 ff.;
Comparetti, *Laminette orfiche* (Firenze, 1910).

[2] Cf. Herodotus, ii. 81.

movement in the Hellenistic age, yet its influence was
strongly felt in secondary forms. Orphic doctrines and
practices were variously appropriated by the popular
philosophers as well as by influential mystery-cults,
and thus their influence continued long after the disappearance of formal Orphic brotherhoods.

In addition to the mysteries of Greece proper, the
eastern lands and Egypt supplied the same type of
religion in still greater abundance. To describe the
oriental mystery-cults in detail is too large a task for
the present. It will be sufficient for our immediate
needs if we note their leading characteristics and observe
the extent of their influence before the rise of Christianity.

The Phrygian cult of the mother-goddess, Cybele,
and her consort, Attis, came to occupy a prominent
place within the religious syncretism of Hellenistic
times.[1] Cybele was a wild nature-deity worshiped on
the top of the mountains, especially on Mount Ida.
The chief seats of her cult were Cyzicus, Sardis, and
Pessinus. She was known, like Demeter, as the source
of all life in nature, and her rites had a correspondingly
orgiastic character. Connected with her was a male
deity, Attis, who personified the death of nature in winter

[1] For detailed information on the Phrygian religion see Showerman,
The Great Mother of the Gods (Madison, 1901); Hepding, *Attis, seine
Mythen und sein Kult* (Giessen, 1903); Frazer, *Adonis, Attis, Osiris* (New
York, 1906²), pp. 219–65; Dill, *Roman Society from Nero to Marcus
Aurelius*, pp. 547–59; Cumont, *Oriental Religions in Roman Paganism*,
pp. 46–72; Toutain, *Les cultes païens*, I, ii, 73–119; Wissowa, *Religion
und Kultus der Römer*, pp. 317–27; Schmidt, *Kultübertragungen*, pp.
1–30; Loisy, "Cybele et Attis," *Revue d'histoire et de littérature religieuses*,
Nouvelle série, IV (1913), 289–326.

and its revival in the spring. The myths about Attis
vary in details,[1] but they all have the same general
import. Attis dies, either at the hand of an enemy or
by self-mutilation, and the goddess mourns until he is
restored to life. The deity's triumph over death is
made the basis of the ritual by which the believer avails
himself of the god's help in effecting a similar victory
for mortals.

The Greeks became acquainted with this Phrygian
religion at least as early as the sixth century B.C. Both
Cybele and Attis were worshiped at various places in
Greece before the beginning of our era, and they were
easily fused with other gods of a similar character
already known to the Greeks.[2] The Phrygian goddess
enjoyed so much prestige by the year 204 B.C. that her
cult was officially introduced into Italy.[3] The Romans
were sore pressed by Hannibal, a plague had carried
off many of the Roman soldiers, and a shower of meteors
had fallen upon the earth. The Sybilline books when
consulted advised bringing the worship of the Phrygian
goddess to Rome. Accordingly messengers were sent
to Pessinus where they procured a sacred meteoric
stone which they conveyed to Rome and installed in
great solemnity on the Palatine in April 204 B.C. Following this the Romans were successful in their conflict
with Carthage, Cybele was honored with a temple, and
from that time on her position was officially established.

[1] Cf. Diodorus, iii. 58 f.; Ovid, *Fasti*, iv. 223 ff.; Pausanias, vii. 17;
Arnobius, v. 5–8.

[2] Cf. Farnell, *Cults*, etc., III, 289–393; Gruppe, *Griechische Mythologie*,
pp. 1519–54.

[3] Particulars are given by Livy, xxix. 10–14.

A glimpse into the character of her worship in Catullus' day (87–47 B.C.) is given in his poem called *Atys* which shows this religion to have been one of great ecstatic frenzy in which the devotee sacrificed his manhood to the goddess, thus assimilating himself to her nature. He performed certain initiatory rites, clothed himself in a special garment, participated in the maddening dance, and became a bondsman of Cybele forever. Catullus' description is at the same time a protest— perhaps to some extent a caricature—but it probably gives a true picture of the orgiastic nature of the cult. Not, however, until the time of Augustus and his successors in the first century A.D. did Cybele-Attis worship really thrive at Rome. The celebration of the yearly festival as it was observed under official patronage in the time of Claudius was an elaborate mystery-drama extending from the fifteenth to the twenty-seventh of March. The death of Attis, mourning for the dead god and rejoicing at his resurrection, constituted the prominent features of the ceremony. The worshipers performed various rites to indicate union with the deity, whose career was represented in a kind of mystery-play depicting the triumph over death.[1]

Thus the Cybele-Attis religion had reached out from its native Phrygian home, gaining official recognition

[1] Cumont, *Oriental Religions*, pp. 58 f., gives a detailed description of this spring festival. The "Taurobolium," as well as the "Criobolium," is not known to have been performed before 134 A.D. Then it appears in Italy, but it unquestionably had an oriental origin and so must have been practiced at a considerably earlier date. It may also have had Mithraic connections. The description given by Prudentius (*Peristaphanon*, x. 1011 ff.) purports to be based on personal observation. A perforated platform was erected over a pit in which the neophyte

and support in the capital of the empire, while Christianity was still making its first appearance in the homeland of the Cybele-Attis cult.

It is a more difficult task to define the religious influences which emanated from the regions of Cilicia and Syria.[1] Tradition supplies a variety of gods and goddesses, but leaves their mutual relations and the details of their worship obscure. Yet, in spite of the chaotic condition of our information, the main lines of religious development are discoverable, and they disclose features fundamentally similar to those of the Phrygian cult. We find here a goddess mother occupying a central place in the cultus, and associated with her is a male deity whose death is lamented and his resurrection celebrated with rejoicing.

placed himself. The steer was killed above and the blood dripped through upon the worshiper who eagerly received it upon his clothing, face, and lips, even drinking it as it struck his mouth. This baptism was believed to purify the neophyte; he died to his old life and arose to a new, having been reborn through the bloody bath. See, further, Cumont, "Le Taurobole et le culte de Bellone," *Revue d'histoire et de littérature religieuses*, VI (1901), 97–110, and *Oriental Religions*, pp. 66 ff.; Hepding, *Attis*, pp. 177–205; Frazer, *Adonis, Attis, Osiris*, pp. 229 f.

[1] See Cumont, *Oriental Religions*, pp. 103–34; Frazer, *Adonis*, etc., pp. 1–216; Vellay, *Le culte et les fêtes d'Adônis-Thammous dans l'orient antique* (Paris, 1904); von Baudissin, *Adonis und Esmun: Eine Untersuchung zur Geschichte des Glaubens an Auferstehungsgötter und an Heilgötter* (Leipzig, 1911); Toutain, *op. cit.*, pp. 35–72; Strong and Garstang, *The Syrian Goddess* (London, 1913); Wissowa, *Religion und Kultus der Römer*, pp. 359–68; Gruppe, *Griechische Mythologie*, pp. 1582–86; W. R. Smith, *Religion of the Semites* (London, 1894[2]); Lagrange, *Études sur les religions sémitiques* (Paris, 1905); Luckenbill, "The Early Religion of Palestine," *Biblical World*, XXXV (1910), 296–308 and 368–79; Paton, "The Cult of the Mother-Goddess in Ancient Palestine," *ibid.*, XXXVI (1910), 26–38.

These ideas in and about Syria seem to have their natural antecedents in Babylonia where Ishtar is the deified embodiment of mother-life. She is the Ashtoreth of the biblical writers, the Ashtart of Phoenicia, the Astarte and Aphrodite of the Greeks. Ishtar is an ancient figure in Babylonia and her position is a fairly stable one throughout all the changes affecting Assyrian and Babylonian religion. Her influence continued to be felt long after many once greater divinities had been forgotten. She is the mother-goddess of prosperity and fertility who teaches men the arts of civilization and has a constant care for their welfare. Associated with her is the male deity Tammuz, a youthful god who is slain, remains for a period in the lower world, and is later revived. As Ishtar personifies the source of life, Tammuz represents life in its natural manifestation— the constantly rotating cycle of birth and death. Hence the prominence of lamentation in his cult, a practice which in the time of Ezekiel had been adopted by Jews and was being carried on by the women, at the north gate of the temple.[1]

The Babylonian Ishtar became Ashtart in Phoenicia, with apparently an important cult. As early as the third century B.C. she is the patron goddess of the kings of Sidon.[2] Both King Tabnith and his father were her priests. The coffin inscription of his son Eshmun'azar tells us not only that Tabnith's wife was a priestess of

---

[1] Ezek. 8:14. For laments for Tammuz see Gressmann's *Altorientalische Texte und Bilder*, I, 93–96; or Prince, "A Hymn to Tammuz" in the *Journal of the American Oriental Society*, XXX (1909–10), 94–100, and "A Tammuz Fragment," *ibid.*, XXXIII (1913), 345–48.

[2] For data see G. A. Cooke, *A Text Book of North Semitic Inscriptions* (Oxford, 1903), *passim*.

Ashtart, but that a male deity, Eshmun, was associated with her in Sidon. Eshmun'azar boasts of his line that it "built the houses of the gods, the house of Ashtart in Sidon, the land of the sea, and we caused Ashtart to dwell there, making her glorious; and we are they who built a house for Eshmun in the holy field, the well of Yidal in the mountain, and we caused him to dwell there, making him glorious."

It is probable that this male deity associated with Ashtart plays a rôle similar to that of Tammuz, but a better known name of the god who figures in this capacity is Adonis. The equivalence of Adonis and Tammuz is now generally admitted, as well as the fact that Aphrodite was a counterpart of Ashtart, or Astarte as the Greeks called her. In remarking upon the different Venuses of mythology Cicero says, "the fourth was a Syrian . . . . who is called Astarte and is said to have been married to Adonis."[1] And the Greek poetess Sappho mentions the weeping for Adonis—an item which shows not only connections with Tammuz, but also the particular character of the cult. The myths about Adonis and Aphrodite as told by various Greek and Latin writers have the same import. The slain—or, in some myths, stolen—god descends to the lower world; Aphrodite agonizes in grief at his disappearance; finally he is restored in the springtime and continues with the revolution of the seasons to die and rise again each year.

The cult of Aphrodite and Adonis fosters the same type of belief and practices as that which meets us in the other mystery-religions. The goddess is the personification of maternal life and the male deity is the

[1] *De deor. nat.*, iii. 23.

embodiment of the redemptive idea—life in action.
The Adonis festival held at the court of Ptolemy II
early in the third century B.C., as described by Theocritus,[1] has a striking general resemblance to the Attis
festival of Claudius' day. A mystic drama depicted
the death of Adonis, lamentation followed his decease,
and his resurrection was greeted with outbursts of joy.
Among the sacred things displayed were representations
of Aphrodite and Adonis joined in wedlock, the death
of the god, the mourning of the goddess, and Adonis'
restoration to life. In the words of Theocritus, the
musician at the sacred festival sings:

The bridal bed for Adonis spread of my own making is;
Cypris hath this for her wrapping, Adonis that for his.
Of eighteen years, of nineteen, is turned the rose-limbed groom;
His pretty lip is smooth to sip, for it bears but flaxen bloom.
And now she's in her husband's arms, and so we'll say good night;
But tomorrow we'll come with the dew, the dew, and take hands
     and bear him away
Where plashing wave the shore doth lave, and there with locks
     undight
And bosoms bare all shining fair will raise this shrilling lay:
O sweet Adonis, none but thee of the children of gods and men
'Twixt overworld and underworld doth pass and pass again;
That cannot Agamemnon, nor the Lord o' the Woeful Spleen[2]
'Nor the first[3] of the twice ten children that came of the Troyan
     queen,
Nor Patroclus brave, nor Pyrrhus bold that home from the war
     did win,
Nor none of the kith o' the old Lipith nor of them of Deucalion's
     kin—
E'en Pelops' line lacks fate so fine, and Pelasgian Argos' pride.

[1] Text and English tr. by J. M. Edmonds, *The Greek Bucolic Poets*
(New York, 1912), pp. 175 ff.

[2] Ajax.   [3] Hector.

> Adonis sweet, Adonis dear,
> Be gracious for another year;
> Thou'rt welcome to thine own alway,
> And welcome we'll both cry today
> And next Adonis-tide.

The cult of these deities spread in Hellenistic times from two chief centers, Byblos in Syria and Paphos in Cyprus. When Paul in Syria and Cyprus centuries later preached his message about the crucified and risen Lord of Christian faith, the Adonis religion was still thriving in these regions. Many members of the Christian missionary's gentile congregation would undoubtedly be perfectly familiar with the mystic drama depicting the death of the god, they would have participated in the rites of the cult, and would have enjoyed the religious satisfactions which that faith gave its votaries.

Another female deity of Syria, whose genealogical connections are obscure, bore the name Atargatis. Her consort was Hadad, who appears in the Zenjirli inscription which Bar-rekub erected in honor of his father Panammu (745–727 B.C.). Here Hadad's name is connected with belief in the immortality of the soul—an idea especially fostered by all the mystery-religions. The lines referring to Hadad read:[1] "Whosoever of my sons shall hold the scepter and sit upon my seat and grow strong and sacrifice to Hadad . . . . and make mention of the name of Hadad, or shall say, May the soul of Panammu eat with thee and may the soul of Panammu drink with thee . . . . may Hadad look favorably upon him!" Furthermore, a passage in

[1] Cooke, *op. cit.*, pp. 180 ff.

Zech. 12:11 which speaks of mourning for Hadadrimmon seems to indicate, as Gunkel thinks,[1] that Hadad was, like Tammuz and Adonis, a dying god in whose ritual lamentation was a characteristic item.

But in Hellenistic times it is Atargatis herself about whom we hear most. Greek writers often refer to her simply as Συρία θεά ("Syrian goddess"), whence the Roman *dea Syria*, popularly corrupted into *Iasura*. Her cult seems to have been widely disseminated over the Graeco-Roman world among the lower classes, especially among the slaves.[2] The great uprising among the slaves of Sicily in 134 B.C. was led by a devotee of the Syrian goddess who affirmed that he was acting under divine guidance and inspired by divine mania. Her worship apparently was of an ecstatic, mystic type like that of Cybele-Attis.

Persia furnished, in Mithraism,[3] one of the strongest redemption-religions that appeared in the Graeco-Roman world. Mithra was an ancient Iranian deity who was

[1] *Zum religionsgeschichtlichen Verständnis des Neuen Testaments*, p. 78, n. 5.

[2] Yet for a time she was highly esteemed, even by the Roman emperor Nero, who "held in contempt all religious rites except those of the Syrian goddess." But this respect was short lived (Suetonius, *Nero*, 66).

[3] Some representative literature on Mithraism is Lajard, *Recherches sur le culte public et les mystères de Mithra en Orient et en Occident* (Paris, 1867); Cumont, *Textes et monuments figurés relatifs aux mystères de Mithra* (2 vols., Bruxelles, 1896–99), *Les mystères de Mithra* (*ibid.*, 1900), English tr., *The Mysteries of Mithra* (Chicago, 1910²), and *Oriental Religions*, pp. 135–61; Dieterich, *Eine Mithrasliturgie;* Dill, *Roman Society from Nero to Marcus Aurelius*, pp. 585–626; Gruppe, *Griechische Mythologie*, pp. 1591–1602; Wissowa, *Religion und Kultus der Römer*, pp. 368–73; Böhlig, *Die Geisteskultur von Tarsos*, pp. 89–107; Toutain, *Les cultes païens*, I, ii, 121–77; Loisy, "Mithra," *Revue d'histoire et de littérature religieuses*, Nouvelle série, IV (1913), 497–539.

subordinated to Ahura Mazda in the classical period
of Zoroastrianism but regained his popularity with new
strength in later times. Already in the Avesta, Ahura
Mazda declares: "Verily, when I created Mithra, the
lord of wide pastures, O Spitama! I created him as
worthy of sacrifice, as worthy of prayer, as myself
Ahura Mazda."[1] Invoked "in his own name and with
the proper words" he brings the worshiper sure help.
He is mediator between the great God, Ahura Mazda,
and man. As the ever-watchful guardian of justice
and truth, he is especially hostile toward evil demons.
He is the enemy of all wickedness and the one who
delivers righteous men from all troubles. Both here
and hereafter he is the hope of those who pray: "Mayest
thou keep us in both worlds, O Mithra, lord of wide
pastures! both in this material world and in the world
of the spirit, from the fiend of Death, from the fiend
of Aêshma, from the fiendish hordes that lift up the
spear of havoc, and from the onsets of Aêshma."

The Avesta also contains a Yasht[2] in honor of a goddess Ardvi Sûra Anâhita (or Anaitis), who is "the life-
increasing and holy, the herd-increasing and holy, the
fold-increasing and holy, the wealth-increasing and holy,
the country-increasing and holy; who makes the seed
of all males pure, who makes the womb of all females
pure for bringing forth." She is the great river that
waters all the earth, making it fruitful to support life.
To her the creator, Ahura Mazda, himself sacrificed
in proper fashion, begging her to aid him in training
up Zarathushtra to found the new religion. As a goddess

[1] The entire Mihir Yasht (X) is given up to the praise of Mithra.
[2] The Âbân Yasht (V).

of fertility she strongly resembles Ishtar, and some
interpreters have therefore concluded that she came
into Persia from the Semitic world.[1] However this
may be, her position was at one time firmly established,
although later her functions were largely appropriated
by Mithra.

In the fourth century B.C. both Mithra and Anâhita
occupied a prominent place in popular faith, notwithstanding their subordinate position in the Zoroastrian
system.   Artaxerxes II is said to have erected the image
of Anâhita in Babylon, Susa, and Ecbatana, a custom
which was not only followed in Persia, but extended
to Damascus and Sardis.[2] From this time on Mithra
and Anâhita take their place beside Ahura Mazda, until
finally the popular movement completely eclipses
Zoroastrianism as the religion of the Persians.   In the
course of this development Mithra alone becomes the
chief deity of the cult, assimilating to himself the principal characteristics of Anâhita.[3] But this was not the
only source from which Mithraism borrowed.   From
Greece it learned to chisel the god's image in human
form, from Babylonia it learned astrology, from Phrygia
it absorbed many features of the Cybele cult; in fact,
its capacity for adjustment to environment is strikingly
exhibited at several points in its career.   Yet Mithraism
had its own distinctive character as a religious move-

[1] So most recently J. H. Moulton, *Early Zoroastrianism*, pp. 238 ff.
On the other hand, G. F. Moore, *History of Religions*, I, 374, thinks
there is "no sufficient ground for the opinion that the goddess herself
was borrowed from the Semites."

[2] Cited by Clement of Alexandria (*Prot.*, V, 65) from Berosus'
Chaldaics.

[3] Herodotus, i. 131, mistakenly assumes that Mithra was a goddess.

ment. The initiated passed through seven grades, assuming respectively at each stage the names Raven, Occult, Soldier, Lion, Persian, Runner of the Sun, and Father. These are survivals from a primitive age when the devotee sought union with the deity by identification with some animal sacred to the god. But when astrological influence made itself felt the seven stages of initiation came to prefigure the passage of the soul after death through the seven heavens to the final abode of the blessed. Each grade was reached by observing prescribed rites of a sacramental character consisting of ablutions, sacred meals, and other appropriate observances.

The religious satisfactions held out to the votaries were numerous. Hope of a blessed immortality and a final righteous judgment were very prominent. Mithra was a mighty hero, mediating between the god of heaven and mortals, and leading the forces of good against the powers of evil. In the mythological age he had performed heroic deeds for the benefit of mankind, thus becoming the special champion of humanity. After a last supper celebrating the success of his redemptive labors he ascended to heaven, whence he now ministered help to the faithful in their conflict with Satan and his hosts. After death the sinful soul was dragged down to the lower regions to be tortured, but a soul with enough good deeds to its credit to balance the bad soared aloft, ridding itself of all impurities and fleshly passions as it passed through the celestial regions. The entrance to each of the seven heavens could be passed only by those who had been initiated and had thereby learned the proper passwords. Mithra was the helper of the soul in its course, he received it in glory at last, and was to preside over a final judgment when he would return to earth, raise the dead, and bring the forces of evil to an end.

The date at which Mithraism made its appearance in the Graeco-Roman world, and the stage of development which it had reached at that time, are as yet obscure questions. In the second and third centuries A.D. it was Christianity's most powerful rival throughout the whole Roman empire. But until the last quarter of the first century apparently it had not gained a foothold outside Asia Minor, although it had been flourishing for centuries in the regions of Armenia, Pontus, Cappadocia, and Lydia, and had been the religion of the Cilician pirates who unsuccessfully contended with the Romans under Pompey in 67 B.C.[1] for the control of the eastern Mediterranean. The cult of Mithra had become so firmly established in Cilicia that Tarsus continued to worship him down to the end of the imperial period.[2] As early as the time of Nero the Mithraic religion was so highly esteemed that the emperor received initiation at the hands of the Magi who accompanied Tiridates on his visit to Rome.[3]

Nevertheless Mithraism seems to have made only a very slight impression upon the coast lands of the eastern Mediterranean. Though the Persian religion is familiar to Greek and Roman writers,[4] it apparently

---

[1] Plutarch, *Pomp.*, 24.   [2] Cumont, *Textes*, etc., I, 190.

[3] Pliny, *Nat. Hist.*, xxx. 6; Cumont, *Textes*, etc., I, 239.

[4] E.g., Herodotus, i. 131-40; Strabo, xv. 3. 13-20; Plutarch, *De Iside et Osiride*, 46 f.; Diogenes Laertius, *Proem*, vi, where older authorities are cited.

was not among the religious phenomena with which they came into daily contact. Furthermore, the absence of Mithraeums in the archaeological remains of the eastern Mediterranean is usually taken as evidence that Persian religion was not influential in this territory. But this lack of positive data may easily be overemphasized. It is still possible that Mithraic forces may have been felt more widely than the present data would seem to indicate. A new mystery-religion might not establish a distinctive existence in territory already pre-empted by several similar types of faith, and yet it might be present, coalescing with them and contributing in turn some items in their development. It doubtless was a characteristic of Mithraism in earlier times—as we know it was later—to associate itself with other faiths, at the same time contributing to their life not a little of its own leaven. This process certainly had been going on in the lands about the northeastern Mediterranean long before Christianity arose, although we may not at present be able to define the exact limits of Mithraic activity within the religious life of that region.

On the other hand, the wide dissemination of Egyptian mystery-religion over the Graeco-Roman world in pre-Christian times is amply attested.[1] Isis and

---

[1] Besides the general works on Egyptian religion (see above, p. 76), special treatments of the present subject may be found in Lafaye, *Histoire du culte des divinités d'Alexandrie Sérapis, Isis, Harpocrate et Anubis hors de l'Égypte* (Paris, 1883); De Jong, *De Apuleio isiacorum mysteriorum* (Leiden, 1900); Schäfer, *Die Mysterien des Osiris in Abydos unter König Sesostris III* (Leipzig, 1904); Dennis, *The Burden of Isis, Being the Laments of Isis and Nephtys Translated from the Egyptian* (London, 1910); Burel, *Isis et Isiaques sous l'empire romain* (Paris,

Osiris, and later Serapis, are the chief deities who figure
in the Egyptian mysteries. Isis and Osiris were very
ancient deities with whom the attainment of immortal
blessedness had been associated from an early date.
Herodotus[1] noted that these divinities occupied a unique
position, in that all the Egyptians worshiped them in
the same way, while the worship of other gods varied.
Herodotus is impressed with the substantially uniform
position which Isis and Osiris hold in the popular faith.
Serapis appears prominently first in the Ptolemaic
period, when his worship became an official cult.   The
ancestry of Serapis is very obscure,[2] but he is practically

1911); Moret, *Rois et dieux d'Égypte,* and *Mystères égyptiens* (Paris, 1911);
Weber, *Drei Untersuchungen zur ägyptisch-griechischen Religion* (Heidelberg, 1911);   Boulage, *Les mystères d'Isis et d'Osiris* (Paris, 1912);
Reisner, *The Egyptian Conception of Immortality* (London, 1912);
Frazer, *Adonis, Attis, Osiris,* pp. 267–400; Cumont, *Oriental Religions,*
pp. 73–102; Dill, *Roman Society from Nero to Marcus Aurelius,* pp. 560–
84; Toutain, *Les cultes païens,* I, ii, 5–34;   Gruppe, *Griechische Mythologie,* pp. 1562–82; Wissowa, *Religion und Kultus der Römer,* pp. 351–59;
Schmidt, *Kultübertragungen,* pp. 47–81; Lévy, "Sarapis," *Revue de l'histoire des religions,* LX (1909), 285–98; LXI (1910), 162–96; LXIII
(1911), 125–47; Sethe, "Sarapis und die sogenannten κάτοχοι des
Sarapis: Zwei Probleme der griechisch-aegyptischen Religionsgeschichte," *Abhandlungen der Königlichen Gesellschaft der Wissenschaften
zu Göttingen* (Philologisch-historisch Klasse, Neue Folge XIV, Nr. 5,
Berlin, 1913); Loisy, "Isis et Osiris," *Revue d'histoire et de littérature
religieuses,* Nouvelle série, IV (1913), 385–421.

[1] ii. 42.

[2] Cf. Cumont. *Oriental Religions,* pp. 74 f., 229, notes 1 and 4.
According to Plutarch (*De Iside et Osiride,* 28), Ptolemy I was instructed
in a dream to transfer the colossus of Pluto at Sinope to Alexandria
where it was named Serapis, the name being derived in popular tradition from Osiris-Apis.   This derivation has recently been defended by
Sethe (*op. cit.*), who maintains that the Greeks mistook the *O* in Osiris
for the article and made "Serapis" from the rest of the compound
word.   But no explanation yet offered can be treated as final.

identical with Osiris, the two names being perpetuated side by side.

The story of Osiris' death and resurrection has many variations, but the central elements of the myth agree. Osiris upon earth had been a king of Egypt, bestowing the gifts of civilization upon mankind.[1] He suffered a violent death and Isis in fierce grief sought him until she recovered the body, which was carefully embalmed.[2] Another tradition told of the dismemberment of the body, the parts being recovered by Isis and the whole restored to life.[3] Osiris then became king of the nether world. Under astral influence his dominion was transferred to the Plains of Aalu in the west where the sun sank out of sight, absorbed in the death of night.

Thus Osiris was the prototype of the virtuous man who sought from religion the assurance of admission into the abode of the blest after death. The road to be traversed by the departed soul was a difficult and dangerous one, consequently formulas were provided for use in warding off demons and procuring divine help. The so-called *Book of the Dead* owes its origin to this demand, already in full force during the period from the Eighteenth to the Twentieth dynasties. If the traveler, on reaching the judgment hall of Osiris, received a favorable verdict, he was permitted to enter the Plain of Aalu where he might lead forever a life of eternal happiness. The believer identified his own career so closely with that of Osiris that the soul of a dead man was actually called "Osiris," and those who gained

---

[1] Plutarch, *op. cit.*, 13.

[2] Herodotus, ii. 86.   [3] Plutarch, *op. cit.*, 18.

admission to the Plain of Aalu could even become gods if they so desired.[1]

Naturally the deities were highly praised for providing mankind with a cultus capable of conferring on humanity these immortal blessings. The feelings of appreciation and reverence aroused by contemplating the experiences of Isis and Osiris in their struggle against their enemy Typhon, who had brought about Osiris' death, is tersely expressed in the words of Plutarch: "But the avenger of Osiris, his sister and wife, Isis, who extinguished and put a stop to the madness and fury of Typhon, did not forget the contests and struggles she had gone through, nor yet her own wanderings, nor did she suffer oblivion and silence to envelop her many deeds of wisdom, many feats of courage, but by intermingling with the most sacred ceremonies, images, hints, and representations of her sufferings of yore, she consecrated at one and the same time both lessons of piety and consolation in suffering for men and women when overtaken by misfortune. And she, together with Osiris, having been translated from the rank of good divinities up to that of gods, by means of their virtue (as later was done with Hercules and Bacchus) receive not inappropriately the united honors of gods and of divinities everywhere, both in the regions above the earth, and in those under ground, possessing the supreme power."[2]

In the time of Herodotus[3] the second most important Egyptian festival was in honor of Isis. Her largest

[1] See in general, on this subject, Wiedemann, *The Realms of the Egyptian Dead* (London, 1901).

[2] Plutarch, *op. cit.*, 27.   Cf. the similar language of Paul in explaining Jesus' exaltation to heavenly honors (Phil. 2:5-10).

[3] vii. 59-61.

temple was in the city of Busiris in the middle of the Delta. In connection with the festival held at this place "all the men and women to the number of many myriads beat themselves after the sacrifice" in memory of the goddess' lamentation for the dead Osiris. Herodotus doubtless could have informed us accurately about the details of the ritual had he not been so reverential toward their secrets,[1] nevertheless he does disclose their general character.[2] The death of Osiris was widely lamented; and the adventures of the dying and rising god were depicted before the eyes of the neophytes in the form of a mystery-play. These ceremonies will, of course, have been accompanied by fitting ritualistic observances and an appropriate interpretation of their significance.

The Egyptian mysteries spread extensively over the Mediterranean world from the beginning of the third century B.C. on. During the rule of Ptolemy I the worship of Isis and Serapis was established at Athens, the latter having a temple at the foot of the Acropolis. In fact, the worship of these Egyptian deities had been a familiar phenomenon in almost the entire territory about the Levant for three centuries before the rise of Christianity. The same deities had also traveled to Rome before the beginning of our era. The cult of Serapis was established in Pozzuoli by the year 105 B.C., when a Serapeum is mentioned in a city ordinance. Tibullus' fiancée, Delia, had been initiated into the mysteries of Isis at Rome, and he appeals to Delia to intercede

---

[1] See above, p. 291.

[2] See especially ii. 170 f. Plutarch's *De Iside et Osiride* and Apuleius' *Metamorphoses* are important additional sources of information.

with the goddess for him as he now lies sick in Corcyra.[1]
At this early date the Egyptian mysteries had pushed
their way into Italy despite the opposition—due in
some measure perhaps to Rome's jealousy of Alexandria—which was raised against them. They anticipated Christianity in incurring persecution, records
of which are preserved for the years 59, 53, 50, 48 B.C.
and 19 A.D.; yet, like Christianity a century or more
later, they seemed only to thrive the better for opposition.

The significance of these mysteries for the people of
the Graeco-Roman world seems to have been in fundamental respects much the same as that of the corresponding Greek, Phrygian, or Syrian cults. Here again we
find a mother-goddess personifying the source of life
and civilization, and associated with her is a consort
who impersonates the hope of triumph in the ever-
present human struggle of life over death. Diodorus
in his *History*[2] gives a description of Isis said to have been
derived from a tomb inscription at Nysa in Arabia.
Apart from the question of the tradition's historicity,
the sentiments expressed, which are repeated in fuller
form in an inscription of Ios,[3] probably represent the
popular conception of Isis' functions as conceived by
hosts of persons in the first century B.C. The goddess
proclaims herself to be the queen of every land, equipped
with divine knowledge to ordain binding decrees. She
has designed the arts of civilization; she taught men mysteries, thus founding religion; government and social

---

[1] Tibullus, i. 3.   [2] i. 27.

[3] Text and translation in Deissmann, *Light from the Ancient East*,
pp. 136 f.

order are her gifts; she is the patroness of life both in nature and in mankind; to Egypt which nourished her she is a perpetual honor.

Plutarch, a Greek interpreter of the Isis-Osiris religion, writing at approximately the same period when the author of the Fourth Gospel interpreted Christianity to the Greeks, follows a more philosophical vein, though he does not deviate materially from the popular faith. He admits that the mourning for Osiris and the rejoicing at his resurrection are symbols of the death and revival of nature, but he also sees back of these outward phenomena something else—shall we say something cosmic and "spiritual"? He calls Isis "the female principle of nature and that which is capable of receiving all generation in virtue of which she is styled by Plato 'nurse' and 'all-receiving,' but by people in general she is called the 'one of numberless names' because she is converted by the Logos [that is, Osiris, who is identified with the Logos, the Word] into, and receives, all appearances and forms." Osiris in his Logos-function, according to Plutarch, brought the rational world into being.[1]

Perhaps Plutarch was the first to expound the significance of Isis and Osiris in these particular terms, though that is by no means certain. But for generations devotees of these gods had been observing the sacred ceremonies of the cult, nourishing piety upon, and deriving consolation from, the memory of these deities' sufferings, and worshiping them with hearts more or less full of appreciation and reverence according to the capacity of the worshiper. An interpretation of

[1] See Plutarch, *op. cit.*, 39, 53 f., and 61.

this religion by a truly mystic spirit has been preserved in Apuleius' *Metamorphoses*. Though the document is from the latter half of the second century A.D., it has the same basal conception of the goddess that appears in Diodorus two hundred years before and in Plutarch midway between these limits. Isis addresses Lucius, who is seeking her favor, in the usual way: "Behold me Lucius, moved by thy prayers I appear to thee, I, who am nature, the parent of all things, the mistress of all the elements, the primordial offspring of time, the supreme among divinities, the queen of departed spirits, the first of the celestials, and the uniform manifestations of gods and goddesses."

The response of the devout soul to this much-revered goddess—a response which may have been made by many a worshiper in his heart long before Apuleius put it into the mouth of Lucius—was naturally one of great appreciativeness and strong religious fervor. After the goddess had received him into full fellowship through the rites of initiation, Lucius uttered a prayer, worthy to stand beside Cleanthes' great hymn to Zeus. In the latter the philosopher speaks forth his reverence for the activities of a divine Providence which man beholds with satisfaction; in the prayer to Isis the mystic soul appreciates none the less the god's activities, but it finds the great reality of religion in the inward certainty of union with the deity. Lucius prays: "Thou, O holy and perpetual preserver of the human race, always munificent in cherishing mortals, dost bestow the sweet affection of a mother on the misfortunes of the wretched. Nor is there any day or night, nor so much as the minutest particle of time, which passes unattended by thy bounties. Thou dost protect men both by sea and land, and, dispersing the storms of life, dost extend thy health-giving right hand, by which thou dost unravel the inextricably entangled threads of the Fates, and dost assuage the tempests of fortune and restrain the malignant influences of the stars. The gods of heaven adore thee, thou dost roll the sphere of the universe round the steady poles, thou dost illuminate the sun, thou dost govern the universe, thou dost tread the realms of Tartarus. The stars move responsive to thy command, the gods rejoice in thy divinity, the seasons return by thy appointment, and the elements are thy servants. At thy nod the breezes blow, the clouds are nurtured, the seeds germinate, and the blossoms increase. The birds as they hover through the air, the wild beasts as they roam on the mountains, the serpents that hide in the earth, and the monsters that swim in the sea are terrified at the majesty of thy presence. But I so weak in capacity for celebrating thy praises, and possessing such slender means for offering sacrifices, have far from eloquence sufficient to express all that I conceive of thy majesty. Not a thousand mouths, and tongues as many, not an eternal flow of unwearied speech would be equal to the task. I will, therefore, use my utmost endeavors to do what, poor as I am, still one truly religious may do—I will figure to myself thy divine countenance and will even preserve this most holy divinity locked up in the deepest recesses of my breast."[1]

The mysteries in general perpetuate a very ancient type of religious activity. In the first instance they represent primitive man's effort to avail himself of the

[1] Apuleius, *Metamorphoses*, xi. 25.

help of nature's forces. His main interest is to persuade these powers to act favorably in his behalf. It would be fatal for his welfare if vegetation should fail to revive in the springtime, if the fields should refuse to yield their increase, or if he were denied descendants to defend and perpetuate the existence of the tribe. So he institutes rites designed to bring about the return of spring, the fertility of the soil, and the propagation of the race. His one fear is that life may fail, and his one desire is to insure himself against such disaster. In this lies the explanation of those crude features of nature-worship, the prevalence of phallic images, and the like, which were present in almost all the mysteries.

At an early stage of development man attained confidence in the power of nature to survive the shock of winter's death. He did not base his assurance on the uniformity of nature's law, as we do, but such uniformity was practically as substantial a thing for his faith as that dogma is for our science. This faith was personified in the form of a dying and reviving god, which was the ancient way of talking about what we term the succession of the seasons. The young deity died and the mother-goddess, source of all life, lamenting his decease, refused to sustain life until he was restored. Thus summer followed winter, and winter, summer. In Hellenistic times this type of religion still made a strong appeal, although it had taken a new turn. Not crops and herds and social groups, but the welfare of the individual soul was now uppermost. Men looked to the deity which formerly guaranteed the perpetuity of nature's life to give the individual a similar assurance.

Thus a god which existed first as a redeemer of vegetation became a redeemer of souls.

As in earlier times man sought to ally himself with the forces of nature in order to obtain their aid, so now his aim was to unite himself to this savior-deity. To accomplish this end various means were employed, including pictorial representations of the redeemer-deity's career, rites of purification by which one became worthy of approaching the god, or other ceremonies designed to effect union between the believer and the worshiper. Some of these rites were crude survivals from the earlier stage of nature-worship, while others breathed a noble spirit of purity and devotion. In any case, the religious impulses were fundamentally the same, although the methods employed for attaining the common goal naturally varied with the education and personality of the worshiper.

One of the most influential factors in the evolution of the mystery-religions was the introduction of astral ideas. Originally the gods of these cults seem, for the most part at least, to have been chthonian deities, and the abode of the blest was also located beneath the earth. When the gods were transferred to the heavens and when the soul of man was given astral connections, these religions had a new and much more effective instrument for use in their special task of insuring man the help of the deity in the attainment of a blessed immortality. This process of development must have begun at a comparatively early date, for it was already in full bloom before the opening of our era.[1]

[1] See above, p. 244.

The realistic features of the mystery-religions were still preserved, notwithstanding this transition of thought from earth to heaven.   With the advancement of civilization the crude rites which had formerly been employed to symbolize or to effect union with the god were considerably modified, but this union was not conceived to be any less real.   The devotee and the deity were still realistically united, although the consciousness of the divine presence might now be expressed in terms of intellectual rather than physical emotions.   This intellectualizing tendency, which had been prompted by astrology and which was stimulated by the development of a world-culture in Hellenistic times, led to a greater emphasis than formerly upon speculative items resulting in a more elaborate mystery-religion theology.   The tendency toward mystical speculation has already been observed, even among Greek philosophers,[1] but it came to fullest expression in connection with the oriental religions.   The movement did not at first produce an extensive formal literature, and such as was produced has not been preserved from earlier times.   Its real spirit is at present best reflected in the writings of the Gnostics, in the Hermetic literature, and in the magical papyri.

The actual ancestry of Gnosticism is now understood to be pre-Christian oriental mysticism, though it is difficult to determine with which oriental religions its genetic kinship is closest.[2]   In fact, the movement itself

---

[1] Cf. above, p. 281ff.

[2] Its oriental origin has gradually gained in recognition since the appearance of Anz's *Zur Frage nach dem Ursprung des Gnosticismus* (Texte und Untersuchungen, XV, 4, Leipzig, 1897), who traces its ances-

is a syncretism embodying elements from various sources. But its fundamental interest is the same as that of all the mystery-religions, namely, to procure salvation for the individual soul through the help of divinity. On this practical religious basis it rears its speculative superstructure. The world of matter and the world of spirit are two distinct entities. The soul of man is a spark of heavenly fire belonging to the divine sphere, but has become so entangled in matter that release is impossible without divine aid. This aid is mediated in the form of revealed knowledge, *gnosis* (γνῶσις), which is a mysterious wisdom attained only by those who have been initiated.[1] Through this divine enlightenment the soul now attains liberation,

try to Babylonia. Bousset, *Hauptprobleme der Gnosis* (Göttingen, 1907), on the other hand, derives the main constituent elements from Persia. An Egyptian origin is affirmed by Amélineau, *Essai sur le gnosticisme égyptien* (Paris, 1887), and the same view has been advocated more recently by Reitzenstein, *Poimandres* (Leipzig, 1904) and *Die hellenistischen Mysterienreligionen* (Leipzig, 1910). The latest writer, De Faye, *Gnostiques et gnosticisme* (Paris, 1913), does not believe it possible to construct the genealogical tree of Gnosticism so far as to discover any one primitive type (p. 447). Other works on Gnosticism are F. C. Baur, *Das manichäische Religionssystem* (Tübingen, 1831) and *Die christliche Gnosis* (Tübingen, 1835); Lipsius, *Der Gnosticismus* (Leipzig, 1860); Mansel, *The Gnostic Heresies of the First and Second Centuries* (London, 1875); Hilgenfeld, *Ketzergeschichte des Urchristentums* (Leipzig, 1884); King, *The Gnostics and Their Remains* (London, 1887[2]); M. Friedländer, *Der vorchristliche jüdische Gnosticismus* (Göttingen, 1898); G. R. S. Mead, *Fragments of a Faith Forgotten* (London, 1900); De Faye, *Introduction à l'étude du gnosticisme* (Paris, 1903); Buonaiuti, *Lo Gnosticismo* (Rome, 1907); Schultz, *Dokumente der Gnosis* (Jena, 1910); Pfleiderer, *Das Urchristentum* (Berlin, 1902[2]), II, 1–179, English tr., *Primitive Christianity* (New York, 1910), III, 113–271; Wendland, *Die hellenistisch-römische Kultur*, pp. 163–87; Bousset, *Kyrios Christos*, pp. 222–63.

[1] Cf. Liechtenhan, *Die Offenbarung in Gnosticismus* (Göttingen, 1901).

at the same time learning the secret of a successful journey to the abode of the blest after death. This abode is in the highest heavens, whither the soul journeys equipped with all necessary armor, both offensive and defensive, for triumphing over its foes. This victory is made possible in the first instance through the work of a savior who, instead of being a concrete historical or mythical individual, is now an abstraction in the form of "light," "truth," "wisdom," "primal man," and the like. The whole scheme of the universe becomes a mighty drama of redemption. This in general was the character of Gnosticism before it was fused with Christianity in the second and third centuries A.D.

The Hermetic literature, though not pre-Christian in its present form, represents Egyptian Gnosticism, elements of which are undoubtedly pre-Christian in origin.[1] These pertain to the welfare of the soul in its struggle to attain salvation through alliance with the deity who reveals true wisdom to the initiate. Thus the believer is reborn to a new life, the god dwelling in him and conferring upon him the gift of immortality. The conversation between Hermes and his son Thot[2] regarding regeneration reveals the characteristics of

---

[1] For literature see above, p. 193, n. 1. Jacoby, *Die antiken Mysterienreligionen und das Christentum*, pp. 30 ff., translates some of the more interesting passages. Reitzenstein, *Poimandres*, pp. 328 ff. prints a portion of the original text, the latest edition of which is Parthey, *Hermetis Trismegisti Poemander* (Berlin, 1854). Mead, *Thrice Greatest Hermes*, contains a translation, introduction, and commentary on the entire Hermetic corpus.

[2] Or "Tat"; cf. Reitzenstein, *op. cit.*, p. 117, n. 2.

the religion.[1]   The father has received the divine enlightenment, and as he talks with the son the latter, too,
experiences the change when he learns the secrets of
wisdom from his father.   Man's great misfortune is
ignorance of God, but one who comes to a knowledge
of the truth has the power and presence of deity within
his breast.   Essentially the same atmosphere pervades
numerous magical papyri.   To cite a single illustration
from the prayer of a suppliant in the so-called "Mithra-
liturgy":[2]   "If indeed it seems good to you permit me,
now held down by my lower nature, to be reborn to
immortality . . . . that I may become mentally reborn,
that I may become initiated, that the Holy Spirit may
breathe in me."[3]

Such, in broad outlines, were the redemption-religions
of the Graeco-Roman world.   In details they exhibit
varying characteristics, but they all alike seek to meet
the widespread demand for an individual salvation to
be procured primarily by the aid of the deity.   The
demand for this type of religion was particularly strong
in Hellenistic times, when national ideals were disap-
pearing and the individual was thrown more specifically
upon his own resources in a vast and varied world.   The
human spirit, conscious of its frailty and helpless at the

[1] See text in Reitzenstein's *Poimandres*, pp. 339 ff.

[2] There is much doubt about this document's being a Mithraic
liturgy (see Dieterich, *Mithrasliturgie*, pp. 225–28, for a summary of
the discussion) but it represents a type of religion widely prevalent in
the ancient world.   Although these documents are of post-Christian
origin, many of the religious items in them are directly descended from
the oriental mystery-religions.

[3] Dieterich, *Mithrasliturgie*, p. 4.

loss of older sanctions, eagerly turned toward those
cults which offered a personal salvation based upon a
divine redemptive transaction. Among the oriental
religions of redemption which attempted to meet this
situation, Christianity was the last to arise, but it ultimately triumphed over all its rivals. We have, finally,
to sketch briefly the beginnings of this triumph.

CHAPTER X

THE TRIUMPH OF CHRISTIANITY

Christians in the first century passed through widely varying experiences, due in large measure to a rapidly changing environment. Jesus' death left his more immediate followers disappointed and bewildered. They had hoped that he would lead them in triumph against the foreign oppressor, but instead he had been crushed by the might of Rome. The favor of God which they thought he enjoyed had been removed; it seemed to them now that he had been abandoned to die on the cross like a common thief.

The disciples escaped being seriously involved in the trouble which cost Jesus his life. He apparently was condemned as a possible messianic agitator, his removal being mainly a precautionary measure, since he had not actively instigated any revolutionary political movement. Indeed, his followers were so few that the authorities took little notice of them after their leader had been removed. It was some time before they were sufficiently numerous or influential to attract attention, but even then hostility against them was prompted by entirely new causes. The persecution of the early Christian community in Jerusalem was not any mere continuation of the enmity which had brought about Jesus' death.

Although the disciples had abandoned Jesus on the cross, their lives were still dominated by memories of personal association with him. He, like John the Baptist and many an older prophet, had proclaimed

God's displeasure with contemporary religious conditions among the Jews. But unlike John, he sought to communicate with men in the daily walks of life instead of calling them to hear the ascetic preacher of the desert. While in sympathy with John, Jesus was not fully satisfied with the latter's message. The call to repentance he doubtless approved, as well as the idea of impending judgment, but the constructive side of John's teaching did not adequately represent the experience of Jesus who thought of God not only as a future righteous judge but also as a heavenly father to be found here and now by all who seek him in a truly worshipful spirit.

Jesus' unique capacity for spiritual communion with the Father suggests the measure of that peculiarly strong attachment by which his closest associates were bound to him. They had been disposed to identify him with the long-expected one who should arise to deliver Israel from the yoke of the foreigner. Probably Jesus had not encouraged them in this specific belief, for he seems to have discountenanced current inclinations toward revolution. At any rate, early Christian tradition generally affirms that previous to his death the disciples, in so far as they associated any idea of messiahship with him, entertained an entirely different conception from that which they came to hold subsequently. While his death shattered their political aspirations, it still left them their vivid recollections of his personality on the basis of which they reared a new messianic faith. They no longer looked for an earthly leader, but for a heaven-sent deliverer in the person of the crucified Jesus. Out of the "Jesus of history" enthroned in their memory they proceeded to construct the "Christ of faith" who became central in their hope.

There were various forces at work in their life tending to bring about the transformation of their faith. In the first place they cherished a great longing for a traditional redemption. This hope, stimulated by the Jews' long period of bitter experience under subjection to foreign rulers, became a central item in the national religion. All were agreed that ultimately God was to be the deliverer of his people, but there were differences of opinion about the program he would follow. The oldest view was to the effect that a natural descendant of David would be elevated to the kingship, but in the interim between the Old and the New Testament another interpretation had arisen. According to this view God would send a deliverer out of heaven, miraculously bringing all earthly rule to an end and establishing an eternal kingdom of righteousness. Although Jesus' death compelled the disciples to abandon their belief in him as the man-Messiah, they still could resort to the conception of a heaven-Messiah.

The transition became complete the moment belief in Jesus' resurrection and exaltation to heaven was established. It is a common opinion nowadays that Jesus had attached to himself the notion of a heavenly Messiah and had cautiously endeavored to induct the disciples into his way of thinking. If he did make this attempt he was wholly unsuccessful in accomplishing his purpose, according to the uniform testimony of synoptic tradition. Even Peter, when at last he confessed belief in Jesus' messiahship, immediately betrayed utter ignorance of the type of messiahship which believers later

attached to Jesus. They admitted that prior to his
death they had not comprehended his meaning which
had now become clear to them in the light of further
developments. Had Jesus himself anticipated the future
course of events? Naturally they believed he had, and
so they recalled words of his which were thought to point
in this direction. But to what extent their interpretation was influenced by their subsequent faith is now very
difficult to determine. One thing, however, is clear:
the disciples did not carry away from Calvary any
ready-made expectation of seeing Jesus alive again.
Although they later believed that he had tried to prepare them for what was to happen, they freely confessed
to a former dulness which had made comprehension
impossible.[1] The most important preparatory items
in the attainment of the disciples' resurrection faith were
their memory of Jesus' personality, and the apocalyptic
form of the national hope to which they now naturally
turned. Then of a sudden certain members of their
company had a revolutionary experience; they believed
Jesus had appeared to them in angelic form, thus proving that he had broken through the gates of Hades
and ascended to heaven. He was now in a position to
discharge the functions of the apocalyptic Messiah.

May we suppose that the early believers were influenced in the attainment of their resurrection faith by
the notion of a dying and rising god as current in the
contemporary mystery-religions? This is not an a priori
impossibility. That such influence may have been felt
even within Jewish circles is suggested by Ezek. 8:14,

[1] See Mark 8:30-32; 9:9 f., 30-32; 10:32-34; Matt. 16:20 f.
17:9, 22 f.; 20:17-19; Luke 9:21 f., 36; 9:43-45; 18:31-34.

and its possibility for the Christians is all the stronger
when we remember that they had probably belonged
originally to the populace. It is not unlikely that popular religion, even among the Jews of Palestine, had
absorbed features from the popular faiths of their neigh-
bors, notwithstanding the hostility which official Judaism
may have felt toward these exotic features.

On the other hand, the fundamental motive behind
the disciples' faith is so genuinely Jewish that the idea
of gentile connections in the first instance seems very
questionable. The earliest Christians were not, like the
devotees of the mystery-religions, paying reverence to a
deity because he, by his triumph over death, was thought
capable of assuring them a similar victory. Jesus'
resurrection was only indirectly beneficial to them; its
immediate worth was for Jesus in that it elevated him to
the position of Messiah.   The members of the early community were not expecting to die but to live to see Jesus
come in glory upon the clouds.   His resurrection received
its primary significance from the fact that it made this
action possible.

Paul, so far as we know, was the first to affirm that
Jesus is the first-fruits and that those who are united to
him by faith triumph over death because of his victory.
Thus Paul took advantage of a notion with which the
Corinthians were already familiar.   Similar influences
probably had been at work in the development of tradition as we now find it in the elaborated accounts of
Jesus' resurrection given in the Gospels.   Since these
narratives in the present literary form have probably all
done service in the propagation of the new religion on
gentile soil, the evangelists may have designed them to

show that Jesus guaranteed immortal life as truly as did the dying and rising Attis, Adonis, or Osiris.[1]

The specific conditions under which the first disciples found themselves after they came to believe in Jesus' resurrection and exaltation determined the main lines of their future activity. The early community seems to have been composed, at the outset, of Palestinian Jews only who had no thought of breaking with their ancestral religion. The distinctive thing about them was their conviction that they had at last obtained the correct answer to that age-long question of the Jewish nation, namely, when will Yahweh effect the salvation of his chosen people? Their answer was a very simple one. It was based upon the conviction that Jesus had been raised from the dead and exalted to heaven whence he would come suddenly and soon to bring an end to the present order of things, miraculously establishing a new age where Israel would be supreme. There would be no more oppression from the Romans, no more desecration of the holy city by the foreign soldiers, no more tribute money paid to the heathen overlords, no more suffering for the people of God, and no longer would any evil thing be found in all the earth.

The notions of later times to the effect that this ideal was to be realized in a place called heaven whither each soul went at death, while the order of things on this planet moved on in normal fashion, was no part of the earliest Christians' thinking. They were not going to heaven; heaven was coming to them. They looked for a new Jerusalem to be let down out of heaven upon a

[1] Cf. Pfleiderer, *Early Christian Conception of Christ*, pp. 84 ff., and Brückner, *Der sterbende und auferstehende Gottheiland*, pp. 34 ff.

renovated earth, and they expected to live to see that event come to pass.   Even when the Gospel of Mark was written, presumably about the year 70 A.D., it was believed that certain persons who had been present with Jesus upon the earth would live to see the new kingdom established.[1]   Thus redemption for God's chosen people was on the verge of realization.

How was this impending redemption to be accomplished?   The first disciples seem to have answered this question simply by referring to the future advent of Jesus and demanding belief in his messiahship.   There is really no justification for suspecting that they at the start had any suspicion of a break with Judaism or that they felt Jesus' death had accomplished anything other than his own transition from the status of a possible man-Messiah to the position of the actual heavenly Messiah.   The Pauline argument about deliverance from the bondage of the law—a phase of thought which the apostle worked out so strongly in his practical conflict with the legalists—had not yet arisen to mar the disciples' sense of unity with Jewish coreligionists.   In fact, they did not regard the law as a burden from which men needed redemption.   It was for them rather a favor which Yahweh had bestowed upon his people, something on which they probably delighted to meditate day and night.

The great redemptive transaction was still to be accomplished through Jesus' return, but its consummation was thought to await the assembling of a proper body of inhabitants for the new kingdom.   These were to be gathered from the chosen people of God, who were

[1] Mark 9:1.

to enter into this new privilege by repenting of their
sins and especially of their apathy or hostility toward
those who were proclaiming that God had chosen Jesus
to usher in the new messianic age. Apart from this
requirement the Jews were to continue as before in the
strict observance of the laws of Moses as a part of their
general purpose to please God and so to induce his
interference on their behalf.

In so far as further requirements were imposed on
believers, these seem to have consisted in an enlarge-
ment of the current stock of ethical and religious teaching
by adding items from the teaching of Jesus. His disciples defended this innovation by identifying him with
the prophet whose coming Moses had foretold: "A
prophet shall the Lord God raise up unto you from among
your brethren, like unto me; to him shall ye hearken
in all things whatsoever he shall speak unto you."[1]
Jesus while upon earth was simply the servant of God
sent to bless the people in turning them away from their
sins. The disciples preached a similar message of
repentance in order to persuade God to send Jesus who
had been made Messiah through his resurrection and
exaltation.

According to this program the distinctively redeeming activity of Jesus still awaits fulfilment. His career
upon earth was a preliminary period of teaching designed
to prepare the people for the final deliverance when
Jesus would appear as Messiah coming upon the clouds.
Not till then would the powers of darkness be set at
naught and the people of God enter into the heritage
of the redeemed. Although Jesus would be the national

[1] Acts 3:22.

deliverer of Israel, the national group was narrowed to include only those who were willing to believe that he had been raised from the dead, exalted to the right hand of God, and inducted into the messianic office. Those who held this faith would receive the blessings of redemption when Jesus came upon the clouds to discharge his messianic functions in accomplishing the salvation of Israel.

Thus Christianity at the outset was a nationalistic religion of redemption, distinctively Jewish in type. The figure of the redeemer, the notion of his special functions, and the definition of man's part in the program were all emphatically Jewish in character. The original items contributed by the disciples were their identification of the heavenly savior with a well-known historical individual, and their accompanying belief in Jesus' resurrection. This was the gospel with which the early preachers hoped to win the Jews for the coming kingdom.

Under the inspiration of belief in Jesus' exaltation to a position of lordship in the realm of angelic beings, and having realized in their own lives an ecstatic experience which they interpreted as a special outpouring of the Holy Spirit, the first disciples began enthusiastically to preach their new faith. But they were far less successful in winning the Jews than they doubtless had expected to be, with the result that they were ultimately forced to form a separate organization and to advocate a religion which they, to be sure, called the true Judaism but which their enemies regarded as a heresy to be vigorously persecuted. If some among their number had not conceived the idea of evangelizing the Gentiles, and had not stated the new religion in such form as to make it intelligible and acceptable to foreigners, it is doubtful whether the new movement would have been able to perpetuate its existence beyond the second or third generation.

The story of Christianity's early triumph is closely bound up with these rapidly changing experiences through which the early believers passed. They began to develop distinctive traits as soon as they undertook the work of evangelization. From the start, apparently, they employed baptism as a purificatory rite in much the same way that John the Baptist had done. Although they were following Jewish precedent, for baptism was already practiced by Jews,[1] they gave it a somewhat new meaning by connecting it directly with faith in Jesus as the coming Messiah. Although they observed the stated forms of religious worship customary among the Jews, their own peculiar interest naturally drew them together in a group apart where their own distinctive experiences were given free expression. There they prayed in the full vigor of their new enthusiasm, they ate together in loving fellowship, recalling their life of association with Jesus. They remembered especially the last meal they had eaten with him and made of it a memorial feast which also prefigured the new messianic banquet to be celebrated when the kingdom came. The antecedents of the Christian meal may have been to some extent Jewish,[2] but it was destined to have its own

[1] See Brandt, *Die jüdische Baptismen, oder das religiöse Waschen und Baden im Judentum mit Einschluss des Judenchristentum* (Giessen, 1910); Oesterley and Box, *Religion and Worship of the Synagogue* (New York, 1907), pp. 255–64; Schürer, *Geschichte*, usw., III, 181–85.

[2] Cf. Bertholet, *Die jüdische Religion*, pp. 317 f.; Bousset, *Die Religion des Judentums*, pp. 530 f.; Schürer, *Geschichte*, usw., II, 663 f., and III, 142 ff.; Josephus, *Ant.*, XIV, x, 8.

peculiar development in connection with the new religion. The first Christians' faith in the exalted Jesus, their consciousness of spiritual endowment, and the activities it prompted, the rites of baptism and the Lord's Supper, were some of the earliest distinctive features developed in connection with the new propaganda.

These things not only furnished Christians a means of differentiating themselves from other Jews, but also supplied items which proved particularly serviceable when the missionaries attempted to make their faith minister to the religious needs of the Gentiles. Jesus was presented as the one imperial authority who could satisfy the craving of men for a national redemption, because his kingdom was other-worldly and so eternal. Those Gentiles who were seeking an individual salvation through union with a deity who could confer upon them assurance of blessed immortality were offered the possibility of union with the risen Jesus who alone had brought life and immortality to light. The attempt to know God through emotional experience, already so widespread among gentile faiths, could be met by Christians through their belief in spiritual endowment. Sacramental religious values were easily conserved by adding to or reinterpreting the rites of baptism and the Lord's Supper. The Gentiles' superstitious fears could be quieted by emphasizing the superior power of the risen Jesus over all inferior spirit-beings. In all of these respects Christians advocated a redemptive religion which gradually lost its original national character in favor of individual, mystical forms.

The process of expansion by which Christianity made conquest of the gentile world begins to appear clearly in the work of Paul. While he was one with earlier Jewish Christians in advocating the nationalistic apocalyptic conception of Jesus' messiahship, there were certain respects in which he went his own way. One of the most conspicuous features of his independence is seen in his attitude toward ceremonial observances. Since he had persecuted the Christians before espousing their cause, it was impossible for him to be as oblivious as the first believers had been to the necessity of a separation between Christianity and Judaism. He, accordingly, was not able to unite with them in advocating the keeping of the law of Moses as the condition of Gentiles' admission into the coming kingdom. He agreed with his predecessors in believing that Jesus would come soon and perfect the work of salvation, yet he devised a relatively new program for the regulation of life in the meantime.

In the first place he said, contrary to the views of the Palestinian Christians, that the age of legalism had passed away. He would no longer know either a Moses or a Jesus according to the flesh. We can hardly infer that he no longer admired the ethical standards of Moses or of Jesus, or that he did not recognize the authority of their words as teachers, for he cites them both as a final court of appeal in certain matters. The thing of which he is confident is that the secret of preparing proper inhabitants for the new kingdom lies not in the keeping of ordinances but in establishing a population of spirit-filled individuals. Before Paul, spiritual demonstration seems to have been viewed more as a luxury than a necessity among believers. He made the indwelling Spirit basal for Christian life, and in doing this he equipped himself with a very important instrument for the propagation of the new movement among Gentiles who had become accustomed, in certain circles, to phrase religion in the language of an emotional experience of the indwelling divine power.

The centrality of the Spirit is one of the clearest items in the religion of Paul. He uses a number of expressions emphasizing this idea. To be a Christian is simply to be a spiritual person, and to have the Spirit is just another way of saying that Christ dwells in one. A Christian without some measure of the Spirit is a contradiction in terms. As the ancients often said that a person possessed by an evil spirit was "in the demon," an expression which corresponds to our notion that the demon was in the person, so Paul in speaking of the believer's union with Christ says the believer is "in Christ," or "in the Lord." For Paul such terms meant the fusion of the divine with the human in realistic fashion. In this general sphere of divine activity there is no essential difference between Spirit of God, Spirit of Christ, Christ, or the Lord tabernacling in the believer.

It is not easy for moderns to comprehend Paul on this point. Our notion of the impenetrability of matter makes it almost impossible to think of Spirit in as realistic a way as the ancients did. Perhaps we can better understand their view by comparison with contemporary Stoic teaching. According to the Stoics man was a living being because he had Spirit ($\pi\nu\epsilon\hat{\upsilon}\mu\alpha$) in him; when Spirit withdrew man became an inert corpse. This thing called Spirit was itself corporeal, pervading and animating the body in much the same fashion that the blood was diffused through the system. But this

Spirit was also divinity, being a part of the great primal force, the divine essence, or God, out of which the world came and by which it was constantly sustained. Thus man from the day of his natural birth was divine, according to Stoicism.

Returning to Paul's conception, we find a similar realism. But Paul is no Stoic in holding that the divine part dwells in man from birth, and that he can attain to salvation simply by realizing his inherent divine powers. Paul does not preach the doctrine of redemption by means of the natural man's living true to his best self. On the contrary, he affirmed the doctrine of a new divine insert. There was no hope of obtaining salvation until the natural man had been reinforced with the Spirit, until he had been recreated by the insertion of a new constituent element. The Christian was a new creature, to use Paul's language. He was a compound of the natural man and the divine Spirit—a Spirit-man, a Christ-man, a God-man; and this new element in his constitution was no mere vague impulse toward righteousness, no mere intangible creation of thought, but a specific quantitative reality. This conception was perfectly natural since it was just as difficult for most men in Paul's day to conceive of incorporeal spirit as it is difficult for men in our time to think of spirit as corporeal. If we dismiss, in imagination, our doctrine of the impenetrability of matter, perhaps we shall be able to appreciate better Paul's point of view. Union with Christ, the indwelling Spirit, meant the presence of a new constituent element in personality.

Only those who were thus Spirit-filled could be partakers in the blessings of redemption. They were already united with Christ and thus anticipated these blessings even before the final act of redemption had been accomplished through the destruction of all evil powers on the day of judgment. The thing of first consequence in the meantime, therefore, was to cultivate the life of the Spirit and enlarge as much as possible the membership of the spiritual community. This was a very plain matter, and had Paul's previous religious training been in Stoicism or in the mystery-religions he could have carried out this program much more simply than he did. But he was too loyal to his Jewish religious heritage to be able to dismiss without further ado the faith of his fathers. Moreover, controversy with opponents and the adjustment of his own experience forced him to interpret history.

One of his problems was how to handle that earlier divine revelation, the Mosaic law, upon which Judaism was founded. In solving this difficulty his thinking proceeded from two premises: first, the natural man cannot meet the full requirements of this law, and, secondly, the spiritual man belongs to a new order of things, is a new creation, and so is no longer under the régime of law. Hence Paul could not affirm that the law was still binding and that the Spirit was given for the purpose of helping man to keep the law. On the contrary, the legal régime had come to an end. Yet it had in the first place been a divine enactment, and as such it must have served an essential function and must have terminated in a fitting climax. Its function had been to teach man, by giving him this unattainable standard of conduct, how wide and ever-widening the gap was between his weak, sinful self and the righteous Deity. How was this chasm to be bridged? That it had been bridged and that Paul now as a Christian had the presence of the Deity in his own life was the second main premise of his thinking as well as the incontestable fact of his experience. He met this problem by affirming that Jesus' death had satisfied the demands of the law, redeeming man from its curse and opening up a new highway of communication between humanity and Deity. Had Paul not been so thoroughly Jewish before his conversion we may safely surmise that he never would have taken such elaborate pains to work out this phase of his doctrine. Even as it was, he did not live by his theory of the atonement; he lived by the Spirit, by his union with Christ, and on this rested his hope of redemption.

One of the most important items to which Paul gave his attention must therefore have been the question of how to establish and maintain union with Christ, the redeemer. How did one become united with Christ? Paul says it has pleased God to save the world through the foolishness of preaching. Furthermore, Paul's preaching was concerned with a subject which seemed to Jews quite unintelligible, while to the philosophers of Greece, it was foolishness. Now this subject which Paul expounded, to use his own language, was "Jesus the Messiah and him crucified," and in expounding this theme the preacher spoke God's wisdom in a mystery. This wisdom, like the kernel of all mystery-religion teaching of the times, could be expounded only by one who had been initiated into the mystery, and so had received the Spirit which searcheth out the deep things of God. The natural man receiveth not the things of the Spirit of God, for these no one knoweth save the

Spirit of God. In other words, to understand the redemptive significance of Jesus' death one must be "perfect" (τέλειος), a word which was applied to a person who had been initiated into the mysteries. Thus Paul tersely remarks, closing the discussion about his qualifications for expounding the wisdom of God, "we have the mind of Christ."

Why did Paul thus depict and expound the crucifixion drama? Why did he "placard" Jesus crucified before the eyes of his hearers, as he says he had done to the Galatians? Of course his object was to induce his audience to perform such action as would bring them into union with Christ and so make them sharers in the Christian redemption. The primary action demanded was the exercise of faith, which meant the acceptance of Jesus as the Savior-Deity, the belief that God raised him from the dead, and the consequent confession of his lordship: "If thou shalt confess with thy mouth Jesus as Lord and shalt believe in thine heart that God raised him from the dead thou shalt be saved." Such a procedure issued either directly or indirectly in the establishment of union with Christ through infilling by the Spirit. Paul assumes that everybody will concede it to have been through the hearing of faith that Christians had received, or had made possible the reception of, the Spirit in the first instance.

While "faith" is the primary act in bringing about union with Christ, just how far it carried one along the way to the ultimate goal is not clear. Certainly the rite of baptism by which one "put on Christ" had a place in the process by which one became a full-fledged "spiritual" person. Paul's remark to the Corinthians about not being sent to baptize but to preach, when isolated from its context, may seem to be a depreciation of the rite.   But if it is read in the light of the context the exact reverse is true.   Paul is glad that he had himself not baptized many of the Corinthians, just because baptism was so very significant.   To have been baptized into the name of an individual made one belong to that individual, hence had Paul baptized any large number of the Corinthians they might the more plausibly have claimed to be "of Paul" and so might really have had some justification for forming a distinctly Pauline party.   But since all had been baptized in the name of Christ, there was no ground for schism.   "Is Christ divided?"   Was Paul crucified for you? or were ye baptized in the name of Paul?"   Of course not! It was only Christ who had been crucified for them, it was into Christ's name only that they had all been baptized, and so they were all one in Christ.   For Paul baptism was universally observed by Christians, and was primarily significant because it effected or consummated the believer's union with Christ: "For in one Spirit were we all baptized into one body, whether Jews or Greeks, whether bond or free; and were all made to drink of one Spirit."   Believers took Christ into them as realistically as though they had drunk down the baptismal waters.

The Lord's Supper was another rite having a similar import, since it was a means of maintaining and strengthening this union.   It is, to be sure, commemorative of Jesus' suffering and so serves to refresh the believer's memory on the great mystery-drama which in the first instance had called forth his faith, but it also served to strengthen his vital union with Christ. Paul is one with his contemporaries in believing that whoever ate at any deity's communion table thereby partook of the deity's substance, hence he warns Christians against taking part in any non-Christian meal. Since the other gods are all evil demons, a Christian who partakes at their table subjects himself to grave dangers. On the other hand, the Lord's Supper should be observed with great solemnity and perfect sobriety, otherwise the participant may fail to discern the sacred body of which he is partaking and so incur the divine condemnation. The Supper, as a memorial of Jesus' martyr-death, is a means of bringing freshly to mind the mystery-drama which Paul originally preached, but it also serves to strengthen substantially the realistic union which exists between the believer and Christ.

In giving baptism and the Lord's Supper this sacramental turn, Paul was pursuing a tendency already prevalent in the religious world of his day. In more primitive times rites of ablution[1] and eating[2] were given a crass magical significance, as when the worshipers of Dionysus devoured the sacred victim raw, believing that they were thereby actually eating the god. In the Graeco-Roman world of the first century A.D. these cruder notions had given place to ideas more refined but none the less sacramentally realistic. When symbolic food took the place of the divine animal, and the form of the deity was accordingly "spiritualized," the

[1] See Kroll, "Alte Taufgebräuche," *Archiv für Religionswissenschaft*, VIII, Beiheft (1905), 27–53; Gruppe, *Griechische Mythologie*, pp. 888 f.; Gunkel, *Zum religionsgeschichtlichen Verständnis*, usw., pp. 83 ff.

[2] Gruppe, *op. cit.*, pp. 731 ff.; Goguel, *L'Eucharistie des origines à Justin Martyr* (Paris, 1910), pp. 293–317.

union which the ordinance effected between the believer
and his god was no less realistic—so far as the absorption
of actually divine essence was concerned—than had been
the case in earlier times. So with Paul the Spirit-
Christ entity, the possession of which constitutes one a
Christian, is made available for everyone on the fundamental condition of faith, is realized in experiential
fulness on the occasion of baptism when the convert
formally "puts on Christ," and is constantly renewed
or strengthened through regular participation in the
memorial celebration called the Lord's Supper.[1]

[1] Note the following typical passages in Paul: on baptism, Gal. 3:27;
I Cor. 1:13 ff.; 6:11; 10:1 ff.; 12:13; 15:29; Rom. 6:3 ff.; Col.
2:11 ff.; and on the Lord's Supper, I Cor. 10:14–22; 11:20–32.   Among
writers who find sacramental conceptions of one form or another in Paul
the more recent are Heitmüller, *Im Namen Jesus, Taufe und Abendmahl
bei Paulus,* and *Taufe und Abendmahl im Urchristentum;* Windisch,
Taufe und Sünde im ältesten Christentum bis auf Origines (Tübingen,
1908); Goguel, *op. cit.,* pp. 135–84; H. J. Holtzmann, *Neutestamentliche
Theologie* (Tübingen, 1911²), II, 191–209, and "Sakramentliches im
Neuen Testament," *Archiv für Religionswissenschaft,* VII (1904), 58–69;
Gardner, *The Religious Experience of St. Paul* (New York, 1911), pp.
102–26; Lake, *The Earlier Epistles of St. Paul,* pp. 210–15, 383–91; see
also along similar lines, Hatch, *The Influence of Greek Ideas,* etc., pp. 292–
309; Anrich, *Das antike Mysterienwesen in seinem Einfluss auf das
Christentum,* pp. 25 ff., 106 ff., 199 ff.; Pfleiderer, *Early Christian Conception of Christ,* pp. 124–33; Reitzenstein, *Poimandres,* pp. 219 ff.,
and *Die hellenistischen Mysterienreligionen,* pp. 77 ff.; Dieterich, *Eine
Mithrasliturgie,* pp. 106 f., 176–79; Cumont, *Mysteries of Mithra,* pp.
150–74; Loisy, "L'Initiation chrétienne," *Revue d'histoire et de littérature
religieuses,* Nouvelle série, V (1914), 193–226.   On the other hand, the
sacramental element is in the main denied by Clemen, *Religionsgeschichtliche Erklärung,* usw., pp. 165–207 (English tr., *Primitive Christianity,*
pp. 212–66), and *Der Einfluss der Mysterienreligionen,* usw., pp. 30–59;
Kennedy, *St. Paul and the Mystery Religions,* pp. 227–79; Teichmann,
"Die Taufe bei Paulus," *Zeitschrift für Theologie und Kirche,* VI (1896),
357–72; von Dobschütz, "Sakrament und Symbol im Urchristentum,"
Studien und Kritiken, LXXVIII (1905), 1–40.

Having attained to union with Christ, what were the consequences for the believer? In the first place he anticipated the blessing of ultimate salvation by being permitted to live upon earth the same type of life which he was to share in much greater fulness when the work of redemption reached its climax in the day of judgment. The Christian, filled with the divine Spirit, in a measure lived the divine life even while on earth and to that extent salvation was a present reality. One was redeemed from the power of sinful desire and fleshly impulses by receiving into one's self the new divine increment, the Spirit, the presence of Christ, which strengthened and directed man in his struggle against evil. The manifestations of this redemption as realized in the present were twofold, one might say: outward and inward. One who is Spirit-filled thereby becomes a divinely dynamic person, and so heals the sick, works miracles, prophesies, discerns spirits, speaks with tongues, and interprets tongues. In fact, the believer's whole life is an outward manifestation of this new divine power which has become resident in him through his union with Christ.

The ethical content of life is also determined by this same standard of the indwelling Spirit. Since the Christian is a Christ-filled man, he must set up just as high an ethical criterion for himself as he does for the Deity. The fact that a Christian has the divine Spirit makes it necessary for him in the ethical realm to reproduce a God-like type of life. This requirement is frequently emphasized by Paul, in his demands that the body be kept pure as a proper dwelling-place for the Spirit, and that the fruits of the Spirit be manifest

constantly. Paul, further, always insisted that man himself must bear the ultimate responsibility for his conduct.
He could not hope for success unless he called in the
divine helper, the Spirit, to support his effort; yet it
was he, and not the Spirit, who took the initiative and
with whom the ultimate responsibility rested. If the
apostle had not imbibed from his Hebrew heritage so
emphatic a notion of personal responsibility and so
purely ethical a conception of God, he might have been
less insistent in his ethical demands as a Christian.
But since his God was the ethical deity of Judaism, the
life of the God-filled individual must measure up to the
highest ethical standards.

The final consequence of union with Christ was participation in his triumph over death, with the accompanying heavenly reward. Those who should live until the
end came would in the twinkling of an eye be freed from
this body of flesh and equipped with a proper spirit body;
and those believers who had already died would be
raised from the abode of the dead to receive their new
spiritual body. Because Christ himself had triumphed
over death they that were Christ's would share a similar triumph. The union which had been established
between Christ and the believer was not for this life
only; the divine part which had entered the Christian
would remain with him even in death, thus assuring him
a place in the kingdom of the redeemed.

But there would be different grades in that new
kingdom. Some would enter with high honors while
others would barely come through the testing fire. Was
this variation due to the Spirit's failure to do its redeeming work as well for one person as it did for another?

Not at all! The future reward was conditioned upon man's own effort in availing himself of the help of the Spirit to produce the fruit of righteousness. The fact that the believer had received the Spirit might insure entrance into the kingdom of the redeemed, but the position he was to occupy under the new régime depended upon how well his works stood the fiery testing of the last great day. Paul had fought for the notion that salvation is by faith, resulting in union with Christ, but he still believed that rewards were conditioned by works.

This was the religion to which Paul endeavored to win the gentile world. It preserved a large number of Jewish characteristics, but it also contained many new features serving to meet certain religious demands distinctive of the Graeco-Roman world in Paul's day. He kept the Jewish figure of the Messiah, but he presented him in a form which transcended that of the Roman emperor who was being worshiped as savior, Lord, son of God, and God. Christianity was the new imperial religion which held out to believers not merely temporary civic blessings but membership in an eternal divine kingdom. The Cynic-Stoic preacher might exhort his hearers to cultivate peace of mind and self-realization of spirit to be exhibited in a life of noble ethical attainment. Christianity, however, not only insisted upon the realization of these values but supplied a new power for making their attainment possible. In this latter respect Paul was more closely akin to the ideal of the contemporary mystery-religions. In his pictorial presentation of the crucified Messiah he was able to stage a more vivid and effective mystery-drama, he believed, than that which one

witnessed in the rites of any other cult. His religion—
like the other mysteries, but more effectively in the belief
of Christians—supplied to initiates the privilege of union
with the dying and rising Savior who ultimately would
confer upon his followers a life of immortal blessedness.

Are we to think of Paul as creating his Christianity
by a process of deliberate selection, in which he first
takes a number of things from Judaism, then further
items from the primitive Christians, and lastly a
quantity of materials from contemporary heathen
faiths? Certainly not! Paul's religion was not an
artificial creation but an affair of real life, the result
of many forces intermingling in the making of his
experience. Because his lot was cast in a time when,
and in regions where, the religious life of humanity was
being molded by a particular environment, because the
human spirit in that day was working out its religious
destiny along these lines, because the more serious
spirits of the time were finding and serving God in this
way, Paul's religion also took this form. He was not
merely stooping to accommodate himself to the needs
of his age; rather he was imbibing its atmosphere,
growing strong in faith and mighty in spiritual stature
as he worshiped and served his crucified and risen Redeemer in the language and under the inspirations
furnished by the world of his own immediate experience.
He vigorously presented to others this new religion of
redemption which satisfied the yearnings of his own
spirit, and they with similar needs also found here
new religious satisfactions. Thus Christianity began its
conquest of the gentile world in those regions where
Paul labored as a pioneer.

We may ask in the next place how those Christians who preserved Synoptic Gospel traditions sought to make their faith a winning religion. Speaking generally, the first three Gospels endeavor to exhibit the superior attractiveness of the new religion by emphasizing two main items: (1) the Jesus of history with his personal ideals of character and conduct, and (2) the Christ of faith whom believers revere almost if not quite to the point of worshiping him.

In the thinking of early Christians the historical Jesus apparently had, apart from mere identity of personality, little in common with the heavenly Messiah yet to be revealed in glory. Attention was fixed mainly on the future. Memory of the earthly Jesus, visions of him risen and glorified, and the disciples' own ecstatic life undoubtedly seemed to them adequate proof of Jesus' present lordship in the realm of heavenly spirits where he was awaiting the proper time for his appearing as Messiah. The manner of his earthly life contrasted sharply with the brilliant exhibition of messianic splendor he was about to make. The later custom of viewing his earthly career as a unique display of messianic functions tended not only to dim the early believers' vivid sense of the kingdom's future manifestation but also to obscure those elements of simplicity and naturalness which belong to their thought of the historical Jesus. We must not forget that there were once Christians who believed Jesus had been made both Lord and Christ through the resurrection, that this was the moment when he had been designated Son of God with power, and that his life upon earth had been in the form of a lowly servant.[1]

[1] Cf. Rom. 1:4; Phil. 2:7 f.; Acts 2:36; 3:13, 26.

The early disciples, on the strength of this faith, were devoutly praying "Maranatha," but in spite of their fervent prayer the Lord delayed his coming. In this delay they saw an indication of duty; they must prepare the world for the Messiah's advent by gathering a band of believers to be citizens of the new kingdom. Hence in their active propaganda they directed attention chiefly toward the heavenly Christ. When preaching to Jewish audiences it was necessary to demonstrate that the risen Jesus was to be Israel's long-expected deliverer, and among Gentiles it was desirable to show that the coming Jesus was not only the savior promised to the Jews but that he was also the divinely appointed redeemer of the whole world. This interpretation gave the new religion the sanctity of antiquity and proved at the same time the folly of Jewish unbelief. In whatever land they preached the early Christian missionaries proclaimed a gospel of redemption centering about the person of the coming Messiah.

Notwithstanding this interest in the Christ of faith there were several forces at work tending to preserve the story of Jesus' life and teaching as a means of insuring the success of the new movement. Memory of Jesus' earthly career formed, as we have already observed, the cornerstone of the new faith for the first disciples. In the light of later experiences they found a new meaning in his words and deeds as meditation brought to mind more vividly the events of the past. Jewish Christians had previously been accustomed to draw inspiration from teachers of repute in earlier times, so they turned all the more readily to Jesus for instruction. The Jews' sensitiveness to ethical demands was also inherited by the early Christians, consequently they were predisposed to preserve this type of tradition from Jesus. Since his personality had impressed them so forcibly it is altogether probable that many of his words and ideals had become indelibly stamped upon their minds. The heritage of religio-ethical teaching which they had received from him not only was a great power in their own lives but became a very significant item in the success of their cause.

The necessity of organizing an independent movement to stand over against Judaism also strengthened interest in preserving Jesus' teaching. As Moses had been the founder of the old religion, so Jesus now became a second Moses, figuring as the teacher upon whose authority the new movement rested. His word was set above that of the ancients, although in the main he supplemented rather than denied what "they of old time" had said. Ultimately believers were able to assemble a body of instruction from him covering not only matters of personal living but also more formal features connected with the organic life of the community. He was believed to have set the example for practicing the rite of baptism, his last meal with the disciples was made the church's model for the Eucharist, and he was said to have authenticated the entire missionary enterprise. For many persons it added much to the strength of the new movement when the authority of a traditional founder could be cited in support of its varied life. There doubtless was many a "Theophilus" in the first century who was anxious to be assured, through some account of Jesus' words and deeds, of the gospel's certainty. The ability of Christian teachers to supply this demand doubtless formed an important item in the strength of the new religion.

Jesus' authority as a teacher was employed also in defining Christianity's relations to rival movements. John the Baptist and his followers were given a high rating, but still they were assigned a subordinate position. Jesus' estimate of contemporary Judaism was much more unfavorable. The disciples cited him to justify their hostile attitude toward the whole ceremonial system. He had taught freedom toward the Sabbath, fasting he had permitted but only in a modified form, he had declared all meats clean, he had criticized the temple cultus, and he had pronounced bitter woes upon the Pharisees, frequently consigning them to eternal perdition. The Christians had, to be sure, reached their full sense of separateness from Judaism only gradually, but once compelled to break their Jewish connections they found much satisfaction in being able to recall Jesus' teaching in their favor. Thus they were able to strengthen their own convictions and buttress the Christians' cause when asked why the Jews had rejected a movement originally so closely associated with Judaism.

In picturing Jesus as an ideal teacher of ethics and religion, Christians were also equipping themselves to meet the needs of the Gentiles. Ever since the time of Socrates a new ethical impulse had been at work in the Graeco-Roman world. In New Testament times this phase of life was being diligently cultivated by the widespread and persistent activity of Cynic-Stoic preachers. Socrates and other similar teachers were presented as models of wisdom and virtue for later generations.[1] The admirers of a teacher would also write accounts of his life and work, lauding his superior piety or knowledge, and often impressing readers with the fact that the hero was no ordinary person.[2] The Gospels, all written in Greek and manifestly intended in their present form to be read by Gentiles, present Jesus as the founder of a new teaching which not only transcends Judaism but inculcates all those ethical ideals to the attainment of which the noblest Stoic teachers were exhorting their hearers. By example as well as by precept Jesus became an ideal character for these circles of gentile thinking. They were accustomed to admire the self-sacrifice and devotion of a teacher to his cause, but the simplicity and sincerity of Jesus' life, and his insistent demand that the disciples follow his example, all constituted elements of attractiveness for the Gentiles among whom this faith was preached.

The Gospels show still another interest in recording the life of Jesus. The evangelists all seek to advance the authority of the new religion by making the Jesus of history an appropriate person to become the Christ of faith. This is a very prominent item in the New Testament biographies and it is this feature which chiefly distinguishes the Gospels from all contemporary biographical literature. However much Christian preachers

[1] For example, Epictetus' references to Socrates, *Disc.*, i. 4. 4; 9. 1, 5; 17. 1; 25. 4; 26. 3; 29. 10; ii. 2. 1; 6. 2; 12. 2; 18. 4; 26. 2; iii. 1. 4; 12. 4; 14. 4; 23. 1; 24. 4; iv. 1. 18; 5. 1; 8. 5; 11. 3.

[2] A few examples of this biographical literature are Xenophon's *Memorabilia of Socrates*, Arrian's *Discourses of Epictetus* and *Anabasis of Alexander*, Plutarch's *Lives*, Suetonius' *Lives of the Caesars*, Diogenes Laertius' *Lives and Teachings of the Philosophers*, Philostratus' *Life of Apollonius*.

aimed to strengthen their cause by appealing to the life
and teaching of the earthly Jesus, they believed nevertheless that faith in the heavenly Christ was the main
bulwark of the new religion.   They not only strove to
emulate Jesus' example as a religious person, but that
example seemed to them so extraordinary as to demand
a supernatural interpretation of his significance.   The
only instrument at hand which appeared to them as at
all adequate for this purpose was the Jewish apocalyptic
hope.

In earlier stages of thinking Jesus' words and deeds
were recorded with a view to demonstrating that he was
worthy of faith as the future Messiah, but ultimately he
came to be regarded as already discharging messianic
functions while on earth.   The non-Markan sections of
the Synoptic Gospels common to Matthew and Luke
depict Jesus mainly as a teacher.   He is assumed to be
a supernaturally endowed individual, but he refuses at
the outset to make his career one of miraculous display.
He finds the acme of his ambition realized in preaching
the gospel to the poor, and is content to await God's
own good time for the revelation of his messianic glory.
This disposition to set Jesus' teaching in the foreground,
deriving evidence of his uniqueness mainly from the
power with which he spoke his message, was a most
appropriate way of approaching Jews who reverenced
above all others those historical personages whom God
had chosen to utter his message.

With Mark, on the other hand, another interest
becomes prominent.   Instead of recording Jesus' refusal
to make any miraculous displays, Mark's account of
the Temptation emphasizes the miracle-element—the

wild beasts are docile in Jesus' presence and he is attended by ministering angels. Furthermore, miracles characterized his ministry from the start and demonstrated his power over the demons who recognized in him the Messiah. People in general might not have eyes to see that this earthly individual actually possessed the authority of the apocalyptic Son of Man, but had they been endowed with the supernatural vision enjoyed by demons they would have perceived not only that Jesus was to be the future Messiah but that his present career was a preliminary exhibition of messianic functions. In stressing this side of Jesus' work Mark made the new religion capable of ministering to a very pressing demand, particularly among his gentile audiences. We have earlier noted the degree to which the common people of the Graeco-Roman world were bound by the fetters of gross superstition, fearing evil demons of all sorts. To such persons the new gospel came as a message of deliverance and protection. They did not need to wait until the end of the world to enjoy the blessings of the new kingdom. Jesus already having been Messiah while upon earth, it was now possible for believers to realize the kingdom's privileges. Victory over demons in the power of Jesus' name was one of its most significant blessings, made possible through Jesus' messianic triumph over Satan.

In the course of time many other reasons were urged in favor of the growing belief that the messianic kingdom had already been really established. Evidence of this was seen in the belief that Jesus had been miraculously begotten, and had been pronounced Son of God, both at baptism and in connection with the transfiguration.

Many of his words and deeds seemed to be a fulfilment of messianic prophecy, and he had finally indicated the messianic significance of his career by his triumphal entry into Jerusalem. Although these items were originally Jewish in character, they were now viewed as part of God's scheme for accomplishing the salvation of all men. The more strongly believers stressed faith in Jesus as actually discharging messianic functions in his earthly career, the more readily could they claim to possess at present a full salvation. Thus a once vivid future hope, growing dim with age, was supplanted by the conception of salvation as a present realization. Jesus had, in the main at least, completed his redeeming work in the past, he had finished his task with the end of his earthly life and his ascent to heaven.

This type of faith finds more complete expression in the Fourth Gospel. Here Jesus is quite exclusively the Christ of faith—not the apocalyptic Messiah, but the pre-existent heavenly Logos. The Pauline and the synoptic eschatological imagery has almost completely vanished. Jesus is still the Son of Man,[1] but not in the Danielic sense as so often with the other evangelists.[2] While John is apparently familiar with this earlier usage,[3] it no longer has any real meaning for him and his circle. When asked, "Who is the Son of Man?" Jesus replies, "Yet a little while is the light among you. Walk while

---

[1] 1:51; 3:13 f.; 6:27, 53, 62; 8:28; 9:35(?); 12:23, 34; 13:31.

[2] In the first three Gospels he is portrayed either in humility and weakness corresponding to the "Son of Man" of Ezekiel and Psalms; or, in line with Daniel 7:13 and later apocalyptic imagery, he is a heavenly being to come in glory upon the clouds. The much-debated question regarding his own use of this term does not concern us at present.

[3] 5:27.

ye have the light that darkness overtake you not. He that walketh in the darkness knoweth not whither he goeth. While ye have the light believe on the light that ye may become sons of light." This is the key to all the fourth evangelist's language about Jesus as the Son of Man. He is the light-bringer, the life-giver, the truth-revealer, the mediator of eternal wisdom. He is a pre-existent heavenly being, come forth from God to communicate divine knowledge to men, to give them the meat and drink of eternal life, to provide them a divine enlightenment, and to bring them into communion with God. His coming is synchronous with the incarnation, and his glorification is complete when he is lifted up on the cross —like the serpent, the symbol of wisdom and healing— in order that he may become conspicuous in the eyes of the people who will find eternal life by believing on him. His redeeming work now having been accomplished, he ascends to heaven "where he was before."

One might trace other terms or ideas through the Gospel of John and find the same general attitude constantly in evidence. According to this evangelist the Christian redemption was fully completed so far as the divine side was concerned through the revelation Jesus made while on earth. He had then exhibited his credentials perfectly, being plainly attested by John the Baptist, fulfilling Old Testament Scripture, performing a series of miracles to support faith, and asserting from the start that he was the heavenly redeemer commissioned to save the world. Hence salvation was to be procured simply by recognizing in Jesus the heaven-sent son of God. It was life eternal to know the only true God, seeing him in Jesus Christ who had been sent to

convey to men the saving light of divine knowledge.[1]
The transition from death—the status of every unbe-
liever—to eternal life, was a present experience, and
judgment was passed at once upon all those who refused
to believe in Jesus. Men brought this judgment upon
themselves in the present by the very act of unbelief.
The program of the earlier Christians, who pictured a
great assize at the end of the age when the Messiah would
come to conduct final judgment, making a complete
manifestation of his messianic power, gives place to an
interpretation of Jesus in which his earthly career contained the full display of his heavenly glory. The eternal
destiny of men is decided by their present choices and
the faithful at death individually were to be taken to the
mansions above to dwell with Jesus forever. Attainment of immortal blessedness was still the supreme end
of life, but it was to be reached by way of faith in Jesus
as a past rather than a future Savior.

Thus Christianity is still a religion of redemption,
although it has lost many of its primitive Jewish features.
This transformation was undoubtedly a very fortunate
one for the new religion's success among Gentiles. Paul
had preached the new gospel in the form of a mystery,
verbally depicting the crucifixion of Jesus before the eyes
of his hearers who were moved to accept the new faith
and received an experience of the Spirit's power. John
presented the new religion in the form of a "gnosis," a
heavenly knowledge, a divine revelation. One who
received this revelation experienced an enlightenment
which constituted a new birth. Paul appealed to persons who had been accustomed to seek satisfaction for
religious needs in mystery-cults, with their pictorial

[1] E.g., 1:18; 3:16; 17:3.

displays of a redemptive transaction and their accompanying rites. Such persons seem to have belonged mainly to the proletariat, who were fond of realism and often measured religion in terms of physical emotion. This for the most part was the type of person attracted to Christianity when preached by Paul in Corinth, judging from the conditions revealed in the Corinthian correspondence. We have already observed within the Graeco-Roman world another religious need, partially satisfied by the mysteries but tending to measure religious values more definitely in terms of "intellectual" emotion and theological speculation. It was this class of individual that John seemingly aimed to reach with his doctrine of the Logos Christ.

While he presents Christianity in language that would naturally appeal to the "intellectual" mystic, there is still in John a touch of realism which at first sight seems to harmonize closely with a very primitive sort of sacramentalism. He allows Jesus to say to Nicodemus that salvation can be obtained only by being born of water and spirit, while on another occasion Jesus affirms that eternal life is obtained only by eating the flesh and drinking the blood of the Son of Man.[1] In this John also shows his attachment to the Christian ordinances of baptism and the Lord's Supper, but it is perfectly clear from the context that the rites had been "spiritualized" although, as in Paul's case, the absorption of the spiritual substance may be realistically connected with the ritualistic observance.[2] While it is

[1] 3:3-14; 6:26 ff.

[2] On the sacramentalism of John see Reitzenstein's various writings (*passim*), and the counter-view of Krebs, *Der Logos als Heiland im ersten Jahrhundert* (Freiburg, 1910).

affirmed very explicitly that one must eat the flesh and
drink the blood of the Son of Man, the context immediately adds, "it is the Spirit that quickeneth, the flesh
profiteth nothing." But the Spirit is not that indwelling,
ecstatic power described by Paul; it is rather the inner
light of a new knowledge—"*the words I have spoken* unto
you are spirit and life." Likewise, the new birth is a
birth into divine knowledge which the Son of Man has
brought down from above. Now all this is a very
realistic matter, the ordinances of baptism and the
Lord's Supper being important factors in the mediation
of these experiential facts. The rites are sacramental in
the sense of being instrumental—perhaps indeed indispensable—in procuring for the believer a realistic
quantity of divine knowledge, but that this knowledge
was resident in the emblems of which the communicant
partook is probably no part of John's thought. It was
what came down from heaven that must be eaten, that
is, the divine wisdom, of which the Son of Man was the
revelation.

Thus the fourth evangelist made a significant contribution toward the expansion of Christianity in the
Graeco-Roman world. Paul and his associates had been
most successful among the lower classes to whom Christianity's new moral earnestness and vivid assurances of
future blessedness made a strong appeal when preached
in the form of a new mystery-religion, but those Gentiles
who were disposed to "intellectualize" the mysteries
responded less readily to Paul's preaching. Furthermore, we must recognize that the apostle, notwithstanding the remarkable manner in which he advocated
salvation for the Gentiles, was still Jewish in much of

his thinking and did not really succeed in formulating a philosophy of Christianity to include important items of religious speculation current in the gentile world. Paul never wholly abandoned the effort to divert the streams of Graeco-Roman thinking into Jewish channels, just as he never gave up hope that the Jewish nation would become the crowning fruit of the gospel tree. This hope had been surrendered when the Fourth Gospel was written. Instead of attempting to turn gentile thinking toward Palestine, it was now discovered that the stream of oriental religious speculation which had entered on its course through the Graeco-Roman world might be made to bear along upon its tide Christianity's new faith and life. Accordingly the supremacy of Jesus the redeemer was newly affirmed in the form of a divine deliverer mediating the knowledge of God to benighted humanity. Formerly this divine help was conceived in various forms, such as the "Son of Man" in the old Egyptian messianic texts, the Adapa of Babylonian legend, the "Primal Man" of Persian speculation,[1] and hypostases like "Light," "Life," "Knowledge," "Truth," which played a rôle in early gnostic speculation. The author of the Fourth Gospel has taken this vague conception of divine deliverance and raised it to the nth power in the figure of Jesus, the pre-existent Son of Man who was one with the Father before the foundation of the world. Thus Christianity was freed from all nationalistic limitations; it was a divinely guaranteed revelation to be obtained through the aid of a truly universal Savior of mankind.

[1] See "Der Urmensch" in Bousset, *Hauptprobleme der Gnosis*, pp. 160–223, and Kristensen, "Die term 'Zoon des Menschen' toegelicht uit de anthropologie der ouden," *Theologisch Tijdschrift*, XLV (1911), 1–38; Reitzenstein, *Poimandres*, pp. 59–116. See also above, pp. 326 ff.

The course of Christians' religious development in relation to their environment during the first century has been traced with sufficient fulness to disclose the general trend in the process of the new religion's expansion. It became a many-sided movement, laying hold upon a wide range of vital interests within the Graeco-Roman world. It came to include, usually in a heightened degree, many religious values which its competitors had been seeking to cultivate before the Christian preachers appeared upon the scene. Being itself of oriental origin it readily assumed many of the features which had made oriental mystery-cults and speculations attractive to many persons in the Roman empire. It was pre-eminently a religion of redemption with a Savior whose figure was more real and whose credentials appeared stronger than those of any mythical dying and rising divinity.

When occasion required, the Christian Savior was readily made the center of a type of speculation capable of appealing to the most vigorous religious thinking of the time. While this new religion was emphatically a faith for the individual soul, it also satisfied the group-consciousness by assembling a new community to constitute the kingdom of God on earth. Its early adherents and missionaries belonged to the masses, consequently it was a vital movement from the start and spread widely with the shifting currents of syncretistic life. To the individual who felt himself drifting hopelessly on this boundless sea, Christianity offered very definite religious guidance. It gave an assurance of salvation for the immortal soul, it appealed to the imagination and emotions, in its sacred rites it answered the current longing for realism, it satisfied intellectual demands as they arose, it awakened conscience by its insistence on rewards and punishments, it sounded a strong ethical note, and in its doctrine of the one true God it gave men a sufficiently large conception of Deity to meet the needs of an enlarging world and an imperialistic age.

But in the last analysis it owed its triumph to the activity of loyal individuals who not only answered the call of God as they heard it in their own lives or discerned it on the pages of history, but who learned, consciously or unconsciously, to read the divine will as revealed in the "signs of the times." They were sensitive to the religious forces within their environment, and so drew inspiration from its life and responded to its needs by conserving, heightening, and supplementing current religious values. Under the guidance of these individuals the genius of the new religion is disclosed in their expanding life. If Christians today would be true successors of those ancient worthies they too must make religion an affair of life and growth commensurate with the needs of the present generation.

INDEXES

SUBJECTS AND AUTHORS

Abelson, 88.
Academics, 255 ff.
Achelis, 42.
Adapa, 367.
Adonis, 74, 300, 307 ff., 336.
Aegesilaus, 294.
Aelian, 57.
Aeschines, 297.
Aeschylus, 53.
Ahura Mazda, 311.
Alexander the Great, 48 f., 51 ff.,
    53 ff., 56, 58, 195, 205 ff., 230 f.,
    359.
Alexander the Prophet, 262.
Allard, 191.
Allegory, 274 f.
Allen, 289.
Allo, 189.
Amélineau, 327.
'Am-ha'arets, 93.
Anâhita (Anaitis), 311 ff.
Ananus, 126.
Anaxagoras, 240.
Andocides, 294.
Anrich, 287, 350.
Antigonids, 59.
Antipater the Stoic, 268.
Antisthenes, 266.
Antony, 212 f.
Anz, 326.
Aphrodite, 74, 210, 306.
Apocalypticism, 360 ff.
Apollonius of Tyana, 233, 290,
    359.
Apollos, 35.
Appian, 54.
Apuleius, 319, 322 f.
Archedemus, 268.
Arellius Fuscus, 233.
Aristobulus, 54.
Aristophanes, 295.
Aristotle, 53, 62, 204 f., 256, 279,
    291.
Arneth, von, 191, 248.

Arnim, von, 263 f., 269, 272 f.
Arnobius, 303.
Arnold, 263 f., 271, 278.
Arrian, 54, 56, 206 f., 233, 359.
Artachaees, 203.
Ashtart, 74, 306 f.
Ashtoreth, 306 f.
Astarte, 306.
Astrology, 243 ff., 248, 312 f.,
    325 f.
Atargatis, 74, 309 f.
Athenagoras, 184.
Athenodorus, 268.
Attis, 74, 185, 300, 302 ff., 336.
Augustine, 184 f.
Augustus, 64, 75, 296, 304.

Babelon, 60.
Bacchic mysteries, 282.
Bacchus, 225, 297 ff., 318.
Bacon, 116.
Badham, 125.
Bäck, 91.
Baldensperger, 104.
Baptism, 185; early practice of,
    340; in Fourth Gospel, 365 f.;
    Jewish, 340; in Pauline usage,
    113; 347 f.
Barnabas, 102.
Bar-rekub, 309.
Baudissin, von, 305.
Bauer, A., 66, 198.
Bauer, B., 278.
Baumgarten, F., 66.
Baumgarten, M., 278.
Baur, F. C., 13, 18, 94, 98 ff., 327.
Baur, F. F., 98.
Behm, 153.
Beloch, 53, 69, 198.
Benn, 254.
Bennett, 90.
Benzinger, 134.
Bergmann, 91.
Berosus, 312.

Bertholet, 79, 104, 170, 176, 245. 340.

Beurlier, 197.

Bevan, 60, 263.

Bischoff, 90.

Böhlig, 108, 310.

Böklen, 194.

Boissier, 197.

Boll, 244.

Bonhöffer, 44, 188, 278.

Bosc, 186.

Bouché-Leclercq, 54, 60 f., 244.

Boulage, 316.

Bousset, 79, 88, 104, 108 ff., 111, 113, 115, 119, 125, 128, 192, 245, 288, 327, 340, 367.

Box, 79, 340.

Brandt, 340.

Brasidas, 203.

Breasted, 76, 219 f.

Brückner, 104, 192, 336.

Brünnow, 222.

Brun, 142.

Buckland, 69.

Büchler, 92 f.

Bultmann, 279.

Bunbury, 49.

Buonaiuti, 327.

Burel, 315.

Calderini, 69.

Caligula, 75.

Carneades, 257.

Carter, 77.

Carus, 186.

Catholicism, 3 f., 7 ff., 13.

Catullus, 304.

Champollion-Figeac, 61.

Chantepie de la Saussaye, 76.

Charismata, 129.

Charles, 104 f.

Cheetham, 287.

Christ, von, 68.

Christianity, Babylonian influence upon, 193; breach with Judaism, 123 ff.; Buddhistic influence upon, 194; Catholic idea of, 3 f.; changes within, 1 ff.; contact with Gentiles, 178 ff.; development of, 2 ff., 34, 36, 333 f.; distinctiveness of, 96; divisions of, 98 ff.; early ex-

tent of, 50 f.; Egyptian influence upon, 193; "essence" of, 19 ff., 90 ff.; expansion of, 102 f., 168, 181 ff.; of Fourth Gospel, 362 ff.; genuineness of, 23 f.; Jewish opposition to, 96 f.; "liberal," 16 ff.; Modernist view of, 20 f.; nationalism in, 339; nature of, 1 ff.; newness of, 35 ff.; origin of, 28, 41; originality of, 188 ff.; of Paul, 341 ff.; persecution of, 124 ff.; Persian influence upon, 194; Protestant idea of, 4 ff.; as a redemption religion, 364 ff.; relation to emperor-worship, 197 ff.; 218 ff.; relation to environment, 19, 26 ff.; relation to Judaism, 32, 78 ff., 84 ff., 106; relation to politics, 196 ff.; relation to Stoicism, 277 ff.; religious setting of, 30 ff.; of Synoptic Gospels, 355 ff.

Christology, 333 ff., 355 ff.

Chrysippus, 268.

Church, 5, 18.

Chwolson, 92.

Cicero, 229 f., 241, 243, 245, 252, 255 ff., 289 f., 295 f., 300, 307.

Cleanthes, 264, 268, 322.

Clemen, 44, 188, 278, 287, 350.

Clement of Alexandria, 125 f., 184 f., 294, 312.

Cleomenes, 206.

Colani, 104.

Colin, 54.

Comparetti, 301.

Conybeare, 192.

Cooke, G. A., 306, 309.

Corssen, 69.

Crates, 267.

Creuzer, 293.

Crinagoras, 296.

Criobolium, 304.

Croiset, 68.

Cumont, 77, 185, 192, 233, 242 ff., 248 f., 287, 302, 304 f., 310, 314, 316, 350.

Cybele, 74, 302 ff., 310.

Cynicism, 266.

Cynics, 74.

Cyrnus, 203.

Dalman, 116 f.
Darius, 56 f.
De Boor, 125.
De Faye, 327.
Deification, 229; of Antigonids, 208 f.; of Bacchus, 318; of Hercules, 318; of heroes, 203 ff.; of Isis, 318; of Osiris, 318; of Ptolemies, 209 f.; of Roman emperors, 211 ff.; of Seleucids, 210 f.
Deism, 10, 187.
Deissmann, 29, 66, 198, 236, 320.
De Jong, 287, 315.
De le Roi, 91.
Demeter, 74, 289, 291 ff., 296, 302.
Demetrius of Phalerum, 242.
Democritus, 242, 259.
Demon possession, 152 ff.
Demons, 155 ff.
Demosthenes, 297.
Dennis, 315.
De Quincey, 94.
De Sainte-Croix, 293.
Destiny (εἰμαρμένη), 243.
Dhorme, 76.
Diadochi, 51.
Diaspora, 30 f., 80, 82, 106.
Diatribe, 279.
Dibelius, 155.
Didache, 116.
Diels, 241, 245, 300.
Dieterich, 192, 247, 294, 300, 310, 329, 350.
Dill, 66, 245, 302, 310, 316.
Dillmann, 104.
Diodorus, 54 ff., 207 f., 295, 303, 320, 322.
Diogenes the Cynic, 294.
Diogenes Laertius, 258, 267 f., 294, 314, 359.
Diogenes the Stoic, 268.
Dion Cassius, 212, 216.
Dion of Syracuse, 207.
Dionysus, 74, 210, 230, 295, 297 ff., 300 f., 349.
Dittenberger, 215 f.
Divination, 248, 274.
Divine descent, of Apollonius of Tyana, 233; of astrologers, 233; of Augustus, 234; of Jesus, 234 f.
Dobschütz, von, 350.

Droysen, 54.
Drucker, 92.
Duchesne, 191.
Dupuis, 186.
Duris, 207.
Duschak, 89.

Ebionites, 94.
Ecstasy, 128 ff., 291 f., 298 ff., 304, 310.
Edmonds, 308.
Edmunds, 194.
Eichhorn, 192.
Elements (στοιχεῖα), 244 f.
Eleusinian mysteries, 282, 288 ff., 296 f.
Eleusinion, 290.
Eleusis, 74.
Elijah, 146 f.
Elisha, 146 f.
Emerton, 192.
Empedocles, 204.
Emperor-worship, 73, 195 ff.
Ennatum, 200.
Entemena, 200.
Epaminondas, 294.
Epictetus, 268 ff., 272 ff., 277 f., 295, 359.
Epicureans, 74, 255, 258 ff.
Epicurus, 258 f.
Epigoni, 52.
Epiphanius, 126.
Epiphany, 235.
Erman, 76.
Eschatology (see Immortality), 163 f., 247, 276 f.
Eschelbacher, 91.
Eshmun, 74, 307.
Eshmun'azar, 306 f.
Essenes, 83, 93, 95, 97.
Ethics, of mysteries, 294 f.; of Paul, 351 ff.
Eumenes, 208.
Euripides, 53, 300.
Eusebius, 125 f., 187.
Everling, 155.
Exorcism, 152 ff.

Faber, 194.
Fairweather, 79.
Farnell, 77, 288 f., 293, 295, 297 f., 300, 303.

Fate (ἀνάγκη), 243.
Felten, 79.
Flamininus, 211.
Forbiger, 49.
Fortune (τύχη), 242 f.
Foucart, 288, 297.
Fourth Gospel, Christianity of, 362 ff.; sacramentalism in, 365 ff.
Fowler, 66, 77.
Frazer, 192, 302, 305, 316.
Frey, 136.
Friedländer, L., 66.
Friedländer, M., 93 f., 175, 327.
Friedlander, G., 87, 89.
Fries, 244.
Frölich, 60.

Garbe, 194.
Gardiner, 219.
Gardner, 60, 350.
Garstang, 305.
Geffcken, 66, 175, 266.
Gercke, 54.
Gfrörer, 186.
Glover, 77.
Gnosticism, 76, 326 ff.
God-fearers, 174 f., 178.
Goedeckmeyer, 256.
Götz, 50.
Goguel, 92, 349 f.
Gomperz, 254, 266.
Grätz, 79, 89.
Gressmann, 104, 199, 221 f., 306.
Grünbaum, 89.
Gruppe, 77, 198, 243, 250, 282, 288, 297, 300, 303, 305, 310, 316, 349.
Güdemann, 91.
Gunkel, 108, 128, 155, 193, 310, 349.

Hadad, 309 f.
Hagnon, 204.
Hahn, 54.
Hall, A. C. A., 5.
Hall, T. C., 66.
Halliday, 248.
Hammurabi, 199 ff.
Harnack, 18 f., 51, 80, 91, 127, 191.
Harper, R. F., 201, 221.
Harrison, 77, 297, 301.
Hart, 88.

Hase, von, 194.
Hatch, 66, 191, 288, 350.
Hauck, 300.
Hausrath, 66.
Havet, 186, 278.
Hebrews, Gospel according to, 129, 133.
Hegel, 10 ff.
Hegesippus, 126.
Heinen, 198, 212 f.
Heinrici, 189.
Heitmüller, 108, 119, 159, 192, 350.
Hellenicism, 53.
Hellenism, 53.
Hennell, 186.
Hepding, 302, 305.
Hephaestion, 206, 208.
Heraclitus, 183, 267.
Hercules, 230, 318.
Herder, 15.
Herford, 88, 90.
Hermes, 328.
Hermeticism, 328 f.
Herodotus, 53, 63, 74, 203 f., 291, 296, 300 f., 312, 314, 316 ff.
Hertzberg, 54.
Hicks, E., 187.
Hicks, E. L., 216.
Hicks, R. D., 258, 263 f.
Hilgenfeld, 104, 327.
Hiller von Gaertringen, 217.
Hirsch, 92.
Hirschfeld, 197.
Hoennicke, 100.
Hogarth, 49, 57.
Holm, 53.
Holsten, 101.
Holtzmann, H. J., 79, 104, 350.
Holtzmann, O., 79.
Homer, 204.
Hopkins, 194.
Horace, 65, 69, 225, 230.
Horodezky, 88.
Horos, 209 f.
Hort, 100.

Idealism, 10, 14.
Immortality, Egyptian doctrine of, 317 f.; Mithraic doctrine of, 313; taught in mysteries, 287 ff., 298; procured by initiation, 292 ff.; Stoic doctrine of, 276 f.

India, 57.
Initiation, 289 ff., 313.
Ipuwer, 219.
Ishtar, 74, 221, 306, 312.
Isis, 74, 209, 229, 315 ff.
Isocrates, 63, 289.

Jackson, 76, 194.
Jacoby, 192, 287, 328.
James, brother of Jesus, 35, 125 f.
James, brother of John, 125.
Jastrow, 76.
Jensen, 193.
Jeremias, 187, 193.
Jerome, 129, 278.
Jesus, 2, 4, 6, 16, 18 f., 21, 27 f.
    29, 34, 37 f., 40 ff.; attitude to
    Judaism, 358; conflict with Jews,
    85, 89 ff.; death of, 92 f., 140,
    331; deification of, 230 ff.;
    exaltation of, 169; imperial
    functions of, 236 ff.; influence of,
    331 f.; lordship of, 109 ff., 116;
    messiahship of, 140; miracles
    of, 360 f.; originality of, 89;
    religion of, 23; resurrection of,
    231 f., 335 f.; significance of,
    89 ff.; as teacher, 360; tempta-
    tion of, 360 f.
Jevons, 294.
John the Baptist, 94, 120, 138,
    147, 331 f., 340, 358, 363.
Josephus, 56, 80, 83, 116, 126, 134,
    136, 152 f., 174, 201, 214, 216 f.,
    248, 340.
Judaism, 31, 79 ff.; apologetic of,
    175 f.; dispersion of, 173 ff.;
    institutions of, 81 f.; mission-
    ary activity of, 170 f., 174;
    parties within, 82 f.; relation
    to Christianity, 78 ff.; spirit-
    uality of, 88.
Julius Caesar, 212 f.
Jung, 50.
Juster, 79 f., 92.
Justin Martyr, 183, 185.
Juvenal, 251.

Kaerst, 59, 198.
Kautsky, 69, 186.
Keim, 79, 191.
Kennedy, 44, 189, 288, 350.

Kiepert, 50.
King, C. W., 327.
King, L. W., 76.
Kingship, religious character of,
    199 ff.
Klein, 92.
Koine, 29.
Kornemann, 198, 206, 210.
Krascheninnkoff, 198.
Krebs, 365.
Kristensen, 367.
Kroll, 245, 349.
Krüger, 175.
Kugler, 193.
Kuiper, 278.

Lactantius, 184.
Lafaye, 315.
Lagrange, 104, 305.
Lajard, 310.
Luke, 174, 350.
Lang, 289.
Lange, 219.
Language of New Testament, 28 ff.
Lehmann, 194, 281.
Letronne, 61.
Lévy, 316.
Lewis, 188.
Liechtenhan, 327.
Lietzmann, 200, 219.
Lightfoot, J., 89.
Lightfoot, J. B., 278.
Lipsius, 327.
Livy, 54, 56, 300, 303.
Lobeck, 288 f., 293 f., 297.
Logos, 183, 185, 263, 269, 272,
    321, 362.
Loisy, 20 f., 288, 298, 302, 310,
    316, 350.
Lord (κύριος), 109 ff., 112 f.
Lord's Supper, 185; early ob-
    servance of, 340 f.; in Fourth
    Gospel, 365 f.; Pauline notion
    of, 114, 348 ff.
Lucian, 262.
Lucius, 322.
Luckenbill, 305.
Lucretius, 241, 245, 258 f.
Lysander, 207.

Maass, 297.
Maccabean revolt, 29.

McGiffert, 42.
Magic, 248 f.
Magical books, 249.
Mahaffy, 54, 61, 210.
Manilius, 243.
Mansel, 327.
Maranatha, 116 f., 356.
Marcus Aurelius, 268 f., 277 f.
Marquardt, 54.
Mathews, 79, 104.
Maurenbrecher, 186.
Maximus of Tyre, 251.
Mead, 193, 327 f.
Messianic hope, Babylonian and Assyrian, 220 ff.; Christian, 105 ff., 226 ff., 333 ff.; Egyptian, 219 f.; Jewish, 103, 105 f., 222 f., 333; Roman, 223 ff.
Meuschen, 89.
Meyer, E., 69, 198, 200.
Meyer, P. M., 61.
Mezger, 20.
Mills, 187, 194.
Miltiades, 203.
Minim, 93.
Miracles, 145 ff., 217, 232 f., 360 f.
Mishnah, 88.
Missions, Christian, 166 ff.; Jewish, 170, 174.
Mithra, 74, 217, 310 ff.
Modernism, 20 f.
Moffat, 125, 194.
Mommsen, 54, 119.
Montefiore, 88, 90 ff.
Moore, C. H., 300.
Moore, G. F., 76, 312.
Moret, 199, 316.
Moses, 86, 144 ff., 160, 173, 184 f., 357.
Moulton, J. H., 29, 77, 312.
Müller, 55.
Mullach, 266.
Murray, 77, 252.
Musonius Rufus, 268.
Mysteries, 74, 287 ff.; Babylonian, 306; Bacchic, 297 ff.; Cilician and Syrian, 305 ff.; Dionysian, 295, 297 ff.; Egyptian, 315 ff.; Eleusinian, 288 ff.; oriental, 302 ff.; Orphic, 300 ff.; Persian, 310 ff.; Phrygian, 302 ff.; Sabazian, 297; ethics of, 294 f.; influence upon Christianity, 334 ff.; theology of, 326 ff.
Mysticism, 281 ff., 326 ff.

Naramsin, 199.
Neo-Platonism, 74, 256.
Nero, 295.
Newman, 7 ff.
New Testament language, 28 ff.
Nicodemus, 365.
Niese, 54, 66.
Nöldeke, 117.
Nösgen, 189.
Norden, 54, 279, 281.
Nork, 89.

Oesterley, 79, 222, 340.
Orient, 64 f., 72 f.
Origen, 86, 184, 186, 295.
Orpheus, 230.
Orphic mysteries, 282, 300 ff.
Orphic tablets, 301.
Orphism, 76, 297, 300 ff.
Orr, 6.
Osiris, 74, 209, 213, 229, 300, 316 ff., 336.
Otto, 77.
Ovid, 303.

Panaetius, 276.
Panammu, 309.
Parousia, 111, 197, 235 f.
Passover, 136.
Pathey, 328.
Paton, L. B., 305.
Paton, W. R., 216.
Patrick, 94.
Paul, 18, 27, 35 f., 38, 51, 97 f., 100 f.; Christ-mysticism of, 346 ff.; Christianity of, 341 ff.; conversion of, 132; debt to gentile religions, 354; doctrine of Spirit, 132, 341 ff.; eschatology of, 110 f.; estimate of Judaism, 179, 345 ff.; estimate of paganism, 179; ethics of, 351 ff.; gentile environment of, 178; gospel of, 101, 172 f.: independence of, 103; miracles of, 147 ff.; missionary activity of, 102; persecuted by Jews, 85; relation to predecessors,

106 f., 118 ff.; relation to Seneca, 278; use of Baptism, 347 f.; use of Lord's Supper, 348 ff.
Pausanias, 303.
Pentecost, 131, 134 ff.
Perdelwitz, 287.
Perdiccas, 58.
Peripatetics, 256 f.
Persephone, 292 f., 301.
Peter, 102, 125.
Petersen, 234.
Petrie, 193.
Pfleiderer, 101, 192, 327, 336, 350.
Pharisees, 30, 82, 87 f., 93.
Philip Arrhidaeus, 58.
Philip V, 211.
Philip of Macedon, 52, 62 f., 207.
Philippson, L., 92.
Philippus, 203 f.
Philo, 83, 134, 159.
Philosophy, 239 f., 252 ff.
Philostratus, 233, 290, 359.
Pindar, 289.
Plato, 28, 53, 185, 204, 256 f., 265, 278 f., 289, 298 ff., 321.
Platonism, 73 f.
Pliny the Elder, 243, 314.
Pliny the Younger, 116.
Plutarch, 55 f., 207, 229, 245 f., 282, 292, 314, 316 ff., 321 f., 359.
Pluto, 292.
Pöhlmann, von, 70.
Poland, 66, 76.
Polybius, 54, 242.
Polytheism, 241 ff.
Pompey, 212.
Porter, 174.
Posidonius, 268, 277, 282.
Preaching, of Cynic-Stoics, 270 ff., 358 f.; of early Christians, 137 f.
Pressensé, 187.
Priestley, 188.
"Primal Man," 367.
Prince, 306.
Promus, 186.
Prophet, 138.
Proselytes, 174.
Protagoras, 204, 240, 265.
Protestantism, 3 f., 7 ff.
Prudentius, 304.

Ptolemaic rulers, 61.
Ptolemy Lagus, 54, 207.
Pyrrho of Elis, 257.
Pythagoras, 273.
Pythagoreanism, 76, 301.

Quandt, 297.

Radau, 187.
Radermacher, 29.
Ramsay, 49.
Rationalism, 10.
Rebirth, 305, 328 f.
Redemption, 286 ff.
Reinach, S., 186.
Reinach, T., 80, 173.
Reisner, 316.
Reitzenstein, 77, 108, 192 f., 287, 327 ff., 350, 365, 367.
Religionsgeschichtliche School, 108, 191.
Renan, 191.
Renault, 258.
Resurrection, of Adonis, 307 ff.; of Attis, 303; of Jesus, 333 ff.; of Osiris, 317; of Tammuz, 306.
Rhode, 295.
Richter, 186.
Riess, 245.
Ritschl, 16 ff.
Robinson, 90.
Rodrigues, 89.
Roma, 211, 213 f.
Roman emperors, 62.
Ropes, 42.
Rosetta Stone, 209.

Sabazius, 297.
Sacraments, in Christianity, 341; in Fourth Gospel, 365 ff.; in Mithraism, 313; in the mysteries, 294, 299 f.; in Paul's letters, 349 ff.
Sadducees, 30, 82, 163.
Salvation, 284 ff.
Sanhedrin, 92.
Sappho, 307.
Sargon I, 199.
Satirists, 251.
Schäfer, 315.
Schanz, von, 68.
Schechter, 88.

Schleiermacher, 15 ff.
Schmidt, 77, 302, 316.
Schneider, 69.
Schöttgen, 89.
Schrader, 193.
Schreiber, 89.
Schürer, 79 f., 88, 93, 104 f., 170, 173 ff., 340.
Schultz, 327.
Schwartz, 125.
Schweitzer, 104, 110 f., 186.
Scott, 104, 176.
Scylas, 298.
Seleucid kingdom, 59 f.
Seleucid rulers, 60.
Seneca, 184, 268 f., 272, 275 ff., 278.
Serapis, 74, 115, 316 ff.
Sethe, 316.
Seydel, 194.
Showerman, 302.
Siegfried, 90.
Sikes, 289.
Smith, G. A., 49.
Smith, William, 49.
Smith, W. R., 305.
Socrates, 53, 183, 240, 265, 272, 358 f.
Soltau, 188.
Son of God, 232.
Son of Man, 105, 109, 361 ff., 365 f., 367.
Sophocles, 53, 289.
Sorley, 100.
Spiess, 187.
Spirit, endowing Messiah, 128 ff.; how obtained, 131 ff.; Christian idea of, 129 ff., 351; Paul's idea of, 341 ff.; Stoic idea of, 343 f.
Spitta, 167.
Stähelin, 173.
Staerk, 66, 170.
Stave, 194.
Steck, 278.
Steindorff, 76.
Steiner, 61.
Steinmann, 69.
Stephen, 35, 85.
Stilpo, 267.
Stobaeus, 291.
Stocks, 29.
Stoicism, 76, 262 ff., 267 ff., 286 f.

Stoics, 74, 183, 255 ff., 343 f.
Storrs, 4.
Strabo, 49, 56, 80, 173 f., 205, 248, 268, 314.
Strack, 61.
Strong, 305.
Suetonius, 75, 116, 212, 214, 216 f., 234, 244, 249, 295, 310, 359.
Suidas, 208.
Superstition, 245 ff.
Susemihl, 68.
Synesius, 292.
Syrian goddess, 310.

Tabnith, 306.
Tacitus, 70, 116, 216.
Talmud, 87.
Tammuz, 74, 306 f.
Tarn, 59.
Tarsus, 268.
Taurobolium 304 f.
Taylor, 300.
Teichmann, 350.
Telesterion, 290.
Tertullian, 184 f.
Testament of Judah, 129; of Levi, 129.
Teuffel, 68.
Thackeray, 79.
Theocritus, 299, 308.
Therapeutae, 93, 97.
Thieling, 54.
Thot (Tat), 328.
Thucydides, 53, 203.
Thumb, 29.
Thureau-Dangin, 199.
Tiberius, 244.
Tibullus, 223, 300, 319 f.
Tiele, 77.
Tindal, 187.
Tiridates, 216.
Titans, 300.
Toland, 94.
Torah, 81 f., 134.
Toutain, 77, 198, 244, 287, 302, 305, 310, 316.
Toy, 76, 79, 193.
Trajan, 49.
Trench, 187.
Trezza, 258.
Troeltsch, 13 f., 70.
Tucker, 66.

Tübingen School, 13, 17, 94, 103, 107 f., 110.
Typhon, 318.

Ueberweg, 254.
Uhlhorn, 191.
Ungnad, 199, 221.
Usener, 192, 258.

Van den Bergh van Eysinga, 194.
Vellay, 305.
Vernes, 104.
Virgil, 223 f., 230.
Vollers, 186.
Volney, 186.
Volz, 104, 128, 145.

Wagner, 66.
Wallace, 258.
Wallon, 69.
Weber, 88, 316.
Wecker, 194.
Weinel, 128, 196.
Weinreich, 153.
Weiss, 104, 108 f., 116, 120, 136, 176.
Weizsäcker, 42.
Wendland, 66, 198, 224, 226, 230, 243, 271, 327.
Wernle, 90 f., 113, 176.

Wettstein (Wetstenius), 90.
Whittaker, 186.
Wiedemann, 76, 318.
Wilamowitz-Moellendorff, 66.
Winckler, 278.
Windelband, 254.
Windisch, 350.
Wissowa, 77, 198, 302, 305, 310, 316.
Witkowski, 29.
Wobbermin, 287, 295.
Wood, 128.
Wrede, 101.
Wünsch, 192.
Wünsche, 90.

Xenophanes, 241, 251.
Xenophon, 28, 53, 63, 267, 359.

Yahweh, 32, 80 f., 118, 128 f., 137 f., 146 f., 201, 222, 336 f.

Zadokite sectaries, 83, 130.
Zagreus, 300.
Zahn, 117, 278.
Zealots, 30, 82, 97, 201.
Zeller, 254, 256, 258, 263, 266, 275.
Zeno, 267 f.
Zielinski, 193.
Zimmern, 193.

SCRIPTURE REFERENCES

Exodus
  8:1—12:51............. 146
  14:21 ff................. 146
  15:23 ff................. 146
  20:18 ff................. 135
  24:11–16, 18........... 135

Numbers
  9:9–11................. 136
  11:29.................. 137
  16:29–35............... 146
  17:5................... 146

Deuteronomy
  5:4 f.................. 135
  18:9 ff................. 144
  18:9–22............... 159

Deuteronomy
  18:15.................. 160
  33:2 f................. 135

I Samuel
  10:5 ff................. 137
  10:6 ff................. 146
  10:10.................. 133
  19:20–24............... 133
  19:23 f................ 146

I Kings
  13:4 f., 28............. 146
  17:1................... 146

II Kings
  2:9–15................. 146
  13:14–19............... 146

Psalms
  68:8.................... 135

Isaiah
  9:1 ff................ 222
  9:7.................... 201
  11:1 ff.............201, 222
  11:2................. 129
  42:1................. 129
  61:1 f............... 138
  61:1 ff.............. 129

Ezekiel
  1:1, 28............. 133
  2:1 ff.............. 133
  2:2 ff.............. 133
  3:12................ 133
  3:12–24............. 133
  3:24................ 133
  8:3................. 133
  8:3 ff.............. 133
  8:14...............306, 334
  11:1............... 133
  11:5............... 133
  11:24.............. 133
  20:26–28, 31, 39......... 159

Daniel
  2:47............... 118
  5:23............... 118
  7:13............... 362

Hosea
  9:7................ 138

Joel
  2:28 ff............ 129

Zechariah
  12:10.............. 129
  12:11.............. 310

Malachi
  4:5................ 147

II Esdras
  14:46.............. 83

Tobit
  6:8................ 152
  8:2 ff............. 152
  11:1–13............ 152

Enoch
  49:1–4..............129
  62:2................ 129

Psalms of Solomon
  17:42.............. 129
  18:8............... 129

Matthew
  1:22............... 177
  2:15, 17, 23........... 177
  3:4................ 147
  3:11, 16........... 131
  3:16 f............. 130
  4:1................ 130
  4:14............... 177
  5:17–19............ 120
  5:17–20............ 177
  5:24............... 117
  7:6................ 167
  7:22............... 159
  8:11 f............. 167
  8:17............... 177
  10:5 f., 23...........167, 177
  10:22.............. 167
  11:5 f............. 142
  11:14.............. 147
  11:25.............. 118
  12:17.............. 177
  12:25 ff........... 130
  12:27.............. 160
  13:14.............. 177
  13:26 f............ 168
  13:35.............. 177
  13:37–43, 47–50......... 167
  15:24..............167, 177
  15:26.............. 167
  16:20 f............ 334
  16:21.............. 232
  17:9...............232, 334
  17:9–13............ 147
  17:22 f............ 334
  17:23.............. 232
  19:14.............. 35
  19:28..............167, 177
  20:17–19........... 334
  20:19.............. 232
  21:4............... 177
  21:33–44........... 167
  22:1–14............ 167
  23:3a, 23b............ 177
  24:14, 34, 45 ff........... 167

Matthew

24:20.................. 177
25:21.................. 169
26:13.................. 167
26:65 f................. 162
27:9................... 177
27:63 f................ 232
28:19.................. 167

Mark

1:6.................... 147
1:8, 10................ 131
1:10 f., 12, 18, 20...... 130
1:10 ff................ 133
1:11.................. 129
1:22, 32 f............. 154
1:25 f., 31, 41......... 153
1:27..............154, 232
2:10, 28............... 232
2:11.................. 153
3:5, 0................. 153
3:17.................. 177
3:23 ff., 29........... 130
3:29 f................ 154
4:39.................. 153
5:13, 23, 25........... 153
5:41..............153, 177
6:5 f., 41, 50, 56........ 153
6:13.................. 154
7:2–4, 11, 19, 34........ 177
7:9–13................ 88
7:29, 32.............. 153
8:6, 22............... 153
8:30–32............... 334
8:31.................. 232
8:37.................. 105
9:1...............168, 337
9:9 f...............232, 334
9:11–13............... 147
9:25.................. 153
9:29.................. 154
9:30–32............... 334
9:31.................. 232
9:38.................. 159
10:14................. 35
10:21................. 116
10:22................. 153
10:32–34............. 334
10:34................. 232
10:46................. 177
12:18, 42............. 177
12:32................. 130

Mark

13:3.................. 177
13:10................. 168
13:24 ff.............. 105
14:2, 32.............. 177
14:63 f............... 162
15:34, 42............. 177

Luke

1:1–3................. 127
1:3 f................. 127
1:15, 35, 41, 67........ 130
1:17................. 147
1:80.................129 f.
2:25 f................ 130
2:31 f................ 178
3:6.................. 178
3:16, 22.............. 131
3:21 f................ 130
4:1, 14............... 130
4:16 ff............138, 142
4:24–27.............. 178
7:22 f................ 142
9:21 f., 36, 43–45....... 334
9:22................. 232
10:9, 17.............. 154
10:21................. 118
11:17 ff.............. 130
12:10................. 130
16:2................. 116
18:16................. 35
18:22................. 117
18:31–34............. 334
18:33................. 232
22:69................. 162
24:7................. 232
24:47................. 178

John

1:1.................. 269
1:18................. 364
1:20 f., 25........... 147
1:33................. 129
1:33a...............130 f.
1:33b................ 131
1:46................. 117
1:51................. 362
3:3–14............... 365
3:13 f................ 362
3:16................. 364
3:34................. 130
4:16................. 117

John

4:22...................... 121
5:27...................... 362
6:14...................... 147
6:26 ff................... 365
6:27, 53, 62............. 362
7:41 f................... 147
8:28...................... 362
9:35...................... 362
11:43..................... 117
12:20, 32................ 178
12:23, 34................ 362
13:31..................... 362
17:3...................... 364
20:22.................... 131 f.

Acts

1:1....................... 127
1:2, 5................... 131
1:8.........131, 144, 167, 178
1:8 f..................... 120
1:23...................... 144
2:1 ff...............120, 131
2:22...............148, 232
2:24, 32................ 232
2:36.................232, 355
2:38...................... 132
2:41...................... 142
2:43...................... 145
3:1 ff.................... 142
3:6, 12–16............. 144
3:13...................... 355
3:15...................... 232
3:17...................... 141
3:20 f................... 105
3:22...................... 338
3:22–26................ 160
3:26...................... 355
4:1–3.................... 144
4:3....................... 131
4:7 ff.................... 144
4:8....................... 131
4:8–12.................. 160
4:10...................... 232
4:33...................... 144
5:3....................... 131
5:15 f................... 145
5:16–18, 28 ff., 40...... 144
5:32...................... 131
6:1—7:53.............. 144
6:3, 5, 10.............. 131
7:51, 55............... 131

Acts

7:54–58................ 144
8:1....................... 144
8:14 ff.................. 120
8:14–17................ 132
8:15 ff., 39............ 131
8:29...............131, 133
8:39 f................... 133
9:3 ff.................... 133
9:17...................131 f.
9:22 ff.................. 144
9:23...................... 125
9:26–30................ 120
9:29...................... 125
9:31.................125, 131
10:2, 22, 35........... 174
10:38................... 129 f.
10:40.................... 232
10:44–47................ 131
10:44–48................ 132
10:47.................... 167
11:15.................... 132
11:15–17, 24, 28....... 131
11:16.................... 131
11:17.................... 167
12:1 ff.................. 125
12:17.................... 126
13:2, 4, 9, 52.......... 131
13:16, 43, 50.......... 174
13:24 f., 26........... 147
13:27.................... 141
13:30 ff................ 232
13:46.................... 144
15:8, 28................ 131
15:13.................... 126
16:6 f................... 131
16:14.................... 174
17:4, 17................ 174
17:31.................... 232
18:2, 24 ff............. 102
18:6..................... 144
18:7..................... 174
19:1..................... 102
19:2, 6................. 131
19:2 ff................. 132
19:11 ff................ 249
19:13................... 159
20:23, 28.............. 131
21:4, 11............... 131
21:18................... 126
22:6 ff................. 133
22:19–21.............. 144

Acts

26:12 ff.	133
26:19–21	144
28:25	131
28:25–28	144

Romans

1:4	161, 232, 355
1:8–15	102
1:13–16	177
1:16	148
1:18–32	179
2:8–16	177
2:14 f.	179 f.
3:9	177
3:9–20	179
3:29 f.	177, 179
4:24	118, 232
6:1–11	114
6:3 ff.	350
6:4	232
6:16	270
8:1–17	131
8:11	232
8:14–17	157
8:17	112, 169
8:38 f.	157
9:1 ff.	119
9:3–5	164
9:22–31	177
9:30—10:4	141
9:31 ff.	179
10:8 f.	161
10:9	107, 171, 232
10:9–14	158
11:1 ff.	119
11:11 ff.	177
11:25–32	141, 170
12:1 f.	277
13:12	111
14:10	111
15:7–13	177
15:18 f.	148
15:18–28	168
15:19, 26–28	120
15:24, 28	51

I Corinthians

1:2	157
1:7	171
1:7 f.	111
1:8 f.	105

I Corinthians

1:11–13	113
1:13 ff.	350
1:18–25	179
1:21	277
1:26	278
1:28	157
2:2	132
2:4 f.	148
2:6	155, 157
2:6–8	140
2:6–10	283
2:8	155, 157, 179
2:10–16	131
3:13	111
3:16, 21 ff.	157
3:23	113
4:5	105, 111
4:17	149
5:3 f.	158
5:5	156
6:3	157
6:9	179
6:9–11	177
6:11	350
6:11–15	114
6:14	118, 232
6:15 ff.	155, 157
7:5	155
7:8–31	172
7:10	118, 150
7:11	149
7:12	150
7:14	299
7:25	118, 150, 182
7:40	182
8:1 ff.	177
8:4	179
8:4 ff.	156
8:5 f.	116, 158
9:1	173
9:4–6	102
9:5	118, 151
9:14	118, 150
9:23–27	112, 169
10:1 ff., 14–22	350
10:1–4	114
10:14 ff.	177
10:16	115
10:19 ff.	155
10:20	179
10:21	157

I Corinthians

11:2, 16	150
11:20–32	350
11:23	118, 150
11:26 f.	118
11:29 ff.	156
11:29–32	156
12:1–10	151
12:2	179
12:8 ff.	147
12:9 ff.	148
12:10	138
12:12 f.	114
12:13	132, 350
12:28	138, 147 f., 152
12:28–30	151
14:1 ff.	131, 138
14:33	150
15:3, 12 ff.	232
15:5 ff.	128
15:5–11	161
15:8	173
15:8 f.	103
15:9	97
15:14 ff.	171
15:23 ff.	111
15:24–27	157
15:25 f.	156
15:25–28	158
15:29	350
15:31	112, 169
16:22	111, 116

II Corinthians

2:11	155
2:14 ff.	112, 169
3:17 f.	131
4:3 f.	179
4:4	155
4:14	232
4:14–17	112, 169
5:10	111
6:15	155
11:14	155
11:22	119
11:24, 32 f.	125
12:7	155
12:7 ff.	156
12:11–13	151
12:12	148
12:13	149

Galatians

1:1	161, 173
1:4	155, 157, 179
1:13	97
1:15 f.	132
1:16	172 f., 177
1:19	118 f., 126
1:22	119, 150
2:1 ff.	150
2:2 ff.	177
2:8	103, 172
2:9	126
2:14 ff.	103
2:20	132
3:1–5	132
3:2	132
3:2–5	131
3:3, 5	149
3:3–5	151, 154, 172
3:8 ff.	177
3:19–29	179
3:26–28	113
3:27	350
4:3	245
4:8 ff.	179
4:9	245
4:29 f.	134
5:6	172
6:15	172

Ephesians

1:20	232
2:2 f., 12	179
2:11	177
3:1, 6, 8	177
4:17	177
4:17 f.	179
5:8, 16	179
6:12	179

Philippians

1:6, 10	111
1:23 f.	156
2:5–10	318
2:5–11	158
2:6	169
2:7 f.	355
2:9	232
2:9 f.	229
2:9 ff.	115
2:16	112

Philippians

3:5.................... 119
3:6.................... 97
4:5.................... 111

Colossians

1:21.................. 179
1:27.................. 177
2:8................... 245
2:11 f............... 114
2:11 ff.............. 350
2:12................. 232
2:13, 18 179
2:20................. 245

I Thessalonians

1:5.................. 148
1:6.............118, 132
1:9.................. 177
1:9 f................ 171
1:10...........111, 232
2:7, 16............. 177
2:14................ 150
2:14 f.............. 125
2:15..............97, 118
2:15 f..........140, 179
2:18................ 155
2:19 f..........112, 169
3:5................. 155

I Thessalonians

3:6.................. 158
3:13................ 111
3:16................ 177
4:3-7............... 177
4:5................. 179
4:15............118, 150
4:15-18............. 111
5:2................. 111
5:23............111, 156

II Thessalonians

1:7................. 179
2:8 ff.............. 157
2:9................. 148

II Timothy

1:11................ 177
4:17................ 177

Hebrews

2:2-4............... 134
12:18-24........... 134

James

5:14-18............ 155

Revelation

22:20.............. 116

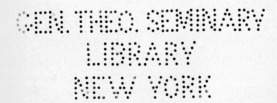